Praise for *Stolen Continents*

"Finally, history through Indian eyes. It's about time ... And Wright's a first-class storyteller."

—*Toronto Star*

"*Stolen Continents* ripped through me like a bullet ... Full of surprises and secrets, the book filled me with sadness and anger ... Ronald Wright has achieved something lasting."

—*The Kingston Whig-Standard*

"A magnificent feat of research, writing, and perception adjustment ... Makes history come alive."

—*Seattle Times*

"A thoroughly documented polemical work of great persuasive force."

—*The Sunday Telegraph* (London)

"Moving and insightful ... Serves to illuminate the moral complexities of our past and to remind us that much business begun in 1492 remains unfinished."

—*Houston Chronicle*

"For five centuries, the Indians of the Americas have doggedly recorded the shocking story of their subjugation by whites ... Ronald Wright has woven their voices into a compelling narrative."

—*The Globe and Mail*

"[Wright] goes about his business with white-hot passion."

—*Los Angeles Times*

"*Stolen Continents* [is] among the most useful, most interesting, best informed, and most wrenching reflections yet inspired by ... Columbus's voyage."

—*Boston Globe*

"A stunning book, a non-fiction tour de force."

—*Calgary Herald*

"Excellent ... Redresses the balance between the invaders and the invaded."

—*Sunday Times* (London)

"Ronald Wright turns his considerable narrative skill to the other side of the story that began in 1492 ... This is a fine and thought-provoking rendering of what [he] calls a 'holocaust that began five centuries ago.'"

—*The Washington Post*

"Mr. Wright .... succeeds, in short, in plausibly maintaining a non-European viewpoint throughout this unusual and fascinating work."

—*The Atlantic Monthly*

"These are real stories, told by a wonderful storyteller."

—*The Gazette* (Montreal)

"A powerful lament for the American Indians ... All who are interested in the clash between European and American cultures should read this well-written book ... They will be moved to compassion and outrage."

—*History Today*

PENGUIN CANADA

STOLEN CONTINENTS

RONALD WRIGHT is the internationally acclaimed, bestselling author of several non-fiction books, including *A Short History of Progress; Time Among the Maya; Stolen Continents*, which won the Gordon Montador Award; and *Cut Stones and Crossroads*. He is also the author of the novels *Henderson's Spear* and *A Scientific Romance*, which won Britain's David Higham Prize for Fiction and was selected as a *New York Times* Notable Book. He was born in England, educated at Cambridge, and now lives in Port Hope, Ontario.

Also by Ronald Wright

Fiction

A Scientific Romance

Henderson's Spear

Non-Fiction

A Short History of Progress

Cut Stones and Crossroads

On Fiji Islands

Time Among the Maya

Home and Away

Quechua Phrasebook

Ronald Wright

STOLEN CONTINENTS

Conquest and Resistance in the Americas

PENGUIN CANADA

Published by the Penguin Group

Penguin Group (Canada), 90 Eglinton Avenue East, Suite 700, Toronto, Ontario, Canada M4P 2Y3
(a division of Pearson Canada Inc.)

Penguin Group (USA) Inc., 375 Hudson Street, New York, New York 10014, U.S.A.
Penguin Books Ltd, 80 Strand, London WC2R 0RL, England
Penguin Ireland, 25 St Stephen's Green, Dublin 2, Ireland (a division of Penguin Books Ltd)
Penguin Group (Australia), 250 Camberwell Road, Camberwell, Victoria 3124, Australia
(a division of Pearson Australia Group Pty Ltd)
Penguin Books India Pvt Ltd, 11 Community Centre, Panchsheel Park, New Delhi – 110 017, India
Penguin Group (NZ), 67 Apollo Drive, Rosedale, North Shore 0632, New Zealand
(a division of Pearson New Zealand Ltd)
Penguin Books (South Africa) (Pty) Ltd, 24 Sturdee Avenue, Rosebank, Johannesburg 2196, South Africa

Penguin Books Ltd, Registered Offices: 80 Strand, London WC2R 0RL, England

First published in a Viking Canada hardcover by Penguin Group (Canada),
a division of Pearson Canada Inc., 1992
Published in Penguin Canada paperback by Penguin Group (Canada),
a division of Pearson Canada Inc., 1993, 2003
Published in this edition, 2009

3 4 5 6 7 8 9 10 (WEB)

Manufactured in Canada.

Library and Archives Canada Cataloguing in Publication data available upon request to the publisher.

ISBN: 978-0-14-316967-3

For Robert Randall
1945–1990

Wayqi, hamawt'a, yachachiq
Friend, scholar, teacher

CONTENTS

PART THREE: REBIRTH

AUTHOR'S NOTE

> How I loathe the term "Indian" . . . "Indian" is a term used to sell things—souvenirs, cigars, cigarettes, gasoline, cars. . . . "Indian" is a figment of the white man's imagination.
>
> —Lenore Keeshig-Tobias, Ojibway, 1990

Any book about the Americas is fraught with problems of terminology. Until 1507, when the name first appeared on a map, there was no "America" and there were no "American Indians." The idea that America might be part of Asia wasn't scotched until 1522, when the survivors of Magellan's fleet returned. The word "Indian" merely commemorates Columbus's mistake. "America" has since become established as a name for the entire so-called New World and, confusingly, for its dominant nation; we are left with the problem of what to call its peoples.

In 1492, Europeans seldom used the term "European"; they defined themselves by their nations and ethnic groups, or as Christians. Ancient Americans did the same, calling themselves Mexica, Maya, Tsalagi, and so forth. In English, these aboriginal people and their descendants should collectively be called Americans, just as the people of Asia are Asians. (That "America" is not a native word is beside the point: neither is "Asia.") This was indeed the primary usage until the eighteenth century, when British settlers became "Americans" in the way that South African Dutch became "Afrikaners."

Today some American Indians call themselves Indians; others dislike the word. The main objection is that "Indian" hides the true diversity, and the true names, of widely differing cultures. (And in Spanish, *indio* became a term of racial abuse.) But one needs a generality to set against "white," "European," and "invader." So I use "Indian." I also use "Native

American," "Amerindian," and the adjectives "aboriginal" and "indigenous." Objections, semantic and political, can be raised to any of them.

These are not the only loaded words. An entire vocabulary is tainted with prejudice and condescension: whites are soldiers, Indians are warriors; whites live in towns, Indians in villages; whites have kings and generals, Indians have chiefs; whites have states, Indians have tribes. Indians have ghost dances, whites have eschatology.[1] In 1927, the Grand Council Fire of American Indians told the mayor of Chicago: "We know that [school histories] are unjust to the life of our people. . . . They call all white victories, battles, and all Indian victories, massacres. . . . White men who rise to protect their property are called patriots—Indians who do the same are called murderers."[2]

Another minefield surrounds the origin of America's peoples. Many American Indians believe that they were created in America, that, in the words of the eighteenth-century Iroquois, they "came out of this ground." Archaeology and genetics suggest that their remote ancestors peopled America from Asia via a Bering land bridge that existed between 15,000 and 35,000 years ago (long before the growth of civilization anywhere on earth). The same lines of inquiry, taken further back, indicate that all human beings came from Africa.

There need be no conflict between sacred tradition and scientific evidence. The traditions are philosophically true. Native Americans have been here since time immemorial; their languages, cultures, and civilizations developed here. They are American in a way that no others can be. Even if we suppose that their ancestors arrived "only" 15,000 years ago (the archaeological minimum), they have been here thirty times longer than anyone else. If we call that time a month, Columbus came yesterday.

Finally, a word on crackpot ideas that the American Indians and their achievements hail from Egypt, Phoenicia, the lost tribes of Israel, medieval Welsh princes, Irish monks, Atlantis, or outer space. Such "theories" are a measure of Europeans' inability to accept Native Americans for who they are. The implication behind them is often subtly racist: that Amerindians could not have done what they did without help.

There is indeed some evidence for occasional contacts across the Pacific, but many of these seem to have gone *from* America, not to it. For example, a South American sweet potato reached Polynesia, where it is known by its Peruvian name. And if there is any link between the discovery of zero by both Maya and Hindu mathematicians, the invention was probably a thousand years earlier in Mesoamerica than India. Tantalizing resemblances between certain art, architecture, and calendrical ideas in Asia and Mesoamerica are still controversial. If they are due to direct contact, it was very rare, mainly late, and of limited cultural and biological significance. No New World artifact has been shown to have an Old World prototype, or vice versa. And Native Americans' terrible vulnerability to Old World disease is proof enough of long isolation. So is the uniqueness of plant and animal kingdoms: not even rats or cockroaches—good sailors both—had reached America before Columbus.

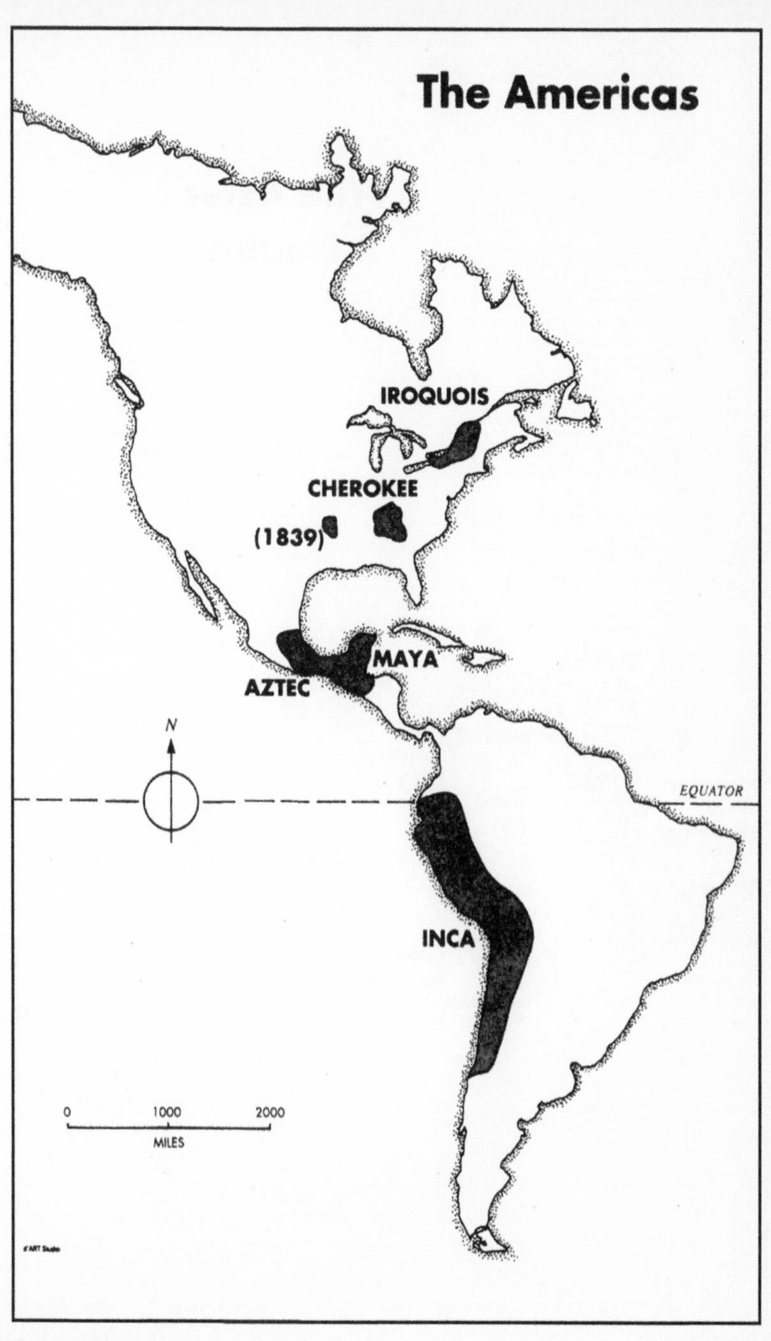

The Americas
IROQUOIS
CHEROKEE
(1839)
MAYA
AZTEC
N
EQUATOR
INCA
0
1000
2000
MILES
d'ART Studio

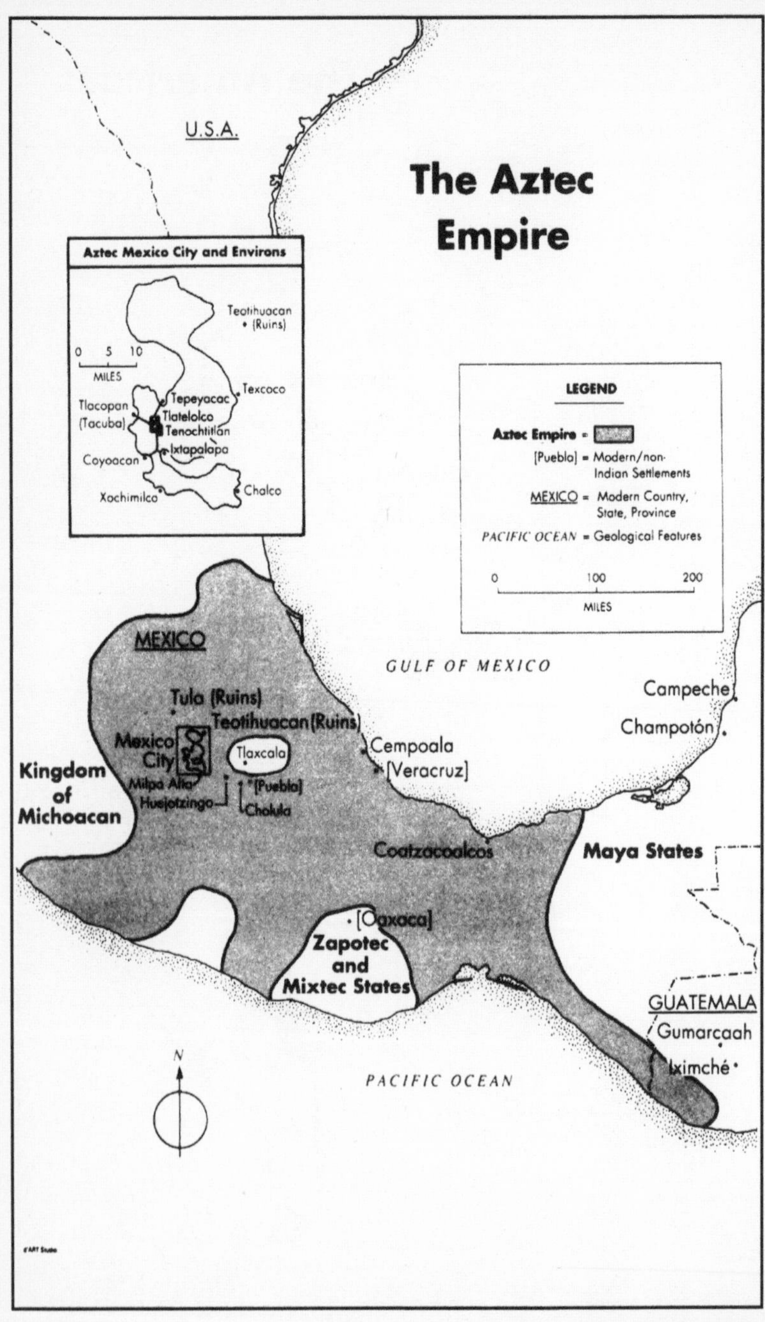

The Aztec Empire
U.S.A.
Aztec Mexico City and Environs
Teotihuacan
(Ruins)
0 5 10
MILES
Texcoco
Tepeyacac
Tlacopan
(Tacuba)
Tlatelolco
Tenochtitlan
Ixtapalapa
Coyoacan
Chalco
Xochimilco
LEGEND
Aztec Empire =
[Puebla] = Modern/non-Indian Settlements
MEXICO = Modern Country, State, Province
PACIFIC OCEAN = Geological Features
0 100 200
MILES
GULF OF MEXICO
MEXICO
Tula (Ruins)
Teotihuacan (Ruins)
Mexico City
Tlaxcala
Cempoala
[Veracruz]
Campeche
Champotón
Kingdom of Michoacan
Milpa Alta
Huejotzingo
[Puebla]
Cholula
Coatzacoalcos
Maya States
[Oaxaca]
Zapotec and Mixtec States
GUATEMALA
Gumarcaah
Iximché
PACIFIC OCEAN
N

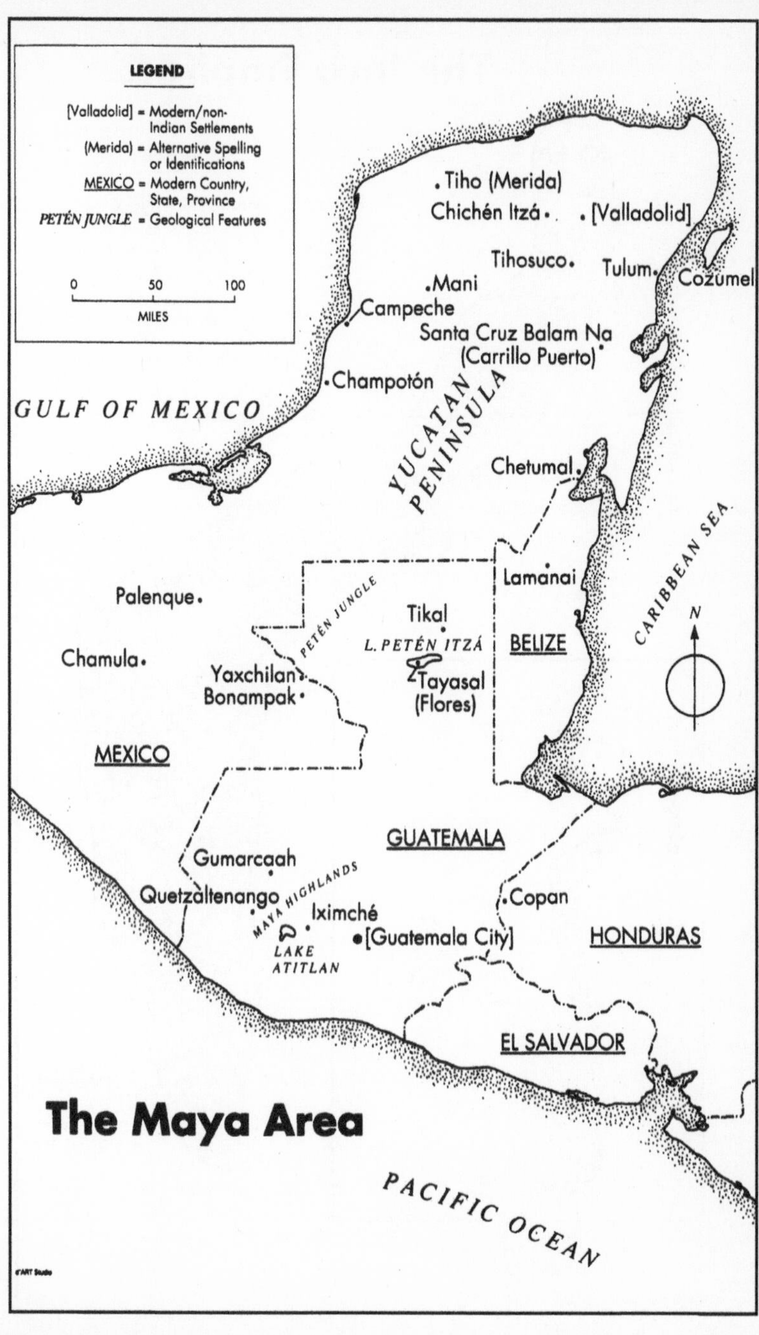

LEGEND
[Valladolid] = Modern/non-Indian Settlements
(Merida) = Alternative Spelling or Identifications
MEXICO = Modern Country, State, Province
PETÉN JUNGLE = Geological Features
0
50
100
MILES
GULF OF MEXICO
Tiho (Merida)
Chichén Itzá
[Valladolid]
Tihosuco
Tulum
Cozumel
Mani
Campeche
Santa Cruz Balam Na
(Carrillo Puerto)
Champotón
YUCATAN PENINSULA
Chetumal
CARIBBEAN SEA
Lamanai
Palenque
PETÉN JUNGLE
Tikal
L. PETÉN ITZÁ
BELIZE
N
Chamula
Yaxchilan
Bonampak
Tayasal
(Flores)
MEXICO
GUATEMALA
Gumarcaah
MAYA HIGHLANDS
Quetzaltenango
Iximché
Copan
[Guatemala City]
HONDURAS
LAKE ATITLAN
EL SALVADOR
The Maya Area
PACIFIC OCEAN

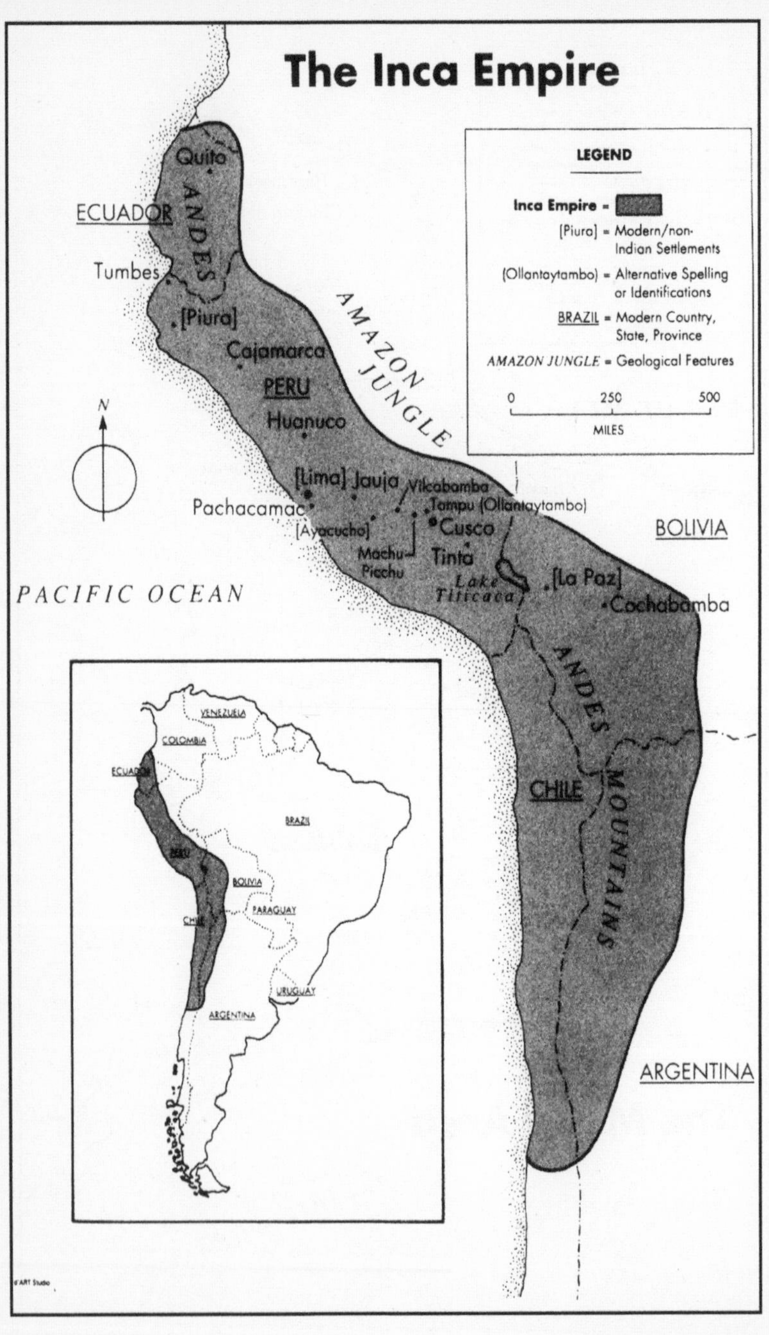
The Inca Empire
LEGEND
Inca Empire =
[Piura] = Modern/non-Indian Settlements
(Ollantaytambo) = Alternative Spelling or Identifications
BRAZIL = Modern Country, State, Province
AMAZON JUNGLE = Geological Features
0
250
500
MILES
N
Quito
ANDES
ECUADOR
Tumbes
[Piura]
Cajamarca
PERU
AMAZON JUNGLE
Huanuco
[Lima]
Jauja
Vilcabamba
Pachacamac
Tampu (Ollantaytambo)
[Ayacucho]
Cusco
Machu Picchu
Tinta
Lake Titicaca
[La Paz]
Cochabamba
BOLIVIA
PACIFIC OCEAN
ANDES
CHILE
MOUNTAINS
ARGENTINA
VENEZUELA
COLOMBIA
ECUADOR
BRAZIL
PERU
BOLIVIA
PARAGUAY
CHILE
URUGUAY
ARGENTINA
d'ART Studio

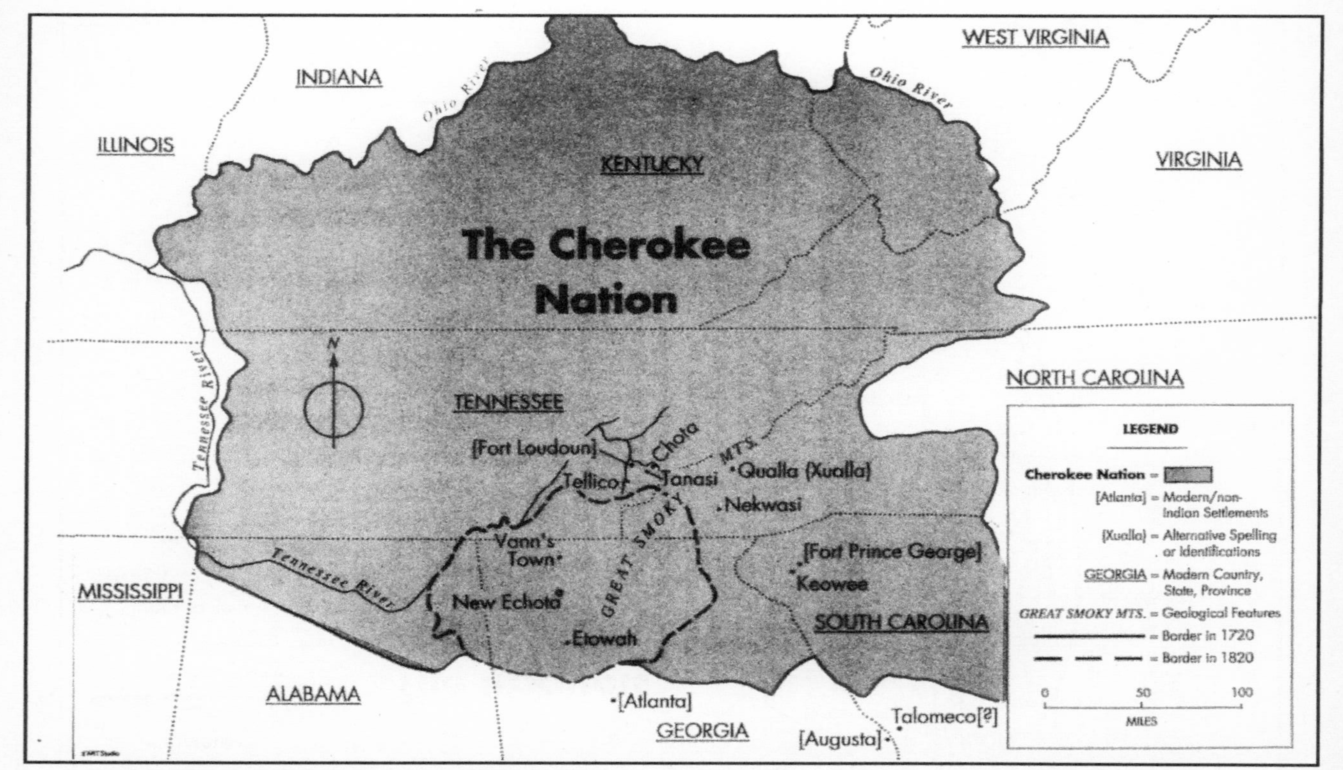
The Cherokee Nation
INDIANA
ILLINOIS
KENTUCKY
WEST VIRGINIA
VIRGINIA
Ohio River
Ohio River
N
TENNESSEE
Tennessee River
Tennessee River
NORTH CAROLINA
[Fort Loudoun]
Chota
Tellico
Tanasi
MTS.
Qualla (Xualla)
Nekwasi
GREAT SMOKY
Vann's Town
New Echota
Etowah
[Fort Prince George]
Keowee
SOUTH CAROLINA
MISSISSIPPI
ALABAMA
[Atlanta]
GEORGIA
Talomeco[?]
[Augusta]
LEGEND
Cherokee Nation =
[Atlanta] = Modern/non-Indian Settlements
(Xualla) = Alternative Spelling or Identifications
GEORGIA = Modern Country, State, Province
GREAT SMOKY MTS. = Geological Features
= Border in 1720
= Border in 1820
0
50
100
MILES

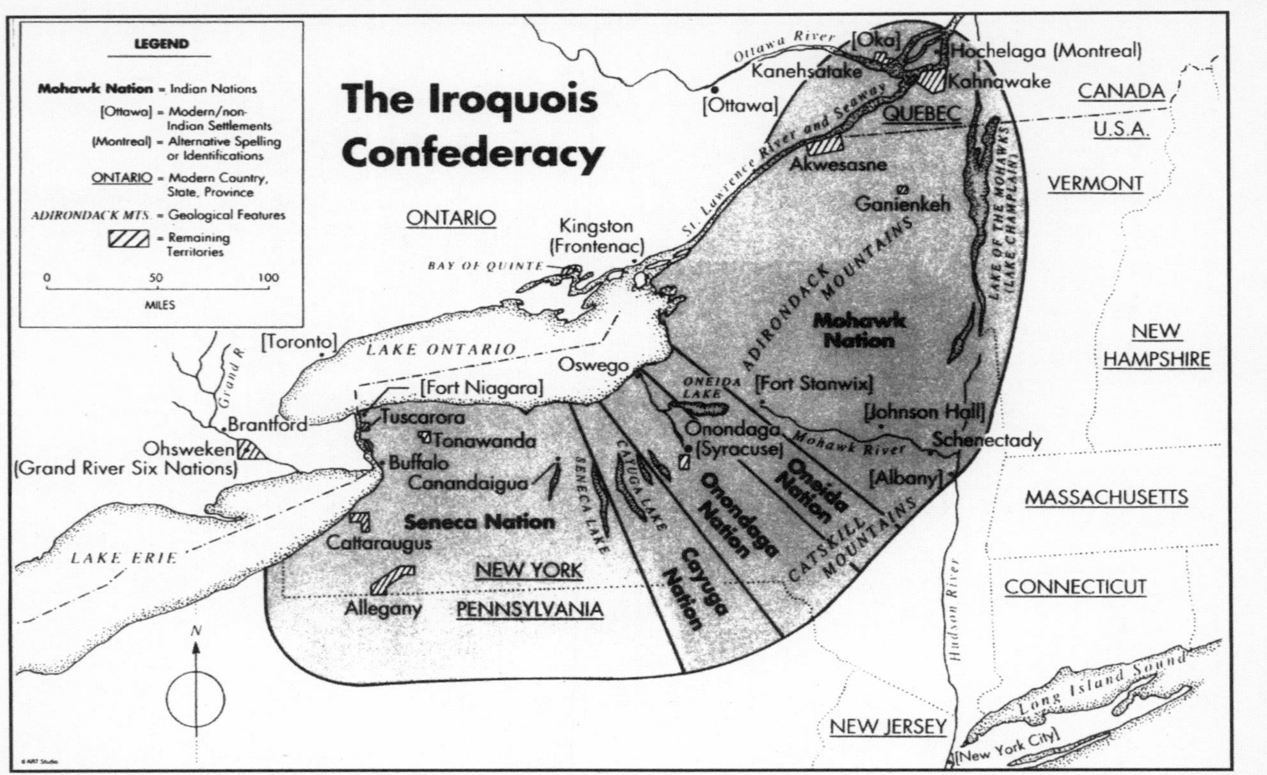

The Iroquois Confederacy
LEGEND
Mohawk Nation = Indian Nations
[Ottawa] = Modern/non-Indian Settlements
(Montreal) = Alternative Spelling or Identifications
ONTARIO = Modern Country, State, Province
ADIRONDACK MTS. = Geological Features
= Remaining Territories
0
50
100
MILES
CANADA
U.S.A.
VERMONT
NEW HAMPSHIRE
MASSACHUSETTS
CONNECTICUT
NEW JERSEY
NEW YORK
PENNSYLVANIA
ONTARIO
QUEBEC
Ottawa River
[Oka]
Hochelaga (Montreal)
Kanehsatake
Kahnawake
[Ottawa]
St. Lawrence River and Seaway
Akwesasne
Ganienkeh
LAKE OF THE MOHAWKS (LAKE CHAMPLAIN)
ADIRONDACK MOUNTAINS
Mohawk Nation
Kingston (Frontenac)
BAY OF QUINTE
[Toronto]
LAKE ONTARIO
Oswego
Grand R.
[Fort Niagara]
ONEIDA LAKE
[Fort Stanwix]
[Johnson Hall]
Brantford
Tuscarora
Tonawanda
Onondaga
(Syracuse)
Mohawk River
Schenectady
Ohsweken
(Grand River Six Nations)
Buffalo
Canandaigua
SENECA LAKE
CAYUGA LAKE
Onondaga Nation
Oneida Nation
[Albany]
Seneca Nation
Cattaraugus
CATSKILL MOUNTAINS
LAKE ERIE
Allegany
Cayuga Nation
Hudson River
N
Long Island Sound
[New York City]

PART ONE

INVASION

PROLOGUE

DISCOVERY

God cannot alter the past, historians can.

—Samuel Butler

History is a set of lies agreed upon.

—Napoleon Bonaparte

History begins for us with murder and enslavement, not with discovery.

—William Carlos Williams

In 1992, the West—by which I mean nations and cultures that are either European or derived from Europe's expansion of the past 500 years—celebrated the quincentenary of Columbus's first voyage from an "old" world to a "new." Conventional history, written by the winners, has always taught us that this "discovery" was one of mankind's finest hours.

The inhabitants of America saw it differently. Their ancestors had made the same discovery long before. To them the New World was so old that it was the only world: a "great island," as many called it, floating in the primordial sea. They had occupied all habitable zones from the Arctic tundra to the Caribbean isles, from the high plateaus of the Andes to the blustery tip of Cape Horn. They had developed every kind of society: nomadic hunting groups, settled farming communities, and dazzling civilizations with cities as large as any then on earth. By 1492 there were approximately 100 million Native Americans—a fifth, more or less, of the human race.[1]

Within decades of Columbus's landfall, most of these people were dead and their world barbarously sacked by Europeans. The plunderers settled in America, and it was they, not the original people, who became known as Americans.

Conventional history, even when it acknowledges the enormity of this assault, has led us to assume that it is finished, irrevocable; that America's peoples are extinct or nearly so; that they were so primitive and died so quickly, they had nothing to say.

Unlike Asia and Africa, America never saw its colonizers leave. America's ancient nations have not recovered their autonomy, but that doesn't mean they have disappeared. Many survive, captive within white settler states built on their lands and on their backs. In the Andes, 12 million people still speak the language of the Incas: the murder of Atawallpa in 1533 and the violence of today's Shining Path are parts of the same story. Central America has 6 million speakers of Maya (as many as speak French in Canada): if Guatemala really had majority rule, it would be a Maya republic. In Canada, in 1990, Mohawks took up arms in the name of a sovereignty that they believe they have never ceded to Ottawa or Washington.

If these facts surprise us, it is because for five centuries we have listened only to the history of the winners. We have been talking to ourselves. It is time to hear the other side of the story that began in 1492 and continues to this day.

> O wad some Pow'r the giftie gie us
> To see oursels as others see us!
>
> —Robert Burns

> The whites told only one side. Told it to please themselves. Told much that is not true. Only his own best deeds, only the worst deeds of the Indians, has the white man told.
>
> —Yellow Wolf, Nez Percé, c. 1877

This book is not about Christopher Columbus. I have little interest here in whether the man was a genius or a fool, a villain or a saint, a good sailor or a lucky one. Neither am I concerned with whether he was indeed the first European to set foot in the Americas, or knew what he had done. Vikings had certainly crossed the Atlantic some 500 years before him; and when he died in 1506, it seems he still thought that he had been to Asia. These are not my points. If Christopher Columbus hadn't reached America from Europe in 1492, somebody else soon would have. Some other European would have his name enshrined in Columbus Circle, British Columbia, and the republic of Colombia. What matters about Columbus, from an Amerindian perspective, is that his voyage initiated a catastrophic invasion from across the world-rim sea.

When I interviewed people for the final chapters of this book, I was told by Dehatkadons, a traditional chief of the Onondaga Iroquois, "You cannot discover an inhabited land. Otherwise I could cross the Atlantic and 'discover' England." That such an obvious point has eluded European consciousness for five centuries reveals that the history we have been taught is really myth. The word "myth" sometimes has a debased meaning nowadays—as a synonym for lies or fairy stories—but this is not the definition I intend. Most history, when it has been digested by a people, becomes myth. Myth is an arrangement of the past, whether real or imagined, in patterns that resonate with a culture's deepest values and aspirations. Myths create and reinforce archetypes so taken for granted, so seemingly axiomatic, that they go unchallenged. Myths are so fraught with meaning that we live and die by them. They are the maps by which cultures navigate through time. Those vanquished by our civilization see that its myth of discovery has transformed historical crimes into glittering icons. Yet from the West's vantage point, the discovery myth is true.

The history of the other side is also mythic. But while Western myths are triumphalist, those of the "losers" have to explain and overcome catastrophe. If the vanquished culture is to survive at all, its myths must provide it with a rugged terrain in which to resist the invader and do battle with *his* myths.

I became interested in pre-Columbian America because I learned nothing about it at school. To British educators of the 1950s and 1960s, history was something that happened mainly in Britain before 1850. A little of Greece and Rome, and a great deal of the Tudors, Stuarts, and Hanoverians, was drummed into unwilling heads over and over. I became bored with this history and began to suspect that there might be alternatives. Reading led me to the Incas of Peru, and they in turn led me to other peoples of South, Central, and North America. Even a schoolboy could see that these cultures had been casually and ignorantly dismissed by Western historiography. Ancient America was criticized for lacking things that Europe had—things deemed epitomes of human progress. The plow and the wheel were favorites; another was writing. It never occurred to Eurocentric historians that plows and wheels are not much use without draft animals such as oxen or horses, neither of which existed in the Americas before Columbus. Far from marveling that civilization arose there despite these "handicaps," historians took the absence of plow and wheel as proof that ancient Americans could not truly have been civilized. In the same spirit they concluded that Maya hieroglyphs were not real writing—though they looked like writing—because no white man had been able to decipher them.

Scholars of today are no longer so naive. Most Maya inscriptions can now be read, revealing magnificent achievements in astronomy and mathematics and adding a thousand years of dynastic records to the human family tree. Archaeologists, anthropologists, linguists, and historians have begun to understand the pre-Columbian world. But Western culture as a whole has not adjusted its myths. Popular history, as taught in schools or gleaned from reference works, is largely unreformed. Take *The Pelican History of the World,* written in 1976 and revised in 1987. It is more than a thousand pages long, yet only ten pages are devoted to indigenous America. The American civilizations are again slighted for lacking the plow and dismissed as "beautiful curiosities in the margin of world history, ultimately without progeny."[2]

Another of Europe's hoariest ideas about America is the self-apotheosis known as the white god myth. According to this, the natives were so overawed by the strange white men, the guns, and the horses that they mistook the invaders for gods. In 1982, the French critic Tzvetan Todorov dressed the white god in new clothes. Amerindians found Europeans so incomprehensible, he claims, that they investigated them by supernatural means, by sorcery and divination, instead of dialogue and empirical tests. America's failure was a failure to comprehend the "Other."

Less influential but more insidious, because of the air of authority perfuming it, was a 1990 *Harper's* essay by Mario Vargas Llosa, Peruvian novelist and presidential candidate. Vargas revives the old myth that the Inca Empire fell because it was an "anthill" society whose subjects had no free will. Ancient Peruvians, he asserts, were so enthralled by their god-king that, without instructions to the contrary, they simply stood around and allowed themselves to be butchered by a handful of Renaissance desperadoes. He concludes that perhaps it was all for the best. Why? Because the conquerors brought to Peru the pearl of individual freedom. At this point, one can recognize Vargas's version of history as political agenda: the indigenous peoples who live in Peru today (and constitute close to half the population) must be swept aside in the name of progress, because modernization, which he equates with "complete assimilation," is "possible only with the sacrifice of the Indian cultures."[3]

The doctrinaire left is often no better than the right. Severo Martínez Peláez, an emigré Guatemalan historian, sees "Indians" as a colonial creation—Indian only because precapitalist exploitation denied them the boons of Spanish culture. For him, the Mayas' very survival is proof of their defeat. The heroic task of socialism is "deindigenization."[4]

Vargas Llosa proposes finishing off the Indian in the name of social Darwinist capitalism, Martínez Peláez in the name of Marx. Neither will allow Amerindian culture even the right to exist.

In recent years, a remarkable body of *post*-Columbian native documents has been unearthed from centuries of oblivion in archives and collections. These works have transformed our knowledge of what happened when the Old World met the New. We can read contemporary Aztec versions of the conquest of Mexico, Inca versions of the famous encounter between Atawallpa and Pizarro. And while scholars are rediscovering these voices from the past, today's American Indians are speaking out for themselves. There is no longer any excuse for ignoring the viewpoint of the "discovered," the vanquished, the colonized. And there is danger in doing so. The civil wars in Peru and Guatemala, and the Mohawk conflict in Canada, are fueled by the ignorance of those countries' white elites. Few things are so dangerous as believing one's own lies.

Felipe Waman Puma, an Inca contemporary of Shakespeare's, called the postconquest world in which he lived and wrote *mundo al revés*, "a world in reverse." For him and his people, the invasion of America turned the world upside down. *Stolen Continents* traces that view of history—the reverse of our usual perception—by presenting the words of people such as Waman Puma. The subject is of course a vast one. I have therefore confined myself to five cultures: the Aztecs of Mexico, the Maya of Guatemala and Yucatán, the Incas of Peru, the Cherokees of the southern United States, and the Iroquois of the Great Lakes. All met the first Europeans to invade their lands; all left accounts of that conflict; all are still here. I make no pretense of giving equal time to the invaders: we have had the floor long enough; our case rests.

These five were among the most complex societies at the time of contact; for this reason they have left the best records. They represent fairly the livelihood of most Americans in 1492, agriculture. Hollywood may have convinced us that the "typical" Indian was a nomadic hunter, but in fact the majority had been living in villages, towns, and cities since long before Columbus.

I sketch their origins and ancient way of life quite briefly. (Another vast topic.) More important for their post-Columbian history is that these five have kept alive their languages, religions, certain arts and sciences, and countless intangibles of culture against all odds. True, they are greatly changed—but so are we. Twentieth-century Europeans are arguably as distant from the world of Columbus as a modern speaker of the Aztec language is from the world of Moctezuma. Cultures grow and ramify and change; they may also die out or be absorbed. These five have been influenced but not extinguished; they have in turn influenced us, perhaps more than we know.

It is a mistake to think of them as curious fossils from the pre-Columbian age. They are living cultures, defining and defending places in the contemporary world. Only the West assumes that modernity and Westernization must be synonymous. Japan, for example, is "modern."

It has taken much from the West, especially technology. Yet it retains its own language, arts, attitudes, social structure, religion, and royal family. It isn't the Japan of the shoguns, but it is no less Japanese.

Two of the five cultures I have chosen are from North America, one from South America, and two from "Mesoamerica"—a useful term for the parts of Mexico and Central America in which complex civilizations arose. Of these three great regions, only Mesoamerica possessed writing as we know it. Most of the indigenous records I quote were written in response to the invasion with the aid of a European tool, the alphabet. The American scripts that did exist were quickly and ruthlessly suppressed; anything in hieroglyphs was likely to end on a missionary bonfire. But within a remarkably short time, Mayas and Aztecs adapted the Spanish alphabet for writing their own languages. Some of their works were intended for a European audience; others—notably transcriptions of pre-Columbian manuscripts—were not. To the Incas, Iroquois, and Cherokees, writing was new, but they quickly grasped its importance for communicating with the invaders. At first they used European scribes and translators. Later they too learned to write for themselves.

These records, like all records, are slanted by secrecy, advocacy, and social attitudes. Complex societies tend to be hierarchical. Great men are remembered; rarely a woman; seldom the common man, as Bertolt Brecht reminds us:

> The books are filled with names of kings.
> Was it kings who hauled the craggy blocks of stone? . . .
> Young Alexander conquered India.
> He alone?

Above all, the records have been edited by chance, by the luck of being preserved. For every word that stands, thousands have been lost, but there are still enough to fill a lengthy shelf. We have an entire book by Inca Atawallpa's nephew, two by Moctezuma's grandson. Iroquois speeches in the colonial records of Pennsylvania and New York run to hundreds of pages. Some parts of the Indian histories exist in detail;

others are completely obscure and may always remain so. Several ancient texts are illuminated by modern oral traditions, telling of the conquest and foretelling the return of Indian kings. To build a story rather than a collection from these pieces, I outline each history, lingering where the native record is particularly rich or important. My narrative is a kind of mortar linking fragmentary inscriptions.

Stolen Continents is divided into three chronological parts corresponding roughly to the initial assault, the colonial period, and the period since the founding of settler republics. I begin the stories of the five in the order of their invasion. The first is the overthrow of the Aztec Empire, ending in 1521; the highland Mayas were next; then the Incas; a few years later the Cherokees were invaded by one of the conquerors of Peru; and soon afterward the Iroquois began to experience regular intrusions by the French, Dutch, and British. The same order—Aztec, Maya, Inca, Cherokee, Iroquois—is followed in each of the three parts. The book therefore ends with the modern Iroquois, whose story suddenly became more urgent than anyone could have imagined. As I was writing, an armed confrontation between Mohawk Iroquois and soldiers erupted onto the television screens of Canada, the country where I live.

Other books like this one could be written: I have said nothing about the Guarani of Paraguay, the Mapuche of Chile, the Yanomami of Brazil, the Navajo, the Blackfoot, the Miskito, and many others with unfinished stories to tell. I have also had to pass over the Caribbean Indians who experienced the first wave of invasion, a period of twenty-six years between Columbus's landfall and the start of serious campaigns against the mainland empires. The islanders were so thoroughly exterminated that they have left not a single account.

The five I have chosen must therefore stand for the many who will never tell their stories because they are extinct. The silence of the Caribbean Taino, the Newfoundland Beothuk, and the Ona of Tierra del Fuego is the most terrible eloquence of all.

> Gold is a wonderful thing! Whoever owns it is lord of all he wants. With gold it is even possible to open for souls the way to paradise!
>
> —Christopher Columbus, 1503

> Empires and churches are born under the sun of death.
>
> —Albert Camus

If there were such a thing as a political globe for the year 1492, with each nation and empire traced in color, the quilt of human powers would be scarcely recognizable today. Much of the world would have appeared as a pointillist canvas of tribal territories, often without fixed boundaries or with interpenetrating rights to the same stretches of land. At a higher level of organization were small city-states and nations, deriving from tribal groups who had become sedentary. Beyond these, dominating large slabs of territory, were two great empires, those of Ming China and the Incas. (The Mogul Empire had yet to be founded; the Ottoman Empire was still in its infancy; and the Holy Roman Empire was, as Napoleon later pointed out, neither holy nor Roman nor an empire.)

Two callow imperialists, seemingly far apart, would meet within a generation: the Castilians of Spain and the Aztecs of Mexico. Both were expanding states with tribal origins; both had quickly gained control over other peoples but had not absorbed them effectively. Of the two, Mexico was by far the larger. The Aztec capital—today's Mexico City—held a quarter of a million people: four times more than Tudor London. The total population under its control was some 20 million.[5]

Europe in 1492 was a small affair. The British Isles had only 5 million people, Spain about eight.[6] Political boundaries were essentially those which had resulted from barbarian migrations after the fall of Rome. The Franks had settled in France, the Germani in Germany, the Angles and Saxons in England, the Vandals and Visigoths in Spain. These patterns have altered remarkably little from the seventh century to the twentieth, though frequent attempts to alter them have made the soil of Europe among the most bloodstained on earth.

European secular government was a tangle of decayed feudal loyalties and personal ambition. The last proper roads had been built by the Romans more than a thousand years before. The rapidly growing cities were unplanned, ramshackle, without sanitation, seething with poverty and disease. If famine struck a region, the state was quite unable to provide relief. Life expectancy oscillated between the high teens and low thirties, lower than in the most deprived nations of today. The achievements of Europe were technological, not social. It had the best ships, the best steel, the best guns; it also had conditions desperate enough to make its people want to leave and use these things to plunder others. Spain, in particular, was scarcely touched by the Renaissance; 700 years of war against the Moors had produced a warrior culture filled with loathing and contempt for other ways of life, not a new spirit of inquiry. The *reconquista* of Iberia, which ended in 1492, would be the model for the *conquista* of America.

Montaigne, whose supple mind exemplifies Western civilization at its best, records in his essay "On Cannibals" a revealing conversation between himself and three Tupinamba captives brought from Brazil to France and exhibited to the boy-king Charles IX in 1562.

> The King talked with them for some time; they were shown our way of living, our magnificence, and the sights of a fine city. [I] asked them what they thought about all this, and what they had found most remarkable. [They said] they had noticed among us some men gorged to the full with things of every sort while their other halves were beggars at their doors, emaciated with hunger and poverty. They found it strange that these poverty-stricken halves should suffer such injustice, and that they did not take the others by the throat or set fire to their houses.[7]

The Tupinamba saw through Europe's alien splendor to the flaws in its society. The answer to their question, as they perhaps knew only too well, was that the poor of Europe were cutting throats and burning houses in America.

Pedro de Cieza de León, a young Spaniard who embarked for the New World after seeing "magnificent specimens"[8] of Inca gold and silver exhibited at Seville in 1534, became one of the most trustworthy European observers of the wreckage in the wake of his countrymen. "It is no small sorrow to reflect," he wrote, "that we Christians have destroyed so many kingdoms. For wherever Christians have passed, conquering and discovering, it seems as though a fire has gone, consuming everything."[9]

Why were Amerindians so vulnerable? Why was America so overwhelmed by Europe that, unlike Asia and Africa, it has never been decolonized? Why are the modern countries of America not really American at all, but imitation Europes built on American soil? Why does none use an American language at the diplomatic level? Why isn't there a single president, prime minister, or monarch with an Amerindian name?

The usual answers—like that retailed in *Harper's* by Mario Vargas Llosa—are self-serving and grounded in assumptions of superiority: the Indians lost because they were primitive, because their societies were weak, because they were few, because they were superstitious, and so forth. Such explanations explain nothing, even by their own false premises. The rolling back of colonialism in the present century has little to do with how "primitive" the natives were upon first contact. Places as diverse as Guinea and New Guinea are today governed by descendants of their original inhabitants. Many parts of ancient America were more advanced (in Western terms) than those. Yet Africans and Papuans have reclaimed a qualified autonomy, while the word "American" does not even mean a native of the continent.

Why was America different? The short answer is disease. As in H. G. Wells's *War of the Worlds*, Europe possessed biological weapons that fate had been stacking against America for thousands of years. Among these were smallpox, measles, influenza, bubonic plague, yellow fever, cholera, and malaria—all unknown in the Western Hemisphere before 1492. Somehow they had not made the journey to the New World with the remote ancestors of the American Indians during the last Ice Age. Perhaps they were frozen to death on the way; perhaps they had not yet evolved. Whatever the reason, Native Americans, having had no exposure, had little or no immunity; they caught the new sicknesses quickly, and infection was extremely virulent. "The Indians die so easily that the bare look and smell of a Spaniard causes them to give up the ghost," one eyewitness wrote.[10] Even today, isolated tribes can be decimated by something as "minor" as the common cold on first contact with missionaries or prospectors. In just two years—1988 to 1990—the Yanomami of Brazil lost 15 percent of their people, mainly to malaria and influenza.[11]

The New World did have some diseases all its own—perhaps syphilis, for one, which appeared in Europe in 1498—but they were few and not mass killers.

It is now clear that Old World plagues killed at least half the population of the Aztec, Maya, and Inca civilizations shortly before their overthrow. The sheer loss of people was devastating enough (Europe reeled for a century after the Black Death, which was less severe), but disease was also a political assassination squad, removing kings, generals, and seasoned advisers at the very time they were needed most.

The great death raged for more than a century. By 1600, after some twenty waves of pestilence had swept through the Americas, less than a tenth of the original population remained. Perhaps 90 million died, the equivalent, in today's terms, to the loss of a billion.[12] It was the greatest mortality in history. To conquered and conqueror alike, it seemed as though God really was on the white man's side.

Survivors of this apocalypse looked back on the pre-Columbian world as an uncontaminated paradise. From a sixteenth-century Maya book:

There was then no sickness;
They had then no aching bones;
They had then no high fever;
They had then no smallpox;
They had then no burning chest . . .
They had then no consumption . . .
At that time the course of humanity was orderly.
The foreigners made it otherwise when they arrived here.[13]

ONE

AZTEC

Proudly stands the city of Mexico-Tenochtitlan,
Here no one fears to die in war . . .
Keep this in mind, oh princes . . .
Who could attack Tenochtitlan?
Who could shake the foundations of heaven?

—*Cantares Mexicanos,* c. 1560

Columbus fell from royal grace, lost his governorship, and died in Spain poor and half forgotten. The gold the invaders stripped from the Caribbean did not amount to much, and when they turned to slavery they found that the merchandise died almost as quickly as they could round it up from burning villages. Expeditions to the mainland were equally disappointing: the Spaniards found no trace of the Orient reported by Marco Polo, who had traveled east from Europe two centuries before. Harangues in Arabic were met with blank stares. The name of Kublai Khan made no impression. Had Polo lied? Then, in 1513, Spaniards struggled across the Central American isthmus, saw another ocean, and began to suspect that these "Indies" were not the ones they sought. By chance, they had passed right between the two regions of greatest wealth and civilization on the continent, Mesoamerica and the Andes.

Though he did not realize it, Columbus himself had made contact with Mesoamericans on his fourth voyage, in 1502. In the Bay Islands off Honduras, his ship met a seagoing canoe "from a province called Maia [Maya] . . . as long as a galley and eight feet wide, all made of one tree . . . in the middle of it there was an awning of palm leaves, no different from the ones on the gondolas of Venice. . . . Under the awning were children, women, furniture and merchandise." The canoe was probably on its way to Costa Rica or Panama from a home port in Yucatán. What is most interesting is the Indian reaction to the Europeans. The crew were walking along the shore, dragging the boat against a stiff current. "On the orders of their master," the Spaniards wrote, the crew "indicated arrogantly to our men that they should make way, and made threats when they offered resistance."[1]

Far from mistaking the strangers for gods, these Mayas—the first to meet Europeans—ordered them to stand aside.

Also in 1502, on the mainland far from Caribbean killing fields, the empire of Mexico had chosen a new emperor from among its princes: Motecuhzoma Xocoyotzin, or Moctezuma II, whom the Spaniards would call Montezuma. Then in his early twenties, "not heavy but lean, slender and with a fine figure," according to an Aztec source, he became the ninth *Tlatoani*—literally Speaker—of the dynasty.[2] His empire was a loose pyramid of city-states dominated by the Triple Alliance of Mexico, Texcoco, and Tlacopan. These three cities stood among a body of lakes in a great valley, 7,000 feet above sea level and surrounded by smoldering volcanoes with icy peaks. The most powerful was Mexico, home of the *Mexica,* as the Aztecs often called themselves. Mexico was then the largest city in the Americas, and one of the half dozen largest in the world.

The next encounter between Mesoamericans and Europeans came in 1511. Several Spaniards shipwrecked off the east coast of Yucatán struggled ashore near Tulum, a walled Maya town whose gaunt stone temples still gaze across the sea. Five of the men were killed on the spot and the rest taken prisoner.

By this time the Spaniards were well established in Cuba, and it dawned on them gradually that an advanced civilization existed on the Yucatán peninsula, just 120 miles to the west. In 1517, Francisco Hernández tried to invade but received a crushing defeat from the Mayas at Champotón. "Though we fought back with swords and muskets and crossbows," wrote one of his men, "they brought us to a bad pass."[3] Hernández died of his wounds soon after getting home. In

1518, Juan de Grijalva skirmished again at Champotón and sailed farther into the Gulf of Mexico, but had to retire when he ran out of supplies.

Hernán Cortés, thirty-three years old and bored with his life as a landowner and politician in Cuba, decided that he would succeed where others had failed. He was a robust man "of good height" for a Spaniard of that day, which probably means he was about five foot four. He had not yet acquired the portliness of later life, but had the high chest and bow legs of a horseman; his eyes, serious but warm, were set in a face too squat to be considered handsome. Like many Castilians of his time, he was consumed by ambition, and he had the talents to pursue it. With his own funds and backing from the governor of Cuba, Cortés assembled a much larger force than previously seen: 11 ships, 600 Spaniards, 200 native Cubans, African slaves, horses, cannon, muskets, crossbows, and the savage war dogs that wore armor, weighed up to 200 pounds, and were routinely fed on Indian flesh. For political reasons, the governor withdrew his support and denied permission to sail, but in 1519 Cortés went anyway.

He stopped first on the east coast of Yucatán, where he learned that two of the Spaniards shipwrecked in 1511 were alive and being held in Chetumal, a city-state that bordered the turquoise lagoon of Bacalar. Recognizing their potential as informants, Cortés sent a ransom to secure their release. One, Gerónimo de Aguilar, a Catholic priest, had so clung to his vow of celibacy that the king of Chetumal made him a guardian of the royal wives. But the other, Gonzalo Guerrero, a young soldier, had gone native. He'd renounced his religion, had his face tattooed in the local style, and married one of the king's relatives.

A joyful Aguilar joined Cortés and began to regale his rescuer with tales of human sacrifice, which he claimed (quite plausibly) had been the fate of his shipmates. He tried to talk Guerrero into leaving with him, but the man of arms had found his place in life among the Maya.

The Spaniards sailed around Yucatán, stopping for a while at a Gulf port on the fringe of the Aztec Empire, a region that was also the ethnic boundary between speakers of Maya and Nahua languages. ("Nahua" is the language family, "Nahuatl" the variety spoken by the Mexica

Aztecs.) There Cortés took a mistress who was fluent in both. Her name was Malintzin, which the Spaniards heard as Malinche or Marina. She proved to be a brilliant schemer with an enduring hatred for highland Mexicans; time after time she would spur Cortés to attack, and save him from fatal mistakes. Using her and Aguilar in tandem, Cortés could communicate with the people he intended to conquer.

By this time, word of the invaders' activities had reached Moctezuma along the trade routes operated by merchant princes in his capital. Unsure of who or what the strangers might be, he sent two officials to spy on them. The men traveled to the Gulf coast and climbed a leafy tree opposite a European ship. This account of their findings was written by Moctezuma's grandson,[4] Tezozomoc, author of two histories, one in Spanish and one in Nahuatl:

> They saw what was drifting there, beyond the shore. And they saw that seven or eight men had left the ship in a small boat and were fishing with hooks. . . . They returned as swiftly as possible to the great city of Mexico-Tenochtitlan, to report on what they had seen.
>
> On reaching Mexico, they went straight to the palace of Moctezuma, to whom they spoke with due reverence and humility. They said to him: "Our lord and king, it is true that unknown people have come. They have arrived at the shores of the great sea, and they were fishing, some with rods and others by casting a net. They fished until late and then got in a small canoe, went back to their two great towers [tall ships], and climbed inside. And there were about fifteen of these people, some with red jackets, others with blue, others grey and green, and yet others of a dirty colour, very ugly, like our *ichtilmatli* [a maguey fiber cloak]; there were also some in pink. And on their heads they wore red kerchiefs and scarlet bonnets, and some had large round hats like small *comales* [tortilla baking dishes], which must have been sunshades. . . . And their flesh is very light, lighter than ours, but they all have long beards, and their hair comes to their ears."[5]

The descriptions were detailed, accurate, and mundane. Although it seemed unlikely that "gods" would wear ugly jackets and go fishing, Moctezuma was disturbed. Unhappily for the Aztecs, he was an insecure and mystical Tlatoani. Ever since hearing the first reports of Spaniards, he had been troubled by omens and nightmares; now he began to worry about an old prophecy concerning a hero or god called Quetzalcoatl, the Feathered Serpent.

According to legend, Quetzalcoatl had sailed away across the sea in ancient times, promising to return in a year called *Ce Acatl,* One Reed. This year, like any in the cyclical Aztec calendar, recurred every fifty-two years; it was the date of Quetzalcoatl's birth and of his death. By an extraordinary coincidence, a year One Reed had begun in February 1519. Cortés's timing was perfect: without knowing it, he had gained a psychological advantage at odds of fifty-two to one. I believe this was the only time that the white god myth had any substance in the conquests of America, and, as we shall see, few Mexicans shared Moctezuma's fears.

Quetzalcoatl was many things: an ancient god and culture hero, a patron of royalty and medicine, a teacher of the arts. He had been worshiped, in various forms, since the dawn of Mesoamerican civilization, 2,000 years before the time of Christ. He was also a semihistorical figure, a prince of the Toltecs, who had preceded the Aztecs. As such he was regarded as a once and future king, an Arthur or a Barbarossa. It is clear from what Moctezuma said later that this worried him most: he thought Cortés might be the ancient ruler himself or a descendant with a prior claim to the Mexican throne. The more the Speaker heard about the strangers, the more these words of prophecy rang in his ears: *If he comes . . . on One Reed, he strikes at kings.*[6]

The Mexica[7] were upstarts and had not forgotten it. A small warrior tribe freebooting through the remains of the Toltec Empire, they had arrived from the north only two centuries before. They were inspired by a tutelar god named Huitzilopochtli who, like the Old Testament Jehovah, specialized in smiting enemies and leading his people to a promised land. When they reached the Valley of Mexico, they liked what they saw: a great basin of fertile volcanic soil with shimmering lakes at its center. This valley, 2,500 square miles in area, had always been the heart of Mexico, as it is today. All the good land was already taken by city-states around the lakeshore, but through a vision of an eagle perched on a cactus eating a snake (still Mexico's national emblem), Huitzilopochtli persuaded the Aztecs to settle in the only vacant spot: a pair of swampy islands. Moctezuma's grandson wrote this foundation legend in epic Nahuatl:

> It is told, it is recounted here how the ancient ones . . . the people of Aztlan, the Mexicans . . . came to [found] the great city of Mexico-Tenochtitlan, their place of fame, their place of example, the place where the *tenochtli* cactus stands amid the waters; where the eagle preens . . . and devours the snake . . . among the reeds, amid the canes.[8]

The Aztecs began modestly, fishing and working as mercenaries in wars between the other states. But soon the muddy cuckoos began to outgrow their hosts. They played one employer off against another and married into the old blood royal of the Toltecs. By ingenious landfilling they made their islands into floating gardens that yielded rich crops of maize, vegetables, and flowers. Under a series of able rulers, the Aztec settlements became twin cities: Tenochtitlan and Tlatelolco, known together as Mexico.

The two cities grew into one, but each had its own central square, temples, nobility, and royal palaces. Tenochtitlan's great plaza, measuring more than a quarter of a mile on each side, held some eighty shrines;[9] Tlatelolco's was almost as big, but much of it was taken up by a marketplace. Like Westminster and London, one was the political hub of the empire, the other its commercial core. Each ceremonial center was dominated by massive flat-topped pyramids supporting dual temples to the gods of war and water. Near these was a great stone court for playing *tlachtli,* a sacred ball game in which teams enacted the eternal struggle between night and day. Though a rite as much as a sport, the game attracted heavy betting from the rich. Beyond the squares were two-story stone palaces of nobles, priests, and wealthy merchants, then thousands of single-story houses belonging to artisans, soldiers, and farmers. The buildings had flat roofs and were brightly painted with bold murals that would one day inspire Mexican painters of the twentieth century. There were also schools, ateliers, shops with hanging signs, and public lavatories. Unlike European cities of the day, Mexico was clean: wastes were hauled away by barge and composted for fertilizer; a thousand men swept and washed the streets each day. Refined Aztecs, who bathed daily, found it advisable to hold flowers to their noses when they met Europeans, who made a point of being filthy.[10] (Spaniards considered bathing an infidel Moorish custom; to be too clean was to risk the attentions of the Inquisition.)

Most of Mexico's streets were canals, laid out on a grid still followed by the modern city plan. Three great causeways with drawbridges ran north, west, and south to the mainland, an aqueduct brought drinking water from mountain springs, and a long dike kept out briny waters to the east. The Spaniards called Mexico "another Venice." The Aztecs, like many American peoples, conceived of their world as a great island; their capital, by both chance and design, was a microcosm of the whole.

Mexico was greater than any Toltec city had ever been, but the fame of the Toltecs had become so inflated that Moctezuma didn't know this. He remembered that he and his people were parvenus, and he felt like a presumptuous butler caught playing lord when the master returns. "It was as if he thought the new arrival was our prince Quetzalcoatl. This is what was in his heart. . . . *He will come here, to see the place of his throne and canopy.*"[11]

> The truth is that in describing the Indian and his lands the white man was describing himself, his own drives and consuming desires.
>
> —Frederick W. Turner, 1974

The strange vessels sailed on, anchoring at last near Cempoala, whose ruins stand not far from modern Veracruz. In the sun its stuccoed temples still have traces of the snow-bright gleam that sent Cortés's scout galloping back shouting that the walls were made of silver.

Moctezuma decided on a policy of appeasement.

> [He] sent five men to greet [Cortés] and to take him gifts. . . . He said to them . . . "It is said that our lord has returned to this land. Go to meet him. Make a speech to him. Open your ears to what he says; listen and remember well.
>
> "Here is what you must take to our lord. This is the regalia of Quetzalcoatl."
>
> There was: a serpent mask of turquoise; a head fan made of quetzal feathers; a collar . . . with a gold disk in the middle; and a shield adorned with gold. [The list continues for more than two pages.]
>
> "Say to him: 'We are sent by your deputy, Motecuhzoma. These are the gifts with which he welcomes you home to Mexico.'"[12]

According to Aztec sources, Cortés gave the messengers a churlish reception aboard his flagship. Like Columbus before him, he was living in a fantasy, expecting at any moment to find a kingdom where gold was common as muck. It was an old obsession, inherited from the barbarian tribes of Europe and the Arab conquerors of Spain. Cortés expected solid gold, lots of it, not weird ornaments of beaten plate with silly feathers and turquoise. "Is this all?" he said to the messengers. "Is this your gift of welcome? Is this how you greet people?" They answered calmly, "This is all, our lord. This is what we have brought you."[13]

Cortés had them thrown in chains and fired a nearby cannon to frighten them. After that he plied them with wine and suggested that they and the Spaniards fight each other in pairs to see who were the greater warriors. The messengers refused, saying that it was not within their warrant from Moctezuma. Cortés insisted, but the Aztecs escaped and hastily returned to Mexico.

The Spanish version of this meeting, written by Bernal Díaz, who was then a young soldier, is quite different. According to him, Cortés "received all this with gracious smiles" and gave in return some glass beads, a crimson cap with a gold badge of Saint George and the Dragon, and an armchair. The one point on which they both agree is that the messengers observed everything minutely. Díaz says that "those skilled painters they have in Mexico" made portraits of the Spaniards and drawings of their ships, guns, horses, dogs, and of the interpreters Malintzin and Aguilar.[14]

Book 12 of the Florentine Codex, a history of the conquest written by Aztecs for Friar Bernardino de Sahagún in the 1550s, quotes at length the messengers' report to Moctezuma. Sahagún was fluent in Nahuatl and used techniques that would stand as good ethnography today. He drew on authors and texts of illustrated Aztec books (known as codices) and on the trained memories of eyewitnesses and professional bards. The history, he adds, "was written in the Mexican language [by] . . . prominent elders, well versed in all matters . . . who were present in the war when this city was conquered."[15] The result is the most detailed Indian account that survives from any of the conquest wars. Written decades before Bernal Díaz, the best European eyewitness, penned his memoir late in life, it is probably the most accurate view from *either* side. Friar Sahagún does not reveal the Aztec authors' names (perhaps to shield them from the Inquisition), but their work speaks for itself as firsthand testimony. Here is the description of the invaders' weapons and appearance, as given to Moctezuma by his messengers:

> "When [the cannon] is fired, a thing like a stone ball comes out of its entrails, raining fire and shooting sparks. And the smoke that comes out of it has a foul smell, like rotten mud, which assaults the brain. If it is fired . . . at a tree, it shatters the tree into splinters—an extraordinary sight, as if someone blew the tree apart from within.
>
> "Their weapons and equipment are all made of iron. They dress in iron; they wear iron helmets on their heads; their swords are iron; their bows are iron; their shields are iron; their spears are iron.
>
> "Their 'deer' carry them on their backs, and these beasts are as tall as a roof.

> "Their bodies are covered everywhere; only their faces can be seen. They are very white, as if made of lime. They have yellow hair, though some of them have black. Their beards are long and yellow, and their moustaches are also yellow. . . .
>
> "Their dogs are huge, with flat waving ears and long, dangling tongues. These have fiery, blazing eyes—yellow eyes, a burning yellow. . . . They are very strong and tireless and agitated. They run panting, with their tongues hanging out. And they are spotted like jaguars." . . .
>
> When Motecuhzoma heard this, he was filled with terror. It was as if his heart grew faint, as if it shrank; he was overcome by despair.[16]

After consolidating his base at Cempoala, Cortés sent one ship to Spain and scuttled the rest. Because the governor of Cuba had forbidden him to sail for Mexico in the first place, Cortés needed the ear of the Spanish king. By sinking his ships he committed every man to win or die.

The Spaniards then marched inland, accompanied by a force of Cempoalans, who were disgruntled vassals of the Aztec Empire. In the mountains between the coast and the Valley of Mexico lay the small republic of Tlaxcala, which had resisted Aztec armies and kept its independence. Tlaxcalan language, religion, and customs were similar to those of Mexico, and they certainly shared the god Quetzalcoatl, who was worshiped throughout Mesoamerica. But they wasted no time agonizing over the identity of Cortés. According to Bernal Díaz, they boasted that they would kill the Spaniards and dine on white flesh with chili sauce.[17] (It is possible that ritual cannibalism was practiced in ancient Mexico, but the evidence is not conclusive. Malintzin, the only person who could understand Nahuatl, may have invented these outrageous taunts.) At any rate, the people of Tlaxcala fought fiercely from the moment the foreigners crossed its border. The Spaniards lost several men and horses to obsidian-bladed wooden broadswords that cut like razors through everything but steel; one horse had its head taken off with a single blow.[18] They won by using artillery, but the Tlaxcalans "had kept their ranks and fought well for a considerable time."[19] Like the Mayas at Champóton, they showed no terror of "gods," guns, and giant "deer."

That night, wrote Bernal Díaz, "we dressed our wounds with the fat from a stout Indian whom we had killed and cut open, for we had no oil."[20]

Tlaxcala sent ambassadors to the Spanish camp with food, hoping to gather intelligence before another fight. Malintzin denounced them; Cortés had their hands cut off and sent them home. Meanwhile, a Tlaxcalan general devised a simple experiment to demonstrate that Spaniards, though hard to kill, were mortal: he held one under water until he drowned.[21]

After another battle with heavy losses, the ruling council of Tlaxcala accepted an offer of peace. Cortés's price was to form an alliance against Mexico. By then the Spaniards were down to only twelve horses and had lost forty-five men, about a tenth of their force, excluding those left on the coast.[22] Several leading Spaniards had already told Cortés that it was time to retreat. Without Tlaxcala's change of heart, he would sooner or later have had to abandon his march on Mexico. "We . . . wondered," Bernal Díaz recalled, "what would happen to us when we had to fight Montezuma if we were reduced to such straits by the Tlaxcalans, whom our Cempoalan allies described as a peaceful people."[23]

The Spaniards and their native allies moved on to Cholula, an ancient city whose public buildings included the largest pyramid in the world.[24] At the summit of this vast structure, which today resembles a natural hill, stood the finest of all temples to Quetzalcoatl. If Moctezuma's fears about the identity of Cortés had much currency outside his own mind, one would expect the Cholulans, who were Mexico's allies, to be in awe of the strange white men. But according to a Tlaxcalan account, they called the Europeans "upstarts" and "foreign savages."[25]

Bernal Díaz reported that Malintzin heard some loose talk and noticed suspiciously large quantities of taco sauce. "So in return for our coming to treat them like brothers, and tell them the commands of our lord God and the King, they were planning to kill us and eat our flesh, and had already prepared the pots with salt and peppers and tomatoes."[26] The Aztec account denies any such plot, blaming Cortés and the Tlaxcalans for an unprovoked massacre.

> Suddenly there were knifings, there were sword strokes, there was death. The Cholulans had suspected nothing. They faced the Spaniards without swords or shields. And so by treachery they were slain. They died like blind men, not knowing why they died by the treachery of the Tlaxcalans.[27]

After this the Spaniards made their famous march over the high saddle between the volcanoes Popocatépetl and Ixtaccíhuatl, the spectacular gateway to the Valley of Mexico. Moctezuma tried some feeble ruses to turn them back at the pass. Most unwisely, he tried to buy them off.

> They gave [the Spaniards] emblems of gold, banners of quetzal plumes, and golden necklaces. And when they gave them these, the Spaniards' faces grinned: they were delighted, they were overjoyed. They snatched up the gold like monkeys. . . . They were swollen with greed; they were ravenous; they hungered for that gold like wild pigs.
>
> They seized the golden standards, they swung them from side to side, they examined them from top to bottom. They babbled in a barbarous language; everything they said was in a savage tongue.[28]

At last the strangers came down from the snowfields and beheld the valley, the Aztec city gleaming at its heart. To Mexicans this was a normal sight; to Bernal Díaz it was a marvel.

> When we saw all those cities and villages built in the water, and other great towns on dry land, and that straight and level causeway leading to Mexico, we were astounded. These great towns and *cues* [pyramids] and buildings rising from the water, all made of

> stone, seemed like an enchanted vision from the tale of Amadís. Indeed, some of our soldiers asked whether it was not all a dream.[29]

> Remove justice, and what are kingdoms but gangs of criminals on a large scale? . . . A gang is a group of men . . . in which the plunder is divided according to an agreed convention. If this villainy . . . acquires territory, establishes a base, captures cities and subdues peoples, it then openly arrogates to itself the title of kingdom.
>
> —Saint Augustine, *City of God,* c. 420

The Spaniards advanced along the Iztapalapa causeway, five miles long, eight yards wide, and built of hewn stone. "Wide though it was," recalled Díaz, "it was so crowded with people that there was hardly room for them all. Some were going to Mexico and others coming away, besides those who had come out to see us. . . . The towers and the *cues* were full, and they came in canoes from all parts of the lake."[30]

Romantic Spanish paintings of the entry into Mexico, done long after the event, show Cortés leading a gallant parade. According to the Aztecs, the Spaniards advanced in fear of ambush, with Cortés leading from behind.

> In front came four men on horses, guiding the others, leading the rest. They kept veering and turning, going back and forth . . . darting down the side streets, examining the houses, constantly looking up at the roof terraces.
>
> Their dogs did the same, their dogs ran ahead. They came sniffing everywhere; they came panting, always panting.
>
> Marching by himself, in front and alone, came one who bore their flag. . . . Behind him were the men with iron swords; they came with their swords drawn, with their swords flashing. On their shoulders . . . they had shields of wood and leather.

> Secondly, in a squadron, came the horses, carrying men on their backs.... These *caballos*—these "deer"—snorted and neighed; they sweated heavily, the sweat flowed from them like water; and the foam from their mouths fell on the ground in drops....
>
> And at the very end, directing from the rear, came their captain [Cortés], who seemed to be their equivalent of our war commander, the *tlacateccatl.*[31]

Mexico City's lakes have since been drained, and the causeway is a boulevard choked with traffic. When this was dug up in the late 1960s to build the Metro, a small round temple came to light. In 1519 it stood on the edge of Tenochtitlan's core; now it parts rush-hour crowds in the middle of Pino Suárez station.[32] This is probably where the Aztec emperor at last confronted Cortés, on a day Eight Wind, which to the Spaniards was November 8, 1519.[33]

The two men were fit and slim and fairly close in age—Moctezuma was the elder by five or six years. He wore his dark hair just over his ears and sported a small goatee. Cortés had a sparse black beard that failed to hide a scar on his lower lip, memento of a knife fight involving a woman. Each leader was attended by his closest followers, the Aztec resplendent beneath a canopy of quetzal plumes, the Spaniard a strange, scaly creature in his carapace of beaten steel. The moment was fraught for them both, but especially for Moctezuma. He had tried flattery, deception, and Danegeld. After what had happened at Cholula, there was little likelihood that the strangers had anything to do with Quetzalcoatl. But from his words, it seems that Moctezuma decided to stick to his original policy of treating Cortés as a king of Mexico returned.

When the two had exchanged gifts, the Speaker gave this speech in the majestic, repetitious style of Nahuatl oratory:

> My lord, you are weary, you are tired. You have come to your land; you have arrived in your city, Mexico. You have come to rest beneath your canopy; you have come to your seat, to your throne.[34]

For a short time they have kept it for you, they have preserved it, those who now are gone, those who have been your deputies: the kings Itzcoatl, Motecuhzoma the First, Axayacatl, Tizoc, Ahuitzotl. For just a short time they have kept and governed the city of Mexico for you. . . .

If only one of them were here to witness, to wonder at what I now see myself! To see what I see: I the last, I the reigning one of all our lords. No, I am not dreaming, I am not sleepwalking . . . I am seeing you now, I have set eyes on your face!

For some time I have been anguishing: I have fixed my gaze on the Region of Mystery. And you have come from clouds, from mists.[35] Just as it was foretold by the kings, by those who have ruled, by those who have governed your city. . . .

So now it has been fulfilled; you have come. With great weariness, with great effort, you have arrived.

Come now and rest; take possession of your royal palaces; give comfort to your body. Enter your land, my lords![36]

Moctezuma may have been pusillanimous, but his words removed any pretext for a "just war." Only five years earlier, the Spanish king, to save his mortal soul, had accepted the principle that foreign peoples, even pagans, could not be attacked without first being given a chance to submit. Conquistadors were supposed to read out an absurd document known as the Requirement, offering this Hobson's choice. By presenting Cortés with the throne of Mexico, Moctezuma had already complied. The Aztec account continues with Cortés's reply.

When Motecuhzoma's speech had ended, and Cortés had heard it, Malintzin then translated it and explained it to him.

And when Cortés had understood Motecuhzoma's words, he replied through Malintzin. He spoke to him in a barbarous tongue; he said in his barbarous tongue:

"Be reassured, Motecuhzoma, have no fear. We love you greatly. Today our hearts are at peace."[37]

Marveling, the Spaniards then entered the strange metropolis. "Who could now count the multitude of men, women, and boys in the streets, on the roof-tops and in canoes on the waterways, who had come out to see us?" Díaz asks his reader. "It was a wonderful sight and, as I write, it all comes before my eyes as if it had happened only yesterday."[38]

The Spaniards and their allies were taken to the center and given lodging in the palace of Moctezuma's late father, Axayacatl. This building, which stood near the greatest pyramid, was large enough to accommodate 400 Spaniards, 6,000 Tlaxcalans, a dozen horses, and all their supplies in comfort. To judge from ruins and paintings of similar structures, it was a complex of connecting halls and garden courtyards. For the next eight months it served as the invaders' base and fortress; within a few weeks it also became Moctezuma's prison.

> Our religion seems foolish to you, but so does yours to me.
>
> —Sitting Bull, Sioux, 1889

> Chacun appelle barbarie ce qui n'est pas de son usage.
>
> —Montaigne, c. 1588

During the unnatural calm that prevailed while the two sides weighed each other, the Spaniards were sightseers in the Mexican capital. Aztec writers do not describe the city in detail because it was as familiar to them as London to Londoners, so we must turn for a while to the European point of view.

First, the foreigners observed closely the possessions and activities of Moctezuma. The Tlatoani lived where the national palace of Mexico now stands, just south of the main pyramid. Besides state rooms, banqueting halls, sleeping quarters, and kitchens capable of serving more than a thousand, his palace held "a great house" of hieroglyphic books detailing the income and expenditure of the Aztec Empire.[39] There were two houses filled with ornate weaponry, cotton armor, and heraldic shields in feather mosaic (a major art form throughout much of ancient America). But what impressed the invaders most were the emperor's zoological gardens, a wonder then unknown in Europe. A large aviary contained "everything from the royal eagle, smaller kinds of eagles, and other large birds, down to multicoloured little birds, and those from which they take the fine green feathers they use in their feather-work. These . . . are called *quetzals*."[40] There were pools for many kinds of waterbird, including flamingos; Cortés, in one of his letters to the Spanish king, added that the waterfowl alone ate 250 pounds of fish a day.[41]

Other parts of the zoo were more sinister. Big cats, wolves, snakes, and small carnivores were kept not merely for amusement; they were mouths of the war cult on which Aztec power was based. "We know for certain," Díaz wrote, "that when they drove us out of Mexico and killed over eight hundred and fifty of our soldiers, they fed those beasts and snakes on their bodies for many days."[42]

At first Cortés commanded his troops not to stray far "until we knew better what conduct to observe."[43] Despite his weapons and his arrogance, he never forgot that he and his men were only 400 Europeans in one block of the largest city any of them had ever seen.

After four days, Cortés and several others were taken to the central square of Tlatelolco, Tenochtitlan's twin, which had been annexed in 1473 to form greater Mexico City. Tlatelolco's vast market, with its stalls, workshops, arbitrators, and every conceivable product from bronze hardware to furniture and chocolate (a Nahuatl word), fascinated them. Here was an aspect of Mexican culture that they could understand and appreciate.

Of all the European and American nations that clashed in the sixteenth century, the Aztecs and Spaniards had the most in common. Both were warlike, mercantile people, avaricious and quick to resort to force. Both believed they had a divine mission to rule the world. In more than one way, they deserved each other.

From the market the Spaniards were taken up Tlatelolco's main pyramid, an artificial mountain raised 150 feet above the human plane. On its flat top stood sacrificial altars and smoking incense braziers; behind these, the houses of the gods—the actual temples—rose another sixty feet into the air. Here, nearly two years later, the Aztec nation would bleed to death. Bernal Díaz:

> Now let us leave the market . . . and come to the courts and enclosures in which their great *cue*[44] stood. Before reaching it you passed through a series of large courts, bigger I think than the Plaza at Salamanca. These courts were surrounded by a double masonry wall and paved, like the whole place, with very large smooth white flagstones. Where these stones were absent everything was whitened and polished, indeed the whole place was so clean that there was not a straw or a grain of dust to be found there. . . .
>
> The top of the *cue* formed an open square . . . and it was here that the great stones stood on which they placed the poor Indians for sacrifice. Here also was a massive image like a dragon, and other hideous figures, and a great deal of blood that had been spilled that day. Emerging in the company of two *papas* [priests] from the shrine which houses his accursed images, Montezuma made a deep bow to us all and said: "My lord . . . you must be tired after climbing this great *cue* of ours." And Cortés replied that none of us was ever exhausted by anything. Then Montezuma took him by the hand, and told him to look at his great city and all the other cities standing in the water, and the many others on the land round the lake. . . . So we stood there looking, because that huge accursed *cue* stood so high that it dominated everything. We saw the three causeways that led into Mexico: the causeway of Iztapalapa by which we had entered four days before, and that of Tacuba [Tlacopan] along which we were afterwards to flee on the night of our great defeat. . . . We saw the fresh water which came from Chapultepec to supply the city, and the bridges that were constructed at intervals on the causeways. . . . We saw a great number of canoes, some coming with provisions and others returning with cargo and merchandise. . . . We saw *cues* and shrines in these cities that looked like gleaming white towers and castles: a marvellous sight. All the houses had flat roofs, and on

> the causeways were other small towers and shrines built like fortresses.
>
> Having examined and considered all we had seen, we turned back to the great market and the swarm of people buying and selling. The mere murmur of their voices talking was loud enough to be heard more than three miles away. Some of our soldiers who had been in many parts of the world, in Constantinople, in Rome, and all over Italy, said that they had never seen a market so well laid out, so large, so orderly, and so full of people.[45]

From the top, the center of Tenochtitlan must have been visible as another great temple complex more than a mile to the south. Recent excavations have shown that the main pyramids of the twin cities were about the same size.[46] They were steep and terraced, probably in four great tiers. On the western side two parallel staircases ran in one flight from bottom to top. Of the two temples built side by side on the summit, one was dedicated to Tlaloc, god of water, rain, and fertility; the other belonged to the Aztecs' warlike patron, Huitzilopochtli. If Bernal Díaz is accurate, Huitzilopochtli also shared his temple with Tezcatlipoca, his "brother." Huitzilopochtli, which can be translated as the Southern Hummingbird,[47] was the day sun, while Tezcatlipoca, the Smoking Mirror, represented the night sky, the north, and the sun's nocturnal journey through the underworld.

When missionary priests learned Nahuatl and came to understand some of the ideas behind the images and rites, they often compared Aztec deities to those of ancient Greece and Rome: "This god called Huitzilopochtli," wrote Sahagún, "was another Hercules."[48] In fact, Aztec religion was more subtle than that. Unlike Zeus and Mercury, the gods of Mexico were not human individuals writ large. Aztec religion was closer in structure to Hinduism: its many gods were interpenetrating and kaleidoscopic, conceptualizations of nature, time, and space.

Aztec cosmology was deeply dualistic, structured by complementary forces: night and day, life and death, fire and water, man and woman, mountain and ocean, future and past. These were reconciled in the supreme Duality, Ometeotl, and in the god-hero Quetzalcoatl, whose name can be rendered Precious Twin, as well as Feathered Serpent, and whose bird-snake symbols unite sky and earth.

The Aztecs believed that the world was impermanent and delicate. They worried constantly that the sun might weaken and die and the universe end in cataclysm—a belief intimately related to the cycles of their calendar. Hieroglyphs on the famous Sun Stone, or Calendar Stone, which now dominates the Mexica Hall of the national museum, told that four previous eras had been created and destroyed; there was no reason to think that the present one, called Motion and destined to end in earthquake, would be any different. The stone also refers to the complex gearing of two time counts, which return to the same starting point every fifty-two years, a period known as the Calendar Round.

When each Calendar Round was complete, the universe was thought to be especially unstable, and great efforts were made to start the new cycle in the proper way. Pottery was broken and replaced, new fire was kindled throughout Mexico, pyramids were enlarged and rededicated with lavish sacrifices. These ideas may seem strange to us in this form, but the theme of gods destroying one world and building another is found in many religions—witness Noah. All over the world people have tended to feel that their own deeds were to blame for natural disasters. In the volcanic lands of America there was no shortage of landslides, floods, earthquakes, and fiery eruptions to fuel this anxiety.

Amerindians always sensed the toll that human life takes from the environment. Man was not seen as separate from, and superior to, the rest of creation; the world that mattered was this earth, not an imaginary hereafter. Humans lived in a reciprocal relationship with nature, and repayment had to be made for the existence they enjoyed at the expense of other life.

During what is known as the Classic period, which lasted for most of the first millennium A.D., repayment had usually taken the form of personal bloodletting by rulers and priests. Occasionally, rival kings were captured and sacrificed, sometimes after a high-stakes ball game played as a substitute for war. But the wholesale immolation of war captives, which has given the Aztecs such a bad press, seems to have arisen only in the last centuries before the Spanish conquest. It was provoked by instability and militarism that followed the Classic collapse, when many great cities were abandoned and populations fell. The causes of the collapse are not fully understood, but there is mounting evidence of environmental change. Perhaps this was natural—a shift in climate—but it may have been caused or aggravated by human activity such as the felling of tropical forests. The Aztecs knew of the catastrophe; it had passed into mythic history, reinforcing their anxiety about the world's impermanence. In addition, they themselves were facing problems caused by a new population boom.

So in their bid for power, the Aztecs, like all imperial nations, made a convenient marriage of politics and piety. They believed they had a sacred mission to prolong the existing age by feeding the sun with human blood. Personal mortification was no longer enough; only hundreds of enemy captives could suffice. Huitzilopochtli shouldered his way into the ancient pantheon and made himself boss of a fanatical cult linking the universe and war.

Human sacrifice was therefore not the persistence of an old "savage" practice among civilized people who should have known better but rather a hypertrophy of sinister elements in their culture, which in more gracious times had been kept in check. Like the modern world, the fifteenth century in Mexico was an age of competition for shrinking resources. What differed were the patterns of war. Modern armies slaughter one another on the battlefield; ancient Mexicans preferred to take their enemies alive and kill them later ritually. Sacrificial death was "flowery death," granting honor and a kind of immortality.

The Spaniards, who considered Islam thoroughly devilish, could not have been more appalled by the Aztec religion. Its fine, philosophical, and poetic side was obscured from them by alien imagery and pools of blood. When they saw the gory altars and carved serpents, the terrifying statues and the racks of skulls, they believed that Aztec gods were genuine demons risen from hell.

Cortés kept preaching to Moctezuma, hoping for a conversion that would justify all he had done—and planned to do—in Mexico. According to Díaz, the Tlatoani replied:

> These arguments of yours have been familiar to me for some time. I understand what you said to my ambassadors . . . about the three gods and the cross, also what you preached in the various towns through which you passed. We have given you no answer, since we have worshipped our own gods here from the beginning and know them to be good. No doubt yours are good also, but do not trouble to tell us any more about them at present.[49]

Cortés would not give up, and he even had the temerity to raise the subject while on Tlatelolco's pyramid. "Lord Montezuma. . . . Allow us to erect a cross here on top of this tower, and let us divide off part of this sanctuary where your Huitzilopochtli and Tezcatlipoca stand, as a place where we can put an image of Our Lady . . . and then you will see, by the fear that your idols have of her, how grievously they have deceived you."[50]

On this occasion Moctezuma's weariness turned to anger. To make such a suggestion here, in the very precinct of the gods, was not only bad manners but sacrilege. It was also hypocrisy. The Spaniards, believers in a faith that commanded "Thou shalt not kill," had a war god of their own: Santiago Matamoros, Saint James the Slayer of Moors. He had been at their side throughout the reconquest of Spain, and his sword was stained with as much enemy blood as the knife of Huitzilopochtli. Spanish histories are filled with accounts of miraculous interventions by Santiago who, in the thick of battle, would ride down from heaven on his charger to smite the heathen. Early in 1492, he had helped defeat the last of the Moors; loot from that victory had outfitted Columbus and opened a new theater of operations. Soon he was known as Santiago *Mata-indios,* Saint James the Indian Killer.

When Mexico fell and the Europeans began building a new town in the Aztec ruins, one of the first things they did was erect a church beside the Tlatelolco pyramid—dedicated to Santiago.

> You will scarcely find traces of humanity [in Indians]; who . . . are so cowardly and timid, that they scarcely withstand the appearance of our soldiers . . . fleeing like women before a very few Spaniards.
>
> —Juan Ginés de Sepúlveda, 1550

Neither Spaniard nor Aztec knew what to do next. Beneath a show of friendship lay mutual fear. From the tense debate over religion it is clear that Moctezuma had at last abandoned any illusions he may have had about Cortés and Quetzalcoatl.

At about this time, the Spaniards broke through a walled-up doorway in their quarters to find several rooms filled with the treasure of Axayacatl, Moctezuma's father. The discovery electrified the invaders, fueling both their greed and fear. "All the gold Montezuma had given us, and all that we had seen in the treasury of his father . . . was turning to poison in our bodies," wrote Díaz who, with many others, urged Cortés to seize the emperor immediately or risk becoming "senseless beasts charmed by the gold and incapable of looking death in the eye." Pedro de Alvarado, who soon proved to be a pathological killer, urged that the Speaker "be got out of his palace by smooth words and brought to our quarters."[51]

A pretext for seizing Moctezuma arose the very next day, when news came from the coast that an Aztec provincial governor had killed several Spaniards sent to demand his fealty. Cortés and an armed squad burst into the Tlatoani's chambers. Malintzin listened to the torrent of Castilian threats and told Moctezuma, "If you stay here, you will be a dead man."[52] The emperor then allowed himself to be frogmarched out of his own palace and into theirs. He summoned the offending governor to the capital and handed him over to the Spaniards for punishment. Under "severe questioning"—a Spanish euphemism for torture—the official and his men said they had acted on Moctezuma's orders.

Having heard what he wanted, Cortés had them burned alive in public. The Mexicans went into shock. They were used to the spectacle of death, but the quick death of an obsidian knife to the heart. Never before had they seen living people set on fire; the alien savagery appalled them. Worse, they now knew that their ruler, whom Cortés had thrown in chains during the execution, was in the hands of the invaders and there was nothing they could do for him without risking his life.

Soon after, a tearful Moctezuma signed papers formally making himself a vassal of Charles V, Holy Roman emperor and king of Spain. He then acquiesced while the Spaniards ransacked his own and his father's treasuries. Much of the treasure was feather mosaic and turquoise inlay, which, as the Aztecs noted sadly, meant nothing to the Europeans.

> The [Spaniards] worked obsessed, like little beasts, patting each other on the back, and their hearts were filled with delight . . . they were transported to the brink of lunacy. They rushed in everywhere, each one grasping for himself. They were utterly possessed by greed.
>
> All of Motecuhzoma's personal riches were taken immediately. This was his own property, precious and wonderful things of every kind: necklaces of heavy gems, anklets of beautiful workmanship, gold bracelets, wristbands, ankle rings with little golden bells, and the turquoise diadem that is the insignia of the ruler, reserved only for his use. . . . They took everything, they seized everything, they appropriated everything as if they had won it. . . .[53]
>
> When they reached the treasury called Teucalco, they hauled everything outside: the quetzal plume headdress, featherwork pectorals, fine shields, golden discs, necklaces of the gods, gold nose pieces, greaves, bracelets, and diadems all of gold.
>
> They stripped the gold at once from the shields and the coats of arms. Then they made a great heap of gold, and they set fire to everything else, no matter how valuable. They burned it all.
>
> They melted the gold into ingots, and of the jades and emeralds they took only what looked good to them; the Tlaxcalans made off with the rest.[54]

The treasure was enormous, though not nearly as big as that which awaited other Spaniards in Peru. The gold alone weighed 162,000 *pesos de oro*—about 19,600 troy ounces.[55] At 1992 gold prices it would be worth close to $8 million, though its purchasing power in contemporary Europe would have been far greater. But by the time the Spanish king, Cortés, and other prominent Spaniards had taken their allotted shares, and filched extra ones, not much was left for the common man. Each foot soldier received a mere hundred pesos. A few were so disgusted that they refused to accept their share; others lost it at cards the same day.

Some Mexican goldwork, featherwork, and hieroglyphic books given earlier by Moctezuma to Cortés had already been sent to Emperor Charles. Cortés may not have liked Aztec art, but he knew that its sophistication would convey far better than words that he had found a high civilization in the Indies. Miraculously, this was seen in 1520 by one of the few Europeans capable of appreciating it, Albrecht Dürer, himself a goldsmith and one of the greatest artists of the day.[56]

> I saw the things which were brought to the King from the new Golden Land: a sun entirely of gold, a whole fathom [six feet] broad; likewise a moon entirely of silver, just as big; likewise sundry curiosities . . . all of which is fairer to see than marvels. . . .
>
> Nothing I have seen in all my days has rejoiced my heart so much as these things. For I saw among them amazing works of art and I marvelled over the subtle ingenuity of the men in those distant lands.[57]

The Spaniards in Mexico now looked for ways to increase their spoil. They pored over Aztec tax records, searched the empire for mines, and seized fertile plantations. They acted as if Moctezuma's submission had substance, as if they had really conquered Mexico. But they had not. Unrest was growing, and when they installed a statue of the Virgin in a temple, the anger in the city became palpable. Instead of fleeing from the sight of the True God, as Cortés had predicted, the Aztec gods made it clear to their priests that they would not tolerate foreign idols on their turf. Moctezuma warned Cortés that the Spaniards had gone too far; if they did not leave Mexico immediately, all would be killed. Cortés protested that he had no ships; Moctezuma promptly sent carpenters to the coast with orders to work to Spanish specifications.

Then, one day early in May 1520, the Tlatoani suddenly seemed a new man. He summoned Cortés to his rooms and told him breezily that more Spaniards had landed. Cortés would no longer have to wait until the ships were ready; he could leave right away. In fact, Aztec spies had already found out that these men were enemies of Cortés, sent by Cuba's governor to punish him for sailing against orders. Moctezuma fondly imagined the European forces annihilating one another.

Cortés took about 250 men and marched to confront his rival on the coast, making the mistake of leaving Mexico City under the command of Pedro de Alvarado. Alvarado's dashing character and blond good looks had made him popular not only with his men but with the Aztecs who, not having seen his dark side, nicknamed him Tonatiuh, or Sun. But even by the standards of his fellow conquistadors, Alvarado was unstable and wantonly cruel.

Just before Cortés had left, the nobility of Tenochtitlan asked permission to hold a kind of Easter festival that involved dancing in Huitzilopochtli's precinct. As the time approached—the night of May 21—Alvarado asked to attend.[58] Both he and Cortés had raised no objection, so long as the dancers were unarmed and no human sacrifice took place. These conditions were observed, but Alvarado massacred the celebrants.

He later made the usual claim that the dancers—perhaps as many as a thousand young noblemen—were plotting an attack, but since they had no weapons and were surrounded by a Spanish guard, his excuse is hollow. Possibly he panicked at the strange music and the eerie vigor of the dancing; more likely he decided this was a good opportunity to kill as many young officers of the Mexican army as he could. The outrage is recorded in all its horror by several Aztec sources, including the eloquent Florentine Codex.

> And so it happened when they were celebrating the fiesta; the dancing had already begun, already there was singing, already one song was entwined with another and the singing echoed like

> crashing waves; at that opportune moment the Spaniards decided to kill the people.
>
> They appeared suddenly, in battle array; they came to seal the exits, the gateways, the passages. . . . And when this was done, they rushed into the Sacred Courtyard to slay the people. . . .
>
> Quickly they surrounded the dancers; then they rushed among the drums. They hacked at the drummer and cut off both his hands; they chopped off his head and it fell far away. Then they ran the people through with iron spears, and slashed at them with iron swords. Some they cut open from behind and these fell to the ground with their intestines hanging out. . . . And when they tried in vain to run away, they merely dragged their entrails and their feet became entangled. There was nowhere they could go.
>
> Those who tried to leave were stabbed and cut down at the gate. But some scaled the walls. . . . Others lay among the dead, and by feigning were able to escape, but if anyone was seen to take a breath they cut him down.
>
> The blood . . . ran like water, like slimy water; the stench of blood filled the air, and the entrails seemed to slither along by themselves. And the Spaniards went everywhere, searching the public buildings, thrusting with their weapons.[59]

The Mexicans, who had borne so much, rose to besiege Alvarado's men. They killed several, wounded others, and set fire to Axayacatl's palace even though it still held their Speaker as well as the invaders.

While this was happening in the capital, Cortés pulled off one of his masterstrokes. The force sent against him, under the command of Pánfilo de Narváez, was the largest yet assembled in the Spanish Indies: 900 men, including 80 cavalry, 80 musketeers, 150 crossbow-men, several heavy cannon, and large quantities of gunpowder. Cortés was outnumbered four to one, but somehow he defeated Narváez on a rainy night at Cempoala and imprisoned him. Then, employing the smooth words for which he was famous—especially that word "gold"—he persuaded the new men to join him in the rape of the Aztec Empire.

No record survives of Moctezuma's thoughts as he saw the foreigners returning in greater numbers than ever. They managed to reach Axayacatl's palace, but their arrival merely worsened the shortage of food and water there. The Aztecs had cut off all supplies and closed the great market to prevent the Spaniards from raiding it. Moctezuma then achieved a coup of his own. Perhaps seeing that war was inevitable and that his people would need a new leader, he persuaded Cortés to release his brother Cuitlahuac, who had been arrested for anti-Spanish activities. Surprisingly, Cortés swallowed the idea that Moctezuma's brother would be able to calm the city and allow the Spaniards to leave.

Cuitlahuac, of course, did no such thing. He summoned the council of nobles, which deposed Moctezuma and made him Tlatoani instead. Cortés responded by forcing Moctezuma to address his subjects from a rooftop, but the fallen monarch could do nothing. The Mexican assault became fiercer and better organized: "The canals were each dredged, widened, deepened. . . . Everywhere the canals were made dangerous."[60] The Spaniards were trapped.

A few days later, probably on June 30, 1520,[61] Mexicans found Moctezuma and the lord of Tlatelolco "dead . . . tossed outside the royal houses."[62]

Who killed Moctezuma? Spanish sources claim that when he spoke to the crowd he was hit by stones. "Though [our men] begged him to have his wounds dressed and eat some food . . . he refused," says Bernal Díaz. "Then quite unexpectedly we were told he was dead."[63] This version, highly suspect, has been accepted by most historians. It is revealing that Díaz distances himself by "we were told." Another Spanish account has Cortés declaring that the ruler died "before I returned from the coast."[64] This cannot be true, as Moctezuma had yet to make his rooftop speech.

Aztec sources give a different story. Chimalpahin, a native historian who based his work on glyphic codices, says, "The Spaniards put Lord Motecuhzoma to death by throttling him."[65] Sahagún, compiler of the Florentine Codex, agrees: "The first thing that [the Spaniards] did was to strangle all the nobles whom they held prisoner, and throw them dead outside the fort."[66] The Texcoco historian Ixtlilxochitl, whose family collaborated with Cortés, has it both ways, adding a macabre twist: "They say that one of [the Mexicans] threw a stone at him, from which he died. But his own subjects say that the Spaniards killed him, stabbing him in the anus with a sword."[67]

So died the emperor of Mexico who, depending on one's reading of his deeds, was either a mystic and a weakling lost in the maze of appeasement or a pragmatist who judged submission to Spain inevitable and tried to arrange the best transition for his people. In the light of what happened next, it is clear that Moctezuma could have destroyed the Spaniards in 1519 if he had tried. It is also clear that the disease they introduced, which respected no frontiers, would have made Mexican independence difficult to sustain against further European invasions.

Shortly after Moctezuma's death, the besieged Spaniards and Tlaxcalans slunk out of Axayacatl's palace and tried to escape by the shortest route, the western causeway to Tlacopan (now Tacuba). For them that night would become *la Noche Triste,* the Night of Sorrow; but the Aztec chroniclers can scarcely conceal their glee at the greatest Indian victory in all the conquest wars.

> When it was dark, when midnight came, all the Spaniards and Tlaxcalans crept out huddled together. The Spaniards went first with the Tlaxcalans behind, and they stuck closely to each other's backs. They were pressed together like a wall. They carried portable wooden bridges, which they put over the canals, and thus they got across.
>
> At that time it was raining lightly. . . . They managed to cross [three] canals . . . but when they got to the . . . fourth, they were seen by a woman who was fetching water. She saw them and immediately cried out: "Mexicans! Come over here! They are going; your enemies are already crossing the canals! They are escaping stealthily!"
>
> Then one of the men at the top of the temple of Huitzilopochtli called out. His cry rang out over the people, everybody heard his shout: "Soldiers, captains, Mexicans! Your enemies are fleeing! Come to attack them. Bring boats armoured with shields. Block the way!" . . .

> Then those with armoured boats drew up in battle order. They pursued [the Spaniards], they rowed furiously, they paddled with powerful strokes, and their boats leapt forward as if whipped . . . they attacked the Spaniards from both sides, they threw themselves upon them. . . . Others came on foot, heading straight for Nonohualco and on towards Tlacopan to cut off the retreat.
>
> Then the crews of the armoured boats launched their darts against the Spaniards. From one side and another the arrows fell.[68] But the Spaniards also shot at the Mexicans. They fired guns and crossbows. There were dead on both sides. The Spaniards were withered by the arrows, and so were the Tlaxcalans. . . .
>
> When the Spaniards reached . . . the Toltec Canal, they collapsed in heaps, as if they had fallen in a landslide. There they all threw themselves into the water, they all leapt from the edge. . . . The canal filled with their bodies, it was blocked with men. And those who came last crossed on the dying and the dead.[69]

About three quarters of the 1,200 Europeans in Mexico City died that night. Several thousand Tlaxcalans also died. Forty-six horses were killed or taken, leaving the Spaniards with only twenty-three.

The Aztecs had won the first round.

> When the Christians were exhausted from war, God saw fit to send the Indians smallpox.
>
> —Francisco de Aguilar, c. 1525

> Had there been no epidemic . . . Cortés might have ended his life spread-eagled beneath the obsidian blade of a priest of Huitzilopochtli.
>
> —Alfred Crosby, *The Columbian Exchange*, 1972

The high number of Spanish dead is unique in all their American campaigns. The Spanish soldier of fortune, product of a warrior culture honed by seven centuries of war, was a most formidable opponent. No American people had weapons that could kill him easily. Aztec broadswords cut like razors through clothing and flesh, but their blades of obsidian—a volcanic glass—shattered against steel armor and Toledo swords. Arrows and darts were feeble compared to the iron crossbow and harquebus (a heavy musket supported on a stand and fired by a smoldering wick). And the Spanish knight at full gallop on an armored mount was the tank of his day.

These advantages, great though they were, had been checkmated by conditions in the Aztec capital. Cavalry was ineffective on streets broken by canals and barricades; matchlocks were snuffed out in the rain; heavy armor, crammed with loot, meant that to fall in the water was to drown. Many Spaniards met a poetic doom, sinking with the weight of Moctezuma's gold. The Aztecs, too, were members of a warrior culture, ready to die in dozens for every Spaniard killed. They knew how to use their city, whose design had served them well before. But when they tried to finish the job by attacking the rump of Cortés's army on a plain, brilliant horsemanship enabled the Spaniards to escape to Tlaxcala.

As soon as the invaders had gone, the Mexicans searched the canals and lake bottom. They gathered all the foreign weapons they could find and retrieved some treasure from the corpses. "Their bodies were white like white reed shoots,"[70] the Florentine Codex vividly recalls. The Aztecs set about repairing temples and streets, confident they would never see Hernán Cortés again.

Perhaps the Spaniards really would have left the country, at least until they had raised a larger force. But a new and sinister ally had come with Narváez and had been hatching all this time—smallpox. The disease was endemic in Europe, as common as chicken pox or measles, and most adult Europeans were immune to it. Its effect on the Mexicans was catastrophic. "More than one half of the population died," wrote a Spanish friar. "They died in heaps, like bedbugs."[71] His estimate is no exaggeration: it fits with known attacks on isolated populations. In 1707, smallpox killed 36 percent of Icelanders who, being European, likely had some resistance.[72] An 1898 outbreak in the Hopi pueblos killed up to 74 percent.[73]

A drawing in the Florentine Codex shows this new death, together with these words:

> After the Spaniards had left the city of Mexico, and before they had made any preparations to attack us again, there came amongst us a great sickness, a general plague. It began in the month of Tepeilhuitl. It raged amongst us, killing vast numbers of people. It covered many all over with sores: on the face, on the head, on the chest, everywhere.
>
> It was devastating. . . . Nobody could move himself, nor turn his head, nor flex any part of his body. The sores were so terrible that the victims could not lie face down, nor on their backs, nor move from one side to the other. And when they tried to move even a little, they cried out in agony. . . .
>
> Many died of the disease, and many others died merely of hunger. They starved to death because there was no one left alive to care for them. . . . Many had their faces ravaged; they were pock-marked, they were pitted for life. Others lost their sight, they became blind.
>
> The worst phase of this pestilence lasted sixty days, sixty days of horror . . . then it diminished, but it never stopped entirely. . . .
>
> And when this had happened, the Spaniards returned.[74]

Among the dead was Moctezuma's brother Cuitlahuac, whose reign had lasted a mere eighty days. In that short time he not only defeated the Spaniards but tried to weld an alliance against them that reached far beyond the borders of his empire. He offered the Tlaxcalans peace if they would kill the hairy refugees among them, an offer debated by the Tlaxcalan senate but declined. He sent ten ambassadors to the king of Michoacan (a state west of the Aztecs'), but smallpox reached that king before the envoys.[75] The biological weapon now loose in Mexico utterly transformed the balance of power.

Again Cortés had amazing luck: at this critical moment, ships intended to supply Narváez fell into his hands. With new men, new horses, and gunpowder, he won over the wavering lords of Tlaxcala and other Aztec enemies, who were many. The Mexican empire had operated rather like the superpower-and-client systems in modern Latin America and Eastern Europe. The Aztecs drained economic surpluses, backed local puppets, demanded cooperation, and toppled any ruler they disliked, but they did not create a true imperial structure. This had worked reasonably well for several generations, but now it crumbled like the legacy of Joseph Stalin. Vassal cities—even Texcoco, a member of the Triple Alliance—made a bid for freedom. Only later, when the nature of Spanish rule became clear, did they rue the day they involved the pale barbarians in their own political schemes.

For their new leader the Mexicans chose Cuauhtémoc, son of Moctezuma's predecessor and grandson of a Tlatelolcan hero—a good choice that strengthened the shaky bond between Mexico's two halves. Alvarado's massacre, the fighting, and plague had reduced the nobility of Tenochtitlan to a shadow. The new "emperor"—little more than the Speaker of his title—did what he could to strengthen the Mexican position with fortifications and political initiatives, but it was too late. The Spaniards, supported by a huge number of local allies, soon overcame all opposition on the mainland. In May 1521, they cut the aqueducts to the island city. The final siege began.

The Aztecs fought tenaciously, block by block, week after week, like Berliners at the end of the Second World War. Their valor and desperation brought them some successes: more than once the invaders saw comrades sacrificed atop the pyramid and bearded heads displayed in triumph. But starvation and disease closed in; defeat was a matter of time.

The last days are commemorated by a lament written in Tlatelolco during the 1520s. One of the first Nahuatl writings on the conquest, it belongs with the great literature of war.

> In the roads lie the broken spears . . .
> Without roofs are the houses,
> And red are their walls with blood.
> Maggots swarm in the streets and squares,
> And the ramparts are spattered with brains.

The waters have turned crimson, as if they were dyed,
And when we drink them they are salty with blood . . .[76]
In shields was our defence,
But shields could not hold back the desolation.
We have eaten . . . lumps of adobe,
Lizards and rats,
Soil turned to dust, and even the worms.[77]

The wonder is that the siege took so long: eighty days as terrible as any in history. As they advanced, the conquerors razed the city they had so admired, devouring it house by house to fill the canals. At the end only the pyramids were left, towering above a wasteland. The home of the Aztecs was again what it had been at its beginning, a muddy island in a lake.

Ixtlilxochitl estimated that four fifths of the defenders died.

When the invaders had overrun everything except the Tlatelolco temple and the docks behind the market, the survivors tried to escape. Many were butchered, raped, and branded into slavery as they fled along the causeways.

Cuauhtémoc and his generals attempted a last stand from a boat, but were taken prisoner.[78] It was the day One Serpent in the year Three House, or August 13, 1521.

Grief is spilling over,
Tears are streaming there in Tlatelolco.
The Mexicans have gone away across the water . . .
Where shall we go? Oh, friends! . . .
Now they abandon the city of Mexico:
The smoke rises; the fog is spreading . . .
Weep, my friends,
Know that with these disasters
We have lost our Mexican nation.[79]

TWO

MAYA

When Columbus discovered America, where were we?

—Ignacio Ek, Maya, 1970

The people who met Columbus in 1502, seized a boatload of Spanish castaways in 1511, and killed Francisco Hernández in 1517, were Yucatec Maya—inhabitants of the Yucatán peninsula, which forms the lower jaw of the Gulf of Mexico. They and their modern descendants belong to just one language group of more than twenty in the Maya family. Altogether there are about 6 million Maya speakers alive today, perhaps the same number that existed when Columbus reached America.[1]

In 1492, the Maya lived, as they had for at least 2,000 years, in small city-states throughout Yucatán, Guatemala, Belize, Chiapas, and parts of what are now Honduras and El Salvador. Each state had its own dynasty, art style, and religious idiosyncrasies, a disunity that came to be the Mayas' strength: the Spaniards could not conquer a single capital and thereby conquer all. Instead, the invaders had the laborious and unrewarding task of crushing one small kingdom after another followed by resistance and rebellion when their backs were turned.

It is therefore hard to say when and where the conquest of the Maya took place. The story lacks a single turning point such as the fall of Mexico, and this makes it difficult to trace. But it is one of the most significant stories, for, as the numbers show, the Maya people and culture have survived to an extraordinary extent. Although some of them were the first Mesoamericans to meet Spaniards, other Mayas were the last to be subdued. One state kept its independence in the Petén jungle until 1697—more than a century and a half after the rest had fallen—while smaller groups lived free in remote parts of the same forest until the twentieth century. The part of the story in sharpest relief, which follows, is the conquest of highland Guatemala in the 1520s. But Guatemala is also where, during the 1980s, the war of conquest was tragically renewed. I shall turn to that in Part 3.

The Maya lands are a rough rectangle more than 200 miles from west to east and 500 from north to south. The top third of the map is the flat limestone slab of Yucatán—dry, scrubby, and riverless in the north, but becoming increasingly wet and forested as one moves south. It grades into the central region, the magnificent Petén rain forest. Yucatán and the Petén are known together as the Maya lowlands. The southern third of the rectangle rises steeply to become the Maya highlands. This—Guatemala proper—is a wrinkled land of pine forests, cool moors, lush valleys, volcanic cones, and crater lakes, geographically and culturally as convoluted as a brain. Eighty percent of the modern Mayas live there, the heirs of ancient city-states whose ruins can still be seen and whose past is not forgotten.

During Mesoamerica's Classic period (A.D. 200–900), the center of Maya civilization was the Petén jungle, the green heart of the Maya world. More than a dozen great cities flourished there, each the capital of a small kingdom; in the very middle of the forest stood the greatest of them all, Tikal. This city, whose overgrown ruins cover twenty-three square miles (ancient Rome, though more densely populated, covered only eight), was inhabited for two millennia and held perhaps 100,000 people at its height. The urban core contains 3,000 buildings, gripped by tall trees alive with birds and monkeys. Five pyramids with ornate stone temples on their summits still rise 200 feet into the air, and when you climb these ancient skyscrapers they lift you above the forest canopy and you stand as if upon an island in the greenery and mist. One of these, prosaically called Temple IV, was the tallest structure in the Americas until the Washington Capitol dome was built—eleven centuries later.

Maya achievements in art, writing, architecture, astronomy, and mathematics rivaled those of ancient Egypt or Classical Europe.

Mathematicians invented the concept of zero and place-system numerals—discoveries that eluded Greece and Rome—and with these intellectual tools the Maya designed a calendar that could measure time precisely over millions, even billions, of years (they often juggled with immense spans of time for astrological reasons). This enabled them to reckon the solar year more exactly than the Julian calendar used by Europe until 1582;[2] they refined the length of an average lunar month to within twenty-four seconds of the figure determined by atomic clocks, and their extraordinary calculation for the synodical period of Venus was out by a mere fourteen seconds per year.[3]

Such triumphs are all the more remarkable when one considers that the Classic Maya were technically in the Stone Age. They had little or no bronze, certainly no iron, and made no practical use of the wheel, though they knew its principle. To Europeans, who think civilization and hard technology are much the same thing, this poses a paradox. The teleological march of stone, bronze, and iron means little in the Americas. It may be a useful yardstick for calibrating Europe's past, but it's useless for taking measure of the Maya—worse than useless, because, like all flawed premises, it blocks true understanding.

The problem lies in our definition of technology. If we think of it merely as gadgetry, the Maya were far behind. If we think of it as the totality of systems devised by a civilization—not only their tools but their social structure, their use of intellect, their familiarity with plants and animals, weather and the environment, their ability to pass down knowledge and put it to work—then we can see how they overcame a lack of hardware. Their astronomical discoveries, for example, were made without telescopes of any kind, but they had the mathematical theory, the record keeping, and the perseverance to refine naked-eye sightings in the crucible of time.

To support cities such as Tikal, the Maya developed a unique form of intensive agriculture in what are now forbidding swamps. A network of canals and raised fields (similar to the Aztec floating gardens) allowed large populations to thrive in jungle, an achievement equaled only by the Khmer of Cambodia somewhat later. The luxuriance of the rain forest became reflected in the leafy baroque of Maya sculpture, in the fantastic regalia of their kings—jade and jaguar skin and iridescent quetzal plumes—in the illuminations of their books, and the painted roof combs of their buildings. But eventually something went wrong. In the ninth and tenth centuries, the social and political order collapsed, as it did in highland Mexico. One by one the great cities fell silent, erecting no more monuments and temples.

By 1492, Tikal had been abandoned for 600 years.[4] Vines and epiphytes draped its pyramids, spotted cats strolled through palace corridors, and wild bees swarmed in the ornate sapodilla lintels of the temple doors. The Maya managed to carry on more modestly in Yucatán and Guatemala, but the Petén jungle became a natural barrier between those regions, growing back over the roads and fields, splitting the Maya world into two constellations of small states. Given more time, the Maya would perhaps have recovered and gone on to new heights, but time ran out with the arrival of the Spaniards.

Only in recent years have scholars come close to decipherment of Maya writing, and they now know that it was a fully developed system combining phonetics and ideographs, as in Egyptian or Chinese. There was much the Maya might have taught us, but from the thousands of their ancient books that could have been read in the sixteenth century, only three survived the Spanish bonfires.[5] One contains the astonishing astronomical data on Venus and other planets. Who can say what has been lost?

> The conquest has not yet ended, and neither has resistance to the conquest.
>
> —Juan Adolfo Vásquez, 1982

Almost as soon as Mexico fell, Spanish war parties exploded over Mesoamerica like Goths after the sack of Rome. The fame of Cortés and the misery of Europe brought thousands more to the land now called New Spain. Not content with the Aztec Empire, the invaders used the native armies they had massed to seek new kingdoms to despoil. There was no such thing as enough: years after America's great nations were in ruins, bands of desperadoes still died in swamps and jungles searching for El Dorado, the Golden One, the ultimate prize, which was of course nothing but an echo from the crash of cities other Spaniards had destroyed.

Invasion was not new to the Mayas, an ancient people who had been attacked by the empires of Mexico time after time. Tikal itself had fallen under the influence of Teotihuacan, a Classic period metropolis whose ruins lie north of Mexico City. Then had come the Toltecs, who took over Yucatán and highland Guatemala for a century or two after the Classic fall. More recently, the long arm of Moctezuma had been reaching in the same direction. His forces had annexed the Pacific coast below the Maya highlands, and the most powerful state of Guatemala—the kingdom of Quiché—was well on its way to becoming an Aztec client. The Spaniards, with their Tlaxcalans and other Mexican allies, would finish the job Moctezuma had begun.

The Quichés, who are today the largest single Maya nation, had had imperial ambitions of their own. Led by aggressive kings in the fifteenth century, they had subdued several of their highland neighbors. But the Maya genius, like the Athenian, was not to be empire builders; the Quiché dominions soon began to drift apart. Most damaging was the secession of the Cakchiquels, a branch of the Quichés who broke away around 1475 to found their own state. The parting was acrimonious, and the two fought border wars for years.

The capital cities of the Quichés and Cakchiquels can still be seen, a mere thirty miles apart as the crow flies, but separated by volcanic cones and the upper gorge of the Motagua River. Fitting relics of a warlike, "medieval" age, they are built on fortified hilltops surrounded by ravines. Their temples are small, their streets narrow, with the palaces of the royal lineages huddled together yet divided by strong walls. Some of this fortification, it seems, guarded against internal enemies, for the records of these Mayas reveal that coups d'état and family feuds were as common in ancient as in modern Guatemala. But today Gumarcaah, the Quiché capital, and Iximché, the Cakchiquel, are tranquil places overgrown with stately pines. No one lives there except the Maya custodians who care for the ruins, and raucous flocks of ravens who wait for an unattended picnic lunch. The architecture shows strong Mexican influence—the thirty-foot pyramids are miniature versions of Tenochtitlan's, and the palace walls were once covered in mural paintings less Maya than Aztec in inspiration. One imagines that the food served in these royal halls was equally swayed by Mexican vogue—the chilies hotter and the chocolate sweeter than Mayas really liked.

Both the Quichés and Cakchiquels had a system of dual monarchy, a king and vice king drawn from two royal lineages. Among the Cakchiquels they were called the *Ahpo Zotzil* and the *Ahpo Xahil.* After the Spanish conquest, survivors of the Xahil family transcribed an account of Cakchiquel history from hieroglyphic to alphabetic writing and added to it in the manner of a journal until the early seventeenth century. In later years this manuscript, known as the *Annals of the Cakhiquels,* and the more famous *Popol Vuh* (a religious text similar to the Old Testament or the Sanskrit Vedas) fell into the hands of church authorities. But by then the fires of the Inquisition had cooled and the books were kept for historical interest. In the mid-nineteenth century they were rediscovered by Guatemalan and foreign scholars, who published early translations in Spanish and French. Several English translations have since been made.[6]

The Xahils' book is terse and matter-of-fact. They reproduce the structure of a hieroglyphic chronicle: a list of events concisely described and precisely dated in the Maya calendar. When they turn to the European invasion and its aftermath, their laconic prose becomes powerful eyewitness testimony of what it was to live through the New World's apocalypse. Their account is balanced, documenting Spanish cruelty and injustice, but also praising Spaniards who tried to help them.

The Xahils begin with the mythic origin of their ancestors, describe their internal politics and wars with the Quichés, and record events from the onslaught of the first smallpox plague until the year 1604. As one writer dies, another takes up the pen. The first author (known to us only by his Spanish name Hernández) is a grandson of Hunyg, a Cakchiquel king who died of smallpox in 1521; both his parents also died then, leaving him orphaned, like so many others. He remembers the arrival at the Cakchiquel court of ambassadors from Moctezuma when he was a little boy in 1510, and he was probably about eighteen when the first Spaniards reached there in 1524. The book opens: "Here I shall write some histories of our first fathers and forebears, those who begot the first people in ancient times."[7] It ends in 1604 with his cousin Pacal Xahil telling their descendants: "This is our genealogy, which shall not be lost, because we know our origin and we will never forget our ancestors."[8] Though the text of the *Annals* stopped nearly four centuries ago, the Mayas of Guatemala still keep that vow.

The following passage recalls the final days of Cakchiquel glory, then somberly describes the effect of smallpox on the nation's royalty. The disease spread outward from Mexico, softening up the native kingdoms before Spanish attack. Of four Cakchiquel kings mentioned, three died: a precise measure of the plague's political effect.[9]

> During this year [1517] our fathers and grandfathers once again defeated the Quichés. . . . Thus your grandfathers became great, oh my sons! . . .
>
> During the twenty-fifth year [1520] . . . the pestilence appeared, oh my sons! First they fell ill with a cough, they suffered nose-bleeds and infected urine. Truly terrible was the number of deaths in this time. Then Prince Vakaki Ahmak died. Little by little deep shadows and dark night enveloped our fathers and grandfathers, and us, too, oh my sons, when the pestilence raged. . . .
>
> Forty days after the epidemic began, our father and grandfather died. On the day Twelve Death [April 16, 1521] died King Hunyg, your great-grandfather. Two days later, our father, the Ahpop Achí Balam, also died. . . .
>
> Great was the stench of the dead. . . . Half the people fled to the fields. Dogs and vultures devoured the corpses. The mortality was terrible. . . . Thus it was that we became orphans, oh my sons! Thus we were left when we were young . . . We were born to die! . . .
>
> One hundred days after the death of the kings Hunyg and Lahuh Noh, Cahi Ymox and Belehé Qat were elected kings; they

> were elected on the day One Serpent [August 13, 1521]; but only one ever took up office, Belehé Qat, who survived [the smallpox]. We were children and we were alone; none of our fathers had been spared.[10]

By an ominous coincidence, the day the Cakchiquels elected their new kings was the very day that Cuauhtémoc of Mexico surrendered to Cortés.

After finishing his account of the plague, Hernández Xahil allows himself a personal note:

> Now one year has passed since our fathers and grandfathers died from the pestilence.
>
> During this year we [a royal "we"] married your mother, oh my sons.... On the day Twelve Water [May 24, 1522] we took a wife.[11]

Although Cortés passed through several lowland Maya kingdoms in the 1520s, he did not attempt their conquest. Perhaps he remembered too vividly the reception Yucatec Mayas had given him and other Spaniards in the past. Certainly he knew that these small kingdoms held no rewards like the treasure of Moctezuma. He preferred to retire to his estates in the lovely Oaxaca valley and from there defend his privileges against churchmen and officials who soon flooded New Spain and tried to tame both Indians and conquistadors. Instead, it was Pedro de Alvarado, slaughterer of the Aztec dancers, who became the conqueror of Guatemala. Behind the sparkling blue eyes and golden beard of the man the Aztecs called Tonatiuh (a nickname that stuck even in Guatemala), there lurked a psychotic mind.

In the Byzantine world of Mesoamerican politics, the Quichés had been aligned with the Aztecs, which at first made the Cakchiquels well disposed toward the Spaniards on the principle that their enemy's enemy was their friend. In 1519 and early 1520, Moctezuma had sent warnings to the Quiché kings about the hairy strangers who had become such unwelcome guests in his capital. Then came news of the emperor's death; a few months later the plague that killed his successor spread to the Maya highlands. No record of the pestilence among the Quichés survives, but they did not escape it; both their kings died.

Two young and inexperienced men succeeded to the dual throne. Forewarned of Alvarado's invasion, they tried to organize a pan-Guatemalan alliance, but the Cakchiquels refused to join. Early in 1524, the kings sent a general named Tecum (or Tecun Uman) to stop the Spaniards in the broad valley of Quetzaltenango. The choice of battlefield was disastrous. Alvarado's force was smaller, but he had 135 cavalry—more than Cortés had ever had in Mexico. (The Spaniards were well supplied from their bases in the Caribbean, where horses, war dogs, and other European animals bred as quickly as the natives died.)

This Quiché account, written a generation later, is very different from the factual but maddeningly brief Xahil *Annals*. Here fact has already been reworked into myth. The battle is shown as a magical duel between Maya and Spanish commanders; the event has become enshrined in the landscape, in the names of a town and of a river that flows from the Mayas' open veins.

> The Spaniards began to fight the 10,000 Indians which this captain Tecum brought with him. . . . They fought for three hours and the Spaniards killed many Indians. There was no counting the number they killed. . . .
>
> Then Captain Tecum launched himself into the air, for he had come transformed into an eagle, covered in [quetzal] plumes that grew from within himself: they were not false. He had wings that sprouted from his body and he wore three crowns, one of gold, one of pearls, and one of diamonds and emeralds. Captain Tecum charged, intending to kill the Adelantado [Alvarado], who came on horseback, and he lunged at the horse to strike the Adelantado, and he cut off the horse's head with a lance. . . .
>
> And when he saw that it was not the Adelantado who had died but the horse, he turned and flew up, so as to swoop down and kill the Adelantado. But then the Adelantado guarded himself with his lance and he speared Captain Tecum through the middle. . . .

And afterwards the Adelantado called all his soldiers to come and see the beauty of the Quetzal Indian. And he told his soldiers then that he had never seen an Indian so gallant, so lordly, and so bedecked in such beautiful quetzal plumes, not in Mexico, nor in Tlaxcala, nor in any part of the nations he had conquered. And for that reason the Adelantado declared that this town should henceforth be called Quetzaltenango [the Quetzal Citadel].

And when the rest of the Indians saw that the Spaniards had killed their captain, they fled. And the Adelantado Don Pedro de Alvarado . . . said that they too must die. And so the Spanish soldiers went after the Indians, and they caught up to them, and they killed every one.

The Indians they killed were so many that they made a river of blood, which became the Olintepeque.[12]

After this defeat, the Quiché kings asked Alvarado for peace and invited him to visit them in Gumarcaah. The ruins of their capital stand on a wooded hill outside Santa Cruz del Quiché, the colonial city that replaced it. The cut stone that faced the buildings was taken years ago, but rough cores of the larger temples still stand among the pines. As he rode into its web of narrow streets and high walls, Alvarado immediately suspected ambush. At least that is how he later justified yet another of his preemptive massacres. Certain spies, he claimed, revealed to him that the Quiché kings were planning to set fire to their city with the Spaniards in it. Alvarado decided to strike first. "As I observed in them such ill will toward the service of His Majesty," he wrote glibly to Cortés, "I burned the lords alive, and I ordered that the city be burnt and thrown down to its foundations."[13]

The story is taken up by the Cakchiquels. Even though they were collaborating with "Tunatiuh" Alvarado at this time, they make no mention of any Quiché ambush, and in their plain words one senses sorrow at the barbarous fate of their enemies, yet kinsmen, the Quichés:

[At] the city of Gumarcaah, [the Spaniards] were received by . . . the Ahpop and the Ahpop Qamahay [the king and vice king], and

> the Quichés paid them tribute. But immediately the kings were put to torture by Tunatiuh.
>
> On the day Four Lizard [March 9, 1524] the Ahpop and the Ahpop Qamahay were burned by Tunatiuh. The heart of Tunatiuh had no compassion. . . .
>
> Immediately afterwards, a messenger from Tunatiuh appeared before the [Cakchiquel] kings, telling them to send soldiers: "Let the warriors of the Ahpo Zotzil and the Ahpo Xahil come to kill the Quichés," the messenger said to the kings. The order of Tunatiuh was obeyed immediately, and two thousand soldiers marched to the slaughter. . . . Three times the soldiers went to collect the Quiché tribute. We, too, went to gather it for Tunatiuh, oh my sons![14]

> Oh! Wake, my country, wake!
> And from your volcanoes hurl fire,
> Burn and destroy the conqueror
> Who comes to put us in chains.
> —Dance of the Conquest, Guatemala, twentieth century

Having broken Quiché power, Alvarado and his allies—mainly Tlaxcalans—moved on to Iximché, the Cakchiquel capital, where they were nervously but hospitably received.

> On the day One Flower[15] [April 14, 1524] the Castilians came to the city of Iximché. . . . The kings Belehé Qat and Cahí Imox went out to meet Tunatiuh. The heart of Tunatiuh was well disposed toward the kings when he arrived in Iximché. Thus, in those days, the Castilians arrived, oh my sons![16]

Despite the fact that the Cakchiquels had never faltered in their friendship toward the Spaniards, Alvarado's heart did not stay "well disposed" for long: "Tunatiuh slept in the Tzupam palace. On the next day . . . he went to the residence of the kings: 'Why are you making war on me, when I can make it against you?' he said. And the kings answered: 'This is not so.'"[17]

Alvarado seems to have been temporarily reassured, for he switched, almost in the same breath, to a policy of divide and rule. He asked the kings who their enemies were and immediately set off to attack them. First he conquered the Tzutuhils, a small nation who lived, as they still do, on the south shore of Lake Atitlan. This lake is the jewel of the Guatemalan highlands, its shining water cupped by a ring of volcanoes that rise from shore to clouds with sweeping grace. But Alvarado did not linger to enjoy the view: he swung down to the coast and east into Curcatlan, the Nahuatl name for El Salvador. Then, having eliminated all forces that could conceivably have forged an anti-Spanish alliance, he turned on the faithful Cakchiquels.

> On the day Ten Flower [July 23, 1524] he returned from Cuzcatlan. . . . Next Tunatiuh demanded one of the king's daughters, and the lords gave her to Tunatiuh.
>
> Next Tunatiuh asked the kings for gold. He wanted them to give him piles of the metal, their vessels and their crowns. And as they did not bring this immediately, Tunatiuh became angry with the kings and he said: "Why haven't you brought me the metal? If you do not bring with you all the wealth of the lineages, I shall burn you and I shall hang you."
>
> Then Tunatiuh sentenced them to pay twelve hundred gold pesos. The kings tried to have this reduced and they began to weep, but Tunatiuh did not relent and he said to them: "Get the metal and bring it within five days. Alas for you if you do not bring it! I know my heart!" Thus he spoke to the lords.[18]

At times of intolerable stress, an individual or an entire people may seek miraculous deliverance; prophets, messiahs, and führers are likely to arise. When the Cakchiquels had managed to scrape together half the gold demanded by Alvarado, such a person appeared among them. "I am the lightning," he said. "I will kill the Castilians; by fire they shall die."[19] Only weeks before, Alvarado had "founded" Iximché as a Spanish city, renaming it Santiago of the Knights of Guatemala. Outraged by this, unable to meet the demand for gold, and inspired by their prophet's desperate visions, the Cakchiquels took to the hills.

> We abandoned our city on the day Seven Vulture, oh my sons!
>
> But Tunatiuh knew what the kings had done. Ten days after our flight from the city, Tunatiuh began to make war on us. On the day Four Death [September 7, 1524] they began to make us suffer. We scattered under the trees, beneath the vines, oh my sons! All our lineages took part in the fight against Tunatiuh. The Castilians then went on the march, they left the city, leaving it deserted.
>
> Immediately the Cakchiquels began to attack the Castilians. They dug pits and holes for the horses and planted sharp stakes so that they would be killed . . . Many Castilians died, and the horses died in the horse traps.[20]

From months of alliance, the Cakchiquels had learned plenty about the bearded strangers. They knew that cavalry was the key to Spanish success, that pitched battles were disastrous. So they waged a guerrilla war from mountains and forests, inventing new tactics such as deadfall pits to unhorse the knights of Santiago. These Mayas, who had once welcomed Alvarado to Guatemala, now fought him tenaciously for five years, one of the longest and bravest actions of the conquest period. With his usual economy, the Xahil historian records his nation's valor, adding an occasional glimpse of his personal life.

> The people would not humble themselves before Tunatiuh. When six months of the second year since our flight from the city had passed . . . Alvarado returned and burned it down. On the day Four Death [February 9, 1526] he set fire to our city. . . .
>
> We did not submit to the Castilians, and we were living in Holom Balam, oh my sons! . . .
>
> Death struck us yet again, but not one of the towns paid the tribute. . . .

> Fifteen months [later] my son Diego[21] was born. We were at Bocó [Chimaltenango] when you were born, on the day Six Dog, oh my son![22]

Finally, on Eight Earthquake, or May 10, 1530, the Cakchiquel kings surrendered at Panchoy, where Alvarado was building a new, wholly Spanish, Guatemala City. Losses from disease, hunger, and fighting, coupled with a growing influx of Europeans, had made it impossible for the Cakchiquels to continue the war. In the same year, the Spaniards conquered other holdouts, notably the Mam and Ixil of the northwestern highlands. The sufferings of war were followed by those of defeat; the Mayas of Guatemala entered the long period of resistance, sometimes passive, sometimes armed, that continues to this day.

Almost immediately, Alvarado resumed the behavior that had provoked the Cakchiquel war in the first place. Hernández Xahil:

> During this year [1530–1531] terrible tributes were imposed. Gold was paid in tribute to Tunatiuh; we had to deliver him four hundred men and four hundred women to go and wash for gold. All the people extracted gold. [Also] four hundred men and four hundred women were sent to work at Pangan, on Tunatiuh's orders, in building the city of the Lord [his new Guatemala City]. All these things, all this, we saw, oh my sons. . . .
>
> In the second month of the third year that had passed since the lords surrendered, King Belehé Qat died; he died on the day Seven Deer [September 26, 1532] while washing for gold. After the death of the king, Tunatiuh came immediately to set up the king's successor. Lord Don Jorge was forthwith installed in office by sole order of Tunatiuh. There was no community election to nominate him. Tunatiuh then spoke to the lords and his orders were obeyed, for in truth the lords feared Tunatiuh.[23]

Thanks to the precision of the Xahil *Annals,* we can assess the impact of the first decade of European invasion on the Quiché and Cakchiquel royalty, a valuable indicator of what was happening to the general population. Of eight kings mentioned (a pair for each kingdom plus their successors), five died of smallpox, two were burned alive, and the lone survivor—Belehé Qat—was worked to death.

The exploitation became so bad that a Crown official, Alonso de Maldonado, was eventually sent from Mexico to stop it. But before he reached Guatemala in 1536, Alvarado slipped away.

> During the course of [1534] Tunatiah left for Castile, making new conquests on his way. At that time the people of Tzutzumpan and Choloma [in Honduras] were destroyed. Tunatiuh went conquering and destroying many towns.
>
> A remarkable thing happened when he was at Tzutzumpan: I heard Hunahpu [the volcano now called Agua] rumble. . . .
>
> On the day Eleven Earthquake [May 18, 1536] arrived the Señor Presidente Maldonado, who came to ease the suffering of the people. Soon the washing for gold stopped, and the tribute of girls and boys was halted. Soon the killing by fire and by hanging also ceased; highway robbery by the Castilians also came to an end. Soon the roads were again travelled by the people, as they had been before the tribute began . . . oh, my sons.[24]

Tunatiuh's absence was unhappily brief. Employing his famous charm, and boasting of his recent conquests, Alvarado cleared himself at the Spanish court, married a highborn wife, and brought her back to Guatemala, bent on squeezing every peso from the Maya. He then worked thousands more to death in the mines and hanged any local kings who tried to shield their people. He enslaved so many that the price of an Indian fell to one twentieth of what it was in Mexico.[25]

> Before the end of the second year of the third [calendrical] cycle . . . Tunatiuh disembarked at Puerto Caballos [now Puerto Cortés] after having gone to Castile. . . .
>
> Thirteen months after the return of Tunatiuh, the Ahpo Zotzil king, Cahí Imox, was hanged. On the day Thirteen Rabbit

> [May 28, 1540] he was hanged by Tunatiuh, together with Quiyavit Caok. . . .
>
> Fourteen months after the Ahpo Zotzil king was hanged, they hanged Chuuy Tziquinú, lord of the city, because they were angry. . . . They took him away by road and lynched him secretly.
>
> Seventeen days [later] Lord Chicbal and Nimabah Quehchun were hanged together, on the day Eight Wind [March 18, 1541].[26]

The Xahils' catalogue of Alvarado's terror ends only with his death. Ever restless, he went on yet another military adventure, in the Guadalajara region of Mexico to suppress the Mixton "revolt." Nearby, he believed, lay the Seven Cities of Cíbola—a fantasy, like El Dorado, that lured many to their deaths.

There Pedro de Alvarado, the quintessential caballero, died beneath a fallen horse. When the news reached Guatemala, his widow promptly took over as governor. Her rule lasted two days.

On the night of September 10, 1541, the rumblings the Xahil annalist had heard deep in the volcano[27] bore fruit:

> Five months after Lord Chicbal was hanged, came the news that Tunatiuh had gone to his death. . . .
>
> On the day Two Knife the volcano Hunahpu erupted; waters burst from inside the mountain; the Castilians perished and died. And there died the woman of Tunatiuh.[28]

An avalanche of ice and mud swept down on the European base and flattened it; 600 were killed. The Maya gods had administered a measure of revenge.

THREE

INCA

> O Peru! Land of metal and of melancholy!
>
> —Federico García Lorca

Stout Cortés never did cross the Isthmus of Darien (*pace* Keats), but among those Europeans who first gazed on the Pacific in 1513 was another squat Castilian, Francisco Pizarro. Pizarro became a wealthy citizen and mayor of Panama, the town the Spaniards built beside the new ocean they called the South Sea. But he was not content with a burgher's life in a frontier port. Hearing rumors of a golden land, far to the south, called Viru or Peru, he resolved to find and conquer it.

Several early expeditions down the South American coast were failures, but in 1526 one of Pizarro's ships intercepted a strange vessel near the equator. It was a great balsa raft of the kind the Incas used for trading with Central America and exploring the Pacific, one of a fleet heading north. Its size and sophistication immediately impressed the Europeans: "It carried masts and yards of very fine wood, and cotton sails in the same shape and manner as on our own ships."[1] The craft had a twenty-man crew and thirty tons of freight—close to what a caravel could hold. The cargo excited the Spaniards more than anything, for here was a showcase of the products of a rich, advanced, and unknown civilization. And there was plenty of that magical substance for which they would risk all.

> They were carrying many pieces of silver and gold for adorning the body . . . crowns and diadems, belts and bracelets, armour for

> the legs and breastplates . . . mirrors decorated with silver, and cups and other drinking vessels. They carried many wool and cotton mantles, shirts and *aljulas* [Moorish-style tunics]. . . . They had some small weights to weigh gold, resembling Roman workmanship.[2]

The golden land of Peru was a fable no longer. The Spaniards seized the ship and three of its crew to train as interpreters (the rest jumped overboard or were marooned). In the following year, under instructions from these captives, Pizarro reached their home port, Tumbes, the northernmost coastal city of the Inca Empire. There he was greeted by a flotilla of ships carrying imperial troops on a campaign against the Puna islanders, notorious cannibals who fourteen years later had the distinction of eating the first bishop of Cusco.[3]

At Tumbes an Inca noble, a high official of the empire, made it his business to visit the bearded strangers. He came on board, examined the ships closely, and asked the foreigners what they were doing. Pizarro did not have enough men to begin his conquest, but he thought he might as well get over the formality of reciting the Requirement, that shabby document intended to remove the stain of innocent blood from the Spanish king's immortal soul. It informed foreign powers that their lands had been "donated" to Spain in 1493 by Pope Alexander VI (better known as Rodrigo Borgia, father of the infamous Lucrezia).

That night off Tumbes the Peruvian heard this:

> I, Francisco Pizarro, servant of the high and mighty kings of Castile and León, conquerors of barbarian peoples, and being their messenger and Captain, hereby notify and inform you . . . that God Our Lord, One and Eternal, created Heaven and Earth and a man and a woman from whom you and I and all the people of the world are descended. . . . Because of the great multitude begotten from these over the past five thousand and some years since the world was made . . . God placed one called Saint Peter in charge over all these peoples. . . .
>
> And so I request and require you . . . to recognize the Church as your Mistress and as Governess of the World and Universe, and

> the High Priest, called the Pope, in Her name, and His Majesty [king of Spain] in Her place, as Ruler and Lord King. . . .
>
> And if you do not do this . . . with the help of God I shall come mightily against you, and I shall make war on you everywhere and in every way that I can, and I shall subject you to the yoke and obedience of the Church and His Majesty, and I shall seize your women and children, and I shall make them slaves to sell and dispose of as His Majesty commands, and I shall do all the evil and damage to you that I am able. And I insist that the deaths and destruction that result from this will be your fault.[4]

Reading this document now, one wonders, like the humanitarian Las Casas, "whether to laugh or cry."[5] It is at once primitive in conception and maniacal in grasp. Nothing proclaims more loudly the arrogance of European man and the meanness of the mental prison he inhabited. One can imagine the smiles of the Maya, who knew the scale of eternity, on being told that the world was made "five thousand and some years ago." And one applauds the chiefs of Sinú, among the first to hear the document, when they answered, "The holy father has indeed been generous with others' property."[6]

How much was rendered into Quechua, the Inca language,[7] is unclear. Conquistadors were not sticklers about such things: the Requirement was largely symbolic, like crossing fingers while telling a lie. Sometimes it was read to empty streets and squares, even from ships at sea; seldom was it well translated. (Much of it is untranslatable outside a European context anyway.) The Inca noble, member of a people known for their reserve, gave no reply. He dined with Pizarro, politely praised the strange food and wine, and invited the Spaniards to visit him in Tumbes. He sent fruits, vegetables, and llamas to the caravels; in return, two Spaniards and an African slave took a gift of chickens and pigs ashore. The Spaniards astonished the Peruvians by firing a harquebus at a target; they were themselves astonished by glimpsing the riches of an Inca temple.

Pizarro left two Spaniards behind to learn the language and sailed back to Panama. He had the evidence he needed to persuade investors, the Crown, and would-be conquerors to join him in a definitive assault on the last great realm of gold. From Panama he went to Spain for a *capitulación* (a royal license to conquer), which was granted after much delay. Pizarro was illegitimate, illiterate, and a poor horseman—all strikes against him at court—but his exceptional tenacity saw him through. Little is known about his appearance, but his character has not gone unremarked. Courageous, ruthless, and devious was the opinion of most who met him. As a Peruvian prince named Atawallpa would discover, Francisco Pizarro was not a man of his word. He returned to Panama in 1530, and at the end of the year sailed again for Peru with his brothers,[8] partners, and about 200 men.

The Spaniards had seen precious metals, strange animals, large ships, orderly towns built of stone and adobe, irrigation canals and fields laid out beneath the hard sun of an arid coast, the crops a brilliant green against tawny desert and the lion-colored foothills of the Andes. But they still had little understanding of what they faced. Despite the visit to Tumbes, they had grasped neither the name of the capital, Cusco, nor of the reigning emperor, Wayna Qhapaq. They had no idea that the empire was 3,000 miles long and several hundred miles wide, stretching from southern Colombia to central Chile, from the Pacific Ocean to the Amazon forest. They hadn't even learned that the builders of this empire were an energetic mountain folk called Incas.

> His Catholic Majesty must know that we found these countries in such a condition that there were no thieves, no vicious men, no idlers. . . . We have transformed these natives, who had so much wisdom and committed so few crimes. . . . There was then no evil thing, but today there is no good.
>
> —Mancio Sierra (a conqueror of Peru), 1589

Peru differed from Mesoamerica as greatly as pharaonic Egypt from Periclean Athens. It shared certain ideas and food staples with that other cradle of American civilization, but human society had made unique responses to its formidable terrain. While Mesoamerica was an urban and entrepreneurial world with busy markets, a large merchant class, competing cities, and a monetary system based on copper and cacao, Peru was rural, centralized, and its primary medium of exchange was labor.

The Inca Empire comprised modern Ecuador, Peru, Bolivia, half of Chile, and northwestern Argentina: a land of desert in the west, endless rain forest to the east, and between these extremes the high plateaus and glacial peaks of the Andes, which form its spine. Civilization had arisen in cool mountain basins and the small hot river valleys that segment the arid coast like cracks across a bone. The oldest temples in Peru are found in both these zones and date from before 2000 B.C. Jungle peoples—then much more numerous than now—contributed certain crops, pharmaceuticals, and religious ideas to the interplay of the "three Perus." Technology, as I've said, is not a good classifier for American cultures, but it bears mentioning that Andean peoples made greater use of bronze than did those of Mesoamerica and were highly skilled in working gold, silver, and platinum, though they lacked iron. They raised llamas and alpacas (domesticated from wild camelids) for wool, meat, and as pack animals.

Little is known of the Incas' intellectual life because they kept their records by quipu, a medium the invaders never mastered. Quipus are strings tied in long fringes, making elaborate use of knotting, color, and position. The system may seem laborious to us, but it was the creation of a society that produced the world's finest weaving and set great store by the practical and metaphorical properties of thread. The conquerors attested to the uncanny accuracy of these records, yet burned whole archives of them without a thought. The system died out with the statisticians and chroniclers who ran it. Modern research on quipus has revealed that the Incas, like the Mayas, had an advanced arithmetic using zero and place notation. They, or their predecessors, seem to have invented this independently, for they reckoned in tens, not the twenties of Mesoamerica.[9]

In statecraft, the Incas had moved far beyond the crude domination of client states practiced by the Aztecs. They created a true empire, with

14,000 miles of paved roads,[10] colonial cities that reproduced the style and institutions of the capital, a state courier service, an official language, and a policy of forging one nation from many ethnic groups by moving people about within the empire. Warfare was a practical matter: the Incas kept a standing army and a network of garrisons, but there was no militaristic cult of human sacrifice. They encouraged independent kingdoms to join their empire peacefully, offering genuine inducements for doing so. Chief among these were safeguards against famine, which only a large state with good stores and communications could provide.

Inca religion was hylotheistic: all matter was divine. The creator, Pachakamaq, was "the soul of the universe" and worship of him or her took forms reminiscent of Shinto and Zen. A diffuse godhead included Pachamama, Mother Earth, and a complex sky deity whose most obvious symbols were the Milky Way, the Rainbow, and Inti, the Sun. The world was alive with numinous rocks, springs, and peaks, known collectively as *wak'a*. These were regarded as shrines to the Creator and as totemic ancestors of human groups. Some wak'as had temples and rock-hewn altars; others were left in their natural state. Inca iconography, like Inca architecture, was largely abstract and geometric, very different from the baroque of Mesoamerica. Buildings and sculpture were adapted to natural formations with a bold simplicity that is almost Scandinavian. There were few "idols" to outrage the invaders; adornment was confined to precious metalwork and sumptuous weaving. Gold and cloth the Spaniards could understand, but the austere and faultless stonework chilled them. To a culture of facade, the perfectionism of the Incas was a constant rebuke that unsettles the conquerors' descendants to this day.

Except for Cusco itself, which had between 50,000 and 100,000 citizens, Andean cities were small. Huánuco, a typical provincial center, was home to only 15,000, and many of its buildings were for itinerant public servants, work parties, and troops. Most people lived on the land in small towns and villages; the movement of supplies—except for coastal trading—was organized collectively by ethnic groups and the state. These economic and political structures, which have seemed "socialist" and "totalitarian" to modern writers, were not necessarily the invention of the Inca rulers. They had their roots in the social organization of ancient farming communities, called *ayllu,* which owned land in common and tried to control a variety of ecological zones in the vertical mountain world. The Andes present severe difficulties to human settlement. One in three crops is lost to hail, frost, or drought; landslides are common, and transportation over snowbound passes can be very difficult. Only by having colonies of ayllu members on the high pastures, the hot lowlands, and the temperate zone in between could a community guarantee its members a balanced diet of fruits, vegetables, corn, other grains, meat, and potatoes. It was often easier to rotate people at different times of the year than to move goods.

The Incas expanded ayllu organization to an imperial scale. They taxed people in labor more than in kind, using it to extend scarce arable land with terracing and irrigation projects. Much of the surplus thus raised supported the Inca royalty and priesthood, the army and bureaucracy, but the Incas returned enough to the people to legitimate their rule. Andean societies, like many others in the Americas, were built on the ethic of reciprocity, not rapacity. The state demanded much of its people, but the people expected—and received—much from the state. Even today, a person rises in Andean village life by gathering wealth and giving large parts of it away (as in the North American potlatch). Since power rested on the ability to control labor and redistribute resources—because people, rather than things, were wealth—it was in the Incas' enlightened self-interest to take good care of their subjects. This alien thinking impressed the better European minds, especially the conqueror and chronicler Cieza de León.

> At the beginning of the new year [officials] used to come from Cusco with their *quipus,* by which it was known how many births there had been that year, and how many deaths. And in these there was great truth and accuracy, without any fraud or deceit. In this way the Inca and the governors knew which of the Indians were poor, which women had been widowed, and whether they could afford to pay their taxes. . . . And in each head province there was a

> great number of storehouses full of supplies and provisions . . . and if there was no war all these supplies were divided among the poor and widows, the old, the lame, the blind, [and] the crippled. . . .
>
> It is no small sorrow to reflect that those Incas, even though they were heathens and idolaters, knew how to keep such good order . . . and that we Christians have destroyed so many kingdoms.[11]

Modern archaeology bears out Cieza's claims: the Inca ruins of Huánuco contain 500 warehouses with a total capacity of more than one million cubic feet.[12]

What is most extraordinary is that the Inca Empire was scarcely a hundred years old when Europeans arrived. Its formation, beginning around 1400, had ended a long period of warring states, which had in turn been preceded by an empire known as Wari-Tiawanaku.[13] The Incas managed to pull these fragments together and draw on the best features of their rivals and predecessors to build their system. Yet the Inca period was no mere copy of things that had gone before: it was a brilliant synthesis of Peruvian civilization, the fruit of thousands of years. The empire's physical remains—its roads, suspension bridges, temples, towns, fortresses, and irrigation canals—can still be seen everywhere, overshadowing what went before and what has followed. Only in the past twenty years has the acreage under irrigation on the Peruvian coast reached its 1520 extent, while food production in the mountains is far lower today than then. So effective were Inca social policies that the Quechua language predominates in the Andes despite centuries of pressure from Spanish. To visit the Andean highlands today is to see a place where something important happened in the past—and nothing comparable has happened since.

It isn't easy to account for the Inca Empire's rapid success, but part of the explanation must be that it was an idea whose time had come. It fulfilled in real terms an order remembered from previous Andean empires and idealized as populations rose and rubbed against one another in chronic strife.[14] Peruvians, like most American peoples, thought of space as a quincunx: four directions united by a central principle. This scheme was writ large in both the structure and name of the Inca Empire, which was not called Peru.[15] Each cardinal direction was a great *suyu,* or province, and together they formed Tawantinsuyu, the United Four Quarters. The capital at the pivot of the four was the unifying principle, and the city's name is no less revealing: *Cusco* is a Quechua word for "navel." Through Cusco, heaven nourished the earth.

The word *Inka* is often translated as "king" or "emperor" and loosely applied to ancient Peruvians as a whole, but its primary meaning in Quechua is "archetype." "*Inka,*" a modern anthropologist was told, "is the original model of all things."[16] The monarch was sometimes called *Sapa Inka,* Unique Inca, or *the* Inca. Like the emperors of Egypt, China, and Japan, he was a god-king, a son of heaven, a child of the sun. His title applied more to the office than the man. Sapa Inkas were born, made love, fought, and died like men, but once secure in office the ruler became the representative of humanity to the gods, and of the gods to man. He was the hub around which the four quarters of the world revolved. In Western terms, a Sapa Inka was Adam, Christ, and king.

> They say that a great plague of smallpox broke out [and] spread to all parts of the kingdom. . . . In the days of the Incas there was very little arable land . . . that was not under cultivation, and all as thickly settled. . . . Now there are few natives . . . their number has diminished to what we now see.
>
> —Cieza de León, c. 1545

While Pizarro was "discovering Peru," the throne of the Tawantinsuyu was occupied by Wayna Qhapaq, the eleventh Inca according to the traditional list of kings.[17] Indeed, only he, his father, and his grandfather were true emperors: the first eight had ruled little more than Cusco and its hinterland. Wayna Qhapaq was crowned in 1493, the year in which Pope Alexander gave the New World to Portugal and Spain. America's quarantine had been broken, but the biological consequences took another thirty-four years to reach Wayna Qhapaq. Though he did not know it until the end, he lived his long and illustrious reign on borrowed time.

In Cieza's account, he was a formidable ruler, "not very large in stature, but sturdy and well made, with a fine face and grave expression; a man of few words and many deeds."[18] Pedro Pizarro, Francisco's cousin and page, was told of Wayna Qhapaq's lighter side: "The Indians say he was a great friend of the poor and that he ordered they should be given special care throughout the land. They say he was affable with his people yet august. They say he could outdrink three men but they never saw him drunk."[19]

In 1527, couriers ran up into the mountains with the news that strange foreigners were probing the fringes of the empire and that two of them—the men Pizarro had left behind—were being held in custody on the coast.[20] The Inca, in Quito consolidating his annexation of Ecuador and pondering whether to push on into what is now Colombia, ordered that the two strangers be brought before him. But at that very moment the Spaniards' invisible allies reached Peru. The pandemic that had devastated the Aztecs and the Mayas may have been carried south by Pizarro himself; more likely it spread overland through Darien and Colombia and then burst upon Wayna Qhapaq's 20 million subjects.[21] As in Mesoamerica, it killed at least half the population and toppled the leadership: Wayna Qhapaq died, past fifty but still in his prime, and so did the son likely to have been his heir.[22] History does not record whether he had time to question the Spanish captives personally, but shortly before his death the Inca warned his children and governors to prepare themselves for an invasion from beyond the known world.

Pachakuti Yamki, an Indian noble writing in southern Peru at the end of the sixteenth century,[23] tells of Wayna Qhapaq's death in a story reminiscent of Pandora's box.

> The Inca went to Quito to rest and to issue new laws and taxes; and then from Cusco came the news that there was a plague of smallpox. . . . And when he turned towards the sea with his entourage, there were seen at midnight, as if surrounding him, a million million people, and it was not known who they were. And

> they say that [the Inca] said they were living souls . . . meaning that so many were about to die in the pestilence. . . .
>
> At dinner time a messenger in a black cloak arrived, and he kissed the Inca with great reverence and gave him a *p'uti*, a small case locked and with a key, and the Inca told the Indian to open it, but he asked to be excused, saying that the Creator had commanded that only the Inca should open it. And seeing that this was so, the Inca opened the box and there came flying out [things] like butterflies or scraps of paper, scattering until they vanished; this was the smallpox plague. And so within two days General Mihacnacamayta[24] died, along with many other captains, and all their faces were covered in burning scabs. And when the Inca saw this, he ordered that a stone house be built in which to isolate himself . . . and there he died.[25]

It is tempting to infer that the Spaniards sent a gift of infected material to the Inca court (as the British later did in North America). But it's unlikely that Pizarro knew enough epidemiology for such a scheme. Pachakuti Yamki's story is symbolic, reflecting the trauma of sudden mass death. Children lost their parents, parents their children; fields and canals went untended, buildings lay unfinished, and vital links were struck from the chain of command.

Had it not been for this plague, the Spaniards would have had to face a shrewd, experienced, and venerated ruler at the height of his powers. As Pedro Pizarro admits: "If this Wayna Qhapaq had been alive when we Spaniards invaded this land it would have been impossible to win, for he was greatly loved by all his vassals. . . . Had the country not been divided by the wars between Waskhar and Atawallpa, we could neither have invaded nor triumphed—not even if more than a thousand Spaniards had come at once."[26]

Wayna Qhapaq's warnings were soon forgotten in the war of succession that broke out between two of his surviving sons: Waskhar, favored by Cusco, and Atawallpa, based in the north. The wars not only divided the Inca royalty but gave restive subjects a chance to revolt. The rule of the Tawantinsuyu, benign though it was, did not go unchallenged; there were always those who thought they could do better on their own, and these elements became active whenever an Inca died and a successor had yet to establish himself.

Just at this moment of depopulation, discord, and civil war, Francisco Pizarro reappeared with 200 men and 70 horses.[27] The Spaniards found Tumbes, where they had planned to set up a bishopric, deserted and in ruins. The extent of the Tawantinsuyu's preoccupation with dynastic troubles is clear from what happened next. Pizarro was able to move south, occupy the fertile Piura valley, enslave what remained of the locals, and start building a Spanish town, complete with a church and town hall.

The Europeans stayed there in San Miguel de Piura—today a dusty, rather stuffy provincial center and a shrine of *hispanismo* for Peruvians who identify with the conquerors—for several months, ignored by the Inca state. During this time they heard tantalizing reports about the war between the brothers. Up in the highlands great armies were clashing, disputing the roads and cities along the backbone of the empire. From time to time word reached Atawallpa that bearded foreigners were pillaging parts of the coast. Waman Puma, a native writer from whom we shall hear more in Part 2, gives an idea of these reports.

> The Christians did not sleep. (This was said because they stayed up late at night.) They ate silver and gold . . . and day and night each one spoke with his papers and writings. And they were all encased [by armor] and their faces completely covered in wool, so that all that could be seen were their eyes. . . . And they had no great lord among them, for all seemed to be equals in their . . . manner of speaking and eating and dressing.[28]

Atawallpa was too busy defeating his brother to take much notice, but he did send a senior official, who "entered as casually as if he had been brought up all his life among Spaniards [and] enjoyed himself for two or three days among us."[29] Pedro Pizarro describes the investigator's methods.

> It was this Indian's intent to count how many people we were, and what sort of men we were, and so he went around provoking the Spaniards by mocking them, and asking them to draw their swords. It happened that he went up to one Spaniard . . . and put his hand on his beard, for which the Spaniard gave him many blows. . . . After having counted the Spaniards, the Indian returned to his lord Atawallpa and told him everything he had seen, and he said that there were about 190, including ninety on horseback more or less, and that they were lazy robbers . . . bearded thieves who had come from the sea, and that they came riding on some llamas like those of Qollaw [Bolivia], which are the largest in this land. . . .
>
> With this Atawallpa was reassured, and he took [us] for nothing.[30]

The incident is important for what it says about the white god myth. Tzvetan Todorov, the French critic who has written about America's failure to perceive the "Other," further claims that ability to detect the "Other" is related in some way to literacy. Because the Incas are less literate than the Mayas and Aztecs, he asserts, they "firmly believe in [the Spaniards'] divine nature."[31] The facts say otherwise. Of the three, it was the Incas who made the most practical investigation of the strangers, and, like the Mayas, they clearly treated them from the start as men. Peruvians certainly found Spaniards strange, but they despised them for their unruly behavior, their lack of hierarchy, and their filthiness. All the actions of Inca Atawallpa, his envoys, and officials point to this. Atawallpa's mistake was the opposite of Moctezuma's: the new Inca, puffed with recent victory, fatally underestimated the barbarians.

> So fell Peru. We gave her greed, hunger and the cross: three gifts for the civilized life. The family groups that sang on the terraces are gone. In their place slaves shuffle underground and they don't sing there. Peru is a silent country, frozen in avarice.
>
> —Peter Shaffer, *The Royal Hunt of the Sun*, 1964

In September 1532, Pizarro set out from his base at Piura with about 170 men and 62 horses. His battle standard has survived, a childish piece of embroidery showing a knight on one side and the Hapsburg arms on the other. Atawallpa, resting with his army at Cajamarca, a highland city in northern Peru, allowed the strangers to climb into the mountains and cross formidable passes unmolested. Because the Incas used no wheels, their roads did not avoid steep inclines—they took the shortest route, often ascending thousands of feet in flights of stone steps. If Atawallpa had wanted to kill the invaders he could have done so easily. Spanish forces of this size were annihilated in such terrain by Inca armies four years later.[32]

But Atawallpa, who now had leisure to examine the foreigners himself, thought he might be able to use them somehow to enhance his victory celebrations. He admitted as much after his capture, explaining that he had planned to breed the horses and make the Spaniards into court eunuchs.[33] His judgment was impaired by arrogance, the arrogance of one who thought he had just become ruler of the world.

There are many versions of the events at Cajamarca on the fifteenth and sixteenth of November 1532, but though they vary in detail and in point of view, they do not differ much in substance. Of interest here are the two main accounts by writers from the Inca side. The earlier and more authoritative is that of Titu Kusi Yupanki, Atawallpa's nephew, who was a small boy at the time his uncle was overthrown but later led the Inca resistance from a mountain stronghold near the famous ruins of Machu Picchu. In 1570, he dictated a document that is part history, part memoir, and part protest to the Spanish regime: "May those who read this letter know that I, the Sapa Inka . . . Titu Kusi Yupanki, first-born son of Manku Inka Yupanki, and grandson of Wayna Qhapaq, who were the natural lords of these realms and provinces of Peru, say this."[34] Most of his *Relación*, which runs to more than a hundred pages, tells the Inca side of the great "rebellion" launched by his father, Manku, in 1536.

His version of what passed between Atawallpa and the Spaniards at their first meeting—on the day before the massacre—is most important for its depiction of an exchange that would become symbolic of cultural hostility and incompatibility in Peru from that day to this.

> Some lowlanders brought two of these *wiraqochas* [Spaniards] to my uncle Atawallpa, who was in Cajamarca at the time. He received them very well and gave one of them our customary drink, which is called *chicha,* in a gold chalice. The Spaniard took it from his hand and tipped it on the ground, which angered my uncle very much. After this, those two Spaniards showed my uncle a letter or a book, or whatever, saying that it was the writing of God and the king. And my uncle, offended by the spilling of the chicha, took the letter . . . and threw it down, saying, "How should I know what you are giving me here? Away with you! Go!"[35]

Thus, each side abused what the other held dear.

Spanish accounts gloss over the spilling of the chicha, but they do mention the frosty reception that Atawallpa gave Hernando de Soto and Hernando Pizarro at some hot springs a few miles outside the city. Atawallpa was a thickset man in his early thirties, a generation younger than the Spanish leader. He had "a large face, handsome and fierce,"[36] was grave with his subjects, but cheerful in private and fond of debate. When the Spaniards came to understand his conversation they found him intelligent and quick with sarcasm.

The Inca was fasting and taking the waters. He told the Spaniards he knew that they had been mistreating his subjects; one lord had sent him an iron slave collar and reported that he had killed three white men and a horse. Hernando Pizarro protested that such a killing was impossible and began to boast of Spanish valor. Atawallpa, who sat on a low stool throughout the meeting, "smiled, as someone who did not think much of us."[37] He kept his composure even when Soto's horse came so close that its breath stirred the *maskhapaycha* on his forehead, the crimson fringe of vicuña threads that was the Inca crown.

Atawallpa assigned the strangers empty buildings on the city square for the night and agreed to visit them the next day, little realizing that he had thereby set his own trap. Cajamarca, now a small city of adobe walls and tile roofs, stands at 9,000 feet (not high by Andean standards) on the edge of a broad valley set like a green cabochon among folds of rock. The Spaniards could see Atawallpa's army, stationed in neat rows of cotton tents on the hills. They estimated 80,000 fighting men and said that the campfires that night were "like a brilliantly star-studded sky."[38]

Only one building of Inca Cajamarca remains, the so-called Ransom Room, a typical structure of large masonry blocks superbly fitted without mortar. Its walls have the usual batter, or incline, giving it a massive and invincible stance; on the inside the usual row of trapezoidal niches circles the room at shoulder height, a decorative feature perhaps used for lamps and statuettes. The roof would have been a steep crest of thatch. On important buildings this thatching was several feet thick, finely woven and sharply trimmed in shingles and geometrical designs, with embossed sheets of copper, silver, or gold on the ridge and corners. Such roofs complemented and relieved the severe stonework.

It is hard to picture Cajamarca's square—now occupied by a fountain, some topiary, and an army of bootblacks—as it looked in 1532. It followed the standard imperial plan designed for public ceremonies and parades.[39] The middle held a terraced platform where the Inca or his representative would sit; around three sides were stone halls, each with a row of large doorways, resembling colonnades. These were intended to shelter the crowd during rainy fiestas; they were also perfect for the ambush the Spaniards had in mind. The invaders hid inside, fully armed, the knights mounted, for most of the day. As hours passed and there was still no sign of the Inca, the suspense grew unbearable. Pedro Pizarro recalled, "The Indians he had spying on us [told Atawallpa] that the Spaniards were all inside the hall, full of fear, and that none were to be seen in the plaza. And it was true what the Indians were saying, because I myself saw many Spaniards who, without knowing it, pissed themselves from pure terror."[40]

Atawallpa came late in the afternoon, so confident of his overwhelming strength that neither he nor his men brought weapons. Files of retainers entered the square through the main gate, each company in uniform, singing a lilting song. After thousands had taken up their places, the Sapa Inka appeared in a rich palanquin carried on the shoulders of his senior lords. When he reached the middle of the square, Friar Vicente Valverde (who later became bishop of Cusco and dinner for the Puna islanders) approached and invited him to speak to Pizarro indoors. Atawallpa said he would not move until the Spaniards had made good everything they had consumed, damaged, or stolen while in his empire, the quipus being very exact in such matters. It seems that Valverde then read Atawallpa the Requirement, and that the Inca replied, "As for the Pope of whom you speak, he must be crazy to talk of giving away countries which do not belong to him."[41]

Here is Waman Puma's account of that bizarre interview.

> Atawallpa Inca went from the baths to the city and court of Cajamarca in all his majesty and surrounded by his captains . . . and on the throne called *usnu,* which is at the middle of the public square, Atawallpa sat. And then Don Francisco Pizarro began to tell him, through the interpreter Felipe (a Wankawillka Indian)[42] that he was the messenger and ambassador of a great lord and that he was his friend and had come only to tell him this. . . . And the Inca replied with majesty that it might be true he [Pizarro] had come from a great lord, since he had come from so far a land . . . but that he [Atawallpa] was also a great lord in his kingdom, and did not need such friends.
>
> After this reply, Friar Vicente approached, holding in his right hand a cross and in his left a breviary, and he said to Inca Atawallpa that he was the messenger and ambassador of an even greater lord and great friend of God [the pope], and that the Inca should become his friend and adore the cross and believe in the gospel of God, and worship nothing else because all else was foolishness. And Atawallpa Inca answered that he worshipped no one but the Sun, which never dies, and the shrines and other gods according to his law. . . .
>
> And the Inca asked Friar Vicente who had told him such things, and Friar Vicente responded, "The book of the gospels." And Atawallpa said, "Give me the book that it may speak to me." And so . . . he took the book and began to leaf through its pages. And the Inca said, "Why does it not speak to me? This book tells me nothing!" And . . . Atawallpa Inca threw the book from his hands.[43]

Valverde called on the Spaniards to avenge the insult to the holy volume. A gun was fired; knights charged out and began killing the unarmed courtiers "like ants," in Waman Puma's words.[44] The massacre took about an hour and a half. When it was over, between 5,000 and 10,000 Peruvians lay dead in the square, including many of the empire's lords. They defended their god-king to the last, supporting the litter on their shoulders even after their hands had been sliced off.[45] The only injury on the European side was a cut suffered by Pizarro himself as he parried another Spaniard's blow aimed at the Inca. Pizarro wanted Atawallpa alive as a hostage and a puppet.

Titu Kusi Yupanki:

> The Spaniards charged out with great fury into the middle of the square, where there was a high throne of the Inca, resembling a fort, which we call an *usnu*. They occupied this and would not let my uncle ascend it. Before he reached the foot, they pulled him from his litter by force, and turned it upside down, they seized his insignia and headband, which among us is the crown, and they took him prisoner. . . .
>
> That square was enclosed by walls and all the Indians were inside like llamas.[46] There were a great many of them and they could not get out, nor did they have any weapons—they had not brought them because of the low opinion they held of the Spaniards; all they had were slings and *tumis* [ceremonial knives]. . . .
>
> The Spaniards killed them all—with horses, with swords, with guns—just as one might slaughter llamas, for nobody could defend himself. From more than 10,000 men there did not escape 200.
>
> And when all were dead they took my uncle Atawallpa to a cell, where they kept him bound all night, with a chain around his neck.[47]

Atawallpa soon saw that the acquisition of treasure interested his captors much more than the imposition of Christianity or King Charles, so he made his famous offer: a roomful of gold and two rooms of silver for his freedom. Temples and palaces were stripped. Llama caravans streamed along the roads to Cajamarca for months, bringing the riches of the empire. From the outside walls alone of the main temple in Cusco came a ton and a half of gold plates.

Gold and silver held no monetary value for the Incas; their significance was purely aesthetic and iconic. Gold was the sweat of the sun, silver the moon's tears; one symbolized man, the other woman. The Peruvians were puzzled by the foreigners' inordinate lust for these metals. Among the many pen drawings with which Waman Puma so ably illustrates his chronicle, he shows a meeting between Emperor Wayna Qhapaq and Pedro de Candía, who went ashore at Tumbes in 1527. Concerned with poetic rather than literal truth (Candía and the emperor never met), Waman Puma dramatized the clash of cultures by having each man speak in his own tongue: "*Kay qoritachu mikhunki?*" asks the Inca. "Do you eat this gold?" And the European answers yes, "*Este oro comemos!*" "We eat this gold![48]

The rooms filled more slowly than Atawallpa had expected, but the quantity gathered was immense: about seven tons of gold and thirteen tons of silver. At a price of $400 per ounce, the gold alone would be worth nearly $65 million. This does not convey its true value at the time; no European king had anything like such a sum at his disposal.[49] As in Mexico, all but a small sample was melted into ingots on the spot. It was a devastating cultural loss, for precious metals were a principal medium of Inca art.

It took the Peruvian goldsmiths about a month to undo their oeuvre, melting down a quarter ton per day. It was no use, of course. When the time drew near for Atawallpa's captors to fulfill their side of the bargain, they put him on trial for treason and condemned him to be burned. The proposed execution appalled the Peruvians not merely for its injustice and cruelty but because the Incas were ancestor worshipers. Dead kings and queens, carefully mummified, behaved as if alive: they threw banquets in their palaces, paraded in Cusco's streets, and with hollow eyes watched dawn after dawn from thrones in the Temple of the Sun.

Without a body, Atawallpa would be denied this busy afterlife. So he agreed to baptism in exchange for death by the garrotte. He died, as

Don Francisco Atawallpa, on July 26, 1533. Some say he was buried in Quito, the home of his mother's people, others that Pizarro cheated him even in death by burning his corpse.

This Quechua elegy, entitled "Atawallpa Wañuy" ("The Death of Atawallpa") was composed in the Quito region:

Like a cloud, the *wiraqochas,*
The white men,
Demanding gold,
Invaded us.

After seizing
Our father Inca;
After deceiving him,
They put him to death.

He with the heart of a puma,
The adroitness of a fox,
They killed
As if he were a llama.

Hail fell,
Lightning struck,
The sun sank,
Night came.

And in their terror,
The elders
And the people
Buried themselves alive.[50]

FOUR

CHEROKEE

> Instead of populating these provinces they have ruined them by wandering in search of the lake of Eldorado or a new Atawallpa; thus they wasted their time and destroyed whatever was there.
>
> —Martín de Urué, 1573

Today there is little to link the chill town of Cajamarca high in northern Peru with the sultry Old South of the United States. But prominent among those who seized and melted Atawallpa's ransom was Hernando de Soto, Pizarro's lieutenant, sometimes described as the "discoverer" of the Mississippi. Soto was many things Pizarro wasn't: literate, legitimate, wellborn enough to be thought a true hidalgo, and one of the best horsemen in the Americas. He was also as turbulent as any desperado.

Soto had spent his teens killing Indians in Panama and his twenties doing the same in Nicaragua. Even before Peru, he was rich enough to lead a comfortable life; at Cajamarca he became an instant millionaire in gold.[1] Pizarro gave him the governorship of Cusco, but Soto was incapable of settling down. He wanted a Peru and an Inca of his own. By 1536 he was in Spain, using his spoils to finance the conquest of "Florida," the Flowery Land, then a vague term for the warmer parts of the North American continent, whose shape was a mystery to Europeans. In May 1539, Soto landed on the Gulf coast of what is now Florida, only six and a half years since his horse's breath had stirred the royal fringe of Atawallpa.

This would not be the only link between Florida and Peru. A month earlier, in the blackened ruins of Cusco, one of Atawallpa's cousins gave birth to a boy fathered by a Captain Garcilaso de la Vega. Fascinated by the nation that had overthrown his mother's people, the boy would go to Spain at the age of twenty-one, calling himself Inca Garcilaso. He never returned to the New World, but the clash between the civilizations of America and Europe reverberated in his mestizo soul and spent itself in writing. From the reports of men who had been with Soto, he fashioned a narrative, *The Inca's Florida,* America's first great literary work in a European language.

Several Spaniards had already tried to conquer Florida and failed. To men who had seen Mexico and Peru, nothing seemed unlikely or impossible. Their minds endowed the mysterious land with an entire geography of avarice: El Dorado; the Fountain of Youth; the Seven Cities of Cíbola. Such fantasies doomed them to roam, marauding like Huns, until they dropped. In 1521, a Floridian arrow killed Ponce de León. In 1526, Vázquez de Ayllón was driven from South Carolina after trying to enslave its people. In 1528, Pánfilo de Narváez, who had transferred an army to Cortés and smallpox to the Aztecs, died on a raft somewhere in the Gulf of Mexico; only four of his men survived an ordeal ending in starvation and mutual cannibalism.[2] And in 1542, the corpse of Hernando de Soto, dead of fever, would be sunk in the Mississippi he "discovered" to save it from desecration by avenging locals.[3]

Not a pretty record. But the mayhem these Europeans brought on themselves was nothing compared to what they inflicted on the people they so casually invaded. Living "off the land," the Spaniards wandered from one town to another, seizing crops from storehouses and fields, often burning what they couldn't take away. To carry the stolen food they needed hundreds of bearers. If a local ruler refused to cooperate, Indians were kidnapped when they came out to greet the whites, snapped into iron collars, and abused until they died or escaped. Troublesome ones were mutilated or burned alive to encourage the rest. Soto's "expedition," honored as such by Spain and the United States, was nothing but a barbarous rampage.

With his share of Atawallpa's gold, Soto had assembled some 600 soldiers, 200 horses, a number of black and Mexican slaves, the usual war dogs, and a vanguard of several hundred swine. (The latter were not merely pork on the hoof; they served to flush out ambushes and root up fields.) The three eyewitness accounts of this invasion are maddeningly vague, and Inca Garcilaso's mellifluous work was written at second hand. Soto made no conquests, though he won battles; he founded no towns, though he razed many. His venture was of no more consequence than those of the Vikings in Newfoundland. It does not matter that he was the "first." What matters here is that he was the last outsider to see this part of North America in anything like its pre-Columbian state. By the time the British and French trod the same ground more than a century later, it had been utterly transformed by the microbes that were the true conquerors of the New World.

Soto's men had little interest in nature; it is hard to reconstruct the landscape in front of their hungry eyes. Their vocabulary for the Appalachians is the same as for the Andes—"very high," "difficult," "very cold," and so forth—like the jottings of a dull schoolchild on holiday. One hardly knows whether they are marching across hot savannas or beneath the shade of mossy oaks. It is clear, though, that they are traversing a landscape profoundly changed by culture. There are roads and paths for them to follow, and whenever they approach a town they speak of riding for miles beside great fields of maize. Their accounts come to life only when they mention something of material value—temples and storehouses, caskets of pearls, a whiff of gold.

The Florida they saw reminded them of Mesoamerica and Peru. They attacked large towns with thousands of inhabitants. They plundered elaborate temples on top of earthen pyramids. They met rulers who wore cotton and feather-mosaic tunics, traveled on splendid litters, and styled themselves children of the sun. Almost every fertile valley was intensively farmed. The only thing missing was the thing they had come for: a great empire with a hoard of gold. Since this was the sole purpose of their journey, they could never arrive. Soto was a fighter, not a settler; the golden prize was always across the next river, over the next range.

His exact route is still in doubt.[4] He headed generally north from Tampa to the southern Appalachians (the Smokies or Blue Ridge mountains), then west until he reached the Mississippi, following information extracted from local prisoners and interpreted by a Spaniard who had spent several years as a captive near Tampa. What concerns us here is the middle of this three-year trek—Soto's encounters with the lowland people later known as Creeks and with their upland neighbors, the Cherokees.

The Spaniards wintered near Tallahassee, then moved north into Georgia in March 1540. They crossed a broad, shallow river that may have been the Savannah to enter a sophisticated state called Cofitachiqui, which was ruled by a beautiful young woman. The capital, Talomeco, was on the hot lowlands that would one day grow cotton and tobacco for the world, perhaps near modern Augusta or Columbia. "The people are very clean and polite," wrote one of Soto's men.[5] Another said, "They are more civilized than any people seen in all the territories of Florida, wearing clothes and shoes."[6] Rodrigo Ranjel, Soto's secretary, gave this account:

> The next day . . . the chief Indians came with gifts and the . . . lady of that land whom Indians of rank bore on their shoulders with much respect, in a litter covered with delicate white linen. And she crossed in the canoes and spoke to the Governor [Soto] quite gracefully and at her ease. She was a young girl of fine bearing; and she took off a string of pearls which she wore on her neck, and put it on the Governor as a necklace to show her favour. . . .
>
> When [she] saw that the Christians set much store by [pearls], she said: "Do you hold that of much account? Go to Talomeco, my village, and you will find so many that your horses cannot carry them."[7]

Inca Garcilaso lingers over Talomeco and its princess. They reminded him of his boyhood Cusco and the Indian mother he had left behind. Yet his fluent description fits well with the terser accounts of men who were there.

> [Talomeco] had 500 houses, all large and of the best materials, better built than the ordinary ones, so that it indeed looked like the seat and court of a great lord. . . .

> Around the temple were eight halls. . . . The Governor and other gentlemen wanted to see what was in them, and they found that they were all stocked with arms. . . . The first hall they saw was filled with lances . . . all very long, and very well fitted with blades of bronze which gleamed in the light like gold. . . . In the second hall were clubs. . . . In the third were axes with copper blades.[8]

Earlier Spaniards had not penetrated this far from the Carolina coast, but they had left behind two legacies for Soto. One was a collection of Spanish artifacts, including iron axes, brought to Talomeco and kept in the temple precinct. The other, predictably, was plague. "About the place," wrote one eyewitness, "were large vacant towns, grown up in grass, that appeared as if no people had lived in them for a long time. The Indians said that, two years before, there had been a pest in the land."[9] Garcilaso adds that the capital itself was a ghost town: "The Castilians found the town of Talomeco without any people at all, because the recent pestilence had raged with more virulence and cruelty in this town than in any other of the entire province. [Near] the rich temple, it is said they found four longhouses filled with bodies from the plague."[10]

Perhaps this explains why the young princess was so generous with her pearls. The wealth offered to the gods and ancestors for centuries had shown itself worthless against an invisible enemy that had crippled her people at a stroke. As for dealing with the all-too-visible invaders now looting her kingdom, she had weapons but few men to wield them. Perhaps she hoped that the strangers would sicken while robbing the tombs and die.

Soto took corn from Talomeco's granaries, then seized the princess and forced her to lead him into the mountains. Gold, he had learned in Peru, was to be found in mountains.

At the south end of the Appalachian chain lived the people called Tsalagi. The Spaniards would render this name as Chalaque, and the English as Cherokee.[11] The Tsalagi had been hearing rumors of "ugly white men" for some time. Then, in May 1540, the strange column of armored men, horses, war dogs, chained slaves, and swine reached the eastern border of their country at a place called Xualla—probably Qualla, North Carolina, where the Eastern Cherokees live to this day.

Soto was in a valley hard below the Great Smoky Mountains. The sweaty lands of Georgia, with its sluggish brown rivers, its swamps and magnolias, was behind him. Here the air was cool, and a trout-filled stream ran fast and clear over gravel shoals between freshly dug cornfields on the valley floor. Slopes covered with giant oaks, hickories, and maples rose steeply to peaks lost in cloud. The trees were in the bright new leaf of spring, but frost lingered in the morning air.

The strangers' reception was hospitable, as usual: "The . . . chief was so prosperous," wrote Soto's secretary, "that he gave the Christians whatever they asked—*tamemes* [bearers], corn, dogs, *petacas* [backpacks], and as much as he had." The Spaniards fattened themselves on Cherokee provisions and cast appraising eyes at the cusps and knife edges of the Smokies looming above them: "It seemed there were more indications [of] gold mines than in all the country [we] had traversed."[12]

In a few days, the white men tightened their horses' girths and trekked westward following serpentine ravines between the peaks. These valleys are dark and thickly wooded today, and the trails seldom open out into a view. Soon after setting off, the lady of Cofitachiqui went into some bushes to relieve herself and promptly disappeared along with a box of her best pearls, which Soto had been planning to extract from her as the price of freedom. Presumably she returned to her ghostly Talomeco; she was never seen again by Europeans.[13]

The Spaniards took five days to cross the mountains, then stumbled sweating, cursing, and hungry into a Cherokee town they called Guasili.[14] The noisy foreigners, who were poor hunters, by this time were not too fussy about what kind of meat they ate: "The Christians being seen to go after dogs, for their flesh, which the Indians do not eat, they gave them 300 of those animals."[15] Inca Garcilaso:

> The lord of the province . . . brought with him 500 noblemen, well attired in rich cloaks of different furs and with great feather headdresses, as is the general custom throughout that land. With such pomp he received the Governor . . . and took him into the town,

> which had 300 houses, and lodged him in his own. . . . This house was on a high [artificial] hill, like other similar ones I have mentioned. All around it was a walkway, where six men could stroll abreast.[16]

This part of the trek is particularly obscure. The Spaniards confused names of places with their rulers, and the strange words later fell differently on English ears. During the plagues and wars that raged for the next three centuries, towns were moved, abandoned, and renamed. Ancient trails are now buried under asphalt, and rivers beneath manmade lakes. The Nacoochee mound near Clarkesville in northern Georgia may be all that is left of the earthen pyramid of Guasili.[17]

Forced to abandon the gold quest for more pressing needs of corn and pasture, Soto led his men south into the piedmont. Their next stop, Chiaha or Ychiaha, was built on an island in a river surrounded by "very rich meadow lands, having many maize fields";[18] nearby were satellite villages protected by stockades. Whether Chiaha belonged to Cherokees or Creeks, it was clearly an important town near the western frontier between them. I would like to identify it with Etowah, which was a Cherokee town until the 1830s. This is a guess that many will argue with, but if Soto didn't go to Etowah, one has to explain why not; by far the largest town in the region, it must surely have drawn him. Its impressive ruins still stand in a meadow about thirty miles northwest of Atlanta. The main pyramid, at sixty-three feet, is the second highest north of Mexico. A ramp or staircase ascends to a spacious square on the flat top, which once supported wooden halls and temples. In front of it is a broad plaza and some smaller mounds, and the whole complex is ringed by a moat through which the Etowah River was diverted. Archaeologists have found marble statues, sheets of copper embossed with designs reminiscent of Mesoamerica, many graves, and traces of a stockade along the moat.[19]

The Europeans were welcomed with genuine hospitality. Relations remained amicable for a week or two, even though the Spaniards were eating up food that Chiaha's citizens had expected to last until the next harvest, some two months off. But when a demand for women sparked a revolt, the wise ruler of Chiaha played the card so many others have played to get rid of barbarians: "[He said] that towards the north there was a province called Chisca, and that a forge was there for copper, or other metal of that colour, though brighter, having a much finer hue, [but] not so much used, for being softer."[20]

It worked. Soto and his men left the Cherokee country forever. Finding no gold in Chisca, they fought and burned their way through Alabama, Mississippi, Louisiana, and Arkansas, ceasing only when Soto died. The fever that killed him was probably of Old World origin—a rare instance of a European leader dying from a disease brought to America in his nation's ships.

Archaeology has confirmed what Soto's chroniclers describe. The peoples of the Mississippi basin and the South had been building ceremonial mounds since before 1000 B.C., at first to cover their dead, later to elevate temples, palaces, and mausoleums. Etowah is surpassed by Cahokia—near modern St. Louis—a full-blown city with several hundred mounds and pyramids.[21] The largest covers sixteen acres and stands more than a hundred feet high. With about 40,000 inhabitants in the thirteenth century, Cahokia was as populous as the London or Paris of that time.[22]

Soto saw such places in their last days. The temples and pyramids were still in use, but the people would never again be numerous enough to build them. The plague that killed the kings of Mexico, Guatemala, and Peru, and half their subjects—"the most severe single loss of aboriginal population that ever occurred"[23]—had struck equally hard in the unknown kingdoms of the north. More had followed. The "tribes" the English would find, though still considerable, were remnants of once-powerful states. Houses had rotted away and woods had crept back into fields. America seemed a virgin land waiting for civilization. But Europe had made the wilderness it found; America was not a virgin, she was a widow.[24]

> The Indians . . . are the Bulwark of this Settlement. . . . Suffer not the Traders to cheat and use them with insolence.
>
> —South Carolina Board of Trade, 1713

The widowing of the land was most severe along the seaboard, where a muggy climate and frequent contact with Europeans prompted wave after wave of pestilence. When the Pilgrims arrived at Plymouth, the Massachusetts and Wampanoag Indians had died so recently and on such a scale that the settlers found empty cabins and cleared fields waiting for their use.[25] Unlike Soto's conquistadors, who had come upon a similar situation at Talomeco, the Pilgrims moved in and stayed.

The Indians who stood the best chance of survival were those living in hill country far from the shore. The most successful of these uplanders turned out to be the Cherokee Nation and the Iroquois Confederacy, distantly related peoples dominating the south and north ends of the Appalachian chain, respectively. Until settlers drove a wedge between them in the 1770s, their spheres of influence overlapped in Kentucky and West Virginia. This made them enemies, though the wars they fought were long-range, low-intensity affairs designed to maintain boundaries rather than to change them.

Hernando de Soto cannot have left a good impression, but Cherokees made no mention of his visit when they began meeting other Europeans late in the seventeenth century. By that time Britain, France, and Holland had established colonies on the eastern seaboard, while Spain controlled the Florida peninsula and vied with the French for the Mississippi. But European control did not spread far beyond coasts and rivers; the mountainous hinterland and the whole of the Great Plains were still independent. Although 200 years had passed since Columbus, white enclaves and surviving Indian nations of eastern North America were more or less evenly matched and mutually dependent for commercial and military alliances.

The Cherokees were doing a brisk trade with the British at the port of Charleston by the early eighteenth century. Europeans, having long ago exterminated their own wildlife, needed pelts and hides; the Cherokees wanted guns, cloth, and steel. The nexus was deer—a creature fond of abandoned fields—which had multiplied in North America as the human population fell. Between 1700 and 1715, a million deerskins were shipped from South Carolina.[26] At first this trade passed through intermediaries, but as the lowland Indians died or moved away, British and Cherokees came face to face.

On the evening of March 23, 1730, in what is now the hilly western corner of South Carolina, 300 citizens of the Cherokee town of Keowee were gathered for public business and entertainment in their "townhouse," or meeting hall. The building was an octagonal structure, perhaps sixty feet across, standing on the largest of several ancient mounds.[27] At the center of the octagon blazed a ceremonial fire, its smoke lost in the conical roof supported by massive painted posts. The flames bronzed the tattooed faces of elderly men and women reclining on their seats of honor, puffing thoughtfully at soapstone pipes. Behind them, like an amphitheater, rose tiers of benches thronged with townsfolk. The air smelled of hickory smoke, tanned buckskin, and strong tobacco. They had gathered to listen to a white man wearing a red frock coat and a curious detachable scalp made of curly white ringlets smothered in talcum powder.

The stranger introduced himself as Sir Alexander Cuming, emphasizing that the "sir" signified he was a Beloved Man of the English king across the sea. He spoke with extraordinary energy, stopping only to shift his scalp and scratch the pale orb beneath it. At times he sounded threatening, and the Cherokees could see that his coat bulged with three brace of pistols, a blunderbuss, and a sword. Normally an armed stranger would not have left the townhouse alive, but the Indians were amused by the audacity of this white man who seemed to them slightly mad, as indeed he was.

Cuming then made a lightning tour of the important towns in the Nation and persuaded several chiefs to convene at the great mound of Nekwasi (now Franklin, North Carolina) on April 3. His idea was to select an "emperor" from one of their number, a certain Moytoy of Tellico, who would in turn swear fealty to Britain. Best known in Charlestown as a high-class confidence man, Sir Alexander was doing all this on his own initiative—perhaps from patriotism, perhaps to divert attention from his finances.

> With great Solemnity Sir Alexander was placed in a Chair . . . Moytoy and the Conjurers [shamans] standing about him, while

> the Warriors stroak'd him with thirteen Eagles Tails, and their Singers sung from Morning 'till Night. . . . After this Solemnity of stroaking was over, Sir Alexander . . . required Moytoy and all the head Warriors to acknowledge themselves dutiful Subjects and Sons to King George.[29]

At least Sir Alexander, who wrote the above, believed this is what he had done. The Cherokees thought they had agreed to a defense and trading pact. Relations between whites and Cherokees were always complicated by a fundamental cultural difference. Europeans, accustomed to hierarchy, assumed that all they had to do was seek out one "king" or "emperor" and make agreements with him. Perhaps when the earthen pyramids were raised, there had been such a Cherokee monarch. But the Cherokee Nation of the eighteenth century was a loose federation of sixty-four autonomous towns united only by language, culture, and kinship. Chiefs led by example; bad ones simply lost their following. "The Savages are an odd kind of people," one British officer noted disapprovingly.

> There is no law nor subjection amongst them. . . . The very lowest of them thinks himself as great and as high as any of the rest, every one of them must be courted for their friendship. . . . So what is called great and leading men amongst them, are commonly old and middle-aged people, who know how to give a talk [and] may influence the minds of the young fellows for a time, but every one is his own master.[30]

This native democracy irked the Crown, but to the colonists it was a revelation. "The equality among the Indians, and the just rewards they always confer on merit," wrote one who knew Cherokees well, "warm their hearts with a strong and permanent love to their country. . . . Their whole constitution breathes nothing but liberty."[31]

To complete his stunt, Sir Alexander invited Emperor Moytoy and several others to travel with him to England and there make obeisance to King George in person. The high chiefs were not at all keen to get into a weird and smelly foreign ship for a month-long journey. Moytoy made the excuse that his wife was ill. Eventually one promising young man agreed to cross the sea; years later he spoke of his decision.

> After some questions were asked about England, and how far it might be to it, not one of our people would consent to go. . . . At night Mr. Wiggan the interpreter came to the house where I was, and . . . pressed me very much to accept of his invitation. I was then a young man but I thought it right to consider before I spoke; I told him that I understood England was a great way off; that I should be long in going there, I should be detained there a considerable time, and would be long in returning, and I did not know how I should get back. But he assured me that the distance was very much magnified and that I might be back at the end of the Summer or at least some time in the Fall, upon which assurance I agreed to go. Early next morning one of our people came to me. . . . He then told me that . . . I should not go alone. . . . accordingly [others] were spoke to and agreed, making in all six, and we immediately got ready and soon set off.[32]

The young Cherokee soon became famous as Attakullakulla, the Little Carpenter, renowned for his "deep, artful, and ingenious diplomatic abilities."[33] (His nickname reflected his skill at making alliances.) North American Indians were generally taller and better built than the wizened, ill-fed European of those days, but Attakullakulla was unusually short and slight, though fine featured and wiry, with an oval face and golden skin. Like any Cherokee man of fighting age, he kept his head shaved except for a spiky topknot bound with beadwork or silver wire. In wartime this scalp lock would be provocatively adorned with feathers, the object of battle being to remove the enemy's hair along with the flesh in which it grew. But Attakullakulla was generally a man of peace—from wisdom, not timidity. He would be the dominant Cherokee leader for most of his life.

His career spans the period I have chosen somewhat arbitrarily to equate with invasion or "conquest." Among the Cherokees and Iroquois, there was no seizure of an Atawallpa or a Moctezuma to concentrate the clash between invader and invaded into a single event. But when the Little Carpenter left for England in 1730, the Cherokee Nation numbered 30,000 people and controlled a territory the size of Britain; when he died in 1780,[34] his people were only 10,000, most of their towns were ruins, two thirds of their land was lost, and his own son had defied him to wage a quixotic guerrilla war against the newly formed United States.

The reluctant ambassadors did not get home for a year.[35] They were entertained at the king's expense and mobbed by London crowds eager to glimpse a "savage." William Hogarth drew their portraits, and Jenny Tite, a well-known tart, picked their pockets. They were taken to plays, to the Tower, Westminster Abbey, Parliament, and Bedlam lunatic asylum, which was considered a tourist attraction at the time. Cherokees thought it impolite to look another person in the eye, let alone stare, but Attakullakulla bore the crowds with good grace. "They are welcome to look upon me as a strange creature," he said dryly to his guide. "They see but one, and in return they give me an opportunity to look upon thousands."[36]

In later years Attakullakulla "was marked with two large scars on each cheek; his ears were cut and banded with silver, hanging nearly down to his shoulders . . . a mode of distinction."[37] To judge from Hogarth's portrait, his ears had not yet reached this venerable state, and his hair seems to be growing in. He is shown wearing a frogged jacket, knee britches, hose, and shoes. He is erect and graceful with an enigmatic smile, a young man formidably bright and confident.

King George received the Cherokees at Windsor Castle in June. Cuming, a showman at heart, had dressed them according to English notions of savage attire: paint, feathers, and breechclouts adorned at the back with horses' tails.[38] At George's feet he laid what he called "the Crown of the Cherokee Nation" together with "four scalps of Indian enemies; all of which His Majesty was graciously pleased to accept."[39] The day went off well, though one of the king's guests had to be dissuaded from loosing an arrow at a royal elk in Windsor Park.

The treaty was ready for signing in September. It was probably Attakullakulla who addressed the Lords Commissioners,[40] taking leave of the British government with this speech:

> The crown of our Nation is different from that which the great King George wears, and from that which we saw in the Tower, but to us it is all one; and the chain of friendship shall be carried to our people. . . . Though we are red, and you are white, yet our hands and hearts are joined together. When we shall have acquainted our people with what we have seen, our children from generation to generation will always remember it. In war we shall always be as one with you; the great King George's enemies shall be our enemies; his people and ours shall be always one, and shall die together.[41]

He then set down the tail of an eagle, a bird symbolizing wisdom and clarity of sight: "This is our way of talking, which is the same thing to us as your letters in the book are to you; and to you, Beloved Men, we deliver these feathers in confirmation of all that we have said."[42]

In return, the English pledged friendship for "as long as the mountains and rivers shall last, or the sun shine," words that became a formula for Indian treaties. They meant, as many have observed, "until the white man needs more land."[43]

> If science produces no better fruits than tyranny . . . I would rather wish our country to be ignorant, honest and estimable as our neighboring savages are.
>
> —Thomas Jefferson, 1812

The Little Carpenter grew up in a town called Tanasi, a name more familiar as Tennessee. Tanasi was one of a string of Cherokee settlements in the fertile highland valley where the Little Tennessee River paused to meander after a westward dash through the Great Smoky Mountains. Its remains now lie beneath the Tellico Dam at the east end of the state that took its name.

The alluvial soil here was deep and black, "equal to manure itself,"[44] enriched by an annual carpet of leaf mold from the deciduous forest that had occupied the valley floor until Cherokees took up corn farming around the time that the Roman Empire fell. (Agriculture spread north from Mexico to the Pueblos, then to the South, and finally to the Great Lakes.) Over more than a thousand years, stone axes had patiently cleared the bottom land beside the Little Tennessee, leaving the valley open or covered only by patches of secondary growth in fallow periods.

The Indians knew better than to remove the thick canopy of giant trees on the surrounding hills. White oaks, straight and tall as columns, grew to a diameter of five or six feet on the lower slopes; on the rocky spurs were pine and hemlock; and along the wrinkled creek bottoms grew chestnut, walnut, and other species offering food to squirrel and man. The European invader regarded these forests as primeval, and their like has not been seen since his steel saws ripped them into boards. But the Cherokees and other Indians had been subtly managing them for thousands of years. By burning undergrowth each spring, they forestalled wild fires and kept the floor open between the well-spaced patriarchs. The young shoots that followed the burn fed deer and buffalo, and these in turn brought wolf and puma; bears searched for berries, roots, and the occasional feast of meat. All these animals provided the two-legged custodian of the woods with flesh, fat, and skin.

Tanasi and its neighbors along the river became known to the English as the Overhill towns because they lay on the far side of the Smokies. They formed one of the three main geographical regions in the Cherokee Nation. The others were the Middle towns, including Nekwasi and Qualla, east of the Smokies, and the Lower towns, centered around Keowee, in the adjacent corner of South Carolina. In effect, the Lower towns controlled the headwaters of the Savannah and several smaller rivers flowing through the Carolinas to the Atlantic, while the Little Tennessee and other rivers of the Overhill territory flowed westward to the Mississippi. The Middle towns straddled this divide, the rivers that rose in their narrow valleys—notably the Little Tennessee and French Broad—cutting westward through the mountains. As the eighteenth century progressed, the Overhill towns, being least exposed to white encroachment and contagion, emerged as the most powerful.

The openness of the forest floor along the Appalachian chain made a ready highway for enemies, especially in fall when the harvest was in and the rivers quiet. Even though most Cherokee towns lay at the heart of the 100,000 square miles controlled by the Nation there was always the possibility of surprise attacks. Usually these came from the Creeks to the south and west, but it was not unknown for Mohawk Iroquois to come raiding all the way from Quebec and New York. Cherokees repaid such visits in kind, vying for the military title *Outacité,* or Mankiller. The rule was the rule of vendetta: a life for a life.

By the time Attakullakulla died, the architecture and layout of Cherokee towns had started to change, but the Tanasi of his youth had held to a pre-Columbian pattern—a pattern strangely familiar from Hollywood films, for white Americans would copy it for the forts they built across the continent. An English trader who penetrated to the Overhill valley in the 1670s described Tanasi (or its neighbor, Chota)[45] as enclosed by a stout stockade made of tree trunks two feet thick and twelve high with a parapet "to defend the walls and offend their enemies." It measured 300 yards square and contained "houses set in streets."[46] The houses were rectangular with pitched roofs of clapboard or bark shingles. The larger ones had two or three rooms. At one end was a fireplace flanked by sleeping platforms covered in bearskins. As steel axes became common, the Cherokees built more in logs, but the house Attakullakulla grew up in was probably of the traditional post-and-wattle construction: "They lash in-and-out canes, and plaster them over with white clay mixed with small pieces of talc, which in a sunshiny day gives to these houses . . . a splendour of unpolished silver."[47] Most Cherokee families also owned a conical "hothouse," a miniature version of the town hall, which doubled as sauna and bedroom in cold weather.

When Attakullakulla went to England, his people could field an army of more than 6,000, which implies a total population of about 30,000. Before the post-Columbian plagues, the Cherokees must have numbered many times that figure.[48] The Nation was organized into seven clans, with membership spread throughout its towns. (According to mythology, an eighth clan had rejected the human way of life to become the bears; townhouses were built as octagons in memory of this.) Descent was matrilineal—reckoned through the mother—and people had to marry outside their mother's clan. Early observers agree that the Cherokees were generally law abiding, but when a serious crime such as murder did occur, revenge was exacted by the victim's clansmen. Like the Incas, the Cherokees looked after their poor, feeding them from community stores and holding dances to raise goods for relief.[49]

In short, the Cherokees were a civilized people, perhaps more so than the settlers who would one day drive them from their homes. Their rapid adoption of white technology during the early nineteenth century—which earned them and their neighbors the name Five Civilized Tribes—was not such a giant step as whites imagined. "Civilization," like "freedom" and "democracy," is a word that kills. I use it in its literal sense, as shorthand for a settled life in towns and cities. If the word means anything at all it means only this. The moral values commonly attached to it are nonsense. Civilized peoples have practiced the Roman circus, the Aztec sacrifice, the Spanish Inquisition, the burning of witches, the gassing of Jews. Uncivilized ones have behaved no worse.

William Bartram, a naturalist and explorer who met the Little Carpenter near the end of his life, found Cherokees "dignified and circumspect in their deportment; rather slow and reserved in conversation; yet frank, cheerful, and humane; tenacious of the liberties and natural rights of man; secret, deliberate and determined in their councils; honest, just and liberal, and ready always to sacrifice every pleasure and gratification, even their blood, and life itself, to defend their territory and maintain their rights."[50]

Women had high status: "It is customary among [us] to admit women to our councils," Attakullakulla told a British governor archly. "[Since] the white people, as well as the red, are born of women, is not that the custom among them, also?"[51] Women could become warriors if they wished,[52] but their usual responsibilities were farming and handling captives—even carrying out torture and execution at the stake. Most war prisoners entered into a loose kind of servitude and were gradually adopted into families who had lost sons of their own.

Although they had no central authority, the Cherokees never warred among themselves. Disputes between towns were vented in tough games of lacrosse, "the little brother of war," which resembled the Mesoamerican ball game in its ritual and political functions.

Oratory was esteemed so highly that a person could rise to chieftainship on the strength of it. Prominent men and women who had earned the title Beloved through skill with weapons or words spoke first in council and had great influence. Some leaders were known to be more active in war, others to work for peace, attracting parties like modern hawks and doves. People debated in the townhouse for days, until harmony—the ideal of Cherokee society—was reached. Political decision was by consensus, not majority decree. Dissenters had the right to withdraw. If a rift was serious, one faction might hive off and found a new town.

Early travelers often said that the Cherokees had no religion. They saw no temples, no idols, and no priests but the "conjurors" who cured the sick and divined the future. In truth, the Cherokees were so deeply religious that there was no seam between holy and profane. The breath of Life Master, the Great Spirit,[53] was in all things: townhouse, field, forest, and home were all temples to him and the earth. The Cherokees' daily worship was a ritual dip in the river, addressed poetically as "Long Man."

Pre-Columbian North America had no writing, except pictographs and mnemonic devices such as wampum—belts and strings of beadwork in symbolic designs and colors, which were exchanged to illustrate important points in formal talks. These needed oral commentary, and whenever the old died en masse from war and plague it was as if a library had burned. "I cannot write as you and your Beloved Men do," a chief of Keowee once said to the governor of South Carolina. "My tongue is my pen and my mouth my paper."[54] There is therefore nothing written in Cherokee from the early years of contact, but Attakullakulla and other leaders did use writing at second hand, dictating letters and speeches that survive in colonial archives. The job of interpreting these was taken very seriously whenever political matters were at stake. "Linguisters"—usually traders who lived with the Indians—translated and wrote down the eloquent native discourse, paragraph by paragraph, as in court and parliamentary records.

The authenticity of these renditions is sometimes questioned, especially when they have literary merit (it being meanly said of translations and wives that the faithful ones aren't pretty, and the pretty ones aren't faithful).[55] But no one knew the risks of poor translation better than the Indians themselves: they often asked for a copy of the written version and checked it later.[56] I therefore believe that their speeches and letters can be taken as the first draft of history. It may not be as satisfactory as if written in the Indians' own hand, but it's as close to their voice as we can come.

> God saw fit to send the Indians smallpox.
>
> —Francisco de Aguilar, c. 1525

> I have seen two generations of my people die. . . . Why will you destroy us?
>
> —Powhatan (father of Pocahontas), 1607

A serious test of the alliance between Cherokees and British came seven years after the diminutive Attakullakulla got home. In 1738, a slave ship brought smallpox to Charleston, and the infection spread with trade goods into the mountains. Half the Cherokee Nation died.[57]

The plague struck hardest in the Lower towns. Skiagunsta, a chief who had seen Sir Alexander Cuming's performance at his townhouse, said sadly, "I live in the Town of Keowee. I call it a town, but there are so few people in it that it scarce deserves the name."[58] When Bartram passed through a generation later, the place had not recovered, and never would.

> The vale of Keowee is seven or eight miles in extent. . . . Within the remembrance of some old traders [it] was one continued settlement; the swelling sides of the adjoining hills were then covered

> with habitations. [They] now exhibit a very different spectacle, humiliating indeed to the present generation, the posterity and feeble remains of the once potent and renowned Cherokees: the vestiges of the . . . Indian dwellings are yet visible . . . as posts or pillars.[59]

James Adair, an Irish trader and writer who lived with the Cherokees for forty years, observed the psychological effects of the disease. Cherokee conjurors, finding no remedy, "broke their old consecrated physic-pots, and threw away all the other pretended holy things . . . imagining they had lost their divine power."[60] Survivors were deranged: "Seeing themselves disfigured . . . some shot themselves, others cut their throats . . . many threw themselves with sullen madness into the fire."[61]

When news of the disaster reached the French at Fort Toulouse (now Montgomery, Alabama), they saw an opportunity to unravel Sir Alexander Cuming's work. An agent of theirs befriended Attakullakulla's main rival, Oconostota (whose name means "Groundhog Sausage"),[62] and tried to turn him from the British. There can hardly have been two people in the Cherokee Nation less alike: the Little Carpenter slight, subtle, and a clever speaker, the Groundhog Sausage a big-boned, blunt-spoken, athletic man, over six feet tall and 200 pounds in weight, with "a head of enormous size."[63] Despite their rivalry, the two held senior positions in Chota. Attakullakulla was Chota's Second Man, its prime minister, while Oconostota was the Great Warrior, its military chief. In theory they answered to the town's *Uku*, or Fire King, a lame uncle of Attakullakulla's known to the English as Old Hop; in practice they took much of the initiative. Under this triumvirate, Chota rose to become the Cherokee capital, and Old Hop inherited the title "emperor" from Moytoy.

Oconostota caught smallpox and survived it, but the first time he looked in a mirror he saw his handsome face grotesquely ruined. Too vigorous a man to ponder suicide, he turned his anger against the source of the disease, the English. The French agent convinced him that the presence of smallpox germs in English goods was no accident, an accusation prescient if not true. Twenty-five years later, during Pontiac's war, the British indeed used germ warfare on Indians. But they had no motive for wishing the Cherokees dead—yet. "It is absolutely necessary for us to be in friendship with [them]," wrote the governor of South Carolina. "While we call them friends we may consider them a bulwark at our backs."[64]

The British captured the French agent and flung him in a Charleston jail. For several years thereafter they suspected the Chota leadership of playing a double game. They were probably right. Throughout most of the 1740s, Attakullakulla was up in Quebec, ostensibly a captive of the Ottawas. But word leaked out that the "captive" spoke often with traders, Jesuits, and even the governor of New France. Governor James Glen of South Carolina became alarmed: "I have heard bad things of the Little Carpenter," he told Old Hop.[65]

Attakullakulla foresaw that the two European powers would soon fight to decide the mastery of North America. Though impressed with British strength during his visit to England, he wanted to assess the competition and make sure the Cherokee Nation chose the winning side. He drew the right conclusion: as the clouds gathered for the so-called French and Indian War (c. 1754–1763), the Little Carpenter opted for Britain. Old Hop sent a reassuring letter to Charleston, not missing the chance to air some hoary grievances.

> Cherokee Nation, April 29, 1752. Caneecatee, commonly called Old Hop of Chota. . . .
>
> I look every day to the rising sun where my brother [Governor Glen] lives close by the great water side. When I was a little boy the white people began to settle thick in the country, and all the ground from that to this was ours . . . but now I find we are disbarred from it. . . . The Lower Towns people received some presents or consideration for it, but neither I nor my people living in the Mother Town of all [Chota] ever got anything. . . . The great King's talk [is] still in our Townhouse in writing. In that talk he desired us to be kind and good to his people, and accordingly we were well supplied for some time, for which reason we assisted the white people in the Tuscarora War. . . .[66]

> As to the Little Carpenter, he is my relation, and I never heard any bad talk of him [though] perhaps he might speak some things in rum drinking which I hope may be forgot.[67]

The Cherokees decided to make their nation a British protectorate in fact as well as word, offering to contribute men to King George's wars if the British would build forts to guard Cherokee towns from the French. It is a measure of the Cherokees' weakened state that they required foreign help to build a stronghold of the kind they used to make for themselves. But for smallpox, the Cherokee Nation would neither have needed nor wanted white garrisons on its territory. In June 1755, Attakullakulla met Governor Glen at the Saluda treaty grounds near Columbia, South Carolina, the midpoint between Chota and Charleston. Attakullakulla, who was fond of props, gave the final address holding his young son by the hand. "What I am about to speak, our father the great King George should hear. We are now brothers with the people of Carolina, one house covers us all. I bring this little child, that when he grows up he may remember what is now agreed to, and that he will tell it to the next generation, that so it may be handed down."[68]

He paused for effect, brandishing a bow and arrow. "These are all the arms we have. . . . Send us guns and ammunition. We fear not the French. Give us arms and we will go to war."[69]

The Little Carpenter then handed Glen a string of wampum and asked for a written transcript in return. He thought he had secured protection from the power most likely to win, with a bonus of trading concessions. The wampum was white, symbolizing the peace intended to reign "forever" between Englishman and Cherokee. It would last four years.

> The Great Being . . . gave us this land, but the white people seem to want to drive us from it.
>
> —Attakullakulla, 1769

In brief, we forced the Cheerake to become our bitter enemies.
—James Adair, 1775

The French and Indian War went badly for the British at first. Their commander in chief, General Edward Braddock, was an arrogant drunkard fresh from the old country who alienated both colonists and native allies. On July 9, 1755, he was routed at Fort Duquesne (Pittsburgh). One of the survivors was a young colonial officer named George Washington, then a rising star in his mid-twenties. Unlike Braddock, he understood the value of Indian troops. "They are more serviceable than twice their number of white men," he wrote. "If they return to their nation; no words can tell how much they will be missed."[70]

But relations with the Cherokees were fatally mishandled. Two Virginia colonels sent to Chota in 1756 capsized their canoes and lost their supplies. By the time the bedraggled envoys reached the smoky warmth of the townhouse, word had also arrived that Virginia frontiersmen were scalping friendly Cherokees for the bounty on Indian "hair." The Little Carpenter had to use all his joinery to prevent his people from doing the same to the colonels on the spot, even though, by Indian law, ambassadors were sacred. "Never shall the hatchet be buried until the blood of our countrymen is atoned for, but let us not violate our faith by imbrueing our hands with the blood of those who are now in our power. They came to us in the confidence of friendship, with belts of wampum to cement a perpetual alliance."[71]

Attakullakulla swore that vengeance would be taken later; the British managed to "soothe the Indians" with apologies and lavish compensation to the bereaved.

In spring 1757, after many delays, Fort Loudoun was completed at the confluence of the Tellico and Little Tennessee rivers a few miles downstream from Chota. Fort Prince George had already been built opposite Keowee to protect the Lower towns. Relations between locals and garrison became cordial in both places. Cherokee women took soldiers for husbands, and Attakullakulla, who enjoyed his rum, went drinking with the commanders. Soon afterward, he traveled to Charleston with prisoners and enemy scalps that he had taken at Fort

Toulouse.[72] (The British justified scalping on the usual grounds for wartime atrocities: "a barbarous method . . . introduced by the French, which we are obliged to follow in our own defence.")[73]

Throughout 1758, Cherokee troops fought beside Virginians, but the alliance was uneasy. Many militiamen were frontier louts who despised "Injuns." Early in 1759, the commander of Fort Prince George, supposedly guarding Keowee's civilians, took part in a drunken rape of Indian women. Young Cherokees killed frontier settlers in revenge. The British might have overlooked these killings if they had still needed Cherokee support, but by then the war was going their way. Quebec fell to General James Wolfe in 1759, and in 1760 Montreal capitulated.[74]

Attakullakulla and Oconostota both saw that the British might now turn on the Cherokee Nation. The Great Warrior and more than thirty chiefs went to Charleston and tried to set things right.

> Your Excellency is the Beloved Man; I am come to talk with you. I come from my governor, Old Hop, at Chota. There has been bad doings at the towns thereabouts, but I was not the beginner of them. Old Hop, my governor, has always loved the white people, and I am come hither to prove it. The path has been a little bad, but I am come to make it straight. . . . There has been blood spilled, but I am come to clean it up. I am a warrior, but want no war with the English.[75]

Governor William Lyttleton, who had succeeded Glen, was unmollified. He seized the ambassadors, marched them to Fort Prince George, and locked them up. The price of their freedom, he told Attakullakulla, would be twenty-four warriors to be executed by the British.[76] The Little Carpenter managed to get Oconostota and two others released, handing over two men who had killed settlers in exchange. More he could not do. Lyttleton returned to Charleston thinking he had shown the Indians what was what. The remaining twenty-nine hostages were kept in a cell built for six. Not long afterward there was a skirmish outside the fort in which the commander, who was one of the rapists, was shot. No other white man died, but the soldiers murdered all their Cherokee hostages.

The outrage was unpardonable in Cherokee eyes because the dead were ambassadors. The Indians rose, attacking the forts they themselves had requested and helped to build. In June 1760 the British counterattacked, burning the Lower towns, cutting down corn and fruit trees as they advanced. But when the whites tried to cross the mountains to relieve Fort Loudoun, Oconostota drove them back with heavy losses. The garrison was reduced to eating horses and dogs. In August, Oconostota and Captain John Stuart, a Scot married to a Cherokee, negotiated terms for capitulation. In return for surrendering the buildings and big guns to Chota, the men would be allowed to leave under escort with their small arms. The Cherokees also promised to care for sick and wounded who could not travel.[77] They honored the latter promise, and Attakullakulla rescued Stuart, but they killed thirty officers in an ambush and took 200 prisoners. To whites this was the basest kind of treachery; to Cherokees it was payment in coin for the murders at Fort Prince George.

Most Cherokees now felt that the score was even: with similar numbers of dead on both sides, the time for peace had come.

Lord Jeffrey Amherst, victorious over the French and no friend of Indians (though many had helped him win his war), would not hear of it. Condemning the Cherokees as "a vile and fickle crew," he ordered 2,600 troops under Colonel James Grant against them. Grant was reluctant. He, too, felt that the war had gone on long enough, saying, "If both sides were heard . . . the Indians have been the worse used . . . and would be glad to make a peace if they knew how to bring it about."[78]

Attakullakulla met Grant's advancing army at Fort Prince George on May 27, 1761, and pleaded for more negotiations: "I am and have always been a friend to the English, although I have been called an old woman by the warriors. The conduct of my people has filled me with shame, but I would interpose in their behalf and bring about peace."[79]

But Amherst was implacable, and Grant carried out the operation in June. The Cherokees, low on ammunition, could do little but harry the flanks of his powerful force. He destroyed all fifteen Middle towns, several square miles of crops, and drove 5,000 refugees—half the Cherokee Nation—into the mountains. One of his officers described the grim campaign with uncommon sensitivity.

> We proceeded . . . to burn the Indian cabins. Some of the men seemed to enjoy this cruel work, laughing heartily at the cruel flames, but to me it appeared a shocking sight. . . . When we came, according to orders, to cut down the fields of corn, I could scarcely refrain from tears. Who, without grief, could see the stately stalks with broad green leaves and tasselled shocks, the staff of life, sink under our swords?[80]

Starving, out of trade goods, out of gunpowder, at the nadir of a population graph that had been falling headlong for two and a half centuries, the Cherokees realized that no sustained war against the British could succeed. In September, a contrite Little Carpenter met Governor William Bull for a long and difficult series of negotiations. The two men smoked from one of the beautiful polished stone pipes that accompanied any weighty discourse, and Attakullakulla began to speak, presenting wampum from each of the towns he was authorized to represent. After three months of meetings a treaty was ready to be signed.

Attakullakulla had done well, using delay as effectively as action. Governor Bull recognized that the war had been provoked by both sides; his terms were less punitive than Cherokees feared and vengeful whites desired. A week before Christmas, about a hundred Cherokees and Carolinian delegates met for the final ratification. A pipe of "a very special character" was lit and smoked, and Attakullakulla took the floor.

> It is so long a time since I heard the talk of the Great King George over the great water . . . but I have always kept that talk, and I will to the end of my days. . . . There is none now in the nation alive but myself of those present when the treaty was concluded with the Emperor of Tellequoh [Tellico], our then headman; and the paper it was wrote upon is still in the Nation. We make use of feathers on such occasions and what I now say may be depended upon. [He bent down and symbolically swept the floor with the plumes.]
>
> Before I came down here last, a great deal of blood was spilt in the path, but it is now wiped away; and I will leave these feathers

> with the Governor as a sure token that no more will be spilt by us and I hope all will be light and clear again.[81]

So ended a cruel and needless war. In 1762, Ostenaco the Mankiller and two other Cherokees made a visit to Britain and came back chastened. The sight of King George III, his castles and armies, and the hordes of white people on the teeming island left a deep impression. Now, like Attakullakulla, they knew what indigenous America was up against. "The number of warriors and people all of one color which we saw in England," the Mankiller said, "far exceeded what we thought possibly could be."[82]

With the French crushed, native nations no longer held the balance of power in North America. From now on, the victorious English saw them not as buffer states but as obstacles to settlement. Even their importance in the fur trade was evaporating; skins were becoming scarcer and many white frontiersmen, having learned Indian skills, wanted the Indians gone so they could take their place.

Foreseeing this, resenting the hostile and disdainful attitude of Amherst, and inspired by the messianic visions of a Delaware prophet, the Ottawa chief Pontiac united the northern tribes and came close to driving Britain from the Great Lakes in 1763. Pontiac lost, but his war was not entirely in vain. In October, King George signed a Royal Proclamation setting a boundary line between white and native America along the Appalachian chain. This document remains the legal basis for Indian reserves, land claims, and aboriginal rights in the United States and Canada to this day. Like much protective legislation decreed in European capitals, the proclamation was not only flouted by unruly colonists but did much to sharpen their thirst for independence.

Most of North America was now nominally British. On King George's birthday, 1764, the "French Indians" surrendered their Gallic medals and were given British ones. Captain John Stuart, the man Attakullakulla had rescued from Fort Loudoun, was installed at Mobile, Alabama, as head of Indian Affairs for the Southeast. One of his first acts was to send two Scots, Alexander Cameron and John McDonald, to live among the Cherokees as Crown agents. Finding the rugged Overhill country and the people who lived there much to their taste, these men married into the Cherokee Nation and established themselves like Highland lairds. McDonald's mixed-blood grandson became the famous Kooweskoowee,[83] known to the white world as John Ross. As Principal Chief in the 1830s, Ross fought President Andrew Jackson's infamous Cherokee removal all the way to the Supreme Court.

With peace came a tide of frontier settlers—desperate people from the slums of Europe and the American seaboard, so hungry for land they were prepared to kill and die for it. Many deemed an Indian a "varmint" and counted it a good day's work to kill one. "No nation," Cameron wrote to John Stuart, "was ever infested with such a set of villains and horse thieves."[84] Using the classic tools of rum and debt, unscrupulous traders forced private land cessions, even though such were forbidden by the Crown. In an effort to regularize this situation, Stuart got the Cherokees to cede a tract of their eastern hunting grounds in 1768.

The speaker on this occasion was Oconostota, elderly, pitted by smallpox, but still gigantic and "very straight for a man of his age."[85] The Great Warrior joked that he "had never run from an enemy, but had walked fast . . . once."[86] Now, however, he wished to emphasize that the time of war was past, mentioning his "white seat," a throne of peace.

> I arose from my white seat in Chota. I gathered together the chiefs and warriors of my nation and hastened to meet [you], that we might smoke on affairs of peace, and that the Great Being above might bear witness to our talk and see the uprightness of our intentions.
>
> The land is now divided for the use of the red and the white people, and I hope the white people on the frontier will pay attention to the line marked and agreed upon. I recommend to them to use kindly such of their red brothers, the Cherokees, as chance to come down into the settlements. We have now given the white men enough land to live upon, and hope in return to be well used by them.[87]

But moving the border did nothing to stop encroachment. Daniel Boone brought swarms of settlers through the Cumberland Gap into what are now Kentucky and Tennessee, deep inside the Cherokee Nation's heartland. These Long Knife frontiersmen, epitomized by Boone and the Crocketts, had acquired Indian technology but little of the Indian's decorum, self-discipline, and reverence for the land. They wore buckskin, ate dried meat, grew maize, took Indian women, and were as quick as any Mankiller to take a scalp. They also cut the timber, dammed the creeks, wore out the soil, exterminated the game, and having done so, pulled up their shallow roots and moved on. "Settlers" is hardly the word for them; the Indians were settled, but most of these white men were nomads. Like the conquistadors, they left a ruined country in their wake.

In July 1769, a despairing Oconostota wrote to Stuart: "The white people pay no attention to the talks we have had. They are in bodies hunting in the middle of our hunting grounds. . . . The whole nation is filling with hunters, and the guns rattling every way on the path, both up and down the river. They have settled the land a great way this side of the line."[88]

The chiefs saw that Stuart and his deputies were powerless; the boundary drawn by King George was endlessly renegotiable and permeable—in one direction and by one race only. To enforce the sanctity of native lands would precipitate a war between the white man and his own militia, a war that was brewing in any case. The best Stuart could do was suggest that the Cherokees get the squatters to pay some rent.

In March 1775, Daniel Boone and Richard Henderson, a land speculator, forced Attakullakulla, Oconostota, and several other aging chiefs into a far more ambitious deal: for £10,000 in trade goods they bought much of modern Kentucky and Tennessee. Some of this land was used by other Indians too, but in effect the Cherokee chiefs signed away nearly half of what remained of their Nation.[89] Perhaps they realized that their only choice was to sell then or see it stolen later. "Time out of mind," the Little Carpenter said bleakly, "these lands have been the hunting grounds of the Cherokees."[90]

And so Tanasi, the log-walled town in which Attakullakulla grew up, became only a name for part of the nation being built by the invaders.

Among those opposed to the sale was Attakullakulla's own son, Tsiyu Gansini, known in English as Dragging Canoe. Unlike his father, he was tall and muscular, with a stern face cratered by smallpox. He had fought the white man's plague; he intended to fight the white man's greed. In accordance with Cherokee right and custom, he disassociated himself from the agreement, even though this meant defying his elderly parent. Soon afterward he and fellow militants seceded, founding new towns in the Chickamauga district near modern Chattanooga. From there they waged guerrilla war against the Long Knife for another twenty years.

Before storming from the treaty grounds, Dragging Canoe delivered this speech, a speech not only eloquent but prophetic:

> Where now are our grandfathers, the Delawares?[91] We had hoped that the white men would not be willing to travel beyond the mountains. Now that hope is gone. They have passed the mountains, and have settled upon Cherokee land. They wish to have that usurpation sanctioned by treaty. When that is gained, the same encroaching spirit will lead them upon other land of the Cherokees. New cessions will be asked. Finally the whole country, which the Cherokees and their fathers have so long occupied, will be demanded, and the remnant of Ani-Yunwiya, "The Real People," once so great and formidable, will be compelled to seek refuge in some distant wilderness. There they will be permitted to stay only a short while, until they again behold the advancing banners of the same greedy host. Not being able to point out any further retreat for the miserable Cherokees, the extinction of the whole race will be proclaimed. Should we not therefore run all risks, and incur all consequences, rather than submit to further laceration of our country? Such treaties may be all right for men who are too old to hunt or fight. As for me, I have my young warriors about me. We will have our lands.[92]

FIVE

IROQUOIS

> We Six Nations of Indians feel we have potentially a superior social system to that of the United States. If only we were left alone, we could redevelop our society . . . which was old in democracy when Europe knew only monarchs.
>
> —Ernest Benedict, Mohawk, 1941

More than 500 miles northeast of the Cherokee Nation, the Appalachian chain flattens and breaks into the Alleghenies, the Catskills, and the Adirondacks, then sinks beneath the largest freshwater system in the world, the five Great Lakes and the St. Lawrence River that drains them into the North Atlantic. The waters are so voluminous (an area the size of Britain) that they mellow the climate, melting winter snow, bringing early spring, and lengthening the season for every crop from grapes and apples to tobacco and maize. In its natural state this land grows thick forests of oak and maple, a deciduous canopy that becomes a slow and splendid sunset every autumn, when the evergreens—cedar clumps in hollows, spruce on limestone escarpments, and windblown pines along the dry ridges of ancient tills and dunes—stipple the reddening hills with veins of jade.

The "three sisters" of American agriculture—corn, beans, and squash—had slowly spread north and east across the continent from Mexico as plant breeders adapted them to cooler zones. Sometime before the year A.D. 1000 they were planted in the deep alluvial soils beside the great water known in the Mohawk language as Onhatariyo, Handsome Lake, which the English would render as Lake Ontario. Farming brought prosperity, population growth, and power to the nations living there; it also brought new political frictions. To resolve these, five related peoples on the south side of the lake formed a remarkable union known as the Iroquois Confederacy or League. The five were the Mohawk, Oneida, Onondaga, Cayuga, and Seneca, living in that order from east to west across the Finger Lakes country of upstate New York, where the Creator had raked his glacial nails through the world. The extent of the League before Columbus is unknown, but at its height during the seventeenth and eighteenth centuries, it was the greatest native polity in North America, its influence stretching a thousand miles from Quebec to Kentucky and from Pennsylvania to Illinois.

On the north side of the lake, in what is now the Canadian province of Ontario, lived the League's main rivals, the Hurons, who fell under heavy French influence soon after 1600. All these peoples spoke languages of the Iroquoian family, to which Cherokee also belongs. To avoid confusion we must here define two terms: "Iroquoian," the broader, covers the whole linguistic and ethnic family, regardless of political ties or geographical location; "Iroquois," whether adjective or noun, refers only to the member nations of the Confederacy. Just as Scandinavians and English are Germanic but not Germans, Cherokees and Hurons are Iroquoian but not Iroquois. A third term, "Iroquoia," is a handy neologism for the Confederacy's home territory. There is one further complication: for centuries the Iroquois League had five nations, all founding members; but after the British and Cherokees drove the Tuscaroras from North Carolina, the latter were admitted, around 1720, as the sixth. Since then, the Iroquois Confederacy has been known as the Six Nations.

These six survive, still fighting for recognition of a nationhood that they believe they never surrendered to the parvenus who built the United States and Canada around them. They also feel an ironic pride that European colonists took the Iroquois Confederacy as a model when contemplating a union of their own. The idea came from Canasatego, an Onondaga sachem who spoke for the Six Nations at the Treaty of Lancaster, Pennsylvania, in the summer of 1744. He was described by one who heard him as "a tall well-made man [with] a very full chest and brawny limbs. He had a manly countenance, mixed with a good-natured smile. He was about sixty years of age, very active, strong, and had a surprising liveliness in his speech."[1] Frustrated by the bickering commissioners of Pennsylvania, Virginia, and Maryland, Canasatego said:

> We heartily recommend Union and a good agreement between you, our [English] brethren. . . .
>
> Our wise forefathers established union and amity between the Five Nations; this has made us formidable; this has given us great weight and authority with our neighbouring nations.
>
> We are a powerful Confederacy; and, by your observing the same methods our wise forefathers have taken, you will acquire fresh strength and power.[2]

Taking notes while Canasatego spoke was Benjamin Franklin, then thirty-eight, already a printer, writer, and philosopher, yet to become the inventor of the lightning rod and coauthor of the American Constitution. Franklin thought about the Iroquois example (as did others) and in 1751 he wrote: "It would be a very strange thing if Six Nations of ignorant savages should be capable of forming a scheme for such a union, and be able to execute it in such a manner as that it has subsisted ages, and appears indissoluble; and yet that a like union should be impracticable for ten or a dozen English Colonies."[3]

So it is that the eagle on the United States shield is the Iroquois eagle and the bundle of arrows in its grasp originally numbered not thirteen but five.[4]

The new Americans gave little credit to the "ignorant savages" from whom they learned. They adorned Washington, their ceremonial center, with the icons of Greece and Rome and put Latin—E PLURIBUS UNUM—in the eagle's mouth. Their historians have even tried to deny or diminish the Iroquois precedent, but the truth is that the settler republic took Indian ideas as well as Indian land.5

A century later, the Iroquois made another impact on Western thought. In 1845, in upstate New York, two young browsers met by chance in an Albany bookshop. One was a school-educated Seneca,

Hasanoanda or Ely S. Parker. (Like the Cherokees, many Iroquois had both native and English names.)[6] Parker would become a sachem of the Confederacy, a general in the army of Ulysses Grant, and the first Indian commissioner of Indian Affairs. The other was Lewis Henry Morgan, a white lawyer whose legal career was giving way to a fascination with indigenous America.

Guided by Hasanoanda, Morgan wrote his influential *League of the Iroquois* (1851), a cornerstone of modern ethnology. He described accurately and in detail for the first time the workings of a Native American government.

> Their whole civil policy was averse to the concentration of power in the hands of any single individual, but inclined to the opposite principle of division among a number of equals. . . .
>
> The government sat lightly upon the people, who, in effect, were governed but little. It secured to each that individual independence, which the Hodènosaunee [Iroquois] knew how to prize as well as the Saxon race; and which, amid all their political changes, they have continued to preserve.[7]

Ever since Columbus, Europeans had dreamed up utopias in America. Sometimes they tried to build their own; more often they destroyed the ones they found. But Morgan's books on the Iroquois influenced a new breed of utopian: Karl Marx and Friedrich Engels.[8] "This gentile constitution is wonderful!" Engels cried. "There can be no poor and needy. . . . All are free and equal—including the women."[9]

On an unseasonably hot October day I visited the Onondaga Valley, where the Confederacy was formed in ancient times. Whites have taken most of the flatland for the city of Syracuse and its vegetable farms, but the billowy hills are unencumbered, a green ocean heaving from a storm.

On a crest just south of the modern city lie the foundations of a building 334 feet long, dated by radiocarbon to at least a century before Columbus sailed.[10] Below, straggling through the woods beside salty Onondaga Creek, is a 7,000-acre Indian reservation—all that remains of the Onondagas' territory. As the central nation of the Iroquois League, the Onondagas have always been its Firekeepers, the hosts of its assembly. In the middle of their reservation stands a new hall, perhaps one-third the length of the ancient one on the hill but still a large building made of logs. Here sits the oldest living parliament in the Americas, and one of the oldest in the world.

That afternoon I met a railwayman named Irving Powless. In his own language he is Dehatkadons, a Confederacy sachem—a successor of Canasatego, whose build, agility, and wit he shares. We sat at a table on the lawn behind his house and swatted at mosquitoes enjoying the last warm days of the fall. He smiled when I mentioned Marx and Franklin. "Both superpowers took our ideas," he said. "But neither got them right."

The longhouse—whether a modern one of timber or an ancient one built like an organic Nissen hut of arched poles and neatly stitched bark—has always been the symbol of Iroquois identity. Each of the Six Nations has its own language, its own name, and its own history, but collectively they call themselves Haudenosaunee, People of the Longhouse.[11] Today such buildings are purely ceremonial, but in ancient times they were the home of a senior woman—a "clan mother"—with her female kin and their husbands and children: perhaps forty to a hundred people all told. The totemic animal of each clan was carved above the door. Inside were partitions and sleeping platforms, hearths, and storage areas for personal belongings and dried foods. Early whites saw longhouses "fifty or sixty yards long by twelve wide with a passage ten or twelve feet broad down the middle."[12] A typical town might have fifty such buildings, and one was said to have 200.[13] In other respects, ancient Iroquois settlements resembled those of the Cherokees. The towns were surrounded by a ditch, rampart, and stockade so strong that the invading English called them castles.

The Iroquois conceived of their union as a great Longhouse with five (later six) partitions. The Onondagas tended the central fire, symbol of government. The Senecas in the west and the Mohawks in the east kept the doors, which meant they bore the main responsibility for defense. The smaller Oneida and Cayuga nations were the "younger brothers."

One roof covered all. As the Incas conceived of Four Quarters radiating from Cusco to the rim of the world, the Iroquois pictured a Tree of Peace rising heavenward from the Longhouse, its four great roots reaching to the corners of the earth. But unlike the Inca Empire, the League was not imposed and run by a dominant nation: its members came together for mutual benefit and to settle ancient feuds.

Onondaga Lake—the smallest of the Finger Lakes that bear the names of the Five Nations—is today hemmed in by a freeway, a fairground, and the bungaloid growth of Syracuse. Somewhere beneath concrete and asphalt lies the spot where the Peacemaker, a divine hero, alighted from a white stone canoe and expounded his Great Law to the warring Iroquois. Eventually he persuaded a snake-haired Onondaga sorcerer, Tadodaho, to relinquish his evil ways and become the first Speaker, or presiding sachem. Thus a negative force in the world was turned to good, and all Speakers from that day to this have carried the name Tadodaho.

The Peacemaker's Great Law was an inspired blend of elective and hereditary rights, of checks and balances. He established a Confederacy Council of fifty *royaneh* (sachems, or lords) chosen by clan mothers—the Iroquois, like the Cherokees, being matrilineal and partly matriarchal. All succeeding royaneh have assumed the names of these ancient founders in the same way that an English lord assumes a place name. When one of their number dies, the elaborate condolence rites serve to install his successor. For this reason they are also known as "condoled chiefs." The royaneh reach their decisions through a series of small caucuses (an Amerindian word, by the way) until all are of one mind. Though sachems are male and elected for life, women have the right to depose them. In addition, anyone of outstanding merit may be elected to the council as a Pine Tree Chief.[14]

Accounts of the League's origin were passed on orally for centuries with the guidance of wampum belts, then written down about a century ago by the Iroquois themselves. They are lengthy documents, part constitution, part mythology, in which governance is sanctioned by holy revelation. Early in this century, the Seneca ethnologist Arthur C. Parker—a great-nephew of Morgan's colleague—gathered and published several of these texts. "Here, then," he wrote in his introduction, "we find the right of popular nomination, the right of recall and of woman suffrage, all flourishing in the old America . . . centuries before it became the clamor of the new America of the white invader. Who now shall call Indians and Iroquois savages?"[15]

Here is the Peacemaker founding the League, in Parker's rendering of the Iroquois Constitution, or Great Law:

> I am Dekanawidah [the Peacemaker] and with the Five Nations' Confederate Lords I plant the Tree of the Great Peace. I plant it in your territory, Tadodaho,[16] and the Onondaga Nation, in the territory of you who are Firekeepers. . . .
>
> Roots have spread out from the Tree . . . one to the north, one to the east, one to the south and one to the west. The name of these roots is the Great White Roots and their nature is Peace and Strength.
>
> If any man or any nation outside the Five Nations shall obey the laws of the Great Peace . . . they may trace the Roots to the Tree and . . . they shall be welcomed. . . .
>
> We place at the top of the Tree . . . an Eagle who is able to see afar. If he sees in the distance any evil approaching or any danger threatening he will at once warn the people of the Confederacy. . . .
>
> The Smoke of the Confederate Council Fire shall ever ascend and pierce the sky so that other nations who may be allies may see. . . .
>
> Whenever the Confederate Lords shall assemble for the purpose of holding a council, the Onondaga Lords shall open it by expressing gratitude to their cousin Lords . . . and they shall make an address and offer thanks to the earth . . . to the streams of water, the pools, the springs and the lakes, to the maize and the fruits, to the medicinal herbs and trees, to the forest trees for their usefulness, to the animals that serve as food and give their pelts for clothing, to the great winds and the lesser winds, to the Thunderers, to the Sun, the mighty warrior, to the moon,

> to the messengers of the Creator who reveal his wishes and to the Great Creator . . . ruler of health and life. . . .
>
> Five arrows shall be bound together very strongly and . . . this shall symbolize the union of the nations.[17]

Besides its political content, the Great Law reflects the profound gratitude that Iroquois, like all Amerindians, felt for the gift of life. The Iroquois ritual year was a round of grateful celebration. In spring, families gathered at their sugar groves for the Thanks-to-the-Maple feast. In May or June came the Corn Planting, followed by the Strawberry Festival when the first wild fruit was tasted. The greatest occasion was the Green Corn Dance, when the first maize had ripened. Finally, in October, when the crops were harvested and stored, the Iroquois honored the Creator with Thanksgiving, yet another custom that the new Americans borrowed from the old.

The loan went unacknowledged. At white Thanksgivings, the thanks, if there are any, go to a white god who helped his faithful survive in a supposed wilderness. The diners then sit down to eat turkey, pumpkin, maize, beans, and potatoes, none of which was known to pre-Columbian Europe. It was the heathen savage, not the Christian God, who fed them.

Euro-Americans do not like to be reminded that their presence in America was essentially parasitic until they grew strong enough to do without the host. If you visit Iroquoia today, you find that an alien historical landscape has been laid down like a rug beneath which the real history has been swept. Iroquois places have been renamed Syracuse, Rome, Ithaca, Homer, Ovid, as if a past could be transferred by logomancy from one world to another.

> Watcher was chief; he looked toward the sea.
> At this time, from north and south, the whites came. . . .
> Who are they?
>
> —*Walam Olum,* Delaware, seventeenth (?) century

With the Faith, the scourge of God came into the country.

—*Jesuit Relations,* 1653

While Soto and his like were invading North America from the south, others began to probe its colder latitudes. In 1534, a middle-aged Breton named Jacques Cartier sailed up the St. Lawrence and kidnaped two boys out fishing from a distant Iroquoian town. After a winter in France, the boys led Cartier farther west, to where tides cease and the St. Lawrence narrows below a tall bluff. Here was their home, Stadacona, where Quebec City now stands. Cartier released the boys—sons of the chief—and made a hasty trip 150 miles upstream to the hilly island now occupied by Montreal.

In the crystalline light of an October afternoon, Cartier climbed Mount Royal and gazed down on a triple stockade and parapet enclosing fifty longhouses. This was the important town of Hochelaga, inhabited by several thousand Mohawks.[18] Recently harvested cornfields stretched across the island and the flats on the south shore toward the Adirondack foothills blazing scarlet and gold. To the west the Ottawa River emerged from a leisurely drift through the Lake of Two Mountains, joined the St. Lawrence, and boiled angrily over limestone shelves and boulders. Like Columbus, Cartier wasn't looking for America; hoping China lay not far beyond the rapids, he called them La Chine.[19]

Hochelaga's ladies prepared a banquet for the strange guests, but the French, fearing poison, spurned it and retired to their boats before dark. They went back to Stadacona and spent the winter in a small fort nearby. Relations with the local people soon deteriorated. Indians began dying of strange diseases: Europeans, holed up in their fort, died of the familiar scurvy. The two boys, who had learned plenty during their stay in France, warned their father that he was being overcharged for trade goods and fed French avarice with tales of a golden kingdom to the west.

Cartier was less gullible than Hernando de Soto; the land of gold failed to lure him to an ignominious death. When spring came he shanghaied ten Stadaconans, sailed abruptly for Brittany, and did not return for six years. By then, nine of his prisoners had died, and he dared not repatriate the lone survivor lest she reveal what had happened. Instead, he told their anxious relatives that all ten were living the good life in France and had no wish to come home.[20] This didn't fool the Indians for a moment—home was not a place they abandoned lightly.

Cartier's lies, violent behavior, and gloomy reports hindered French efforts to build a colony in Canada until the seventeenth century. But like the Spaniards, the Frenchman left invisible conquerors behind. The fate of his captives—a mortality of 90 percent—was but a sample of the great death consuming the Americas. When Samuel de Champlain retraced the same route in 1603, Stadacona and Hochelaga had vanished. The pre-Columbian world glimpsed in its last hours by Cartier had crumbled like the contents of a violated tomb.

It is impossible to say exactly how many people were living in what are now the United States and Canada in 1492. But it's clear that the old guess of around one million is absurdly low—a guess cherished for so long because it reinforced the myth of the empty land and hid the enormity of native America's depopulation.[21] Good modern estimates range between 7 and 18 million.[22] How many of those were Iroquois? Hard to say, but being settled and powerful peoples, the Five Nations must have accounted for several hundred thousand before the great pandemic of the 1520s. They were probably not more than 75,000 a century later.[23] Archaeology confirms that Iroquoia once had numerous "castles" like Hochelaga, as well as temple mounds that the Senecas said were built by their ancestors between the thirteenth and fifteenth centuries.[24] A Dutch settler observed, around 1650, "the Indians . . . affirm, that before the arrival of the Christians, and before the small pox broke out amongst them, they were ten times as numerous as they now are."[25]

The number of whites in eastern North America is more certain: in 1600 only a handful; in 1700 about a quarter of a million; and by 1800 more than 5 million.[26] Against this immense demographic shift, the Iroquois, like so many others, struggled for survival. It had always been Iroquois practice to replace people killed in battle by adopting prisoners of war. Around 1640, after a decade of smallpox, they perceived that the only way to maintain their strength would be to incorporate their enemies en masse. The first targets of this policy were the Hurons, who had fallen to a mere 10,000 but were still serious competitors in the fur trade. "The design of the Iroquois, as far as I can see," a Jesuit wrote in 1643, "is to take, if they can, all the Hurons . . . to make them both but one people."[27] At first the Iroquois tried diplomacy; when that failed, the Mohawks blockaded the trading corridor to Montreal. Then, in March 1649, a thousand Iroquois troops gathered near the Christianized Huron towns of St. Ignace and St. Louis and poured out of the frozen woods in a dawn attack. By nine o'clock the towns were in flames. According to Jesuit sources, vengeful heathens "baptized" the priests in boiling water; impressed by the bravery of Father Jean de Brébeuf, they roasted and ate his heart.[28]

The Hurons never recovered as a nation. A few fled west and north; a small band of loyal converts moved to Quebec City, where their descendants live today. But most merged with the Five Nations. This in itself was not new—Indian nations, like modern ones, were ethnically fluid and complex; the homogeneous "tribe" of popular imagination seldom existed. But the scale was new. By the 1660s many of Iroquoia's citizens were Hurons and Algonquins who had "become Iroquois in temper and inclination."[29] The same happened with captured whites: European features discernible among modern Iroquois often have a long pedigree. "When white persons of either sex have been taken prisoners young by the Indians," Ben Franklin noted, "in a short time they become disgusted with our manner of life, and . . . there is no reclaiming them."[30]

By this means, the Five Nations not only survived but became the principal buffer state between the colonies of France and Britain. "Those Five Nations," Governor Thomas Dongan of New York wrote to London in 1687, "are . . . the awe and dread of all the Indians in these parts of America, and are a better defence to us than if they were so many Christians."[31] Iroquoia's location was even more strategic than that of the Cherokees, for the foreign powers' main bases—Quebec and New York—lay immediately north and south of it. The Longhouse's western "door," guarded by the Senecas, overlooked the Niagara peninsula that divides Lake Ontario from Lake Erie. Here, within sight of the spray from the great falls, the French periodically maintained a fort. The eastern "door," guarded by the Mohawks, commanded the great geological fault that scores the continent from Montreal to New York City, dividing the Adirondacks from the Green Mountains of Vermont. The southern half of this 300-mile ditch is filled by the Hudson River, the northern half by the long narrow Lake of the Mohawks. In 1609, Samuel de Champlain "discovered" this lake, gunned down the first Mohawks he met, and gave it his own name.

Champlain's burst of musket fire was the first shot in a three-cornered war that lasted until British and Mohawk forces took Montreal in 1760. This in turn was followed by the American War of Independence, in which the Six Nations for the last time held a balance of power. As with the Cherokees, I have chosen that war to mark the end of the initial "conquest," though in fact the invaders never won a conclusive victory over the resilient Iroquois. As we shall see, echoes of these old conflicts are still heard.

In 1664, Louis XIV gave orders "totally to exterminate" the Five Nations, but the best his generals could do was the usual burning of castles and cornfields.[32] In the same year the English displaced the Dutch from North America. New Amsterdam became New York; Fort Orange, where the Mohawk River turns south into the Hudson, became Albany. The Iroquois transferred their trading alliance—known among them as the Two Row Wampum—from Holland to Britain. In 1687, the French crossed the Niagara River and hacked at the Longhouse's western door, reporting to King Louis that they had destroyed more than a million bushels of corn and "a vast quantity of hogs."[33] The Five Nations soon took revenge, wiping out all French forts and settlements west of Montreal. A jubilant delegation went to Albany and gloated over their triumph to Governor Dongan.

> The French can have no title to those places which they possess, nay not to Cadarachqui [now Kingston] and Mount Royal [Montreal] nor none of our lands towards the Ottawas . . . for by what means can they pretend them? Because they came to the

> Mohawks' country formerly, and now latterly to the Senecas' country, and burnt some bark houses and cut down our corn?— If that be a good title then we can claim all Canada, for we . . . plied the French home [until] they were not able to go over a door to piss.[34]

> Savages we call them, because their Manners differ from ours, which we think the Perfection of Civility; they think the same of theirs.
>
> —Benjamin Franklin, 1784

The Iroquois history of their invasion by Europe is recorded, like that of the Cherokees, as a long series of negotiations with the invaders. Many early speeches have survived, partly because of better record keeping in the northern colonies but also because the Iroquois were the finest orators of North America.

The thrust of Six Nations diplomacy was to keep both foreign powers unsure of Iroquois intentions, to extract the maximum in trade goods, to yield the minimum of territory, and to keep the encroaching squatters at bay for as long as possible. To the north of Iroquoia, Lake Ontario provided a natural barrier, and the French were in any case half-hearted settlers: during the 150 years that France controlled Canada, only 27,000 migrants came from the mother country.[35] They multiplied to 65,000 by 1760, but that was nothing compared to the numbers of British in New York and Pennsylvania.

Diplomacy and politics are always theater. In oral societies, whether the Six Nations of the Iroquois or the seven kingdoms of Anglo-Saxon England, this is axiomatic: every legal deed had to be done before witnesses, the more the better. Anyone who reads the minutes and transcripts of conferences involving the Six Nations will be impressed by the way Europeans were forced to adopt Amerindian protocol. They had to acquire a rich metaphorical language—planting the tree of peace, straightening the roads, sweeping the house, stoking the council fire, and so forth—to fix each clause in memory, like headings and illustrations in a text. (Some of this imagery—burying the hatchet, for example—came into general English usage.) Europeans had to learn the intricacies of making and presenting wampum and other gifts, reciprocity being the key to all discourse. They had to remember the correct kinship terms that signified political status. They were given names to be passed, like the sachem titles of the League, from one incumbent to the next. Iroquois always called the governor of New York "Corlaer," the name of the Dutchman with whom they negotiated the original Two Row Wampum treaty in the 1640s.[36] The governor of Quebec was "Onontio," a translation of Montmagny, the first incumbent's name; and the Penns of Pennsylvania were dubbed "Onas," an Iroquois word for pen.

To these metaphors the British added one of their own: the "Covenant Chain," symbol of the ties between indigenous nations and the Crown. Just as "roads" had to be swept and straightened, the "chain" had to be cleaned of rust, burnished with loving hands, lengthened with extra links, mended with new ones, and so forth.

William Bull, who represented South Carolina at an Albany conference, gives an idea of what these negotiations were like.

> There were about 130 men from the Six Nations, their wives and children made up above 300. They made huts for themselves on the hills. . . . Here they had fresh meat, bread and beer served to them every day, the cost each day amounting to £85 our currency. . . .
>
> On the 4th of July . . . they condoled with His Excellency on the death of the Prince of Wales, and His Excellency returned the condolence on the loss of several of the warriors and sachems [for] they never proceed upon business till the ceremony of condolence is performed. . . .
>
> On the 6th, the Governor [sat] in a chair in the street, before his house, and the council of this province, and the commissioners from South Carolina, Boston, and Connecticut being seated on each side of him, and the Indian Secretary seated at a table before him, and the Six Nations seated on logs placed in the street. . . . He then cautioned them against the artifices of the

> French, and proposed to them to destroy the French Fort at Niagara on their land. . . .
>
> On the 8th of July they answered the Governor, paragraph by paragraph.[37]

Of the many great orators who spoke for the Six Nations in the mid-eighteenth century, Canasatego—the brawny Onondaga who influenced Benjamin Franklin—was the star. Franklin was the government printer at the time and returned the favor by publishing transcripts of the conferences at which Canasatego and other speakers shone. Snapped up by both whites and Indians, they also sold well in faraway London as specimens of Americana.

Tough, wily, and convivial, Canasatego used humor as an effective ingredient of his veiled threats. When the English produced rather stingy tots of rum at the end of some difficult talks, he contrasted the generosity of the foreign powers. "It turned out unfortunately that you gave us it in French glasses," he said. "We now desire you will give us some in English glasses."[38] Which must have left the English wondering just how familiar Canasatego was with the size of French tumblers and whether the names of the glasses were reversed when he talked business in Quebec.

Canasatego's years of wrangling with the Penn brothers bore little fruit until open war broke out between the French and British in the early 1740s. War between the invaders was always the Iroquois' most advantageous time, for their forces were still strong enough to decide the outcome. After dropping his usual threats, Canasatego turned even the paucity of his gifts into a demonstration of what settlers and their livestock were doing to Indian hunting grounds.

> We know our lands are now become more valuable. The white people think we do not know their value; but we are sensible that the land is everlasting, and the few goods we receive for it are soon worn out and gone. . . . Besides, we are not well used with respect to the lands still unsold by us. Your people daily settle on these lands, and spoil our hunting. We must insist on

> your removing them . . . for they do great damage to our cousins the Delawares. . . .
>
> It is customary with us to make a present of skins whenever we renew our treaties. We are ashamed to offer our brethren so few; but your horses and cows have eaten the grass our deer used to feed on.[39]

George Thomas, deputy governor of Pennsylvania, replied that efforts had already been made to remove illegal squatters: "Some magistrates were sent . . . and we thought no persons would presume to stay after that," he said glibly. Canasatego was not so easily fobbed off. "These persons who were sent did not do their duty. So far from removing the people, they made surveys for themselves, and they are in league with the trespassers."[40]

In June 1744, two years after the above exchange, representatives of the Six Nations, Pennsylvania, Virginia, and Maryland met at Lancaster for a fortnight of hard bargaining. It was here—on July 4, oddly enough—that Canasatego recommended the Iroquois style of union to the colonies. That speech, momentous in retrospect, was overshadowed at the time by his address of June 26 to the governor of Maryland. In this he painted a large canvas: the entire history of contact between the natives and invaders of North America. His outrage is the same outrage aboriginal leaders express today when they find that the white man's self-serving pieces of paper carry more weight in white courts than the huge fact that the Indians were in America first, since time immemorial.

> When you mentioned the affair of the land yesterday, you went back to old times, and told us you had been in possession of the Province of Maryland above one hundred years; but what is one hundred years in comparison of the length of time since our claim began? Since we came out of this ground? For we must tell you, that long before one hundred years, our ancestors came out of this very ground, and their children have remained here ever since. You came out of the ground in a country that lies beyond the seas, there you may have a just claim, but here you must allow us to be

> your elder brethren, and the lands to belong to us before you knew anything of them.
>
> It is true, that above one hundred years ago the Dutch came here in a ship. . . . During all this time the newcomers, the Dutch, acknowledged our right to the lands. . . .
>
> After this the English came into the country, and, as we were told, became one people with the Dutch. About two years after the arrival of the English, an English governor came to Albany, and finding what great friendship subsisted between us and the Dutch, he approved it mightily, and desired to make as strong a league, and to be upon as good terms with us as the Dutch were. . . .
>
> Indeed we have had some small differences with the English, and, during these misunderstandings, some of their young men would, by way of reproach, be every now and then telling us that we should have perished if they had not come into the country and furnished us with strouds [blankets] and hatchets and guns, and other things necessary for the support of life. But we always gave them to understand that they were mistaken, that we lived before they came amongst us, and as well, or better, if we may believe what our forefathers have told us. We then had room enough, and plenty of deer, which was easily caught; and though we had not knives, hatchets, or guns, such as we have now, yet we had knives of stone, and hatchets of stone, and bows and arrows, and those served our uses as well then as the English ones do now.
>
> We are now straitened, and sometimes in want of deer, and liable to many other inconveniences since the English came among us, and particularly from that pen-and-ink work that is going on at the table.[41]

The Onondaga stopped and wagged his finger at the secretary jotting down his words.

Most Iroquois came away from the Treaty of Lancaster feeling they had done well. They were laden with £1,100 worth of trade goods, for which they had relinquished some land occupied by non-Iroquois over whom they may or may not have been overlords—not a bad haul for a dubious claim.[42] With this and the concomitant brightening of the covenant chain, they felt they were in a strong position to defend Iroquoia during any forthcoming hostilities, and possibly to profit from them.

But both sides had promised more than they could deliver: The colonial governments could not control their unruly "settlers," who were in fact always on the move, driven by a predatory shoal of land sharks at their backs. And when the Franco-British war became serious, the Iroquois were unable to bring their western allies to the British camp.

> Indian-hating still exists; and, no doubt, will continue to exist, so long as Indians do.
>
> —Herman Melville, 1857

No prominent Mohawks were present at the Lancaster talks in 1744, an absence that marked the beginning of a rift in the Longhouse that persists to this day. As the eastern doorkeepers, sandwiched between Albany and Quebec, the Mohawks had the closest contact with both English and French. This gave them great diplomatic and trading leverage, but also exposed them to the brunt of such frontier ills as disease, rum, and squatter invasions. By the 1740s, many had started to withdraw from their old southern heartland along the Mohawk Valley, which runs westward from Albany to within a few miles of Oneida Lake; some had been moving north for a century, repopulating towns along the St. Lawrence where their ancestors had greeted Cartier. The most strategic of these was Kahnawake (Caughnawaga), clustered around a Catholic mission on the south bank across from Montreal. (Six thousand Mohawks live there to this day, and in 1990 unfinished business with the white invader led them to blockade one of the city's freeways for two months.) Mohawks thus had a foot planted in each colonial camp, a high-stakes game that made the rest of the Six Nations uneasy, especially the important Senecas and Onondagas.

The Mohawks thought Canasatego, for all his fine words, had made a serious mistake at Lancaster, trading away too many powers. In 1750, the Onondaga statesman died suddenly. Although he was well past sixty, many thought his death suspicious, especially when the Mohawk leader Thayanoge, known to whites as Hendrick, nimbly stepped into his shoes. Hendrick was one of four Mohawk chiefs who had gone to England to visit Queen Anne in 1710, but the British now suspected him of being a French sympathizer. This he denied, yet exploited. In 1753, Hendrick went to New York City and complained bitterly about British neglect to the governor, Admiral George Clinton.

> We are come here to remind you of the ancient alliance agreed on between our respective forefathers: We were united together by a covenant chain and it now seems likely to be broken not from our faults but yours. . . .
>
> My heart aches because we Mohawks have always been faithful to you . . . especially in this last war [when] there was no assistance given you but by our Nations, and had the war lasted some time longer we would have torn the Frenchmen's hearts out. . . .
>
> You sit in peace and quietness here whilst we are exposed to the enemy. . . . It is by your means that we stand every hour in danger.

Hendrick then moved to the matter of settler encroachments and abuses in the Mohawk Valley.

> When our brethren the English first came among us we gave and sold them lands, and have continued to do so ever since, but it seems now as if we had no lands left for ourselves. . . .
>
> We desire our brother [Governor Clinton] to let us see the patents [title deeds] . . . by this we shall know who have cheated us.
>
> I am going to tell you how many persons we design to drive away from our lands. Viz. Barclay, Pritchett's wife who lives just by us and who does us a great deal of damage by selling us liquors and by that means making us destroy one another. . . . We let her have a little spot of land and she takes in more and more every year.[43]

At last Hendrick came to the sting in the tail of his speech. The Six Nations had, he said, received wampum from the French with an invitation to talk. Of course, he added craftily, the Gallic intent was doubtless to invite the Mohawks to a feast and murder them.

Despite the seriousness of this, Governor Clinton did not give Hendrick a good answer. The Mohawk went away in anger.

> When we came here to relate our grievances about our lands, we expected to have something done . . . and Brother you tell us that we shall be redressed at Albany. But we know them so well, we will not trust to them, for they are no people but Devils. . . .
>
> The covenant chain is broken. . . . You are not to expect to hear of me any more, and Brother we desire to hear no more of you.[44]

When news of this reached London, Clinton's superiors were appalled. He had broken with the Iroquois on the very eve of what came to be known in America as the French and Indian War (c. 1754–1763) and in Europe, where it began two years later, as the Seven Years' War. "When we consider of how great consequence the friendship and alliance of the Six Nations is to all His Majesty's colonies and plantations in America in general as well as to New York in particular," the Lords of Trade wrote to Clinton, "we cannot but be greatly concerned. . . . Fatal consequences . . . must inevitably follow from a neglect of them."[45] To patch things up, the British sent William Johnson, a trader and agent who had lived in the Mohawk Valley for years, to Hendrick with gifts, promises, and an invitation to the Albany Congress of 1754.

Despite the best efforts of Benjamin Franklin, who aired his scheme for an Iroquois-style union of the colonies, the Albany Congress failed to produce concerted action against the French. The Crown then appointed the vain and drunken General Edward Braddock to be commander in chief over all British forces in North America. Braddock, who had little use for colonists and less for Indians, alienated the Iroquois just as he had the Cherokees. When the British were routed at Pittsburgh in 1755, Scarouady, an Oneida chief, let fly about arrogant brass from the old country.

Brother:

It is now well known to you how unhappily we have been defeated by the French. . . . We must let you know that it was the pride and ignorance of that great general that came from England. He is now dead, but he was a bad man when he was alive. He looked upon us as dogs and would never hear anything that was said to him. We often endeavoured to advise him, and to tell him of the danger he was in . . . but he never appeared pleased with us, and that was the reason that a great many of our warriors left him and would not be under his command. . . .

Those that come from over the great seas . . . are unfit to fight in the woods. Let us go ourselves, we that came out of this ground. We may be assured to conquer the French.[46]

In response to such criticism, the Crown set up a Department of Indian Affairs with two divisions, north and south. William Johnson (now Sir William) was chosen to head the northern half, making him the counterpart of the Cherokees' old friend John Stuart. The choice was popular with the Mohawks: "We love him, and he us," said Hendrick's brother.[47] The department worked tolerably well as a liaison with the Six Nations but was powerless to restrain encroaching settlers, one of whom was devious old Johnson himself. He set himself up in style at Johnson Hall, a grandiose Georgian mansion in the heart of the Mohawk Valley, about fifty miles west of Albany. There he met and married Molly Brant, elder sister of a remarkable boy, Joseph Brant, the Mohawk war chief who would opt for Britain in the Revolutionary War.

By October 1758, the tide of war was turning in favor of the British. Despite all their bluster and assurances of support, the Six Nations had remained effectively neutral until then. Finally, in 1759, Johnson got the Senecas to destroy Fort Niagara, the French stronghold on the limestone neck between lakes Erie and Ontario. Later the same year Wolfe took Quebec in a brutal campaign that cost him his own life. Lord Jeffrey Amherst then took Ticonderoga on Lake Champlain, giving him control of the water corridor from New York to Montreal. And in

September 1760, Kahnawake Mohawks ferried a British army across the La Chine Rapids, and Montreal capitulated without bloodshed.[48]

With the French conquered, Indians throughout eastern North America began to hear rumors that the British would now turn against them. There was similar talk within the Six Nations of driving all whites from Iroquoia.[49] This mistrust was aggravated by General Braddock's successor, Amherst. Always an Indian hater, he abandoned his native allies, leaving many to starve amid the wreckage of cornfields and orchards destroyed in the fighting. He stopped their payments and did nothing to halt renewed settler intrusions.

These provocations added up to another war, one linked to the name of the Ottawa chief Pontiac, though he was only one of its leaders. And it became transformed into a holy war.

The indigenous peoples were in the midst of a crisis that threatened every aspect of their lives. They had experienced two centuries of population collapse and accelerating cultural change. Old ways no longer worked; new ones required the adoption of repugnant alien values. The future offered them survival—if it offered survival at all—only at the exorbitant price of becoming like the invaders.

Such a predicament has been faced by many peoples at many times in history, though nowhere on earth has it been faced on such a scale and for so long as in the Americas. A threat from which there seems to be no escape often triggers a religious response: cultures, like individuals, become open to messages from God, resulting in what anthropologists call a revitalization movement or crisis cult. A prophet offers a way—usually presented as a return to an ideal past—which is in fact a new way, synthesizing tradition and change. Such prophets may be doomed, like Joan of Arc, or they may change the world, like Jesus and Mohammed.

In 1762, a Delaware named Neolin, the Enlightened, returned from a spiritual journey to the Creator's dwelling place. There the Master of Life had shown him why his people suffered and given instructions for revival.

> I am the Maker of Heaven and Earth, the trees, lakes, rivers, men, and all that thou seest . . . and because I love you, you must do my

> will; you must avoid also that which I hate; I hate you to drink as you do, until you lose your reason; I wish you not to fight one another. . . .
>
> The land on which you are, I have made for you, not for others: wherefore do you suffer the whites to dwell upon your lands? Can you not do without them? . . . Before those whom you call your [white] brothers had arrived, did not your bow and arrow maintain you? You needed neither gun, powder, nor any other object. The flesh of animals was your food, their skins your raiment. But when I saw you inclined to evil, I removed the animals into the depths of the forests. . . .
>
> Drive from your lands those dogs in red clothing [the British], they are only an injury to you. When you want anything, apply to me. . . . Do not sell to your brothers that which I have placed on earth as food. . . . Become good and you shall want for nothing.[50]

Neolin's preaching gave Pontiac and the others planning the reconquest of North America exactly what any such movement needs: an ideology capable of inspiring extraordinary deeds and sacrifices. The message was carried from town to town, together with plans for a general rising in May 1763, Pontiac quietly dropping the taboo against steel and guns. "Then will the Great Spirit give success to our arms; then he will give us strength to conquer our enemies, to drive them from hence, and recover passage to the heavenly regions which they have taken from us."[51]

Fort after fort fell to the insurgents. Two thousand settlers, most of them illegal squatters, were killed. The turning point, as so often in the contest for America, came with plague. But the scourge was no longer left in the hands of God. Lord Jeffrey Amherst secured his place in history as the inventor of modern germ warfare with this notorious command: "Infect the Indians with sheets upon which smallpox patients have been lying, or by any other means which may serve to exterminate this accursed race."[52] Fort Pitt's commander offered to parley with besieging chiefs; he then made them a gift of contaminated blankets. The epidemic raged all summer. One by one, the leaders who survived it were compelled to sue for peace.[53]

The only positive outcome for the Indians was the Royal Proclamation of 1763, which, as noted in Chapter 4, sealed the fate of Britain's colonies by setting limits to a colonial system based on an expanding frontier.

In 1768, at Fort Stanwix, which stood at the head of the Mohawk River in a place today called Rome, the Iroquois ceded their land to the east and south. The Mohawk Valley passed into the hands of Scots driven from *their* ancient home by highland clearances.[54]

Scottish immigration was craftily orchestrated by Sir William Johnson, who claimed 100,000 acres for himself.[55] Foreseeing the American Revolution, Johnson also played his other role assiduously, cultivating Iroquois ties with the Crown. He had first noticed the precocious ability of his Mohawk wife's little brother Joseph during the French and Indian War, when the boy, aged thirteen, distinguished himself in battle. Johnson saw to his education, first at an Anglican mission, then at the boarding school that later became Dartmouth College. Joseph Brant emerged with a thorough command of English, Latin, and Greek, besides at least three of the Six Nations' languages. But Thayendanegea, as he was known among the Mohawks, paid a price for his bicultural dexterity: he embraced the white world too warmly, and this, along with his rash temperament, made it hard for him to distinguish between the interests of his own people and those of the British. Brant is still praised by Canadians—and blamed by Iroquois—for involving the Confederacy in the Revolutionary War, an involvement that broke the back of the Longhouse and hastened the fall of Iroquoia. A few months after "the shot heard round the world" was fired in April 1775 at Concord, Massachusetts, Joseph Brant and Guy Johnson—nephew of Sir William, who had died the year before—were invited to England to forge an Iroquois-British alliance against the rebels. Indians were still treated as celebrities in London, and Mohawks in particular had captured the public imagination (there were even street gangs called Mohawks who affected spiky haircuts). Brant, then thirty-three, stayed at The Swan With Two Necks, was interviewed for the *London Magazine* by James Boswell, and painted in a rather saccharine style by George Romney. A more revealing portrait, done later in Brant's life, shows an august figure with a lined brow, head shaven but for a wispy topknot, sad eyes, and more than a passing resemblance to Mikhail Gorbachev. Boswell was disappointed to meet a man who could discuss the classics in good English; he had wanted "the ferocious dignity of a savage."[56]

Early in 1776, George III and the colonial lords received the Mohawk leader. Self-assured in any company, Brant used his leverage to speak bluntly about land.

> The Mohawks, our particular nation, have on all occasions shown their zeal and loyalty to the Great King; yet they have been very badly treated by his people in that country, the City of Albany having an unjust claim to the lands on which our Lower Castle is built. . . . We have been often assured by our late friend Sir William Johnson . . . that the King and wise men here would do us justice; but this . . . has never been done, and it makes us very uneasy.
>
> Indeed it is very hard, when we have let the King's subjects have so much of our lands for so little value, they should want to cheat us in this manner of the small spots we have left for our women and children to live on. We are tired out in making complaints and getting no redress.[57]

Before leaving England he repeated that Iroquois support was conditional on land violations being "settled to our satisfaction whenever the troubles in America end," adding that the government's failure to redress past wrongs was "a flatter of surprise to all the Indian Nations."[58]

While Brant was away, the Iroquois League remained aloof from the white civil war. Flying Crow, a Seneca, dryly rebuffed the Crown agent who came with assurances that Britain would win: "If you are so strong, Brother, and they but as weak as a boy, why ask our assistance?"[59]

The Six Nations had no wish to be drawn, yet again, into fighting foreigners' wars. They declared themselves neutral, but warned that the first side to molest them would become their foe. At this critical time smallpox attacked the Onondagas, the Firekeepers at the Confederacy's heart. The losses, requiring condolence rites and new elections, crippled the Six Nations' parliament. In January 1777, a delegation told the British:

> Brother: We are sent here by the Oneida chiefs, in conjunction with the Onondagas. . . . They gave us the melancholy news that the grand council-fire at Onondaga was extinguished. We have lost out of their town by death ninety, among whom are three principal sachems. We, the remaining part of the Onondagas, do now inform our brethren that there is no longer a council fire at the capital of the Six Nations.[60]

Taking advantage of Onondaga's weakness, the British held a council at Oswego on Lake Ontario's southeastern shore. They invited Brant and other sympathetic Iroquois to "eat the flesh and drink the blood of a Bostonian."[61] The colorful phrase was coined by Guy Johnson—Boswell should have got his savagery from him. By then the rebels had committed several outrages, including an attempt on Brant's life. Brant talked four of the Six Nations into fighting for the Crown and assumed command of Iroquois loyalists.[62] The Oneida and Tuscarora, who did not attend the council, took the rebel side: the Confederacy was split in two.

Despite Guy Johnson's barbarous imagery, Iroquois conduct was restrained. Brant forbade torture and protected civilians as best he could; in a letter he demanded that the enemy do the same.

> You Bostonians [rebels] may be certified of my conduct towards all those whom I have captured. . . . Many have I released. Neither were the weak and the helpless subjected to death. It is a shame to destroy those who are defenceless. . . . I have always been for saving and releasing. These being my sentiments, you have exceedingly angered me by . . . threatening and distressing . . . prisoners. Let there be no more of this conduct. Ye are, or once were, brave men.[63]

But rebel propaganda characterized all Indian victories as massacres, painted Brant as a monster, and accused him of atrocities during battles at which he wasn't even present. George Washington ordered that Iroquois not "merely be overrun but destroyed." In 1779, General John

Sullivan cut down orchards and crops, burning 500 houses and nearly a million bushels of corn.[64] Colonel Daniel Brodhead, in an infamous attack that became known as the "squaw campaign," dodged Indian armies but slaughtered women and children. The whites were notorious rapists, though the Indians were not: "Bad as these savages are," General James Clinton wrote, "they never violate the chastity of any woman."[65]

Rebel atrocities served only to stimulate the Indian war effort, Brant's troops shattered frontier militias and wiped out settlements throughout New York, Pennsylvania, Ohio, and Kentucky. The Iroquois were winning, rolling back the settler tide, as George Clinton, the first American governor of New York, admitted to Congress in 1781: "We are now . . . deprived of a great portion of our most valuable and well inhabited territory, numbers of our citizens have been barbarously butchered by ruthless hand of the savages, many are carried away into captivity, vast numbers entirely ruined. . . . We are not in a condition to raise troops for the defence of our Frontier."[66]

Then, in the autumn of 1782, the British suddenly gave up. They urged the Iroquois to go home and withheld supplies to finish the job, even though vengeful settlers began pouring west as soon as hostilities ceased. Brant was in despair; perhaps he was also disillusioned. "We the Indians wish to have the blow returned on the enemy as early as possible," he wrote. "We are . . . as it were between two Hells."[67]

In 1783, at the Treaty of Paris that ended the Revolutionary War, Britain betrayed her native allies. All who had held the covenant chain were abandoned to the mercy of the new republic without a word on their behalf.

PART TWO

RESISTANCE

SIX

AZTEC

Our fathers, our grandfathers—did they know these monks?
—Andrés Mixcoatl, Aztec, c. 1533

To be a gringo in Mexico. Ah, that is euthanasia!
—Ambrose Bierce, c. 1913

After defeat comes occupation, that bland term redolent of property transfer that is used to describe the loss of a nation's autonomy. The invaders do not go home; they arrive in greater numbers and variety: viceroys, administrators, merchants, and missionaries intent on conquering and occupying the mind.

I call the middle part of this book, which corresponds in Latin America to the three centuries of direct European rule, Resistance. (For the Cherokees and Iroquois, the period is much shorter and complicated by the early independence of the United States.) Resistance to foreign occupation may take an organized military form, like that of the French to the Nazis, or be more subtle—a matter of belief, a surreptitious rejection of all or part of the invader's enterprise. When the occupation is as long and irreversible as it has been in the Americas, resistance passes through many phases before it is either crushed conclusively or manages to achieve a partial solution to the dilemma of conquest and survival.

All five peoples in this book have resisted successfully to the degree that they are all survivors, but they have taken different paths. As we shall see in the third and final part, which brings their stories from the nineteenth century to the present, it is possible to discern a qualified rebirth. But this doesn't mean that resistance and the need for resistance have ended. In the colonial period, Euro-Americans and Native Americans began a parallel history on the same soil, a forced marriage that has been violent, unequal, and unhappy but cannot be dissolved. For as long as indigenous America wages a psychological—and sometimes physical—war to survive, its history is unfinished.

Of the five, the Aztecs alone may be something of an exception. The first Aztec chapter closed with a lament that says, "We have lost our Mexican nation." In Part 3, I suggest that the parallel histories of Indian and European have drawn closer in Mexico than elsewhere, that the marriage may have become less painful and more fruitful, that a new Mexican nation may have been born. The colonial Aztec sources examined here in Part 2 illuminate the begetting of that nation.

When Cuauhtémoc, nephew of the dead Moctezuma, surrendered from a canoe in August 1521, he touched Cortés's dagger and said: "I have done everything in my power to defend my kingdom and save it from your hands. Since fate has run against me, I beg you to kill me now. This is as it should be. With this act you will end the Mexican kingship, just as you have destroyed my city and killed my subjects."[1]

But for four more years Cortés denied Cuauhtémoc a good death. He kept him alive, periodically pouring oil on his feet and setting them alight, in hope of learning the whereabouts of the gold lost on the Night of Sorrow, the Aztecs' short-lived triumph. The fallen emperor would reply only that the heavy ingots the Spaniards themselves had forged were sunk too deep in the mud for anyone to find. Finally, in 1525, after he made a quixotic bid for revenge, the Spaniards "seized Cuauhtémoc . . . and baptized him, and it is not certain whether they named him Don Juan or Don Fernando. And after baptizing him, they cut off his head and nailed it to a silk-cotton tree in front of the temple of Yaxdzan."[2]

With him was beheaded the Aztec polity. Though there would be rebellions in other parts of New Spain, the Valley of Mexico never seriously challenged Spanish power. Not in a material way; spiritual resistance was another matter.

To consolidate his victory, and improve the future of his soul, Cortés invited Franciscan missionaries to follow the military conquest with a religious one. In 1524, twelve friars arrived—a number deliberately evoking the apostles. Until then the old religion had continued openly, though without human sacrifice. The crestfallen war gods went hungry on their pyramids, but elsewhere the rhythms of Mesoamerican worship were followed as before. There were still priests to burn incense, still daykeepers to read the calendars and keep the ritual count of twenty days and thirteen numbers to which every action, human and divine, was geared. And in houses and fields, humble folk made offerings at family shrines.

Huitzilopochtli, apotheosis of Mexico City's power, had been discredited, but that didn't mean that an entire cosmology and philosophy, developed over thousands of years, was finished. In the sixteenth century, neither Spaniard nor Mexican thought of religion as merely a compartment of life. To both, faith was all of knowledge and existence, history and destiny, the personal and the exterior world. But unlike Christianity, Mesoamerican religion was not absolutist. It thrived on diversity; it held that different peoples had—and needed—different forms of thought and worship. Aztec gods were demanding, but they had never claimed to be the *only* gods. Most Aztecs thought that conversion to Christianity was simply a matter of ousting Huitzilopochtli and admitting Christ, the Virgin, Santiago, and so on, to the ancient pantheon in his place. After all, the supreme Creator, known as Life Giver or the Duality, seemed little different from the Spaniards' *Dios*.

The Franciscan apostles made it clear that this would not be sufficient. They intended nothing less than the tearing down of an entire culture and its rebuilding stone by stone from different plans. Mexican thinkers who had survived the conquest were appalled. Vanquished but not yet cowed, the priests of Quetzalcoatl (the Feathered Serpent, patron of learning and culture) decided to confront the priests of Christ in a remarkable debate. Even more remarkably, this dialogue was written down in Nahuatl (Aztec) and sent to Rome, where it lay in the Vatican's Secret Archive for 400 years. Forgotten until 1924, it is an extraordinary record of one civilization defending its view of the world against another.

The debate took place in central Tenochtitlan, perhaps not far from the great Quetzalcoatl temple that Bernal Díaz saw before the conquest.

The door, shaped like a snake's mouth, reminded him of medieval paintings of the jaws of hell: it "contained great fangs to devour souls," he wrote.[3] By 1524, the square where it had stood was a demolition site; the Spaniards were camping in ruined palaces while chain gangs of Mexican prisoners cleared the wreckage to make way for the strange architecture of the conquerors. Whenever an Aztec stone image came to light, the masons were told to break it in pieces, but sometimes, when backs were turned, they could rebury their old gods deep in the waterlogged rubble that still reeked of death and fire. A mile away, in Tlatelolco, where the Aztecs had fought to the end, the Spaniards had already begun a church to Santiago, the war god who bested Huitzilopochtli. These were mere outward signs of the cultural transformation that Europe intended to perform.

The Christians spoke first, saying they had brought the Truth and that Mesoamerica's gods were demons sent by the devil. When the friars finished, a Mexican noble rose to his feet and "with courtesy and refinement" gave a reply.

There are those who guide us,
Who govern us,
Who look after us,
Who make the offerings and burn the incense;
And these priests of Quetzalcoatl, as they are called,
Show us how to venerate our gods,
Whom we serve, as wings and tails serve the birds.
They are the ones who must know the litanies . . .
It is they who see, who observe,
The orderly progress of the skies,
And how light is divided from darkness.
It is they who are reading, they who are telling what they read,
They who loudly turn the pages of the books.
They who have in their grasp the red ink, the black ink,
And the paintings;
They lead us, they guide us, they show us the way.
They ordain how the year is borne[4] and counted,

How the count of days and destinies, the cycle of twenty,
Follows its course.
This is their vocation;
It is they who speak of the gods.[5]

These remarks served to introduce the priests, who came forward to answer the Christians. Our image of Aztec priests is not a favorable one: according to Bernal Díaz, they were sinister figures in black robes, their long hair matted with sacrificial blood. Here, on the other hand, they appear as wise and melancholy figures, arguing eloquently that "their ancient ways of thought about the divinity can be and should be respected."[6]

You have said to us that we do not know
The Lord . . . of the heavens and the earth.
You have said that our gods were not true.
This is a new word that you speak,
And by it we are disturbed,
We are unsettled;
Because our ancestors,
Those who have been,
Those who have lived upon the earth,
Never spoke in such a manner.
They gave us their way of life,
They held our gods to be true,
They worshipped them,
They honoured them . . .
They taught us
That [the gods] gave us our sustenance:
Everything there is to eat and drink,
All that supports life:
Maize, beans, amaranth, and sage.
It is to them that we turn
To ask for water and for rain. . . .
And now, must we destroy the ancient principles of life? . . .

Listen, [Franciscans]:
Do not force something on your people
That will bring them misfortune,
That will bring them catastrophe. . . .
It is already enough
That we have lost our government;
That it has been taken from us,
That it has been crushed. . . .

This is all that we can answer,
That we can reply,
To your breath,
To your word,
O, my lords.[7]

But the Franciscans had come to Mexico with the intention of building the Kingdom of God on earth. Here in the New World, they thought, Christianity could be recut from the original template, with none of the failings it had suffered in the Old. Men with such a mentality were of course quite unmoved by pleas for religious tolerance.

There had always been a millenarian cast to the followers of Saint Francis, who had himself come within an inch of heresy. Many believed that their founding saint was the angel of the apocalypse who had unlocked the seal of the sixth age of Revelation; the gospel would now be preached throughout the world and then would come the Antichrist. The Franciscans saw Christendom's sudden leap across the Atlantic—which had opened the way to China and Japan, the last strongholds of darkness—as a sure sign that the millennium drew near. Was not Charles V the prophesied world emperor? And had not Mexico fallen to Catholicism just as northern Europe fell to the Lutheran heretics? Were these not signs that the hosts of good and evil were assembling for Armageddon? As they watched the Mexicans die almost as fast as they could baptize them, the Franciscans saw God's mercy in the plagues: surely He was killing these new Christians to save them from the horrors of the final days?[8]

On New Year's Day, 1525, the friars drove the Mexican priests from their temples and began the "first battle against the devil."[9] Thousands were "converted" in mass baptisms. Motolinía, one of the twelve, baptized nearly half a million in his career.[10] The Aztec nobility took Christian names, adopted new rituals, and sent their children to doctrinal schools. Mesoamerican society split into factions: genuine converts and traditionalists who worshiped in secret as before. Aristocratic members of the latter, if exposed, were tried by the Inquisition and burned in public.[11] The new religion could be as bloody as the old.

Belief in an exclusive patent on truth was new and repugnant to Mexicans, but millenarian thinking was not. They too conceived of succeeding ages, each one ending in cosmic cataclysm. This was likely to happen at the completion of a Calendar Round—a fifty-two-year cycle of the Aztec calendar—which Mexicans dreaded just as Europeans had dreaded the year 1000 anno Domini.

The Calendar Round in which the conquest occurred ran from 1507 to 1559. It had begun without incident, but then had come the disturbing reports from the Caribbean coast, the omens, the arrival of the strangers in the year of Quetzalcoatl, followed in short order by Moctezuma's death, by smallpox, and by the fall of the great city. Now, while the friars preached, the plagues continued. Lords and elders died; holy men were burned alive. The strangers seized the best of everything: land, food, gold, the prettiest girls. New weeds and blights attacked the crops; cockroaches and rats scuttled ashore from stinking galleons and appeared for the first time in Mesoamerican cities, carrying with them virulent sicknesses. Other new animals—pigs, cattle, sheep, goats—ruined the canals and fields. For many Mexicans these disorders were a sign that this Calendar Round would be the last, that they were living through the end of the world.

The measured, cerebral mood of theological debate was replaced by metaphysical vertigo. Among those who could neither accept the new faith nor practice the old, prophets and messiahs arose. In 1533, in Texcoco (the lakeshore city that had defected from the Triple Alliance to Cortés), one Andrés Mixcoatl, announcing he was a god, handed out hallucinogenic mushrooms and railed against the missionaries.

> Why are you forsaking the things of the past? . . . Don't you realize that all the friars say is only lies and falsehood? They have brought nothing to help you; they do not know us, nor do we know them. Our fathers, our grandfathers—did they know these monks? Did they see what they preach, the God they talk about? They did not. On the contrary. . . . we, we are eating what the gods give us; it is they who are feeding us, are teaching us and giving us strength.[12]

Another prophet, Martín Ocelotl, went further. He identified the friars as *tzitzimime,* demons from the stars who threatened to descend to earth during solar eclipses and at the end of each Calendar Round. In other words, the Christians were apocalyptic beings whose presence on earth meant that this was indeed the end.

Although Ocelotl was captured and silenced in 1537, his ideas took root and ramified. A generation later, as the "binding of years" approached—the liminal moment at the completion of the Calendar Round—a third prophet began to teach that the world would return violently to something like its pre-Columbian state. Grotesque and ironic punishments would descend on all who had taken up European ways.

> Do you know what our ancestors used to say? When the binding of years takes place and total darkness falls, the *tzitzimime* will come down and eat us, and there will be transformation. Those . . . who have believed in [the Spanish] God will turn into something else. Whoever eats beef will turn into cattle; whoever eats pork will become pig . . . whoever eats hen will become hen. . . . All will perish, will cease to exist. . . . The term of their lives, the number of their years, will be up.[13]

But despite rejections of Europe such as these, the dominant form of Mexican resistance to the invaders would turn out to be syncretic. Syncretism—the growing together of new beliefs and old—is a way of encoding the values of a conquered culture within a dominant culture.

It would allow the Franciscans to think they had succeeded—and allow the Aztecs to think they had survived.

> Where we go to die, do we yet have life? Is there yet . . . a pleasure land, O Life Giver? Delicious flowers, songs, perhaps, are only here on earth.
>
> —*Cantares Mexicanos,* 1560s

> Where do we come from? What are we? Where are we going?
>
> —Paul Gauguin, c. 1896

Modern visitors to the Mexica hall in Mexico's spectacular Museum of Anthropology cannot fail to notice a monolithic sculpture of the earth goddess Coatlicue, Lady of the Serpent Skirt. To Western eyes she is overwhelmingly sinister, her head composed of two serpent heads, nose to nose, giving her a grotesque countenance with great fangs and a lolling bifid tongue. She wears a necklace of hearts and hands, with a pendant skull; around her waist is a skirt of interwoven snakes, and her feet clasp the ground with lizard claws. She once stood in the main square of Tenochtitlan near the Calendar Stone and other sculptures.

To a sixteenth-century friar raised in a creed that regards the quintessential creature of the earth as evil ("On thy belly shalt thou go"), Coatlicue's image was a nightmare. Yet to Aztecs, Coatlicue was not terrible at all: her reptilian body was the planet, the hearts were human life, the hands human ability, and the skull was a reminder that there is no life without death, Also called Tonantzin, Our Mother, she was the wife of Quetzalcoatl; together they formed the heavenly pair, the Duality, Ometeotl.

The early friars noted that Our Mother's main shrine stood on the hill of Tepeyacac, at the end of the northern causeway leading out of Mexico City. "Innumerable crowds came from a hundred leagues around to celebrate the feast days of this goddess."[14] In 1531, while haunting the ruined temple on this very spot, Juan Diego, a baptized Aztec, received a visit from the Virgin Mary. The date is significant, for it coincides with the second great plague to sweep through Mexico. The Virgin told Juan that she had cured his uncle of smallpox; she then caused a painting of herself to appear miraculously on his cloak. Years later, the miracle was accepted as genuine by church authorities all too eager to believe it. At the time there were doubts.

> They used to make many sacrifices there in honour of this goddess . . . and now that the Church of Our Lady of Guadalupe has been built there, they also call her Tonantzin. . . .
>
> This is something that must be corrected, because the proper name for Our Lady the Mother of God is *not* Tonantzin.[15]

To Mexicans there was no difference. The cult of Our Lady of Guadalupe grew and grew until she became the patroness of Mexico, as indeed she always had been. And today those of her worshipers who speak Nahuatl still call her Tonantzin.

The friars who came to New Spain soon realized that the only way to transform Mexican culture was to understand it. To that end they became America's first ethnographers. Many had difficulty with the Nahuatl language and the daunting complexity of Mesoamerican belief. But one, Bernardino de Sahagún, stands out as a man of genius. To him we owe the preservation of many early Aztec sources, including the account of the conquest I quoted in Part 1. "The physician," he wrote, "cannot advisedly administer medicines to the patient without first knowing . . . from which source the ailment derives."[16] So at the Franciscan college in Tlatelolco he gathered hundreds of hieroglyphic codices and as many "reformed" native priests and nobles as he could. He helped the Mexicans adapt the Roman alphabet to Nahuatl and set them to work transcribing and relating "idolatrous things, as well as human and natural things"[17] in their own words. The result was the Florentine Codex, twelve volumes of Aztec history, science, and lore. But despite his fascination for the alien world beneath his scrutiny, Sahagún never forgot the end that justified his means: he was learning about Aztec culture in order to kill it.

In 1550, Charles V ordered that all Indians learn Castilian and become Hispanicized. In the 1570s the Inquisition forbade further work in native tongues.[18] The honeymoon period of gathering material in Nahuatl, and the complementary process of translating Catholic texts into it, came to an end. Sahagún ignored the imperial decrees, but late in life he began to bowdlerize his informants' work, cutting, paraphrasing, and moralizing as he went. He intended to boil down the raw data into a sort of handbook for future missionaries. Had he finished, he would probably have destroyed the original texts, thereby silencing the authentic Aztec voice.

The early work of Sahagún and others like him helped stimulate a twilight renaissance of Aztec culture. Old men, born before the invasion, took advantage of this opportunity to record all they could from the pre-Columbian past, from the conquest itself, and from the years of chaos and despair that followed. Some of what they wrote was straightforward; other material was deliberately obscure, abounding in metaphor, allusion, and poetic imagery. One manuscript in particular has intrigued and puzzled scholars since its rediscovery at the National Library of Mexico in the 1880s. Known as the *Cantares Mexicanos,* it is a collection of cryptic songs or verses that appear to combine ancient mythology, elegies from the conquest, and comments on the new Christian order. Like the cult of Tonantzin-Guadalupe, the latter material is highly syncretic, identifying Dios with Life Giver, speaking of ancient god-kings and Jesus Christ in the same breath.

Some passages are openly sarcastic:

> We, mere Mexicans, are off to marvel on the sea, the [Spanish] emperor commanding us: he has told us, "Go and see the holy father."
>
> He has said: "What do I need? Gold! Everybody bow down! Call out to God *in excelsis!*" . . .
>
> It would seem that at the pope's [St. Peter's, Rome], where the cavern house of colors stands, are golden words that give us life.[19]

Here, by contrast, is the legend of Nacxitl Topiltzin (another name for Quetzalcoatl) with no visible postconquest influence—the part telling of the Toltec king's expulsion from his city of Tula and journey to the east:

> In Tollan [Tula] stood a house of beams. Still standing are the serpent columns. Nacxitl Topiltzin left it when he went away. . . .
>
> That the mountain collapses, I weep. That the sands have risen, I grieve. Gone is my lord. . . .
>
> Alas we weep, O Lord, O praised one! What of your home, your place of rain? What of this lordly realm of yours that you abandoned . . . ?
>
> You were painted in stone and wood before you went away, yonder in Tollan where you came to rule. O [Quetzalcoatl], your name will never be destroyed, because your vassals will be weeping.
>
> Before you went away you built a turquoise house, a serpent house, yonder in Tollan where you came to rule. O [Quetzalcoatl], your name will never be destroyed.[20]

Early translators regarded the *Cantares* as a collection of Aztec poetry, albeit corrupted somewhat by postconquest "noise." Noting that kings such as Moctezuma and Netzahualcoyotl of Texcoco sometimes spoke in the first person, they deduced that Aztec potentates, like Tudor monarchs, routinely dashed off verses in their quieter hours.

John Bierhorst has recently made new translations of these difficult texts, offering a fresh and compelling interpretation. He sees them as "ghost songs" composed by members of a revitalization movement to summon the ancestors and relive the glories of the past. As such they belong with a vast cycle of crisis cults that span the Americas from the mid-sixteenth century to the late nineteenth. The Sickness Dance of Peru (1560s), the Delaware Prophet (1760s), the Plains Ghost Dances (c. 1870–1890), and many Qthers share a desperate belief that the plagues could be stopped, the dead brought back to earth, and the indigenous world miraculously restored.

Certainly the conditions for such a movement existed among the Aztecs of the 1560s and 1570s, when most of the *Cantares* were composed. By 1568 the indigenous population of New Spain had shrunk to about 2.6 million, perhaps a tenth of what it had been when Cortés landed fifty years before.[21] The psychological impact of such a catastrophe is incalculable: Mexican culture had always been preoccupied with death; now the recent dead—parents, brothers, sisters, children, and cousins still in memory—outnumbered the living ten to one.

The songs seem to be addressed directly to kings and war heroes of the past. These personages, often referred to as flowers—a standard Aztec metaphor for the glorious dead—are invited to "descend" to earth, apparently to speak through singers who have consumed hallucinogens or are entranced. "I've drunk a fungus wine," says the singer on several occasions. Those who have sampled psilocybin mushrooms can imagine their effect on demoralized, nostalgic Aztecs. One pictures these survivors—elderly, scarred and blinded by smallpox, maimed by Spanish steel—gathering behind closed doors late at night to beat the carved drums, call upon their fallen kings, and relive the battles they won and lost. "The earth rolls over, turns over. It's raining javelins: these lords are pouring down."[22]

Metaphors, kennings, and imagery are luxuriant and complex. Jade, turquoise, and the color green symbolize life; birds, like flowers, can be fighting men; Eagles and Jaguars are knightly orders of the Aztec army. Here is a ghost song to Moctezuma:

> Moctezuma, you creature of heaven, you sing in Mexico, in Tenochtitlan. Here where eagle multitudes were ruined, your bracelet house stands shining—there in the home of God our father.
>
> There and in that place they come alive, ah! on the field! For a moment they come whirling, they the eagles, ah! the nobles. . . .
>
> Your name and honor live, O princes. Prince Tlacahuepan! Ixtlilcuechahuac! You've gone and won war death.
>
> Sky dawn is rising up. The multitude, the birds, are shrilling. Precious swans are being created. Turquoise troupials are being created.
>
> Lucky you, arrayed in chalk and plumes. O flower-drunk Moctezuma![23]

> Quetzalcoatl . . . was the father of the Toltecs, and of the Spaniards because he announced their coming.
>
> —Friar Diego Durán, c. 1590

For more than a hundred years, population collapse kept the balance of power shifting steadily in favor of the Spaniards. With their hold on the conquered empire thus strengthened, they could afford to neglect local allies who had helped them win it. Native states like Tlaxcala, theoretically recognized by the invaders as semiautonomous republics, felt the weight of colonial abuse. Powerless yet proud, their rulers resorted to literary protest: long letters in Nahuatl, detailing exploitation and betrayal, to the Spanish king. The following was penned in 1560 by the council of Huejotzingo, a city-state that had supported Cortés on his march between the volcanoes:

> Catholic Royal Majesty. . . .
>
> When your servants the Spaniards reached us and your captain general Don Hernando Cortés arrived . . . not a single town surpassed us here in New Spain in that first and earliest we threw ourselves toward you. . . .
>
> And when they began their conquest and war-making, then also we well prepared ourselves to aid them, for . . . we went in person, we who rule, and we brought all our nobles and all of our vassals to aid the Spaniards. We helped not only in warfare, but also we gave them everything they needed; we fed and clothed them. . . . We gave them the wood and pitch with which the Spaniards made the boats [used on Mexico City's lakes]. . . .
>
> Our lord sovereign, we also say and declare before you that your fathers the twelve sons of St. Francis reached us. . . . When they entered the city of Huejotzingo, of our own free will we honored them and showed them esteem. When they [told us to] abandon the wicked belief in many gods . . . we did it; very willingly we destroyed, demolished, and burned the temples. . . .

> Quietly and peacefully we arranged and ordered it among ourselves; no one, neither nobleman nor commoner was ever tortured or burned for this, as was done on every hand here in New Spain. . . .
>
> But now we are taken aback and very afraid and we ask, have we done something wrong, have we somehow behaved badly . . . or have we committed some sin against almighty God? [For] now this very great tribute has fallen upon us, seven times exceeding all we had paid before. . . . And we declare to you that it will not be long before your city of Huejotzingo completely disappears and perishes, because our fathers, grandfathers, and ancestors knew no tribute and gave tribute to no one, but were independent, and we nobles who guard your subjects are now truly very poor. Nobility is seen among us no longer; now we resemble the commoners. As they eat and dress, so do we. . . . Of the way in which our father and grandfathers and forebears were rich and honored, there is no longer the slightest trace among us.[24]

Huejotzingo still exists; I once attended a fiesta there commemorating all the wars of Mexican history: there were dancers dressed as Aztecs, as Spaniards, as Maximilian's Frenchmen, as Polk's Americans, as Zapatistas. They wore feathers, mirrors, tunics, huge sombreros, leering masks; they drank mescal from Coke bottles; they carried old but lethal muzzle loaders and amused themselves by dancing up behind a gringo and discharging their weapons inches from his ear.

Huejotzingo still exists, but the process lamented by the city's lords 400 years ago has long since reached completion. The native society, once stratified with a range of classes and professions, was ground down into a general peasantry. Whites took the place of the ancient lords, mestizos the jobs of scribes and artisans.

This happened all over Spanish America; indeed, it happens everywhere colonialism reaches. Yet in Mexico it was more than a one-way street, and it produced unusual results. Although many of the lordly families became indistinguishable from the peasants within a few generations, some assimilated into white society and thereby changed it; a cultural blending occurred. Creoles (Mexican-born whites) adopted almost as much from the Aztecs as the Aztecs borrowed from them. They developed a taste for tortillas, turkey, chilies, tomatoes, and chocolate, not as new ingredients for European dishes but as a cuisine. Spanish encroached on Nahuatl, but in so doing became deeply Mexicanized. Preconquest gods survived in Catholic robes. And a distinctly Mexican aesthetic still lives in vigorous folk art and boldly painted architecture. In Mexico—and only in Mexico—the word for a paint shop, *tlapalería,* is a native word.

Elsewhere in Spanish America cultures did not blend easily. Europeans in Peru and Guatemala remained aloof and disdainful of everything indigenous; and Indians, finding little to admire in the foreign ways, emphasized the disjunction between themselves and the invaders. In these regions, the mestizos—the hybrid people who emerged in between—tended to ape the whites and reject their indigenous side. Consequently, modern countries such as Peru and Guatemala are not new nations but cloned offshoots of the old Spanish empire, still internally divided between conqueror and conquered. Their politicians and intellectuals sometimes talk about achieving the kind of *mestizaje*—racial and cultural mixing—that they see in Mexico. But what they usually mean by this is the assimilation of Indians to white ways, not a genuine meeting in the middle. And precisely because they offer nothing to Indians but extinction as a people, they do not succeed.

Why did this blending of cultures occur in Mexico and nowhere else?[25] Partly it was because the capital city remained the same, forcing the two societies into close contact at the center. New Spain was the gem in the Spanish Empire's crown; the best minds and administrators came to Tenochtitlan. But it was also because Castile and Mexico could recognize each other's institutions. Both had merchants, markets, money, tribute, and martial religions, which were either unknown or took different forms among the Incas and other peoples. Spaniard and Aztec were not incompatible.

Descendants of the Mexica ruling class joined with their conquerors to share in whatever the new empire seated at their capital could offer, leaving the weight of Spanish exploitation to fall on the lower echelons and remote provinces such as Huejotzingo. Chimalpahin, a nobleman who lived a century after the conquest, was typical of this new generation of privileged Aztecs. Though he received a thorough Christian education, Chimalpahin retained a deep interest in the Mexican past. In 1620, he began to compile a history, *Relaciones Orginales,* from "old accounts . . . made in the time of the lords, our fathers, our forebears."[26] He refers explicitly to "paintings"—codices passed down in his family from preconquest times. Much of his book is a straight rendering of these from hieroglyphic into alphabetic Nahuatl. His canvas is large, covering over 2,000 years of history and mythology. Each paragraph begins with a date—in both Aztec and Christian calendars—followed by a brief outline of events (he devotes only two or three pages to the conquest). But sometimes he adds observations of his own, among which is a revealing passage about race in Mexico.

> Women who came from Spain . . . married men of Mexico, and from there came the mestizos. Equally, the daughters of some of our most esteemed Princes, as well as some young women of the servant class, were impregnated by Spaniards and thus more mestizos were born—a thing which happens every day.
>
> Some of these keep their mixed origins a secret and hide the fact that they have come from us, the Natives. . . . Other mestizos, in contrast, do us honour and are proud to have come from native blood. . . . The pure Spaniard likes and esteems us, he looks after us and does not make fun of our names. . . .
>
> We need to remember that at the beginning of mankind and of the world, there was only one couple—our first father Adam and our first mother Eve—from whom all of us without exception have descended; moreover, despite the fact that human beings have divided into three different races, we all live on the same Earth.
>
> Three of the great Lord Motecuhzoma's children [produced mestizos] but these still carry in their veins the fine blood that comes down from Motecuhzoma.[27]

Chimalpahin's history reflects a meeting of worlds at the patrician level. That meeting bore fruit in the eighteenth century, when creoles and mestizos began to sense a national identity. Gradually the Mexica Aztecs ceased to exist as a people during the colonial period, while simultaneously a new people, both Aztec and Spanish, came painfully into being.

One could do worse than to choose August 13, 1790—269 years after Cuauhtémoc's defeat—as the day the Mexica became the Mexicanos. On that day, workers paving Mexico City's central square unearthed the colossal statue of Tonantzin-Coatlicue, Our Mother, Lady of the Serpent Skirt. The Calendar Stone reappeared later the same year. The finds galvanized Mexico: crowds gathered, and to each sector of late colonial society the ancient sculptures delivered a powerful message. Indians silently contemplated their ancestors' work, mestizos dreamed of revolution, and criollo intellectuals saw with new eyes the Mexican past. "I was . . . moved," said one who wrote a book on the stones, "to reveal to the literary world some of the vast knowledge that the Indians of this America possessed in arts and sciences in the time of their heathendom."[28]

The Spanish authorities, thoroughly alarmed, had the sculptures dragged to a cloister and reburied. But the passion unearthed with the stones could not be so easily interred. One of its more bizarre yet influential manifestations came four years later, when Servando Teresa de Mier, a Dominican friar, began preaching at the shrine of Guadalupe that Saint Thomas the Apostle and Quetzalcoatl were one and the same.

European theologians had long been puzzled, even disturbed, that the Bible made no mention of America. Aztecs had had to explain away a similiar flaw in their own chronicles. Why, they asked themselves, had Quetzalcoatl allowed apocalyptic barbarians to arrive under cover of his prophecy? Fray Servando constructed a fantastic bridge across the chasm between the Old World and the New: Quetzalcoatl was really a Christian; Mexico had received the word of God long before Spain itself; Tonantzin was indeed the Virgin Mary. *Therefore* the religious justification of the conquest was false. The diabolical religion that horrified the early friars had never existed except in their own eyes. "I repeat," said Fray Servando, "that the Spaniards and the missionaries, who saw the devil everywhere, have bedeviled everything. . . . I enter without fear the serpent's jaws that formed the entrance into the temple of Quetzalcoatl."[29]

This was heresy; but it was also nationalism.

SEVEN

MAYA

> Those who have a unilinear view of time cannot come to terms with the idea of cyclic time: it creates a moral vertigo since all their morality is based on cause and effect. Those who have a cyclic view of time are easily able to accept the convention of historic time, which is simply the trace of the turning wheel.
>
> —John Berger, *Pig Earth*, 1979

The volcanic revenge that fell like a biblical scourge on the Spanish base in Guatemala may have had symbolic value for the Maya, but they did not intend to rely on a deus ex machina to save them. Nor could they accept the syncretic solution adopted by the Aztec nobility. The Maya were determined to engineer their own survival. Aware of the immensity of time, and that their own history was measured in thousands, not hundreds, of years, they prepared to outlive the Spaniards as they had outlived the Toltecs and others. As before, the Maya acquired elements of the victors' culture but did not merge with it. From the sixteenth century to the twentieth, they have ignored the European when possible, accommodated him only when unavoidable, taken from him what they could use, fought him tenaciously whenever he has threatened to break the stalemate between his civilization and theirs.

Chapters on Maya resistance could be written for every part of their world, but the largest and most revealing body of colonial Maya records survives from the Yucatán peninsula.

Spanish conquest of Yucatán had not been easy or rewarding. The first serious attempt had been made in 1528 by Francisco de Montejo the Elder. He set up a base at the crystal lagoons of Xel-Ha on the east coast and, aping Cortés, burned his boats. But there was little to eat and few Indians to subdue. The Yucatec Maya simply retired behind their best defense—the endless thorny bush—which they have always used against invaders as the Russians use their winter. They set ambushes, destroyed supplies, and poisoned wells. After eight years of this, an exasperated Montejo wrote to his king: "No gold has been discovered, nor is there anything [else] from which advantage can be gained. The inhabitants are the most abandoned and treacherous in all the lands discovered to this time, being a people who never yet killed a Christian except by foul means and who have never made war except by artifice."[1]

Those who know the peninsula today, with its straight asphalt roads and quiet villages smelling of orange trees and tortillas, may find it hard to imagine why this porous limestone slab, devoid of mountains, rivers, and lakes, should have presented so many problems for the Spanish knight. But Maya roads were built for sandaled feet, not cavalry: the stone surface wore out the horses' shoes; the bush tore at the rider yet gave no shade; there were no springs, ditches, or ponds. The water lay hidden in caves and sinkholes: without Maya help, it was hard to find and harder to get. Men sweated in their armor; horses dropped from thirst. Worst of all, there was no incentive. Although Yucatán had magnificent cities dating from the Classic period—Chichén Itzá, Uxmal, Tiho, and others—it was a poor country; there was no gold to seize, and in the unvaried karst there could be no mines. Even the soil was mean: a thin dusting of red dirt on the bedrock. The bush that sprang from it offered a living to deer hunters, beekeepers, and shifting corn farmers, but not to would-be hacendados.

When word got out about Peru, all conquistadors in Yucatán left for the riches of the Andes. The Mayas thought they had seen the last of the "eaters of custard apples," as they disdainfully called Spaniards. But Europe's unseen allies—first disease, then famine caused by the death of countless farmers—fought on in the peninsula. By conservative estimates, the population fell from 800,000 to 250,000 between 1520 and 1547.[2]

Eventually, Spaniards who found no fortune elsewhere came back to Yucatán, thinking that at least they could displace the native kings and live idly at Maya expense. In 1542, the Montejos founded a Spanish capital among the empty buildings of a Classic city called Tiho or Ichcaanziho, renaming it Mérida after a city of Roman ruins in Spain.[3] From there they established control across most, but never quite all, of the peninsula.

In the year 1545, says a Maya chronicle, "Christianity began with the fathers of the order of Saint Francis [who] arrived, clutching our redeemer Jesus Christ in their hands."[4]

Four years later, a small, brittle friar named Diego de Landa arrived in Yucatán with a new batch of Franciscans. He had a Roman nose, sallow complexion, and a weak chin. His face hung from his cheekbones like a limp flag, and his eyes seemed permanently downcast in a studied expression of piety. He wanted to be Yucatán's Sahagún, the man who would penetrate the body of Maya culture and drive a stake into its demonic heart.

The peninsula may have lacked gold and resources, but it possessed one great treasure: the bulk of the ancient knowledge that had come down from Classic times. In the towns of Yucatán lived priests and sages literate in the ancient script. They had personal libraries filled with history, mythology, tracts on medicine and beekeeping, astronomical tables predicting the rising and setting of planets, the timing of eclipses, and many other things that we can only guess at now.

If his own account can be believed, Landa began well. Throughout the 1550s, he traveled along the white stone roads from town to town, winning the confidence of Maya lords. They listened to him in a spirit of encounter and told him whatever he wished to learn. They taught him Maya, talked of their past and their ancestors' achievements, and even brought out their precious hieroglyphic manuscripts. The books were made of vellum or paper finished with gesso, but instead of being bound at the spine like European volumes, their pages were joined, like the panels of a screen. Folded when not in use between Jaguar-skin covers, they could be read sheet by sheet or opened to a full length of twenty feet or so. The Mayas let Landa ponder the strange calligraphy, the numerical tables, the illuminations whose intricacy and draftsmanship rivaled parchments he had seen in the scriptoria of Europe.[5] The

Mayas, who valued knowledge, did not yet suspect that this man of knowledge from another world would try to murder their past.

The Yucatec Maya no longer used the Long Count calendar of the Classic period, although they knew of it. Instead, they kept a cycle of *katuns,* thirteen twenty-year periods, or "decades." The katun wheel revolved every 260 years (13 times 20) and was believed to have a cyclical influence on history.[6] The Maya did not see time as we do, as linear progress advancing from a dim past to a glittering future or, in Christian terms, from epiphany to apocalypse. They saw it as they saw the heavens, as a series of interlocking cycles ascending in scale from the constant ticking of the days to the ponderous rhythms of planets and stars. Thousands of years of observation had taught them that celestial events recurred: the earth, the moon, the sun, the planets, all revolved at different speeds but formed repeating patterns over spans of time. Like Newton, the Mayas made no distinction between astronomy and astrology. In the heavens they saw the structure of time, and they believed that heavenly time structured life on earth. For them there could be no great event that was not foreshadowed, no triumph or disaster without precedent, and without echo in the galleries of time.

On that day, dust possesses the earth,
On that day, a blight is on the face of the earth,
On that day, a cloud rises,
On that day, a mountain rises,
On that day, a strong man seizes the land,
On that day, things fall to ruin,
On that day, the tender leaf is destroyed,
On that day, the dying eyes are closed.[7]

A European mind asks, What day is this? Does it lie in the past or future? Is it the day the Toltecs invaded Yucatán? Is it the day the Spaniards arrived? Is it the Day of Judgment? Is it the war of the end of the world? To a Maya mind it is all of those.

The Maya viewed the Spanish conquest in the light of other invasions they had suffered and survived, and they were certain that their wise men had foretold it. Cynics may say that they had plenty of time to foretell it: after all, Mayas had met Columbus in 1502, Mayas had captured Spaniards in 1511 and pumped them for information about their fellow barbarians, and Mayas had driven off the invaders several times before the 1540s. That is not the point. The point is that by believing they had foreseen the conquest, they established control over events that were otherwise uncontrollable. By linking the new conquest to previous ones, they gave themselves the confidence that they would survive yet again. They merged pre-Columbian and post-Columbian history to create "prophecy-history," a uniquely Maya genre that serves two purposes: it is a powerful indictment of the European invasion, and its very seamlessness is a proclamation of resistance, an assurance that the Maya world continues.

The documents containing this material are known as the Books of Chilam Balam, written in the Maya language but using Spanish letters. These are the Yucatec Maya equivalents of the Quiché *Popol Vuh* and the Cakchiquel *Annals*. But unlike those texts, crystallized within decades of the conquest, the Chilam Balam were living books, copied, recopied, and expanded from the sixteenth century to the nineteenth. Every Yucatec town of any size possessed one: they were part bible, part community charter, part almanac, part chronicle. More than a dozen exist today. Within them, like fragments of Greek sculpture in medieval walls, lie archaic texts transcribed from pre-Columbian codices that died on Inquisition bonfires. In order to avoid the same fate, and because Maya sages excelled in puns, allusions, and riddles, the books of Chilam Balam are deliberately obscure. "They are not intended to make sense to outsiders," one translator writes, "and they don't."[8] Be that as it may, the Maya view of European rule is clear.

> With the true God, the true *Dios,*
> came the beginning of our misery.
> It was the beginning of tribute,
> the beginning of church dues . . .
> the beginning of strife by trampling on people,
> the beginning of robbery with violence,

the beginning of forced debts,
the beginning of debts enforced by false testimony,
the beginning of individual strife.[9]

Balam is the Maya word for jaguar, a synonym for godhead; a *chilam* is a priest, spokesman, or oracle; so we can translate Chilam Balam as Spokesman of God or Jaguar Prophet. There may also have been one particular Chilam Balam, a famous and influential figure who lived through the first years of the invasion. According to the book of Maní (a town not far from Uxmal, one of Yucatán's finest Classic ruins), such a man went into trance and foretold the conquest in these words:

> Know all of you that the time has come . . . the rulers as well as the people shall suffer. The symbol of this Katun [twenty-year "decade"] will be the head of a tiger with broken teeth, the body of a rabbit or a dog, with a spear piercing his heart. . . . When these times arrive in these Provinces of Mayapan and Ziyancaan and in this peninsula which will be called Yucatán, you will leave as dying deer. . . . Vultures will enter the houses in your villages because of the great numbers of dead Mayas and dead animals. . . . The [land] will be sold, and all the people will be moved. . . . You will be seen bowing your heads to the archbishop. . . . You will have to follow the True God called Christ. . . . Heaven and earth will thunder, for then, sorrowfully, our rulers' time will end and that which was written on the monuments will be fulfilled. . . .
>
> The invading foreigners will establish their quarters in Ichcaanziho. . . . Your government will tumble down . . . everything will be razed and destroyed. . . . You will be brothers-in-law to the Spaniards, and you will wear their clothing, their hats, and speak their language. . . . The tiger will roar, and the deer that fell into the trap will be heard agonizing until he dies.[10]

For the Maya—people of the *may,* another name for the 260-year katun cycle—mastery of time was the root of political power. The katun counts conferred a mystical authority comparable to Europe's divine right of kings. In pre-Spanish Yucatán, warfare among the petty states had been restrained by sharing out the right to "seat the katun." This right rotated through important cities and towns of the peninsula (including several that had lain in ruins since the Classic period). In theory, each lord was king for twenty years. The ingenious system did not always work smoothly and could be subverted by tinkering with the time machine. Rival lords set up rival calendars and fought over them as bitterly as Europeans once fought over the date of Easter.

The Spanish conquest brought added chronopolitical complications. The new invaders had a calendar of their own, a rather crude and clumsy one in Maya estimation. This new count had to be neutralized by being "contained" in Maya time. Once they had geared Spanish time to the katun wheel, Mayas could be sure it would eventually run out. At most, they gave the Spaniards one full round of thirteen katuns. Oddly enough that is almost exactly how long the Spanish Empire did rule Yucatán.[11]

Working in the Spaniards' favor was a long-standing enmity between the Xiu dynasty of western Yucatán, whose territory included the city of Tiho, and the Itzá dynasty in the east, whose ancient seat was Chichén Itzá. The Xiu quickly accepted Christianity and emphasized its inevitability in their "prophecies." The Itzá, on the other hand, resisted the new faith and stressed the evils of foreign domination. But Xiu connivance with the invaders did not save them from the excesses of Spanish rule. On the contraty, their closeness to the Franciscan missions at Mérida and Maní, the Xiu family seat, exposed them to the scrutiny of Diego de Landa.

As soon as he began to understand the nature of Maya time, Landa condemned it: "If it was the devil who arranged this count of *katuns,* he must have set it up in his own honour; if it was a man, he must have been a great idolator."[12]

In 1562, something in Landa snapped. He discovered to his horror that despite the twelve monasteries and 200 churches the Franciscans had built (with Maya labor) in Yucatán, the Mayas were not, after all, good Christians.[13] In a cave near Maní a cache of "idols" and ancestral bones came to light. When the locals were asked about this, they admitted to worshiping there to ensure good rains, crops, and hunting.

The full repertoire of the Inquisition was not supposed to be unleashed on recent converts, but Landa and his colleagues weren't going to let petty regulations get between them and God's truth. According to a Spaniard who saw them at work, they "ordered great stones attached to [the Indians'] feet, and so they were left to hang . . . and if they still did not admit to a greater quantity of idols they were flogged as they hung there, and had burning wax splashed on their bodies."[14] Under such interrogation, the Mayas revealed anything they could think of, including human sacrifice.

Were these revelations really news to Landa? If so, it is impossible not to marvel at his naïveté and arrogance. How could he expect to have eliminated "idolatry" in only twenty years? How could he torture and kill people for venerating ancestral bones, for feeding the little gods of the cornfield, for burning incense in the crumbling temples of the Classic period? (Maya still do all these things, and the Catholic church has at last learned to tolerate them.) How could he fail to see that many of the confessions were merely the raving of people in agony?

Landa's victims were hard pressed to find enough idols to suit him. Ancient sites were ransacked. Mossy statues and muddy skulls, calcified pots and rotting figurines, were torn from ancient temples, dug from tombs, retrieved from labyrinthine caves. One wonders whether this was not his real objective: not so much to uncover living idolatry as to purge Yucatán of its past, of the physical proof of Maya greatness.

Landa was one of those who destroy not only what they fear but what they admire. He personally supervised the pulling down of Maya buildings he considered to be "of astonishing height and beauty."[15] He personally seized hundreds of hieroglyphic books and threw them on the bonfires.

> These people . . . used certain characters or letters with which they wrote in their books about their ancient things and sciences. . . . We found a great number of books in these letters of theirs, and because they contained nothing but superstition and the devil's falsehoods, we burned them all, which upset [the Mayas] most grievously and caused them great pain.[16]

Diego de Landa was, in short, another Caliph Omar, who is said to have condemned the library of Alexandria with these chilling words: "If what is written in the books agrees with the Book of God, they are not required; if it disagrees, they are not desired. Therefore destroy them."

Determined to attack the nobility as well as the humble corn farmer, Landa held a full-blown auto-da-fé at Maní, complete with dunces' hats, robes, and all the other paraphernalia the Ku Klux Klan would one day borrow from the Holy Office. An enormous pile of Maya artifacts, books, and bones was torched. Bloody penitents, already torn by weeks of "questioning," were publicly flogged, some to death. Altogether 4,500 Mayas were tortured and 158 died during or after interrogation. Countless others were maimed for life: muscle tissue destroyed, tendons broken, hands "like hooks,"[17] to say nothing of mental wounds. About thirty committed suicide to escape Landa's salvation.[18]

The friar defended his purge by sending to Spain forged letters praising his actions and purporting to be from Maya lords. Don Francisco de Montejo Xiu, a Maya so loyal to Spain that he had added the name of Yucatán's conqueror to his own, wrote the other side of the story to King Philip:

> Sacred Catholic Majesty:
>
> After we learned the good, in knowing God our Lord as the only true god, leaving our blindness and idolatries . . . there came upon us a persecution of the worst that can be imagined; and it was in the year '62, on the part of the Franciscan religious, who had taken us to teach the doctrine, instead of which they began to torment us, hanging us by the hands and whipping us cruelly, hanging weights of stone on our feet, torturing many of us on a windlass, giving the torture of the water, from which many died or were maimed.
>
> [Then] came the Dr. Quijada [chief Crown official in Yucatán] to aid our tormentors, saying that we were idolaters and sacrificers of men, and many other things against all truth. . . . And as we see ourselves maimed by cruel tortures, many dead of them, robbed of our property, and yet more, seeing disinterred the bones of our baptized ones, who had died as Christians, we came to despair.

Not content with this, the [friars] and thy royal Justice, held at Mani a solemn *auto* of inquisition, where they seized many statues, disinterred many dead and burned them there in public; made slaves of many to serve the Spaniards for from eight to ten years. . . . The one and the other gave us great wonder and fear, because we did not know what it all was, having been recently baptized and not informed; and when we returned to our people [the friars] seized us, put us in prison and chains, like slaves, in the monastery at Mérida, where many of us died; and they told us we would be burned. . . .

Then came as governor don Luis de Céspedes, and instead of relieving us he has increased our burdens, taking away our daughters and wives to serve the Spaniards, against their will and ours; which we feel so greatly . . . because our ancestors never took from one his children, nor from husbands their wives to make use of them, as today does your majesty's Justice. . . .

Diego de Landa, chief author of all these ills and burdens [has written letters] saying that your majesty approved the killings, robberies, tortures, slaveries and other cruelties inflicted on us; to which we wonder that such things should be said of so Catholic and upright a king as is your majesty. . . .

The religious of San Francisco of this province have [also] written certain letters to your majesty and to the general of the [Franciscan] order, in praise of fray Diego de Landa and his other companions. . . . May your majesty understand that [the letters] are not ours, we who are chiefs of this land. . . . May fray Diego de Landa and his companions suffer the penance for the evils they have done to us, and may our descendants to the fourth generation be recompensed for the great persecution that came on us.

May God guard your majesty. . . . From Yucatán, the 12 of April, 1567.[19]

Eventually Landa's rampage caused so much unrest that even Yucatán's conquistadors expressed their pity for the Indians to the king. Landa was summoned to Spain to justify his conduct. While there he wrote a glutinous memoir—the famous *Relation of the Things of Yucatán*—dripping with nostalgia for the Maya and their land. He presents himself as a scholar, an expert, a sympathetic student of the New World, the equal of other Franciscans such as Sahagún. But Landa's work is brief, shallow, and unreliable compared to his—little more than a defective catalogue of what he had destroyed. The *Relación*'s importance to Maya studies is a measure not of its quality but of the thoroughness of its author's purge.

Despite the outcry from Indians and Spaniards, Landa was exonerated. In 1573, he returned to Yucatán as its bishop; he died there six years later.

The Mayas mourned the loss of their codices and put as much as they could remember of them into the books of Chilam Balam.

> Time present and time past
> Are both perhaps present in time future,
> And time future contained in time past.
>
> —T. S. Eliot, "Burnt Norton"

Maya resistance was greatly helped by geography. Yucatán's waterless bush, Guatemala's cloud-wreathed mountains, and the "poverty" of both places in European eyes weakened the grip of the invaders. Between these two inhabited zones lay the old Maya heartland of the Petén—30,000 square miles of rain forest studded with Classic ruins—where the Spaniards seldom penetrated. Contrary to the myth of discovery, Europeans had no interest or ability in wilderness; their civilization did not spread where there were no people to rob or harness. Europe's presence in the Americas was strictly parasitic until the industrial age.

But the Petén jungle was not completely uninhabited. Small groups lived among the overgrown buildings of a few Classic cities. There were also some newer towns, tiny by Classic standards, but boasting a temple or two. The largest of these lay in the very middle of the forest on an island in a long freshwater lake not twenty miles from the ruins of Tikal. Called Tayasal, or more accurately, Tah Itzá, it ruled a ring of satellite villages around the shore, like a miniature Mexico. Despite occasional visits from outside—including one from Cortés in 1525—it kept its freedom for more than two centuries after Columbus, a living remnant of the pre-Columbian world. So, despite the fury of Landa's bonfires, Maya mathematicians and astrologers were still writing hieroglyphic books when Sir Isaac Newton published his *Principia* in 1687.

As their name suggests, the rulers of Tah Itzá were closely related to those who had built the great Toltec-Maya city of Chichén Itzá in the northeast of the peninsula. The Itzá run through the books of Chilam Balam, portrayed as heroes or villains according to the writer's sympathies. Probably of Gulf coast origin, they had themselves invaded Yucatán in the years of chaos after the Classic fall. But though they had once been outsiders, speaking Yucatec Maya poorly and indulging in the dubious practice of calendrical revision, the Itzá later became as Maya as anyone and heroes of the resistance against Spain.

When the Spaniards overran Yucatán in the 1540s, large numbers of Itzá moved south to join their cousins in the jungle. And for the next 150 years, any Maya for whom the abuses of friars and landlords became intolerable could flee to the Petén. This trickle of new blood kept the free state alive, replacing losses from malaria, yellow fever, and other African diseases that now made life in the jungle nasty and short.

From the Chilam Balam of Chumayel:

> A record of the katuns and years when the province of Yucatán was first seized by the foreigners, the white men. It was, they say, in Katun 11 Ahau[20] . . . when they arrived. . . .
>
> It was after the town of Zaclactun was depopulated, after the town of Kinchil Coba was depopulated, after the town of Chichén Itzá was depopulated, after . . . the great town of Uxmal, as it is called, was depopulated. . . .
>
> Then the great Itzá went away. . . . They did not wish to join with the foreigners; they did not desire Christianity. They did not wish to pay tribute, did those whose emblems were the bird, the

> precious stone . . . the jaguar. . . . Four four-hundreds of years and fifteen score years was the end of their lives . . . the measure of their days. Complete was the month; complete, the year; complete, the day; complete, the night; complete, the breath of life . . . when they arrived at their beds, their mats, their thrones.[21]

The "four-hundreds of years" are the *baktuns* of the Long Count calendar, remembered though not used since Classic times. (A baktun equals twenty katuns.) The figures given amount to 1,900 years in our arithmetic, the span, the Maya believed, of their civilization.[22] Archaeology confirms that the first tall pyramids were built in the second and third centuries before Christ, so the Chilam Balam of Chumayel was right. That this information was still accurately preserved in 1782, when a Maya scribe named Juan José Hoil copied the existing manuscript, is impressive evidence of the colonial Mayas' knowledge of their past.[23]

Hoil was still adding to the text as well as copying it, and for the same reasons that his Classic ancestors had run the Long Count back and forth over millions of years, although his concerns were more mundane: "3 Ahau. On this 18th day of August, 1766, occurred a hurricane," he wrote. "I have made a record [to see] how many years it will be before another."[24]

The manipulation of time that strengthened Maya resolve also had its dangers. The 260-year katun cycle became so hypnotic in colonial times that it could induce a fatal resignation. It is written in the Chilam Balam books that the Itzá were always uprooted in a Katun 8 Ahau. In other words, they moved every 260 years.[25]

> 8 Ahau [672–692?] was when Chichén Itzá was abandoned. . . .
>
> 8 Ahau [928–948?] was when Chakanputun was abandoned by the Itzá. . . . This was always the katun when the Itzá went beneath the trees, beneath the bushes, beneath the vines, to their misfortune. . . .
>
> 8 Ahau [1185–1204] was when the Itzá men again abandoned their homes. . . . For thirteen folds of katuns they had dwelt there. . . .

> 8 Ahau [1441–1661] was when there was fighting. . . . Their town was abandoned and they were scattered [to Tayasal?].

After this litany of Itzá upheavals, the writer turns to the katun in which Yucatán was conquered and evangelized: "11 Ahau [1539–1559] was the name of the katun when the Maya . . . were called Christians; their entire province became subject to St. Peter and the reigning King of Spain."[26]

Only those Maya who stayed in northern Yucatán were "called Christians." The Itzá at Tayasal most definitely were not. Several times during the seventeenth century intrepid friars undertook the long and difficult journey from Mérida to the jungle stronghold, which they described as bristling with idols. Some preached peacefully; others ranted about idolatry; a few went too far and ended on the sacrificial block. The Itzá king, who always bore the name Can Ek, told them each time that conversion was out of the question for the moment. However, he hinted, things might change in—when else?—the next Katun 8 Ahau.

Barring calendar revisions, the next Katun 8 Ahau began in 1697. Shortly before that, one of Can Ek's nephews traveled to Mérida and offered to capitulate. It is hard to fathom his motives. Clearly there were different factions at Tayasal, some of which were weary of isolation from the rest of the world. But it also seems that many Itzá were convinced that further resistance would be useless because it was ill fated, because, once again, the dreaded 8 Ahau had come around. The wheels of time, seen and measured in the heavens, dominated Maya civilization as the wheels of machinery do ours.

The Spaniards responded crudely to Can Ek's overture, invading rather than negotiating, and doing so before the end of the previous katun. Tayasal repulsed the first assault, but in 1697, only months before the beginning of 8 Ahau, it fell to a two-pronged attack from Yucatán and Guatemala.

So many "idols" were found there that the Spanish army spent a whole day smashing them. King Can Ek was led away in chains.

The god Quetzalcoatl, Feathered Serpent or Precious Twin. An example of Aztec sculpture combining realism and iconography. *(Musée de l'Homme, Paris)*

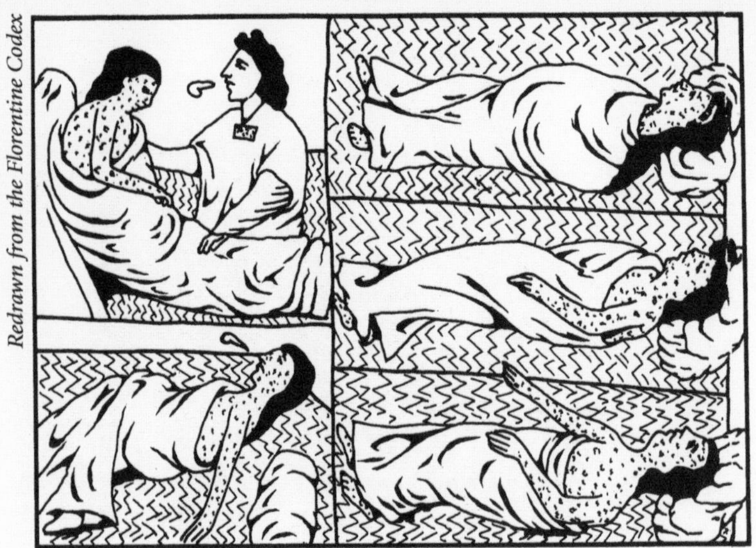

Smallpox victims as portrayed in the Florentine Codex, compiled c. 1550 by surviving Aztec scribes.

The Aztecs attack the Spaniards in the palace of Axayacatl. From the *Lienzo de Tlaxcala,* a pictographic record painted in the 1550s, showing battles in which the Tlaxcalans fought as Spanish allies.

Above: The Night of Sorrows, when the Aztecs drove the Europeans and Tlaxcalans from Mexico City. The Spaniards try to escape using wooden towers and ladders. *Lienzo de Tlaxcala.*

Below: The great city of Tenochtitlan, the Aztec capital, re-created by the twentieth-century Mexican painter Diego Rivera. The mural is in the National Palace, Mexico City.

Bob Schalkwijk

Ian Graham

Tablet of the Scribe, a Maya relief of the late Classic period (A.D. 600–900) from the ruins of Palenque, Mexico.

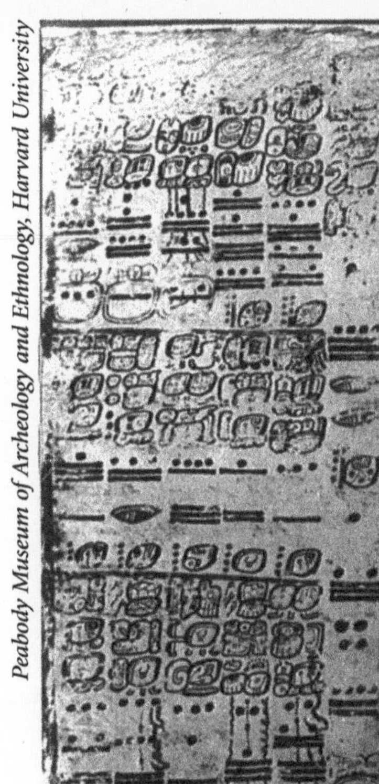

Peabody Museum of Archeology and Ethnology, Harvard University

Left: A page of the Dresden Codex, one of only four pre-Columbian Maya books to survive. The hieroglyphic manuscript contains highly accurate calculations for the movement of Venus.

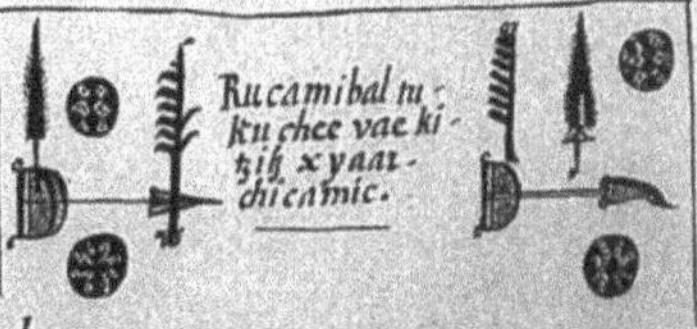

A page of the *Annals of the Cakchiquels,* written in the Cakchiquel Maya language using the Roman alphabet between 1550 and 1604.

University Museum, University of Pennsylvania

Jean-Marie Simon

Ixil Maya women and a U.S. military adviser at Nebaj, in the Guatemalan highlands, in 1982—one of the worst years of the civil war.

Institut d'Ethnolgie, Paris

The capture of Tupa Amaru, last king of the Inca free state in 1572—forty years after his uncle Atawallpa was overthrown by Pizarro. Drawn by the Indian chronicler Felipe Waman Puma, c. 1600.

Below: The beheading of Tupa Amaru in Cusco, the Inca capital, a few weeks later. From this event stems the modern belief that when the severed head has grown a new body, the Inca king will return in triumph.

Institut d'Ethnolgie, Paris

Ronald Wright

A colonial Inca noblewoman in pre-Columbian dress, painted in Cusco in the seventeenth or eighteenth century. The portrait is in Cusco's Archaeological Museum.

Ronald Wright

A nobleman of the same period. Such latter-day Incas, led by Tupa Amaru II, a direct descendant of the king beheaded in 1572, tried to overthrow Spanish rule in the 1780s.

Peter Robertson

Despite Spanish efforts to eradicate Andean culture after the 1780 rebellion, conch trumpets are still played by the heirs of the Incas, to "evoke the sorrowful remembrance of their past."

Cusco today: a porter beside the walls of an ancient Inca palace.

Ronald Wright

Thomas Gilcrease Institute

The Cherokee chief Cunne Shote, painted during his visit to England with Ostenaco the Mankiller in 1762.

Thomas Gilcrease Institute

Chief George Lowrey, painted by George Catlin in the 1820s.

Ronald Wright

Chief Vann's house, built about 1803, in the old Cherokee Nation.

Thomas Gilcrease Institute

Pupils at the Cherokee Female Seminary, built by the Cherokee Nation after its expulsion in 1838 to what is now Oklahoma.

New York State Museum

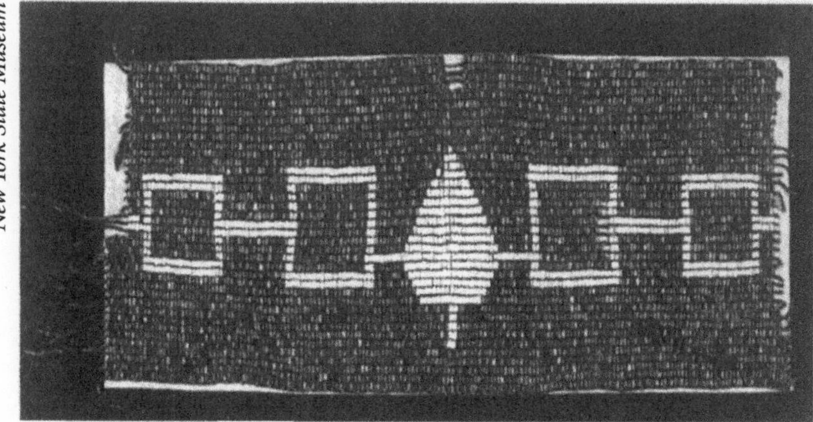

The Hiawatha Wampum Belt, recording the foundation of the Five Nations Confederacy in pre-Columbian times. The pine tree in the center represents the Onondaga Nation; the four links are the Seneca and Cayuga nations, to the west, and the Oneida and Mohawk nations, to the east. Today this symbol is the motif of the Iroquois flag.

Courtesy National Archives of Canada

The Mohawk sachem Hendrick, one of four Iroquois leaders to visit Queen Anne in London in 1710.

Courtesy National Archives of Canada

Brant, also a Mohawk, during the 1710 visit to London.
The queen commissioned John Verelst to paint these remarkable portraits.

Thayendanegea, or Joseph Brant, probably a grandson of the Brant who visited Queen Anne. He split the Iroquois Confederacy by siding with Britain in the American Revolutionary War.

Smithsonian Institution

Smithsonian Institution

Brant's rival Sagoyewatha, or Red Jacket, the great Seneca orator who confounded the Christian missionaries.

Canapress Photo Service/Tom Hanson

The Mohawk revolt at Oka, Quebec, in 1990:
a triumphant Warrior atop an overturned police car.

> The first rulers are driven from their towns. Then Christianity shall have come here. . . .
>
> The descendants of the former rulers are dishonored and brought to misery; we are christianized, while they treat us like animals. There is sorrow in the heart of God. . . .
>
> Oh Itzá! Your worship is of no avail. . . .
>
> Who will be the prophet, who will be the priest who shall interpret truly the word of the book?[27]

Tayasal fell, but the victory was hollow. When the conquerors entered the island town they found it empty; those inhabitants who had not died fighting in the water had swum to the mainland and vanished into the woods. Their descendants became cultural guerrillas in the deepest parts of the Petén. To present no target for invasion, they pared Maya life to its essentials, abandoning their books and statues, building in straw not stone, moving from one clearing to another, using Classic ruins as their temples. Several hundred, known as the Lacandón, lived in this way until modern times along the Mexico-Guatemala border. When archaeologists finally entered the dripping vaults of Palenque, Yaxchilan, and Bonampak, they smelled the resinous tang of recent Maya incense perfuming the ancient statues and reliefs.

To answer the question "Who will be the priest?" requires a short detour into the present. Logging roads now reach into Lacandón villages; the leaders have sold mahogany and bought pickup trucks; and many, under the grim assault of American fundamentalism, have become evangelical Christians. But a hundred or so remain defiantly "heathen" as I write. These are led by a patriarch who is somewhat older than this century. His name is Chan K'in, Little Sun, and he is considered by many to be the last of the Maya priest-kings, though he modestly denies that role.

I visited him a few years ago at his one-room house of sawn planks. Two wives, the elder half his age, the younger with a baby on her back, were grinding corn at a wobbly table covered in oilcoth. Chan K'in sat in a hammock, clutching a huge cigar in his arthritic hand. He wore the Lacandón shift of homespun cotton, and his long mane fell thick and dark about his shoulders. His black eyes sparkled beneath mobile, bushy brows; it was impossible not to think of the old smoking god in the seventh-century reliefs at Palenque—or of Groucho Marx.

Chan K'in gets many visitors: anthropologists, tourists, would-be Castanedas. He speaks good Spanish and will discuss anything from the merits of Maya tobacco—a holy plant—to the future of the world, which he believes will be short. He has lived long enough to see the present creation dying around him. With the prophetic melancholy of Chilam Balam, he thinks that the apocalypse foretold by ancient calendars is near.[28]

Chan K'in and his people may be the lineal heirs of Tayasal, but their story is only one of many. King Can Ek also had other, ideological progeny who would continue to challenge Spanish rule in the Itzá territory of eastern Yucatán. Though Tayasal was gone, the ideal of Maya freedom that it stood for was not so easily destroyed.

In 1761, the Maya rebelled at Cisteil, about thirty miles from Chichén Itzá. A charismatic leader took the name Jacinto Can Ek, crowned himself king in the local church, and declared that the time had come to drive the white invaders into the sea.

His reign was brief. The Spaniards crushed the rebellion within weeks, and executed its leader with their usual panache. His limbs were broken and "his flesh torn off with pincers while he was still alive. Then his body was burned and the ashes thrown to the wind."[29] Eight of his colleagues were hanged and quartered. Lesser rebels were deprived of their right ears.

To the Spaniards, Can Ek of Cisteil must have seemed a curious epilogue to their conquest of Yucatán. In fact, he was only a prelude to the most successful Indian *re*conquest of all: the great Caste War that began in 1847 and established a Maya free state that lasted until the twentieth century.

EIGHT

INCA

> I desire his Catholic Majesty to understand why I draft this account. It is to unburden my conscience. . . . The realm has fallen into such disorder that it has passed from one extreme to the other.
>
> —Mancio Sierra (conquistador), 1589

When Francisco Pizarro murdered Atawallpa in 1533, he was not yet a conqueror; the Inca's death was merely the culmination of a chain of killings. Smallpox had killed Wayna Qhapaq, the last great emperor of Tawantinsuyu; Atawallpa had killed Waskhar, his rival and brother; Pizarro had killed Atawallpa. The Spaniards had been in Peru for two and a half years, but they had not yet occupied the capital. Cusco was stripped but otherwise whole, a distant mountain city that only three Spaniards had seen, and from which they had returned in wonder.

Cusco, the Navel of the earth, lies at the apex of a valley more than 11,000 feet above sea level in southeastern Peru. Bald red hills, washed green during the wet months, shield it from Andean squalls, and peaks higher than 20,000 feet float like icebergs on the horizon. The city's whitewashed adobe walls and sway-backed terra-cotta roofs could belong to a Spanish town. But as one's lungs get used to the crisp air, and one's eyes to the crystalline light, the Inca city can still be found beneath the later encrustations. Curious megaliths stand in the plaza gardens as if left there to graze; stretches of faultless ashlar masonry lie within gimcrack churches of rubble and mud. One wall may have been untouched since the reign of Wayna Qhapaq, its charcoal stones pillowed and snug as if sensing the pressure of their neighbors; another may be an ugly scar of conquest, precisely cut blocks piled up chaotically like a wrongly assembled puzzle.

Above the plaza looms a battered headland where the Incas built their greatest monument, the fortress-temple known as Saqsawaman, Royal Hawk.[1] Three towers, one of them round and cleverly supplied with water by a pressure siphon, once overlooked the city from the summit. Only their foundations can be seen today, but on the far side of the hill survive the bastions of the entire complex—a triple zigzag terrace, half a mile from end to end, made of blocks weighing up to 200 tons. "Some of these stones," observed Cieza de León with his usual precision, "are twelve feet wide and more than twenty high . . . thicker than an ox, and all so delicately seated that a coin will not fit between them. . . . It will last as long as the world exists."[2] A hard-headed viceroy wrote to his king: "I saw the fortress that . . . Wayna Qhapaq built . . . a thing that shows clearly the work of the Devil . . . for it seems impossible that it could have been made by the strength and skill of man."[3]

For the Incas, Cusco was a model of their empire. Modern Cusco is equally a model of Peru—a shoddy European superstructure on an abiding native base. The graft has never taken: whenever earthquakes rock the Andes, Inca buildings emerge unscathed from their prisons of colonial rubble. This example is not lost on the Incas' descendants. In their Quechua language, earthquake is *pachakuti. Pacha* means "world" or "time"; *kutiy* is the verb "to overturn." The word for earthquake is also the word for revolution.

In November 1533, a whole year after the Cajamarca massacre, a Spanish army at last reached the Inca capital. Forces loyal to the dead Atawallpa fought several actions on the way, but without success. The Spaniards' numbers had been swelled by new arrivals, and the farther south they moved the more the local population tended to regard them as deliverers from a usurper. Without benefit of hindsight, many in Cusco saw Pizarro's intervention as a lucky twist to their own civil war. They were delighted when he crowned a new Inca with the crimson fringe snatched from Atawallpa's brow.

The city celebrated with pomp and prodigious beer drinking that went on for a month. Wayna Qhapaq and other mummified ancestors paraded through the streets on their litters, the last time they would ever do so openly. (Centuries later, some were found hidden inside images of Catholic saints, which are also carried around on feast days.)

Pizarro's puppet was Manku Inka Yupanki, a young son of Wayna Qhapaq and a half-brother of Atawallpa. Manku's reign was ably chronicled by his own son, Titu Kusi Yupanki, whose *Relación* is not only the best history of the conquest and its immediate aftermath through Inca eyes—it is the sole autobiographical account by a leading figure from *either* side.[4]

Soon after Manku's coronation, which included an oath of allegiance to Spain, the Spaniards foolishly began to abuse him, stripping another $30 million in gold from palaces and shrines.[5] No Dürer ever saw the Inca treasures, but Pedro Pizarro gives a glimpse of them:

> There were so many warehouses of very fine clothes . . . of thrones; of food; of coca leaves. . . . There were cloaks made of sequins . . . very delicate, and a wonder to see the workmanship. . . . There were many storehouses of copper crowbars for the mines, and of sacks and ropes; of cups and plates in silver. . . . In one cave were twelve llamas of silver and gold, lifelike and life size. . . . There was also a gold effigy whose discovery caused the Indians great pain, for they say it was a figure of the first lord [Manku Qhapaq, founder of the dynasty].[6]

Inflamed by power and greed, the Spaniards clapped Manku Inka Yupanki in irons, raped his women in front of him, even urinated on his face.[7] With typical Andean stoicism, the Inca kept his composure. "Is this what Wiraqocha [God] commands," he asked icily, "that you take by force everyone's property and wives? Such is not the custom among us."[8]

When he had had enough, Manku summoned his lords and generals secretly and, according to Titu Kusi, gave the following speech:

> My brothers and sons, I have called you together here over the past few days so that you may see the new kind of people that have brought themselves to our country, which are these bearded ones

> here in this city. Because they told me they were *wiraqochas,* and appeared to be so in their dress, I commanded you to serve and obey them as you would serve my own person . . . thinking that they were worthy people sent from afar, as they themselves claimed, by Tiqsi Wiraqochan, which is to say by God.
>
> But it is clear to me that everything has turned out the very reverse of what I expected, because—know this, my brothers—these people have given me plenty of demonstrations since entering my country that they are the children not of Wiraqocha but of the devil.[9]

The word *wiraqocha,* a Quechua term for whites then and now, has misled many into thinking that the Incas took the Spaniards for gods. Wiraqocha, it is true, was another name for the supreme deity, Pachakamaq. The word means "sea of fat" and refers to the associations of the Creator with the Milky Way, moisture, animal fat, the sea, and the color white. The Andean world was and is structured by a system of complementary opposites resembling the Chinese yang and yin. In Peru the two halves, or moieties, are called *hanan* (upper) and *hurin* (lower); they may or may not have anything to do with actual height, though the vertical terrain of the Andes supplies the metaphor. Man, sun, fire, mountains, and so forth, belong to the upper moiety; woman, moon, water, sea, and coast to the lower. And—most important here—present and center are upper; past and periphery are lower.

Although Wiraqocha had created all things, including the sun, he belonged to the lower moiety. He was, in a sense, "opposed" to the solar power of the Inca kings. The Spaniards fitted into the lower moiety very neatly: they were white, they came from the sea, they opposed sun worship, they worshiped a god resembling the Peruvian Creator; and they were from the rim of the known world.

The Incas believed that history was a succession of ages divided one from another by a cataclysmic epoch—a pachakuti—an "overturning of the world." This upheaval reversed the polarity of the moieties: what was upper became lower, and vice versa. The previous pachakuti had been the formation of the empire itself by an Inca who took Pachakuti as his name. As soon as the full implications of the Spanish conquest became clear, the years that began with smallpox and ended in foreign rule were seen as the next pachakuti. The solar power of the Incas, radiating from their mountain capital, had been eclipsed by the oceanic power of the Christians at Lima on the coast. Upper and lower had reversed.

Just as the Maya used prophecy to contain and subvert the invasion, the Incas employed their scheme of revolving ages to imply that the new order—unnatural and destructive from the Andean point of view—could not be accepted and would one day be reversed. For the past order is not irrevocable; it remains latent in the underworld, awaiting a return: one pachakuti demands another. This is the meaning of the words in the elegy for Atawallpa: "The elders and the people buried themselves alive." Nearly five centuries later, Andeans still expect the righting of their world.

Manku began planning the return of Inca power early in 1536. He promised the Spaniards more treasure if they would let him hold his royal hunt, a yearly event in which Inca nobility took part. It was ideal cover for what he had in mind. Again he spoke to his most trusted men.

> I have learned by experience, and you have now seen for yourselves . . . how vilely [these bearded people] have repaid me for all I did for them. They have given me a thousand insults, they have imprisoned me and chained me up like a dog by the feet and by the neck; and worst of all, they have done this after giving me their word that they were with me and I with them, that we had become allies. . . .
>
> I will now remind you . . . how many times you have begged me to do what I now intend. . . . Send your messengers throughout the land, so that in twenty days from now everybody shall be here in this city. Make sure the bearded ones know nothing. I shall send to Lima my general Kisu Yupanki, who governs that province, and instruct him that on the same day that we attack the Spaniards here, he and his men shall fall upon them there.
>
> Soon we shall annihilate them, until none remains; and then we can awake from this nightmare and rejoice.[10]

When the rains ended in April, Manku got away to Calca, a town in what is now called the Sacred Valley of the Incas. I once walked over the 14,000-foot puna country that lies between Cusco and Calca. Manku and his loyalists crossed these same treeless uplands broken by dark outcrops and glittering tarns beneath a cobalt sky. In April the llama pastures would have been a deep military green, shot with tiny, brilliant blooms. Perhaps he spent the night, as I did, in the town of Little Cusco, whose ruins stand hidden on a bluff above the Willkamayu, the Holy River.[11]

Even today, the Sacred Valley remains utterly transformed by Inca civilization. Its river runs dead straight, prevented from meandering through the precious bottom land by megalithic walls. Sweeping terraces, as precise as map contours, climb the valley walls to towns and temples contemplating icebound peaks. It is a landscape as artificial as Versailles, yet wholly harmonious with its natural setting.

At Manku's signal, the Tawantinsuyu rose against the Spaniards. Early in May 1536, Inca troops took Cusco's great fortress and soon had the invaders cooped up with their black slaves and local collaborators in a palace on the central square. These palaces were miniature towns inhabited by a mummified king and queen and their descendants. Each covered an entire block and had only one or two entrances; inside, rooms and galleries faced onto garden courtyards, pools, and fountains. The perimeter walls were twenty or thirty feet high, made of superb masonry more than a yard thick. Stocked with food and water, such buildings were virtually impregnable. Their one weak point was the beautiful thatched roofs.

First Manku cut Cusco's pipes and channels. Then, in what must have been the most painful decision of his life, he gave the order to burn the Navel of the world. According to both European and Peruvian writers, the only building that failed to ignite was the one that held the Spaniards. Christians attributed this to intervention by the Virgin Mary, whom they saw descend from heaven and smother the blaze with her skirts. Titu Kusi's explanation was more prosaic: "Negroes were on the roof putting it out."[12]

Spanish defeat, which seemed certain at first, became elusive as time passed. Manku had the satisfaction of seeing his chief tormentor, Juan

Pizarro,[13] killed by a stone from an Inca sling, but the Spaniards managed to retake the fortress. As usual, their trumps were armor and cavalry. Little by little, they demolished the terracing around Cusco to allow mounted sorties. They burned or mutilated every captive and made a special point of attacking the women who fed and clothed the Inca army.

Manku maintained the siege for twelve months, but his victories took place elsewhere. His troops killed a thousand Spaniards, many times the number that had marched on Atawallpa.[14] The survivors included only those in Cusco, those in Lima with Francisco Pizarro, and a force in Chile led by Diego de Almagro with the help of an Inca quisling. In April 1537, Almagro's force returned to Cusco and raised the siege, but by then he and the Pizarros had fallen out, and the Spaniards were as deeply divided as the Incas.

Manku moved his headquarters farther downriver to Tampu (now Ollantaytambo), the last broad valley before the Willkamayu plunges through the eastern Andes to become the Amazon. Stupendous Inca engineering can be seen here on a mountain spur. Tier upon tier of terraces ascend to a work under construction when the emergency began. Stones as big as trucks still lie on their ramps, waiting to be fitted into temple walls. Manku had several of these set up quickly for defense. "And so they made one of the greatest forts that exist in Peru," Titu Kusi wrote proudly, "in the year and a half that [my father] was at Tampu."[15]

From here Manku continued the war with innovative tactics. He forced Spanish prisoners to make gunpowder for captured guns, he himself rode a horse into battle, and he mired one Spanish attack by diverting a river. To the young Titu Kusi, these were his father's finest days.

> Messengers arrived in the town of Tampu from the engagements that had taken place at Lima and Jauja. . . . The Indians had been victorious, and they brought my father many Spanish heads, also two live Spaniards, a black man, and four horses. They arrived with great rejoicing . . . and my father showered them with honours, and exhorted all the rest to fight like that.[16]

After retaking Jauja, Manku's general Kisu Yupanki began the final assault on Lima. His siege of the strange new city went well at first, but when he tried to sweep down into its streets his army was shattered by cavalry. This proved to be the turning point of the war.

The notion that the Tawantinsuyu fell without a fight is false. The Incas fought as bravely as the Aztecs, and they killed just as many Spaniards, but it was too late. Regardless of Kisu Yupanki's tactical mistake, the eventual outcome was inevitable. The population was collapsing from disease; Spaniards were strengthened daily by a gold rush. "At this time," Inca officials recalled, "an infinite number of people arrived from Spain, having seen the . . . great riches taken to Spain from Cajamarca. . . . Every day ships from Panama, Mexico, and Nicaragua put into the port."[17]

Peru's isolation from the rest of the world had been broken forever. Centuries of domination from Lima, the invaders' beachhead, had begun.

Deciding he could not hold the Tampu valley for long, Manku made a strategic withdrawal deep into the Vilcabamba (Willkapampa) range of the Andes. There, where precipitous mountains covered with an olive fleece of cloud forest rise from the hotlands of the upper Amazon, he created what is known as the Neo-Inca state—a fragment of the old Tawantinsuyu where sun worship and the rule of the god-kings could continue. The famous ruins of Machu Picchu may have been part of this territory, but they were not, as some have thought, its capital. The frontiers of Vilcabamba fluctuated, sometimes embracing much of the old Antisuyu—the eastern quarter of the Inca Empire—at others shrinking to an embattled stronghold only a hundred miles across. As the Europeans grew stronger, the free Incas moved their headquarters to the very edge of the jungle; there they built a substitute Cusco of adobe and fieldstone in a steaming valley 8,000 feet below their ancient home.

The conquistadors, meanwhile, were disputing the empire's corpse among themselves. Manku tried to exploit these white wars fought with Indian blood, but it cost him his life: some Spaniards he was sheltering killed him during a game of quoits. Titu Kusi, then about fifteen, saw it happen: "While my father was going to set up the hob for play they all fell upon him with daggers, knives, and swords."[18] The boy escaped, but the assassins did not. Caught on their way to Cusco, they were given, says Titu Kusi with grim satisfaction, "very cruel deaths."

Regents held Manku's throne until 1557, when Sayri Tupa received the royal fringe. The new Inca took the dramatic names Manku Qhapaq Pachakuti, evoking the founder of the dynasty and the hope for a change of worlds.[19] But the quisling Incas of Cusco poisoned him in 1561, after he had negotiated a truce.[20] The fringe was then taken by the future author of the *Relación*. Those who knew Titu Kusi describe a shrewd yet emotional man with a generous spirit, quick to anger and to laugh. About thirty when he came to power, he was stout and tall for an Andean, "with some marks of smallpox on his face; his expression rather severe and manly."[21] His leg was scarred from the fight with his father's assassins.

By then things were very bad in Spanish-occupied Peru. The wars between Inca and Inca, Inca and Spaniard, and Spaniard and Spaniard had wrecked the intricate machinery of the Tawantinsuyu. Supplies were exhausted, records destroyed, bridges burned. The population fell to 1.3 million by 1570 and reached a nadir of 600,000 in 1630. Even taking a conservative figure for precontact levels, this is a decline of 93 percent.[22] With no one left to tend them, irrigation channels burst their banks, contoured fields returned to scrub and dune, Inca cities became eerie ruins blackened by fire and littered with rotting goods for which the invaders had no use. Cusco was little better, a squalid medieval town thrown up on the fragments of its greatness.

In this atmosphere of doom arose a chiliastic cult—the Taki Onqoy, or Sickness Dance. Like North America's ghost dances, it sought to bring back the lost world by supernatural means. Believers gathered the remains of their totemic shrines broken and desecrated by missionaries, and danced before them until a worshiper, entranced, began to speak in tongues, prophesying that a plague would kill the invaders but spare the Indians—a pathetic reversal of reality.[23]

Spanish sources claim that Titu Kusi was planning a military campaign at the same time. But the Taki Onqoy failed, and Titu Kusi had to find other ways to save his kingdom. Aware that paganism was the ideological excuse for Spanish attack, he agreed to let a few friars preach in Vilcabamba. He even had himself baptized—for the second time in his life. (As a boy he had spent four years in Spanish Cusco.) This policy might have worked if the ruthless Francisco de Toledo had not become viceroy in 1569. Determined to crush the free state, Toledo first prepared the ground by hiring chroniclers to discredit the Incas and praise the conquest as a liberation.

Titu Kusi's *Relación*, written in February 1570, was his answer to the viceroy's propaganda. In it the Inca vigorously defends his father's conduct, hoping to convince the king of Spain that Manku's sons, not the puppets living softly in Cusco, are the rightful lords of Peru. Manku, he claims, had welcomed an alliance with Spain from the start; he made war against the Spaniards only because their behavior became intolerable.

This was true, more or less, but it did no good. A year after writing his book, the Inca died as suddenly as his predecessor had. Suspecting Spanish poison, his people killed all foreigners in Vilcabamba, including the friars. Titu Kusi was succeeded by Manku's youngest son, Tupa Amaru.[24] The new Inca banned Christianity and closed the frontier, which gave Toledo the *casus belli* he sought.

After smallpox struck Vilcabamba in 1572, a Spanish army penetrated to the jungle city and burned it.[25] Inca troops fought with desperate bravery, charging bare-chested into harquebus fire, but it soon became clear that the free state—which might otherwise have survived as an American Ethiopia—was lost.[26] Tupa Amaru and his court fled into the forest, their escape hindered by the queen's pregnancy. The royal couple was captured while resting beside a campfire in a clearing; with them was a small golden image of the sun. They were dragged in chains to Cusco, where Toledo was waiting to savor his triumph. After a sham trial, and despite pleas for clemency from many Spaniards who thought the Inca should be judged only in Spain by his fellow monarch, the viceroy had Tupa Amaru beheaded in the square before a vast crowd of mourners.

Toledo, a master of the big lie, asserted that the Inca had made a dramatic scaffold confession, admitting to the crowd that worship of the sun was false. He then had Tupa Amaru's head stuck on a pike, whereupon thousands gathered each night to venerate it. "No punishment,"

Toledo wrote, "could have sufficed to prevent the adoration they made,"[27] which rather damages his claim that the Inca had publicly renounced divinity.

The tragedy had been anticipated years earlier by Manku in a speech he gave when he withdrew into the Vilcabamba mountains. First he reminded his subjects how well the Incas had ruled them: "Reflect on how long my grandparents and great-grandparents and I myself have looked after you and protected you, cared for you and governed . . . making provision that you had plenty, so that it behoves all of you not to forget us, not in your lifetimes, nor the time of your descendants."

Then, acknowledging that Spanish domination might be long, he prescribed a covert antagonism that remains the model of Andean resistance to this day.

> What you can do is give them the outward appearance of complying with their demands. And give them a little tribute, whatever you can spare from your lands, because these people are so savage and so different from us that if you don't give it to them they will take it from you by force. . . .
>
> They did with me as you have seen . . . taking from us our property, our wives, our sons, our daughters, our fields, our food, and many other things that we used to have in this land. . . .
>
> I know that someday, by force or deceit, they will make you worship what they worship, and when that happens, when you can resist no longer, do it in front of them, but on the other hand do not forget our ceremonies. And if they tell you to break your shrines, and force you to do so, reveal just what you have to, and keep hidden the rest.[28]

Europeans usually left their trophy heads to rot; in Tupa Amaru's case they took it down and buried it.

But as we shall see, the Inca's head still lives.

> Lord Inca, will your heart allow
> That we be scattered and lost,
> Broken, dispersed,
> And trampled by the foreigners?
> —"Apu Inka Atawallpaman," eighteenth (?) century

In the Andes, writing was—and still is—seen as something sinister, a tool of foreign domination. Atawallpa was killed because he rejected the invaders' holy book; Manku dismissed the Bible as "painted sheets"; and the ordinary people found themselves cheated, drafted, jailed, and dispossessed by arcane paperwork.

Even so, several Andeans followed Titu Kusi's example, taking up the pen where the sword had failed. They did so to communicate with the foreign power in the hope that they could influence it, and for that reason wrote mainly in Spanish. Four Andean writers—Titu Kusi, Pachakuti Yamki, Waman Puma, and Inca Garcilaso de la Vega (author of *The Inca's Florida*)—wrote to refute the foreign version of what had happened in Peru, a false history that they rightly saw as a form of oppression in itself.

By far the best-known work is Garcilaso's *Royal Commentaries*. First published in 1609, it became a seventeenth-century bestseller.[29] The young Inca had moved to Spain in 1559, made himself a master of Renaissance learning and style, and used these gifts to shape the image of ancient Peru in the European mind.[30] Influenced by More's *Utopia* (which had itself been inspired by early reports of Amerindian societies), he portrays the Tawantinsuyu as the ideal state.

From the English translation of 1688:

> The Incas were not only contented to bestow on their subjects their food and raiment, but many other presents . . . as if they had been stewards or masters of families, whose office was to make provision for others, rather than Kings. . . . Hence proceeded that great love and affection which the Peruvians bore towards their kings, that even to this day, though they are become Christians, they cannot forget the memory of them, but are ready on all occasions . . . to evoke their names. . . . We do not read in all the

> histories of Asia, Africa, or Europe that ever those kings were so gracious to their subjects as these.[31]

Any author who hoped to elude the Inquisition had to profess total acceptance of Christianity's monopoly on truth; he could no more express doubt of official dogma than could a Russian in the age of Stalin. Garcilaso therefore had to finesse the problem of the Incas' paganism, claiming that the Incas, like More's Utopians, had come as close to Christian ideals as was possible through natural reason. By their intellect and altruism they had, he wrote, "glimpsed the true God"; indeed (and here he was on very thin ice), Manku Qhapaq, the first Inca, had been set on earth by divine Providence to pave the way for Christian revelation. In short, the Inca Empire was to the New World what the Roman Empire had been to the Old. His unspoken conclusion was that both those empires fell to barbarian invaders.

Garcilaso succeeded in founding the utopian tradition of Western writing on the Incas. Yet the Utopia he saw was not merely a product of his imagination. Andean writers who had never heard of Thomas More drew similar conclusions. So did mythology, folk plays, songs—the entire oral tradition of the Andes. Whatever the flaws of the Tawantinsuyu, it soon came to be regarded as a golden age.

Garcilaso's success was not shared by other Andean writers. Their manuscripts lay ignored for centuries; none was published until modern times, and even now they are known only to specialists. Apart from Titu Kusi, who used a translator, these authors wrote in broken Spanish distorted by Quechua syntax. Their thinking is equally uncomfortable in European clothes. Yet these very "faults" make their work of unique importance, for their rambling prose and strange conceptions are doorways to the Andean mind.

The most important of all is Felipe Waman Puma. Little is known about him except what he tells us in *The First New Chronicle and Good Government*, his monumental work of 1,200 pages and 400 drawings. Born not long after Atawallpa's death, Waman Puma would have been in his thirties when Tupa Amaru died. He grew up in the hinterland of Ayacucho, between Cusco and Lima; his family may have been quipu readers or artists in Inca times. But Waman Puma, wanting to reach the ear of the Spanish king, inflated his social status, claiming that his mother was related to Wayna Qhapaq.

The author portrays himself in several of his drawings: a beardless face with a mild, earnest expression framed by shoulder-length hair. As he goes to Lima, aged eighty, to send his book to Spain, he gives us a touching portrait of his life on the road—"poor, naked, and travelling in winter" with his son Francisco, his horse Guía, and his dogs Amigo and Lautaro. Evidently he loved animals, as Andeans still do.

It seems that Waman Puma was, for a time at least, a sincere convert to Christianity. By his own account he had learned Spanish and doctrine from a mestizo half-brother, a "saintly Franciscan hermit" devoted to the poor. Waman Puma read chronicles, devotional works, and something of Las Casas. In his early years he worked for a Spanish friar intent on rooting out "idolatry." But as he traveled the broken roads of the Tawantinsuyu, talking to the few elders who remained, he became horrified by what he saw. He was, he realized, living through an apocalypse, a stalled pachakuti, a moment of chaos that refused to end. One order had been thrown down, but a new order had not been instituted: "This world upside down," he wrote to King Philip III, "is a sure sign that there is no God and there is no king."[32] The Spanish emperors, he complained, had failed to fill the Incas' shoes. They had been unable to create a government that worked; they seemed indifferent to their subjects' welfare, and by extracting wealth without redistributing any of it, they violated the Andean law for legitimate exercise of power.

> [Why] do you wish to run the lives of foreigners when you cannot run your own? Why do you demand from the poorest man his mule, but never ask if he needs any help? . . .
>
> And so I dared, as a vassal of your royal Crown, and as a nobleman of his kingdom of the Indies of the New World . . . to write and illustrate the said *New Chronicle and Good Government* . . . in service of God and of Your Majesty, and for the welfare, increase, and protection of the Indians of this realm.[33]

It took him thirty years, from 1585 to 1615. Somehow he got paper and ink, somehow he protected his burgeoning manuscript and himself as he traveled through the Andes asking questions, prying into atrocities. He begins by describing in detail how the Incas governed, then gives a history of the conquest, which in effect denies that a conquest ever took place. Like Titu Kusi, he stresses that the Incas were willing to become allies of Spain, even to accept Christianity. His motive is the same as Titu Kusi's—to undercut any legal pretext for the invasion. Also, anticipating the Mexican Fray Servando by 200 years, he claims that an apostle had reached Peru long before the Spaniards.

The rest of his book is detailed reportage, backed by shocking illustrations, of the chaos and cruelty of European rule. In words and drawings, Waman Puma shows torture, murder, rape, extortion, corruption, and wanton destruction of public works. Having delivered this vehement attack on colonialism, he suggests a remedy, a way for the Spanish king to set things right. This is nothing less than an appeal for independence within a loose international structure resembling the modern British Commonwealth—perhaps the first appeal of its kind. Taking as his model the Inca Empire with its four great quadrants united by the Sapa Inka on his throne in Cusco, Waman Puma proposes a new Tawantinsuyu comprising the whole world as he conceives it: "the Indies" (America), "Guinea" (Africa), "Grand Turkey" (Asia), and "Rome" (Europe). Each sector is to be internally self-governed by its native kings; Spanish officials must leave and be replaced by native ones. Philip, king of Spain and Holy Roman emperor, may preside as the unifying fifth principle, the "Monarch of the World": an Inca for the whole earth.

But this new Inca, unlike the old ones, is to reign, not rule; he must not meddle in each kingdom because he has already shown his incompetence.

> You should consider that all the world belongs to God, and that thus Castile is of the Spaniards, and the Indies of the Indians and Guinea of the Negroes. Each of these are the lawful owners of their lands. . . .

The Indians are the natural owners of this realm; the Spaniards are the natural owners of Spain. . . . [Here] the Inca is king, and no Spaniard nor any priest has the right to intrude, for the Inca was the possessor and lawful sovereign. . . .

You should consider that in the time of the Incas . . . people had much faith in God and were loyal, and very charitable, and humble, and they raised their sons and daughters with discipline and teaching. . . . And [now] the people of this life are lost . . . there is no justice. Everything is by self-interest and the lust for aggrandisement. . . .

In the time of the Incas there was none of this greed for gold and silver. But now there are many thieves: Indians, Negroes, and most of all the Spaniards, who flay the poor Indians and injure them and rob them. And not only that, for they take their wives and daughters—especially the priests. . . .

And consider . . . Don Francisco de Toledo, the viceroy, who in his pride wanted to be greater than a king . . . and who passed judgement on the King of Peru! If only Your Majesty had sent a judge here then to behead *him* on the same scaffold! . . .

Consider the poor Indians and their works . . . that in every town they built irrigation canals from the rivers and springs, the lakes and reservoirs. In ancient times they built them with so much effort . . . and with the greatest skill in the world, so that it seems as if every Indian [that ever lived] raised up a stone. And all this was sufficient for the large number of people that there used to be here. And thus throughout the kingdom all the land produced food, whether jungles, deserts, or the difficult mountains of this realm. . . . And the Inca kings ordered that . . . nobody should damage or remove one stone, and that no livestock should enter the said canals. . . .

But now this law is no longer kept, and so all the fields are ruined for lack of water. Because of this the Indians lose their farms. . . . For in these times the Spaniards release their animals, their mule trains, cows, their goats and sheep, and they cause great damage. And they also take the water, and break the irrigation canals, so that they could not be repaired now for any amount of money. And the little water that remains, they take even that from the poor Indians. And so the Indians abandon their towns.[34]

Consider that the Indians were not barbarous or simple, but that they had a law [even] before there was an Inca. And from that time forth they had an Inca law and an Inca king.[35]

And since [one of these kings] was my grandfather . . . I propose: first, a son of mine, a great-grandson of Tupa Inka Yupanki, as prince of this realm . . . second, a Negro prince in the kingdom of Guinea; third, a king of the Christians of Rome . . . and fourth, a king of the Moors of Grand Turkey—the four to be crowned, with their sceptres and robes.

And in the middle of these four parts of the world shall stand the Majesty and Monarch of the World, King Philip. . . .

[But] the monarch does not have jurisdiction.[36]

Waman Puma's manuscript cannot have reached the Escorial. If it had, it would almost certainly have been destroyed. Somehow the *New Chronicle* made its way to northern Europe, perhaps in the hands of a Protestant who knew political dynamite when he saw it. But if so it was never used. The work lay forgotten for three centuries, until it was found accidentally at the Royal Copenhagen Library in 1908.

There was a darkness all over the earth until the ninth hour. And the sun was darkened, and the veil of the temple was rent in the midst.
—Luke 23:44–45

The Inca military resistance of the sixteenth century and intellectual response of the seventeenth fertilized each other and bore fruit in the Age of Reason. During the eighteenth century, more than a hundred revolts and rebellions broke out in various parts of Peru.[37] Many were small and easily crushed; some were the work of mestizos and creoles. But the majority were native uprisings, and the most successful were led by blood descendants of Inca kings.

The Spaniards thought they had stamped out the royal family when Viceroy Toledo executed Tupa Amaru in 1572. (The Inca's only son—taken captive to Lima—died conveniently soon afterward.) But they were blinded by their own culture: they hadn't got rid of the daughters. Tupa Amaru's daughter Juana married one Diego Felipe Kunturkanki, native lord of a province south of Cusco.[38] Their family kept the name and memory of Tupa Amaru alive for more than 200 years.

By the eighteenth century, the Andean population had started to recover.[39] A precarious modus vivendi had been worked out between the conquered and the conqueror at different levels of society. Most Spaniards lived idly in Lima on income from their estates; Indian communities fought tribute and draft by subterfuge and endless litigation.[40] Andeans professed to be devout Catholics, but their ancient religions survived beneath a thin Christian veneer, as Manku Inka had foreseen. Toledo and other viceroys had found that Peru was ungovernable without reviving some aspects of the Inca system, and they had had to confirm Inca administrators and ethnic lords in their positions. These native aristocrats, known as *kurakas,* became the middle men, the interpreters and brokers, between the Andean and European worlds. The best of them tried to shield their people from the brunt of Spanish rule; the worst used their positions to enrich themselves.

The flower of kuraka society, descended from Inca nobles, though not through Manku's line, lived in Cusco and cherished the memory of their ancient greatness. As their position in the colonial hierarchy became more secure, they led a romantic revival of Inca culture. While the Inca collaborators of the sixteenth century had put on Spanish finery and aped European ways, their eighteenth-century descendants returned to Inca dress. They wrote plays and verse in Quechua. They read Garcilaso's *Royal Commentaries* and compared his utopia with what they saw around them: roads, terraces, aqueducts—the material legacy of the Inca state—lying everywhere in ruins.[41] They staged historical pageants that dwelled on the massacre at Cajamarca—and sometimes Pizarro lost. From Cusco's thriving school of Indian painters they commissioned portraits of themselves and their ancestors in the regalia of the Tawantinsuyu. Several can be seen in the city's churches and museums: noblewomen in sweeping skirts richly woven with geometric heraldry exactly like those their forebears had worn at the Inca court; their menfolk, carrying ceremonial shields and scepters, in tunics of fine vicuña cloth, feather garters below their knees, diadems on their heads, their chests resplendent with sun disks of beaten gold. Even Catholic images were given Inca clothes, leading the bishop of Cusco to complain, "They adore the true God only when they see Him dressed like the Incas."[42]

Among those who read Inca Garcilaso's *Royal Commentaries* in the eighteenth century was José Gabriel Kunturkanki Tupa Amaru, the great-great-great-grandson of the Inca beheaded by Toledo. He was kuraka of the province of Tinta on the windswept altiplano between the watersheds of Cusco and Lake Titicaca. An educated man typical of his class, he "spoke Spanish perfectly and Quechua with special grace."[43] He had a steady private income from his mule trains, which plied between highlands and coast. This business took him often to Lima and Cusco, where for years he tried to alleviate the burdens of his people in the courts. Not only were they being worked to death in the mines, but they were forced to buy useless and shoddy Spanish goods in an ill-conceived scheme to stimulate the imperial economy. This lucrative monopoly was held by *corregidores,* hated judges and tax collectors. Increasingly frustrated by the futility of litigation, José Gabriel began to meet others who thought that legal protest was a waste of time. In November 1780, after all peaceful efforts had failed, he hanged the corregidor of Tinta and proclaimed himself Inca Tupa Amaru II. It is said that he raised the revolt with these Quechua words: *Manañam kunanmanta wakchakayniykiwan wiraqocha mikhunqañachu!* "From this day forth, no longer shall the Spaniard feast on your poverty!"[44] So began the greatest challenge to Spain's rule in America since the sixteenth century.

Tupa Amaru II was then about forty years old. Contemporary sketches show him as a robust and handsome man with the classic hawk profile of the Amerindian and sleek black hair that hung long beneath a tricorn beaver hat. After the first victory over Spanish troops, he and his wife, Micaela, who bore arms and fought beside him, sat for a portrait dressed in the robes of an Inca king and queen.[45]

The war lasted three years and cost 200,000 lives. South American nationalists have tried to appropriate it as a "precursor" of the creole independence achieved forty years later; economic determinists have seen it merely as a tax revolt. It was both of those, but much more. Recent anthropological findings leave no doubt that it was, as Spaniards at the time feared, a native independence movement intent on reinstating Inca sovereignty throughout the Andes.

The return of the Inca fulfilled the deepest desires of the Andean peasantry. They knew their history, and they had charged it with the power of myth. They remembered the Tawantinsuyu as a golden age. The Incas who had died—Atawallpa, Manku, and especially Tupa Amaru I—had fused into an archetypal figure, *Inkarí*, the Inca messiah. Down in the underworld, where the old order existed in a latent state, the head of their king, cut off by the Spaniards, was preparing itself for a triumphant return. Slowly the head was growing a new body; when this was complete, Inkarí would emerge and transform the world. Upper and lower would again reverse; the Inca would be king and the Europeans would be vanquished.

Tupa Amaru II was culturally and politically adroit enough to be different things to different people. He freed all black slaves, his liberal ideals attracted sympathetic mestizos and creoles, he may have intrigued with British agents, and he calmed royalists by declaring himself loyal to the Spanish Crown. In this last point he followed Waman Puma, professing to believe that the distant monarch was good and just though his minions were not. But to his own people, Tupa Amaru was nothing less than the once and future king. Many believed that if they died fighting with their savior, they would rise again on the day he was crowned in Cusco.[46] It is said that on the night before he rebelled, Tupa Amaru prayed to the old gods in the ancient temple of Raqchi, whose columned hall still stands not far from Tinta.

The rebellion spread swiftly through the southern Andes and was loosely coordinated with an Aymara revolt in Bolivia. But the need to consolidate a southern front caused a fatal delay in the Inca's march on Cusco. By the time he reached his ancestors' capital, the Spaniards had had time to prepare. As in Manku's day, several prominent Incas sided with Spain. Some of these thought they had better claims to royal blood (though they hadn't); others were exploiters with good reason to fear an end to the colonial system. Loath to cause a bloodbath, the Inca besieged the city and sent this letter to the town council on January 3, 1781:

> Ever since I began to liberate the natives of this kingdom from the servitude in which they find themselves . . . it has been my object to avoid deaths and hostilities. . . .
>
> Mine is the only blood that has come down from the Incas, the sovereigns of this realm. This has prompted me to seek by all possible means an end to abuses . . . against the unfortunate Indians and other persons, and against the provisions of the very kings of Spain, whose [beneficial] laws I know from experience have been suppressed and ignored . . . ever since the conquest here. . . . This is so notorious that I need no further proof than the tears that have flowed for three centuries from the eyes of my unhappy people. . . .
>
> My desire is that this type of official [corregidor, etc.] be abolshed entirely; that their *repartimientos* [monopolies and extortions] shall cease; that in each province there shall be a chief magistrate [chosen] from the Indian nation itself [and] that in this city a Royal Audience be established with a resident viceroy presiding, so that the Indians may have ready access and recourse. That is the whole thrust of my enterprise for now.[47]

Perhaps the town council didn't like the tone of his "for now." They did not surrender; a week later, after an inconclusive battle, the Inca withdrew. He intended to return to Cusco in triumph after making gains elsewhere, but it was not to be. As the war grew fiercer, it became more racial in character, something Tupa Amaru had tried to avoid. Many Indians could not resist settling old scores with the whites, whom they reviled as *pukakunka,* an early use of the term "redneck." Sympathetic mestizos began to desert; in April 1781, a series of defeats and betrayals led to the capture of the Inca and his immediate family.

They were taken to Cusco, imprisoned, and interrogated. Their torturer, José Antonio de Areche, was an official "visitor" originally sent from Spain to look into the abuses that had sparked the rebellion. Areche made free with inquisitorial techniques, wrenching Tupa Amaru's right arm from its socket in efforts to learn the names of his associates. But the Inca would not talk. Instead, he smuggled letters to relatives and allies still at war and tried several times to escape. Some of his notes survive, written in a pathetic left-handed scrawl with the only ink available, his own blood. To Areche the Inca would say only: "There are no accomplices here but you and I. You the oppressor, and I the liberator. Both of us deserve to die."[48]

On May 18, 1781, Tupa Amaru II was executed in the same square that had seen the death of his ancestor two centuries before. He was made to watch as his wife, uncle, and eldest son had their tongues torn out and were then garrotted. The Spaniards reserved a special fate for the Inca: his limbs were tied to horses, which were spurred in the four directions, "a spectacle never before seen in this city." But despite a month of torture the Inca's frame resisted this symbolic rending of the Tawantinsuyu. After being stretched in midair "like a spider," he was taken back to the scaffold and chopped into pieces. A Spanish eyewitness wrote:

> They cut off his arms and feet. They did the same with [Micaela], and from the others they took the heads, to send to different towns. The torsos of the Indian and his wife were taken to Piqchu [the hill from which Tupa Amaru had besieged the city], where a bonfire had been lit. They were thrown in and burned to ashes and these were then cast into the air and into a stream that runs nearby. Thus ended José Gabriel Tupa Amaru and Micaela, whose pride and arrogance were such that they named themselves monarchs of Peru.

Quechua epics on the death of earlier Incas insist that the universe convulsed in horror: *Hail fell . . . the sun sank, night came.* At the death of Tupa Amaru II, nature imitated faith. The same witness:

> Some things took place which seem to have been wrought by the Devil to confirm these Indians in their errors, omens, and

> superstitions. I say this because although it was a very dry time of year with fine days, *that* day dawned so overcast that the face of the sun was hidden . . . and at noon, when the horses were stretching the Indian, a great squall of wind arose, and then a downpour so fierce that everyone—even the guards—ran for cover. For this reason the Indians declare that heaven and the elements grieved at the death of the Inca, whom the inhuman and impious Spaniards were killing with such cruelty.[49]

Though the Inca died, his followers continued the war for more than a year, killing thousands of whites in revenge. Smaller revolts broke out in other parts of the ancient empire and even beyond its borders. One by one they were crushed; Spain emerged victorious but shaken.

Visitor Areche sent a long report to Madrid. He recommended removing some abuses, but his main thrust was ethnocide: the destruction of a nationality by eradicating its leaders, identity, and culture. With the fanaticism that Spain has used against her Moors and Jews, Areche planned to extinguish "the illusory nation of the Indians," a plan still dear to some Hispanic Peruvians of today. Rebel Incas were killed or exiled; all Incas lost their titles, their hereditary kurakaships, their robes, even their family portraits "which abound in the houses of Indians who hold themselves to be noble . . . to vaunt their ancestry." All Indians were to be taught Spanish within four years; Quechua song, music, and theater were banned.

> The Indians must not perform plays and other public functions that they use to preserve the memory of their ancient Incas. . . . Likewise, the trumpets and horns that the Indians use in their ceremonies must be forbidden amd taken away, [especially] those called *pututu*—marine shells with a strange and mournful sound by which they evoke the sorrowful remembrance of their past . . . and the day of the conquest, which they hold in dread.[50]

But the Incas were not to be forgotten, and Inkarí would live again.

NINE

CHEROKEE

> We are almost surrounded by the whites . . . and it seems to be their intention to destroy us as a people.
>
> —Dragging Canoe, Cherokee, 1776

On April 19, 1775, the friction between Britain and its colonists ignited into open warfare at Lexington and Concord—near Boston—Massachusetts. The Revolutionary War began. Only one month before, Attakullakulla (the Little Carpenter), Oconostota (Groundhog Sausage), and other elderly chiefs had relinquished the Cherokee Nation's sovereignty over what are now the states of Kentucky and Tennessee for £10,000. After finishing his prophetic speech against the deal, Attakullakulla's son Dragging Canoe turned to one of the land speculators, his smallpocked face alight with anger: "You have bought a fair land, but there is a black cloud hanging over it. You will find its settlement dark and bloody."[1] Those words may be taken as the opening salvo in another war—the war of resistance that Dragging Canoe, his followers, and allies waged against the settler republic for nearly twenty years. Attakullakulla knew that such a war was hopeless, that the invasion could not be stopped. In the long run, Cherokees would take the path of accommodation, accepting cultural and political change with extraordinary resilience and adaptability. Perhaps even Attakullakulla could not guess that within fifty years his people would have their own constitution, supreme court, script, and newspaper. Certainly he could not foresee that having made such a transformation in accordance with the white man's wishes, they would still be driven from their homes, just as his son had warned.

When the American colonists rebelled, most Indians thought that their interests lay with the distant king whose Royal Proclamation had drawn a line beyond which his subjects were not to pass. Indeed, a white civil war seemed a good opportunity to strengthen that line, to halt its perforation and westward trend. In spring 1776, as soon as the rivers were thawed and the trails dry, delegates from the Iroquois Confederacy, the Shawnees, the Delawares, and other northerners set out on a mission to unite all Indian nations from the Great Lakes to the Gulf of Mexico. In mid-May they reached Chota, the Cherokee capital, in its cool valley behind the Great Smoky Mountains. The time had come to make a common front against the white invader, the envoys said, adding that what they had seen on the way had only increased their sense of urgency.

> We have been seventy days upon our journey. When we attempted to pass through that country from Pittsburgh to the [Cherokee] Nation, which but very lately used to be Shawnee and Delaware hunting grounds, and where we used to see nothing but deer, bear, and buffalo, we found the country thickly inhabited [by whites] and the people all in arms. . . . Our salt springs and our buffalo grounds had numbers of inhabitants and fortified places round them. We were obliged to go down a great way on the other side of the Ohio and to take a round of near 300 miles to avoid being discovered.[2]

In the 1960s, shortly before the Tellico Dam drowned the historic Little Tennessee Valley where Chota, Tanasi, Tellico, and other towns of the Overhill Cherokees stood, archaeologists uncovered the foundations of Chota's great townhouse—the Cherokee parliament where these talks were held. Only postholes remained, but they were enough to show that the building was an octagon sixty feet across, its conical roof supported by eight massive pillars, representing the eight clans, arranged around a central fire. Henry Stuart, brother of John, the British Superintendent of Indian affairs, also traveled to Chota for the conference, anxious to gauge the Indians' sympathies. He reported, "The standard of war was erected, the flagstaff and posts of the Town House were painted black and red. . . . Every young fellow's face in the Overhill Towns appeared blackened, and nothing was now talked of but war."[3]

The first speaker was a Mohawk representing his own nation and the Iroquois League to which it belonged. He illustrated his speech with a belt of white and purple wampum.

> I suppose there is not a man present who cannot read my talk. The [frontiersmen], whom we call the Long Knives, have without any provocation come into one of our towns; they murdered our people and the son of our great Beloved man. . . . Our nation is fighting now, and I am sent here to secure the friendship of all nations, for our interests are one. At this time we must forget all quarrels among ourselves and turn our eyes and our thoughts one way.[4]

A Shawnee closed the meetings. He unfurled a splendid war belt, "about nine feet long and six inches wide, of purple wampum strewed over with vermilion," the latter signifying white man's blood. When the uproar this caused in the smoky townhouse had subsided, he began to speak.

> In a very few years our Nation, from being a great people, are now reduced to a handful. We once possessed land almost to the seashore, but the red people who were once masters of this whole country, now have hardly enough ground to stand on.
>
> The lands where we but lately hunted . . . are thickly inhabited [by whites] and covered with forts and armed men. Whenever a fort appears in our neighbourhood, you may depend there will soon be towns and settlements. It is plain that they intend to extirpate us, and I think it better to die like men than to diminish away by inches.[5]

Dragging Canoe gladly accepted all the war belts offered. His father and the other elders remained "dejected and silent" on their seats of honor near the central fire. Remembering the cost of previous wars, they did not accept the belts.[6]

Among those who spoke for peace was Attakullakulla's niece, Nancy Ward, an example of womanly power in the Cherokee Nation. (Her second husband was a white trader, hence her name.) She had distinguished herself in battle against the Creeks in 1755, fighting on with her first husband's gun after he fell dead. This earned her the rank of Beloved—a Cherokee title akin to knighthood—and gave her a strong voice in council. She sympathized with white Americans, perhaps because she was married to one and because she shared her uncle's view that the rebels might win.

Both she and Dragging Canoe exercised their right to go their own ways. He defied his elders and prepared for war; she told the settlers of his plans. Neither deed was treachery by Cherokee law. Nancy's warning enabled the squatters to withstand Dragging Canoe's attack, but her magnanimity was not reciprocated. Instead, rebel troops overran the Cherokee Nation, burning innumerable towns. In 1777, the elders were forced to sue for peace. To end a war they had not waged themselves, they had to give up most Cherokee land in the Carolinas, including what was left of the Valley and Middle towns. They narrowly avoided ceding all that remained north of the Little Tennessee River, the "Long Man" on which Chota itself stood. This land was saved by an eloquent appeal from Onitositah (Corn Tassel), Oconostota's most trusted adviser. Slightly younger than his chief, he was a "stout, mild, and decided man" widely respected by both Indians and whites for his integrity. His address on this occasion is one of the great Native American speeches on record, even though, as his interpreter admitted, "the manly and dignified expression of an Indian orator loses nearly all its force and energy in translation."[7]

> When we enter . . . into treaties with our brothers, the whites, their whole cry is *more land!* Indeed, formerly it seemed to be a matter of formality with them to demand what they knew we durst not refuse. But on the principles of fairness, of which we have received assurances during the conducting of the present treaty, and in the name of free will and equality, I must reject your demand. . . .
>
> Let us examine the facts of your present irruption into our country, and we shall discover your pretensions on that ground.

What did you do? You marched into our territories with a superior force . . . your numbers far exceeded us, and we fled to the stronghold of our extensive woods, there to secure our women and children. . . . You killed a few scattered and defenseless individuals, spread fire and desolation wherever you pleased, and returned again to your own habitations. . . .

Your laws extend not into our country, nor ever did. You talk of the law of nature and the law of nations, and they are both against you.

Indeed, much has been advanced on the want of what you term civilization among the Indians; and many proposals have been made to us to adopt your laws, your religion, your manners and your customs. But, we confess that we do not yet see the propriety, or practicability, of such a reformation, and should be better pleased with beholding the good effect of these doctrines in your own practices than with hearing you talk about them. . . .

You say: Why do not the Indians till the ground and live as we do? May we not, with equal propriety, ask: Why do not the white people hunt and live as we do? . . .

We wish, however, to be at peace with you, and to do as we would be done by. We do not quarrel with you for killing an occasional buffalo, bear or deer on our lands when you need one to eat; but you go much farther; your people hunt to gain a livelihood by it; they kill all our game; our young men resent the injury, and it is followed by bloodshed and war. . . .

The great God of Nature has placed us in different situations. It is true that he has endowed you with many superior advantages; but he has not created us to be your slaves. *We are a separate people!* He has given each their lands, under distinct considerations and circumstances; he has stocked yours with cows, ours with buffaloe; yours with hog, ours with bear; yours with sheep ours with deer. He has, indeed, given you an advantage in this that your cattle are tame and domestic while ours are wild and demand not only a larger space for range, but art to hunt and kill them. They are, nevertheless, as much our property as other animals are yours.[8]

The peace treaty was supposed to remove the main irritant for Cherokees—illegal settlements—but this part of the bargain was never kept by the Americans. Dragging Canoe had no choice but to withdraw from the Cherokee Nation. Followed by many who had lost their homes to war, encroachment, and to the peace, he founded new towns farther west, near modern Chattanooga. From there he fought on for another seventeen years.

For a while he was supplied by Henry Hamilton, lieutenant governor of Canada, who paid so generously for rebel scalps that he was nicknamed the Hair Buyer.[9] But the following year, at the Treaty of Paris, the British betrayed the Cherokees, the Iroquois, and all their other native allies. In the same year smallpox struck the Cherokee Nation again, killing 2,500.[10]

In 1785, as the United States began to consolidate itself, Congress negotiated its first federal treaty with the Cherokees, an enlightened document known as the Hopewell Treaty. "The Indians," it read, "may have full confidence in the justice of the United States."[11] For once there were no demands for land. Nancy Ward, Beloved Woman of Chota, replied for the Cherokee Nation:

> I have a pipe and a little tobacco to give to the commissioners to smoke in friendship. . . . Your having determined on peace is most pleasing to me, for I have seen much trouble during the late war. I am old, but I hope yet to bear children, who will grow up and people our nation, as we are now to be under the protection of Congress and shall have no more disturbance.[12]

But Congress could no more restrain the frontiersmen than the British could. Rough whites on the fringe of the Union despised the intellectuals at its core. They hated Indians, and they wanted Indian land. Dragging Canoe and the Long Knives continued to fight it out, with countless atrocities on both sides: Dragging Canoe killed settlers like chickens, among them Davy Crockett's grandfather. As usual, peaceful and defenseless Cherokees bore the brunt of reprisals for the militants' deeds. Whites led by John Sevier created the breakaway "state" of Franklin—a den of racism and intransigence—and forced the Overhill towns to cede all land north of the Little Tennessee.[13] In 1788, they murdered a party of old chiefs under a flag of truce, including Corn Tassel, whose eloquence had saved that land only eleven years before. After this the Cherokees lost heart, gradually abandoning their capital and other Overhill towns. A 1799 visitor to Chota found a mere five houses; by 1813 only one Cherokee was living there.[14]

Near the end of his life, Dragging Canoe avenged the murder of Corn Tassel, and in 1791, the year before he died, his brother Badger helped Little Turtle and other northerners rout the army of General Arthur St. Clair in the Old Northwest.[15] History has judged Dragging Canoe harshly, seeing him as provoker, not provoked. But many distinterested observers agreed with Duc François de La Rochefoucauld, who traveled in the region at the time: the whites, he wrote, "are in the wrong four times out of five."[16] The Indian nations east of the Mississippi then had fewer than 125,000 citizens all told, while the settler republic had 3 million. From the Great Lakes to the Gulf, Dragging Canoe and others like him held off an incomparably larger, richer, and more ruthless people for a generation.

> Our Nation was alone and surrounded. . . . We were forced to leave our towns . . . and now we live in the grass as you see us. But we are not yet conquered.
>
> —Dragging Canoe, 1779

In the autumn of 1794, leaders representing all Cherokee factions signed a peace with the Americans that would prove more durable than most. The United States, for its part, built Tellico Blockhouse near the ruins of Fort Loudoun to keep settlers from crossing the Little Tennessee. From there it began to supply the Cherokees with plows, spinning wheels, and other implements intended to transform them into European peasants. This acculturation policy, originally George Washington's idea, was not motivated purely by idealism: if Indians adopted intensive farming and made cloth to sell instead of hides, it was thought, they would need less land and could therefore be induced to cede the rest. "You will unite yourselves with us," Thomas Jefferson told the indigenous race, "join in our great councils . . . and we shall all be Americans . . . your blood will run in our veins and will spread with us over this great continent."[17] Jefferson might have asked himself why people who had occupied every corner of the continent for thousands of years should need to spread across it; but his words (an early expression of the "melting pot") at least offered them a place.

Some Cherokees believed him. Seeing that "savages" had no rights, they thought their right to exist would be respected if they became what the whites called civilized. The transformation was not just a matter of adopting new technology. It involved overturning many of the values and practices of Cherokee life and replacing them with others that seemed immoral, sacrilegious, and repugnant. Their culture had already undergone great change during the eighteenth century, but its fabric had remained intact. They had borrowed firearms, horses, livestock, crops, and iron, but these were tools, not templates. Men still hunted; women still grew corn. Descent was still reckoned by matrilineal clans; no laws were needed but those of custom and no enforcement but social pressure. Few Cherokees spoke English; fewer were Christian. Sacred ties with the land, the universe, and with each other were strained but yet unbroken.

Farming itself was not an issue: the Cherokees had farmed for thousands of years. But this new kind of farming involved deep changes in the relationships between the sexes and with the land. Men's and women's roles, though valued equally, were not interchangeable. Women had a special affinity with maize and earth, both of which were female beings; men helped with heavy work such as clearing and digging, but they didn't tend plants. It was probably more difficult, culturally, for Cherokee men to replace their wives in the fields than it would be for modern Catholics to accept a female pope. To Thomas Jefferson, field work was "unjust drudgery" for women, a consequence of "barbarism."[18] He thought he was liberating Indian women by turning them into housewives.

With the abandonment of Chota and the other Overhill towns, the Nation's center of gravity shifted to the rich red soil of northern Georgia and southern Tennessee, where the Cherokees' neighbors were not whites but Creeks. Two decades of relative peace enabled the population to recover slightly, to about 13,000. The compact, stockaded towns were gone, replaced by straggling farmsteads along valley bottoms. By 1809 many families had begun to follow the white man's way. Cherokees owned more than 1,500 spinning wheels and 500 plows, plus watermills for grinding corn and wheat. In 1796 there had not been one road in the Nation; by 1809 hundreds of miles were traversable by wagon, including the federal turnpike between Augusta, Georgia, and Nashville, Tennessee.

Because Cherokee society was matrilineal, any white man who married a Cherokee became a citizen. Their children were regarded as full members of the Nation, not, as in other parts of the Americas, mestizos, Métis, or half-breeds. Many of the leaders who emerged after 1794 were bilingual offspring of such unions. They were the catalysts of what the whites called progress, but nobody from one world or the other could imagine the strain of belonging to both. The problems were those which arise wherever a stable, collective system and one based on expansion and individual profit collide. It was, for instance, impossible to run a store or plantation profitably without violating the ethic of reciprocity fundamental to most Amerindian societies. To obtain respect in the native world, people had to redistribute wealth; for esteem in the white world, they had to hoard it. To a Cherokee, sufficient was enough; to a white, more was everything. And once wealth *was* accumulated, who should inherit it? The mother's clan? The father's son? Land belonged to the Nation, but who owned the expensive improvements—barns, workshops, mills, and stately houses—that the "progressives" built upon it? There had always been greater and lesser persons in Cherokee society, but now class based on wealth began to oust rank earned by merit.

Those who experience rapid acculturation often pay a cruel price in self-esteem, falling victim to alcohol and violent behavior. One such was James Vann, a half-blood and the wealthiest man in the Cherokee Nation at the dawn of the nineteenth century. Enriched by the federal turnpike near his farm, he owned a tavern, several ferries, more than fifty black slaves, a distillery, and one of the finest brick houses in what is now Georgia. It stands just west of Chatsworth, lovingly restored and run as a tourist attraction by the state that dispossessed his people. On its walls hang portraits of Cherokee chiefs of the period, startling figures in silk shirts and turbans, their earlobes stretched and hung with silver disks like those of the Incas. Vann had four wives—at least two at once—and thought nothing of keeping vast sums of cash under his bed. When sober he was upright and generous, when drunk aggressive and cruel. He encouraged missionaries to settle near his farm so they could educate his children, but had no use for Christianity himself. When Moravian preachers tried a last-minute conversion at what they imagined to be his deathbed, he sprang up, drained a bottle in one gulp, and chased them from the house.[19] Vann was not the sort of man to die shriven and at home. He had too many enemies. One night in 1809, a rifle poked anonymously through a tavern door and blew his brains out.

For Vann's children and other young Cherokees who began attending mission schools, the problems of acculturation were not only ethical but metaphysical. They were told that their legends were ridiculous, that their healers consorted with demons, that their Master of Life was the Father of Lies. They were made to forsake their own Holy Land—every numinous rock, spring, mountain, grove, and ancient mound in the Nation—and acquire a new one, one they would never see, with names like Jordan, Galilee, and Golgotha. Their fathers had violated Cherokee reciprocity; they now had to reject the Cherokee view of the world and who they were.

At about this time, Thomas Jefferson emphasized that Indians who did not wish to blend with whites had one other option. They could remove west of the Mississippi where, he assured them, they could live as they pleased. One of his motives for the Louisiana Purchase had been to acquire a "wilderness" into which the republic could drive any Indians it could not assimilate. In 1808 the United States began to push hard for removal of the entire Cherokee Nation, not shrinking from the use of bribes and threats when promises failed. About 2,000 Cherokees, convinced they would be forced from their homes anyway, did trickle westward, but the idea was anathema to most. True, the West offered a chance to continue traditional ways, but traditionalists, being the least acculturated, were the most reluctant to abandon sacred geography and ancient graves.

These same traditionalists had neither shared in the rewards of change to a Euro-American economy nor wished to. To exploit the earth in these ways was blasphemous: plows ripped her open far more ruthlessly than digging sticks, causing erosion, and the dearth of game showed that the world was dying. In 1811 their anxieties became manifest in a cult sometimes called the Cherokee ghost dance. A shaman named Tsali said that he and his wife, while traveling in the mountains, heard a great noise; the heavens opened, and they saw countless Indians riding to earth from the sky on black horses. The leader was drumming, and he said:

> Do not be afraid. We are your brothers and have been sent by the Great Spirit to speak to you. He is displeased with you for accepting the ways of the white people. You can see for yourselves—your hunting is gone and you are planting the corn of the white men [wheat]. Go and . . . plant Indian corn and gather it according to the ways of your ancestors, and do away with the mills. The Mother of the Nation [the maize goddess] has abandoned you, because the grinding breaks her bones. She wants to come back to you, if you will get the white men out of the country and go back to your former ways.[20]
>
> You yourselves can see that the white people are entirely different beings from us; we are made from red clay; they, out of white sand. You may keep good neighborly relations with them, just see to it that you get back from them your old Beloved Towns.[21]

The messages were similar to those heard in other parts of the Americas in crisis—the Taki Onqoy of Peru, the Aztec prophecies of the 1530s, Waman Puma's appeal. The Creator, Tsali said, had made different peoples in different lands; the presence of whites in America was unnatural and wrong. The Master of Life never intended Indians to live like whites; the ills he sent would vanish only when the Indians returned to their own ways.

Many had doubts about Tsali's teachings. Progressives were openly scornful. Then, in August 1811, a comet blazed in the sky for weeks, and in December earthquakes shook the mountains. Soon after that a doubter known as the Duck fell dead in public. He died, significantly, at Etowah, the large Cherokee town surrounding the great earthen pyramids that Soto may have climbed.

A similar movement took hold among the Cherokees' neighbors and traditional enemies, the Creeks. It was influenced by the Shawnee prophet Tenskwatawa, a brother of Tecumseh. Like the prophet who had inspired Pontiac fifty years before, he spoke of a final war to drive out the invaders.[22] Whites, the Creator had told him, "are not my children, but the children of the evil spirit. They grew from the scum of the great water. . . . They are numerous, but I hate them. They are unjust; they have taken away your lands which were not made for them."[23]

The Creek Nation, which still held most of Alabama and parts of Georgia, had also been following the acculturation path. A serious split had developed between wealthy progressives and militant anti-acculturation Red Sticks, so named for their vermilion war clubs. When the Red Sticks saw the whites embroiled in the War of 1812, they rebelled against the chiefly establishment and began to carry out the prophet's commands: "Kill the cattle . . . destroy the wheels and looms, throw away your ploughs and everything used by the Americans."[24]

When the Red Sticks wiped out a United States garrison at Fort Mims in 1813, the Creek civil war became part of the larger war in North America.

The Cherokee Nation was torn by similar divisions, but although the ghost dance revived certain customs and forced many Cherokees to think hard about where they were going, it did not bring armed conflict with progressive chiefs or the United States. Remembering the Revolutionary War, the Cherokees judged that the Americans would win again. If they proved themselves loyal allies, they reasoned, surely the United States would cease its effort to uproot them from their ancient home.

In 1813 several hundred Cherokees enlisted under the command of a bush lawyer turned general, Andrew Jackson. Old Hickory, as he became known for his intractable personality, was forty-six, gaunt, shrewd, violent, one arm crippled by dueling wounds—the latest from a duel with his own brother. Of Carolina frontier stock, he hated Indians but was more than willing to employ them as high-grade cannon fodder. His Creek War, hailed by Jackson as a victory for civilization, was notorious for the savagery of white troops under his command. They skinned dead Creeks for belt leather; and Davy Crockett, who was there, told how a platoon set fire to a house with "forty-six warriors in it" and afterward ate potatoes from the cellar basted in human fat.[25]

The decisive victory came in March 1814 at Horseshoe Bend, fifty miles northeast of Montgomery, Alabama. In this action, a Cherokee chief named Junaluska saved Andrew Jackson's life. This didn't stop Old Hickory from winking while his Tennessee troops shot livestock and terrorized civilians for amusement on their way home through the Cherokee Nation.[26] And in the vindictive peace treaty by which he dispossessed all the Creeks—friends as well as foes—Jackson took more than 2 million acres in northern Alabama that belonged to the Cherokees.[27] No sentimental obligation would stop him from opening the country for settlers from Tennessee to the Gulf.

The Cherokees were now encircled, and Andrew Jackson would devote the next twenty years to getting rid of them.

> I tremble for my country when I reflect that God is just.
>
> —Thomas Jefferson, 1784

> I never apologize for the United States of America. I don't care what the facts are.
>
> —George Bush, 1988

Among those who fought as officers in Jackson's army were Kahnungdatlageh, He-Who-Walks-on-the-Mountaintop, known in

English as Major Ridge,[28] and Kooweskoowee, or John Ross, who had more Scots blood than Cherokee in his veins but was deeply loyal to the Nation. Unlike the generation before them, these men achieved a synthesis of Cherokee identity and cultural change. Their solution was nationalism, the creation of a Cherokee polity with a written constitution that would enshrine the ancient sense of kinship with the land and transform ethnic ties into a sovereign republic like the one the Americans were building around them.

This new commitment to Cherokee land and unity had crystallized during the first removal crisis in 1808. At a council held that year, Major Ridge thundered against those chiefs who favored selling out, and his words became, in effect, a manifesto for that remarkable experiment known as the Cherokee Renaissance:

> My friends, you have heard the talk of the principal chief [Black Fox]. He points to the region of the setting sun as the future habitation of this people. As a man he has a right to give his opinion; but the opinion he has given as the chief of this nation is not binding; it was not formed in council in the light of day, but was made up in a corner—to drag this people, without their consent, from their own country, to the dark land of the setting sun. I resist it here in my place as a man, as a chief, as a Cherokee, having the right to be consulted in a matter of such importance. What are your heads placed on your bodies for, but to think; and if to think, why should you not be consulted? I scorn this movement of a few men to unsettle the nation and trifle with our attachment to the land of our forefathers! . . .
>
> I, for one, abandon my respect for the will of [such] a chief, and regard only the will of thousands of our people. Do I speak without the response of any heart in this assembly, or do I speak as a free man to men who are free and know their rights? I pause to hear.[29]

Ridge heard deafening applause. Thirty years later, he and his son, John Ridge, having yielded to removal themselves, would be assassinated for treason.

Those thirty years saw the Cherokee Nation remake itself in the image of Western civilization. It built a new capital dubbed New Chota (usually written Echota) in honor of the old Mother Town. It codified its laws, adopted a constitution, and in wealth, literacy, and good order came to surpass the frontier society thirsting for its land. The betrayal of this indigenous nation that fulfilled every condition asked of it by the newcomers still casts a shadow today, for it was a betrayal of white America's own ideals.

The site of New Echota, near Calhoun, Georgia, is today a state museum, an eerily broad and empty field with a few small buildings dotted about. Two or three are original; the others have been reconstructed or brought from somewhere else. Nothing remains of the Cherokee parliament but its trace on the ground. The acres of grass, waterlogged and emerald green when I was there one spring, seem to be hiding something. New Echota did not feel to me like a town, not even a ghost town. It felt like a cemetery from which the graves had been removed. It was hard to believe that anyone had ever lived there. It was even harder to imagine how this industrious but modest place could ever have threatened the United States.

By the mid-1820s more missionaries had entered the Nation; the schooling they offered was in demand, but conversions were few.[30] Several children had been sent away for higher education in the East. Among these were John Ross, John Ridge, and the latter's cousin Kuhleganah Watie, who became famous as Elias Boudinot. They were all exceptionally able. Sam Houston said of Ridge and his son: "These Indians are not inferior to white men. John Ridge was not inferior in point of genius to John Randolph."[31]

Such a view was not shared by Andrew Jackson, war hero, senator, and future president: "They have neither the intelligence, the industry, the moral habits, nor the desire of improvement," he insisted. "Established in the midst of another and superior race . . . they must necessarily yield . . . and ere long disappear."[32]

Despite what Jackson said, it was the Cherokees' very success that doomed them. Indians were not expected to succeed, least of all on the white man's turf. Frontiersmen willing to tolerate the drunken, exploitable Indian whose women and property could be taken, and who could be counted on to die out in a generation or two, were incensed by the prospect of a native nation competing with their own for a place in North America. Georgia's 1802 Compact with the Union had included a clause that Indians in the state's territory would be expelled by the federal government. The Cherokee Nation was not Georgia, but that awkward fact did not hinder the campaign to uproot them. "Build a fire under them," Jackson said to Georgia's congressmen. "When it gets hot enough, they'll move."[33]

Two outstanding developments gave the Cherokees weapons to fight that fire: a script for writing their language and a national newspaper printed at New Echota. Several missionary linguists had tried and failed to write Cherokee in the Roman alphabet. Unknown to them, an illiterate Arkansas Cherokee with a game leg and a fondness for pipe smoking had also been trying to master the "talking leaves" that conferred such advantages on whites. In English he was called George Guess or Guest; his Cherokee name was Sequoyah. He spoke no English and knew nothing of writing except that it existed. His leg, withered since birth, consigned him to an interior, reflective life. He became a fine silversmith—an ancient Cherokee craft—and had a gift for drawing. He was a bookish man in a nation without books. A portrait shows him as slight and fine boned with thoughtful, distant eyes, a turban on his head, and a calumet planted in his mouth like Sherlock Holmes's meerschaum.

About 1809, after an argument with friends on the nature of writing, Sequoyah began from mere curiosity to devise signs for words. It became an obsession. He neglected his farm and his family; he ignored those who laughed at him or feared him as a dabbler in the occult. He kept going when his wife and neighbors threw his early work into the fire. In twelve years he trod much of the ground covered by entire civilizations over centuries. He began with pictographs (a drawing of each object), then tried ideographs (abstract signs), but abandoned these approaches when he realized how many characters would be needed. Once he had decided on a phonetic system, it was a matter of finding one that best matched the structure of Cherokee. At last, around 1821, Sequoyah discovered that by breaking words into syllables, every sound in the language could be represented by eighty-six characters. These were initially of his own design; later he took letters from the Roman and Greek alphabets (regardless of their usual values) to allow easy use by a printing press.

The result, which looks rather like Russian Scrabble, was the first full writing system invented by Native Americans since the Ancient Maya had perfected theirs. It proved very easy to learn; most Cherokees mastered it in days. "Guess's alphabet is spreading through the nation like fire," wrote an astonished missionary.[34] By 1825 the majority of adults were literate, a higher proportion than in most "civilized" nations of that day, including the United States.

Inventions do not catch on unless they fill a need. Sequoyah's system succeeded because it allowed the Old Settlers—those like himself who had already moved West—to write home. At one stroke he broke the monopoly of letters enjoyed by whites and the acculturated ruling class. These leaders and missionaries soon embraced his invention. In 1826 Ridge's brilliant and devout young nephew Elias Boudinot—perhaps the most acculturated of all though he was only one-sixteenth white[35]—went on the lecture circuit, soliciting funds for a press with a Sequoyan font and rallying sympathetic easterners to the Nation's cause.

Then only twenty-two, Boudinot had already acquired the gravity and pursed mouth of a Puritan gentleman. He embodied the Jeffersonian ideal of what the Native American should become: physically Amerindian, mentally European. He preferred a white man's name to his own and married a white woman. (Her neighbors burned the couple in effigy.) But few have spoken so eloquently of the Indian's dilemma—the dilemma of all who cross cultural frontiers. Here is a short excerpt from "An Address to the Whites," which he wrote for his 1826 tour. He seems to accept the superiority of the invaders' religion and culture, yet speaks of white ignorance and white atrocities against his race, even drawing a connection with the conquest of the Aztecs. He wants acculturation but not assimilation, envisioning the Cherokee state as a sovereign ally, not a subordinate, of the United States and as a model for all indigenous Americans.

What is an Indian? Is he not formed of the same materials with yourself? For "of one blood God created all the nations that dwell on the face of the earth." Though it be true that he is ignorant, that he is a heathen, that he is a savage; yet he is no more than all others have been under similar circumstances. Eighteen centuries ago what were the inhabitants of Great Britain?

You here behold an *Indian,* my kindred are *Indians,* and my fathers sleeping in the wilderness grave—they too were *Indians.* But I am not as my fathers were. . . . I have had greater advantages than most of my race; and I now stand before you delegated by my native country to seek her interest . . . and by my public efforts to assist in raising her to an equal standing with other nations of the earth. . . .

It needs not the power of argument on the nature of man, to silence forever the remark that "it is the purpose of the Almighty that the Indians should be exterminated." It needs only that the world should know what we have done in the last few years. . . .

It is not necessary to present to you a detailed account of the various aboriginal tribes, who have been known to you only on the pages of history, and there but obscurely known . . . to place before your eyes the scenes of Muskingum [a notorious massacre by whites][36] and the plains of Mexico, to call up the crimes of the bloody Cortés and his infernal host. . . .

My design is to offer a few disconnected facts relative to the present improved state, and to the ultimate prospects of that particular tribe called Cherokees to which I belong. . . . At this time there are 22,000 cattle; 7,600 horses; 46,000 swine; 2,500 sheep; 762 looms; 2,488 spinning wheels; 172 waggons; 2,943 ploughs . . . 18 schools [in my nation]. . . . Yes, methinks I can view my native country, rising from the ashes of her degradation, wearing her purified and beautiful garments, and taking her seat with the nations of the earth. . . .

There is, in Indian history, something very melancholy. . . . We have seen everywhere the poor aborigines melt away before the white population. I merely speak of the fact, without at all referring to the cause. We have seen, I say, one family after another, one tribe after another, nation after nation, pass away; until only a few solitary creatures are left to tell the sad story of extinction.

Shall this precedent be followed? I ask you, shall red men live, or shall they be swept from the earth? With you and this public at large, the decision chiefly rests. Must they perish? Must they all, like the unfortunate Creeks, (victims of the unchristian policy of certain persons, [i.e., Jackson]) go down in sorrow to their grave?

They hang upon your mercy as to a garment. Will you push them from you, or will you save them? Let humanity answer.[37]

Elias Boudinot got the printing press with special type. In 1828 he began publishing the *Cherokee Phoenix,* a weekly newspaper carrying articles in both languages. An inspired and witty editor, he wrote columns that were copied by sympathetic papers throughout the United States. For the first time since Inca Garcilaso (who had himself written about Cherokees two and a half centuries earlier) an Amerindian voice reached a wide audience through the printed page.

> No State can achieve proper culture, civilization, and progress . . . as long as Indians are permitted to remain.
>
> —Martin van Buren, 1837

> I fought through the Civil War and have seen men shot to pieces and slaughtered by thousands, but the Cherokee removal was the cruelest work I ever knew.
>
> —Georgia volunteer, c. 1870

In the same year that the *Cherokee Phoenix* first appeared, Andrew Jackson replaced John Quincy Adams at the White House. As in more recent times, the cowboys had hijacked the republic. Jackson's United States would be no liberal utopia but a white settler conquest-state bent on expanding at the cost of Indians and blacks. The ideals the Cherokees had adopted with such fervor were no longer held by those in charge.

Emboldened by this, Georgia declared the Cherokee Nation's existence null and void. It became a crime for the Cherokee parliament to meet within state limits, which according to Georgia included New Echota, Etowah, and most other towns. Discovery of gold lent urgency to this aggression. Georgia made it illegal for Cherokees to dig their own minerals, while white prospectors, assisted by the brutal Georgia Guard, invaded their land.[38] The Indians who ended up in white courts over the trouble that ensued were forbidden to testify—even in their own defense—on the grounds that they were not Christian. The Cherokees' federal agent pointed out that Muslims were allowed to testify in British courts, saying, "The religion of the Cherokees is as good as that of Mahomet."[39] But his logic did no good. The real reason was that Indians were not white.

In 1830 Congress narrowly passed Jackson's Indian Removal Bill, which affected all of the Five Civilized Tribes: Cherokee, Creek, Choctaw, Chickasaw, and Seminole. One by one the others gave in and left; the Cherokees did not. John Ross, who had been elected Principal Chief in 1828, saw, as Dragging Canoe had seen sixty years earlier, that "the advancing banners of the same greedy host" would follow the Indian everywhere. Determined to fight removal all the way, he went to Washington and took the Cherokee case to the Supreme Court.

While there, he met delegates from the Iroquois League and gave them a timely warning:

> Brothers: The tradition of our Fathers . . . tells us that this great and extensive Continent was once the sole and exclusive abode of our race. . . . Ever since [the whites came] we have been made to drink of the bitter cup of humiliation; treated like dogs . . . our country and the graves of our Fathers torn from us . . . through a period of upwards of 200 years, rolled back, nation upon nation [until] we find ourselves fugitives, vagrants and strangers in our own country. . . .
>
> The existence of the Indian Nations as distinct Independent Communities within the limits of the United States seems to be drawing to a close. . . . You are aware that our Brethren, the

> Choctaws, Chickasaws and Creeks of the South have severally disposed of their country to the United States and that a portion of our own Tribe have also emigrated West of the Mississippi—but that the largest portion of our Nation still remain firmly upon our ancient domain. . . . Our positon there may be compared to a solitary tree in an open space, where all the forest trees around have been prostrated by a furious tornado.[40]

In two landmark cases—*Cherokee Nation v. Georgia* (1830) and *Worcester v. Georgia* (1832)—Chief Justice John Marshall handed down decisions that remain the foundation of Native American political status in the United States to this day. Indian nations, he said in the first case, were "domestic dependent nations." By that definition (as controversial and ambiguous now as then) he seems to have meant that they were semisovereign protectorates of the federal government. In the second case, the Supreme Court ruled that the writ of Georgia did not run within the Cherokee Nation.

"It is glorious news!" Boudinot wrote home from Washington.

Jackson remarked, "Marshall has rendered his decision; now let him enforce it."[41] From then on it became clear that Old Hickory was prepared to violate the Constitution to get rid of the Indians.

Ross, a stocky man with the dark eyes of a Cherokee and the mutton-chop whiskers of a Scot, was equally stubborn. He would not give up. In this he was supported by at least four fifths of the Cherokees, especially the more traditional with deep religious ties to their homeland. The more acculturated, however, began to think that resistance was useless, that the Nation should accept the inevitable and seek the best possible terms. Even Boudinot and the Ridges came around to the latter view. "We all know," John Ridge wrote to Ross, "that we can't be a Nation here, I hope we shall attempt to establish it somewhere else!"[42]

The leadership split into two factions: Ross's National Party and the pro-removal Treaty Party. Ross sacked Boudinot as editor of the *Phoenix* and found someone else who would continue to thunder against removal. But in 1835, the Georgia Guard seized the printing press.[43] In violation of the Supreme Court ruling, they harassed and arrested hundreds of Cherokee citizens, including the Cherokee chief justice. He, Ross, and other key figures were imprisoned during crucial stages of the final talks.

And so, on December 29, 1835, in the parlor of Elias Boudinot's fine house on the square of the Cherokee capital, the pro-removal faction put their names to the infamous Treaty of New Echota. Boudinot, the Ridges, and several others signed away the last 20,000 square miles of the Cherokee Nation for $5 million and the promise of land in "Indian Territory," now Oklahoma. Some had perhaps been bribed; most believed sincerely that they were doing the best thing for their people. They knew the ancient penalty for ceding Cherokee land without consensus, and many would pay it. "I have signed my death warrant," said the elder Ridge prophetically. Elias Bodinot spoke with his usual eloquence: "We can die but the great Cherokee Nation will be saved. . . . Oh, what is a man worth who will not dare to die for his people?"[44]

In May 1836, the fraudulent treaty came before the United States Senate. John Quincy Adams denounced it as an "eternal disgrace upon the country." Jackson bullied it through: it passed by one vote.

The Cherokees were given two years to get out, years during which they were invaded more than ever by those impatient for the rich carcass of the nation they had built. In June, Major Ridge protested to Jackson:

> The lowest classes of the white people are flogging the Cherokees with cowhides, hickories, and clubs. We are not safe in our houses—our people are assailed by day and night by the rabble. Even justices of the peace and constables are concerned in this business. This barbarous treatment is not confined to men, but the women are stripped also and whipped without law or mercy. . . . We shall carry off nothing but the scars of the lash on our backs.[45]

General John E. Wool, sent to enforce the removal, agreed: "The whole scene since I have been in this country has been nothing but a heartrending one. . . . The white men . . . like vultures, are watching, ready to pounce upon their prey and strip them of everything they have."[46] Wool also confirmed that the Cherokees were "almost universally opposed to the treaty. . . . So determined are they in their opposition that not one . . . would receive either rations or clothing from the United States lest they might compromise themselves."[47]

It is one of history's darkest ironies that a Cherokee had saved Jackson's life in 1814. This man, Junaluska, went to Washington to make a personal appeal. Jackson listened impatiently, then said, "Sir your audience is ended, there is nothing I can do for you."[48] In the best Cherokee tradition, Junaluska kept his temper, but later, when he saw a woman die after being torn from her home, he raged: "Oh my God if I had known . . . I would have killed him that day at the Horseshoe."[49]

In the summer of 1838 the United States army rounded up all 16,000 Cherokees and confined them for months in disease-infested camps. The trek west, begun that autumn, has been known ever since as the Trail of Tears. For the whole winter, the hungry, frostbitten people shuffled at bayonet point across a thousand miles of frozen woods and prairie. By the time it was over, 4,000—one quarter of the Cherokee Nation—had died. Among them was Quatie, the wife of Chief John Ross.

William Wirt, the former attorney general who took the Cherokee case to the Supreme Court, said: "We may gather laurels on the field of battle, and trophies upon the ocean, but they will never hide this foul blot on our escutcheon. *Remember the Cherokee Nation* will be answer enough to the proudest boasts that we can ever make."[50]

TEN

IROQUOIS

Every man of us thought, that by fighting for the King, we should ensure to ourselves and children a good inheritance.

—Thayendanegea (Joseph Brant), c. 1804

When the Treaty of Paris ended the Revolutionary War in 1783, Britain's abrupt withdrawal from North America below the Great Lakes left enormous questions of sovereignty unanswered, or even unasked. The thirteen ex-colonies were mere enclaves on the edge of a continent still controlled largely by its original inhabitants. The United States was just a seed of what it has become, its population little more than one percent of what it is today. The doctrine of Manifest Destiny, the Americans' brand of divine right, had yet to be concocted; few thought that their country would ever expand beyond the Mississippi. Not until 1805 would Lewis and Clark, with a lot of native help, be the first whites to cross from Atlantic to Pacific.

Though much of the continent was unknown to the new Americans, the old Americans understood its geography quite well. The Iroquois' origin legends show that they knew they lived on a broad land mass rising to the Rocky Mountains, then falling to another ocean. They, and many other peoples, called their continent Great Island or Turtle Island. Before the invaders came, they had thought that it was the only island in a vast primordial sea. After 1492, they learned that there were others—Europe, Africa, Asia—each with its own plants, animals, and people. Native Americans saw (and still see) their Great Island as a sacred gift. They loved it and had no desire to leave it. They found it hard to understand why the intruders had not felt the same.

Despite the whites' advantages in technology, numbers, and resistance to disease, their progress by 1783 was modest. They had been living in North America for two centuries and outnumbered the Indians east of the Mississippi by thirty to one, yet they had penetrated no more than a few hundred miles from early beachheads such as Jamestown and Plymouth Rock. If their advance had continued at the same pace for the *next* two centuries, white America would not reach far beyond the Mississippi today.

Neither Indian nor invader could have known how quickly the rules and pace of the game were about to change. Western civilization, primed by the immense transfer of bullion and food crops from the New World, was beginning to industrialize. To an extent that is only now being examined, native America's stolen assets—gold, maize, and potatoes—bankrolled her own destruction. Steamships, railways, and machine guns were only a few decades in the future. These would transform the Old World's ability to overwhelm the New.

Iroquois resistance took place in this context of accelerating change. At first it seemed that a military struggle might still be possible; later it became clear that only a subtle, cultural resistance might save the Six Nations—Mohawk, Oneida, Onondaga, Cayuga, Seneca, and Tuscarora—from annihilation.

Deeply in debt at home and abroad, the triumphant rebels saw native land as a substitute for their worthless paper currencies. Unpaid troops could be rewarded with it, foreign loans perhaps floated on the strength of it. With the Crown gone, the Royal Proclamation of 1763 could be torn up and thrown away. Even before the Revolution, George Washington had confided to a business associate, "I can never look upon that proclamation in any other light (but I say this between ourselves) than as a temporary expedient to quiet the minds of the Indians."[1]

In 1784 the Thirteen Fires, as the Iroquois dubbed the ex-colonies, took advantage of the Six Nations' disarray to force a new treaty at Fort Stanwix. The young republic created the fiction that it had "conquered" the Indians. The negotiators humbled them by discarding the old diplomatic language, especially the terms "brother" and "nation," and "any other form which would revive or seem to confirm their former ideas of independence."[2] They then forced the Six Nations to give up all claims to land and vassals in what are now Ohio, western Pennsylvania, and even the western corner of New York. In return, Congress magnanimously "gave" the Six Nations a few shreds of their own territory, the rest being the price of peace. Even the Iroquois nations that had fought *for* the Americans—the Oneida and Tuscarora—were treated little better.

In the same year, Joseph Brant, the rash and charismatic Mohawk who had broken the back of the Longhouse, led about a thousand Iroquois loyalists north to what is now Canada. The great founding wampum belt of the Confederacy was literally cut in two, as ominous an act as the quartering of Tupa Amaru far to the south only three years before.[3]

In 1785 and 1786, the Americans forced equally obnoxious treaties on what were then called the western Indians: the Shawnees, Delawares, Miamis, and others living in the Ohio country, the Old Northwest. George Washington himself had been a principal speculator in these very lands before the Revolution.[4] Frustration of his shady dealings by the mother country had been one source of his rebel fervor, and he meant to reap his reward. These western nations, which had formerly relied on the Iroquois buffer state, found themselves on the front line of white expansion. In the late 1780s they had to form their own confederacy to confront the Thirteen Fires and the squatters who recognized no law but the gun. Between 1783 and 1790, 1,500 whites and a similar number of Indians died in sporadic fighting throughout the Ohio valleys and woodlands.[5]

The more moderate of the Six Nations' leaders tried to intervene. In 1790, the great Seneca chief Cornplanter went to Philadelphia, then the Union capital, hoping to renegotiate the offending "conquest" treaties.

> You demanded from us a great country as the price of that peace you had offered us—as if our want of strength had destroyed our rights. Our chiefs had felt your power, and were unable to contend against you, and they therefore gave up that country. There were but few chiefs present, and they were compelled to give it up; and it is not the Six Nations only that reproach us for having given up

> that country. The Chippewas, and all the nations which lived on those lands westward, call to us, and ask us, "Brothers of our fathers! Where is the place which you have reserved for us to lie down upon?" What they agreed to has bound our nation; but your anger against us must, by this time, be cooled, and though our strength has not increased, nor your power become less, we ask you to consider calmly, were the terms dictated to us by your commissioners reasonable and just?[6]

George Washington's response was to invade. But in 1790 and again in 1791, the western confederacy under the brilliant command of Little Turtle (Michikinikwa) routed American forces on what is now the border between Indiana and Ohio. On the second occasion, General Arthur St. Clair lost two-thirds of the United States regular army.[7]

In March 1792, a more conciliatory Washington addressed the Iroquois at Philadelphia. This time he observed their ancient protocol.

> Sachems and Warriors of the Five [*sic*] Nations: I assure you that I am desirous that a firm peace should exist, not only between the United States and the Five Nations, but also between the United States and all the nations of this land—and that this peace should be founded upon the principles of justice and humanity, as upon an immovable rock. [And] that you may partake of all the comforts of this earth, which can be derived from civilized life, enriched by the possession of industry, virtue and knowledge. . . .
>
> I am aware that the existing hostilities with some of the western Indians have been ascribed to an unjust possession of their land by the United States. Be assured that this is not the case. We require no lands but those obtained by treaties. . . .
>
> I deliver you this white belt of wampum, which I request you will safely keep.[8]

The reply was given by a Seneca orator and statesman known to the whites as Red Jacket. Born around 1750 at Old Castle on Seneca Lake, he fought against the Americans from 1776 to 1782 but did not distinguish himself in arms. Joseph Brant disliked him and thought him a coward. Red Jacket's gifts were not those of a man of action: he was a thinker and speaker, which is all he claimed to be. Many considered him the finest orator of his place and time, Indian or white. His fame was such that he attracted a full-length biography within a few years of his death in 1830. "If he lacked firmness of nerves," its author wrote, "he nevertheless possessed unbending firmness of purpose, and great moral courage. His intellectual powers were unquestionably of a very high order. He was a statesman of sagacity, and an orator of even surpassing eloquence."[9] Red Jacket's speeches earned him chieftainship and the name Sagoyewatha, He-Keeps-Them-Awake. (His English name came from a wardrobe of scarlet coats given him by the British.) A portrait shows him at about fifty, a lean, stiff man with thin lips and a severe brow. Unlike Brant, he had no white education and spoke little English; he was traditionalist in outlook, unimpressed by white civilization, defending always the right of Indians to be Indian. In his reply to President Washington, he accepts the offer of civilization's "blessings" only if his people may adjust gradually and without duress. But first he extracts a legal reading from the president's softened position, establishing that the Iroquois are not conquered nations.

> The president, in effect, observed to us that we of the Five Nations were our own proprietors—were freemen, and might speak with freedom. This has gladdened our hearts, and removed a weight that was upon them.... This is the source of the joy which we feel. How can two brothers speak freely together, unless they feel that they are upon equal ground? ...
>
> The president further observed to us that by our continuing to walk in the path of peace, and hearkening to his counsel, we might share with you the blessings of civilized life.... You enjoy all the blessings of this life; to you, therefore, we look to make provision that the same may be enjoyed by our children. This wish comes from our heart; but we add that our happiness cannot be great if in the introduction of your ways we are put under too much constraint....

> We, your brothers of the Five Nations, believe that the Great Spirit let this island [America] drop down from above. We also believe in his superintendency over this whole island. It is he who gives peace and prosperity, and he also sends evil. But prosperity has been yours. . . .
>
> The king of England and you Americans strove to advance your happiness by extending your possessions upon this island, which produces so many good things. And while you two great powers were thus contending for those good things . . . the whole island was shaken and violently agitated. Is it strange that the peace of us, the Five Nations, was shaken and overturned?
>
> But let me say no more of the trembling of our island. All is, in a measure, now quieted. Peace is now restored. The peace of us, the Five Nations, is now budding. But there is still some shaking among the original Americans, at the setting sun [the western Indians]; and you the Thirteen Fires, and the king of England, know . . . the cause of this disturbance. . . .
>
> Let us therefore make this observation: That when you Americans and the king made peace [in 1783], he did not mention us, and showed us no compassion, notwithstanding all he said to us, and all we had suffered. This has been the occasion of great sorrow and pain, and great loss to us, the Five Nations. When you and he settled the peace between you . . . he never asked us for a delegation to attend to our interests. Had he done this, a settlement of peace among all the western nations might have been effected. . . .
>
> Brother! Have patience and continue to listen. The president has assured us that *he is* not the cause of the hostilities now existing at the westward. . . . We wish you [in that case] to point out to us of the Five Nations *what you think is the real cause.*[10]

Despite Red Jacket's closing barb—a favorite tactic of his—Washington still insisted on the boundary line "agreed" at Fort Stanwix in 1784. When Red Jacket, Cornplanter, and other Iroquois relayed this news to the western confederacy, it provoked weary anger. "Eldest Brothers. . . . We have been informed the president of the United States thinks himself the greatest man on this island. We had this country long in peace before we saw any person of a white skin; we consider the people of a white skin the younger."[11]

The Iroquois ambassadors went back and told Washington bluntly, "If peace does not take place the fault must arise from your people. . . . Send forward agents who are men of honesty, not proud land jobbers, but men who love and desire peace."[12]

The Americans and the Iroquois met again at Buffalo Creek in June 1794. This Seneca town has become Buffalo, New York, a grim industrial city surrounded by refineries and chemical plants leaking their poisons into the Niagara River. The infamous Love Canal toxic dump is not far from here; the eastern wood bison, for which the place was named, has been extinct for more than a century. Cornplanter again warned Washington:

> Brother: You wish to be a free people in this country, who have come from the other side of the water; and why should not we, whose forefathers have lived and died here, and always had possession of the country?
>
> We, the Six Nations, have determined on the boundary we want established, and it is the warriors who now speak. . . . We want room for our children. It will be hard for them not to have a country to live in after that we are gone. . . .
>
> We now call upon you for an answer, as Congress and their commissioners have oftentimes deceived us, and if these difficulties are not removed, the consequences will be bad.[13]

But the Americans had been arming while they were talking. General ("Mad") Anthony Wayne, a man very different from his predecessor St. Clair, had prepared a well-drilled army of 3,000 men. On August 20, 1794, he routed the western Indians at Fallen Timbers, near what is now Toledo, Ohio, and followed up by burning fields and houses throughout their country.

Before the import of these events was fully apparent, the Six Nations remaining in the United States succeeded in renegotiating the hated

Stanwix treaty. The Americans realized that the contest with Britain was still undecided and that the Iroquois, especially the Seneca at the "western door," were in a position to influence its outcome. With the loss of so much land farther east, Canandaigua, at the north end of the slender lake of that name in the Seneca country, had become the geographical center of the compressed Six Nations. In the fall of 1794, as the maple forest reddened the slopes above the narrow waters, George Washington sent Colonel Timothy Pickering, a commissioner the Indians knew as Connisauti, the Sunny Side of the Hill.[14] Pickering withdrew the offending notion of conquest, restored some territory, and offered an annuity of $4,500 to be spent on "clothing, domestic animals, [and] implements of husbandry." Most significantly, the United States recognized the sovereign jurisdiction of the Iroquois as being equivalent to its own in cases of crime committed by each other's nationals.[15] Worried by the Mohawk presence in Canada, Pickering then wrote to Joseph Brant, hoping the generous terms might lure him back to the United States. "I consider the whole six [nations] as forming one confederate nation. . . . By the terms of the present treaty, the complaints which were the immediate occasion of it have been removed . . . all appeared to be satisfied. . . . To me it seems like a new era."[16]

Brant was not taken in by Pickering's euphoric tone. In his reply he sternly advised a United States withdrawal from the Ohio country and seems to have recovered a healthy cynicism toward both white powers.

> My principle is founded on justice [i.e.] your relinquishing part of your claims in the Indian country. . . .
>
> As to the business of the white nations, I perceive it at present to be a lottery: which will be uppermost cannot be known until drawn. . . .
>
> Our situation is the same, as we will have whites to deal with whose aims are generally similar.[17]

Brant's last sentence turned out to be as prophetic as anything uttered by Chilam Balam or Dragging Canoe. Repeated encroachment on the sovereignty of the Six Nations by both Canada and the United States would lie at the root of many troubles over the next two centuries.

Our religion is not one of paint or feathers; it is a thing of the heart.
—Follower of Handsome Lake, Seneca, c. 1905

Although Canandaigua was a modest diplomatic success for the Six Nations, 1794 saw their population bottom out at a mere 4,000. The following years were years of diaspora and disillusionment. Some migrated west to join nations that still were free. Others moved to the lands Brant had obtained on the Grand River, only forty miles northwest of Buffalo. Soon there were almost as many Iroquois on the British side of the border as below it. After the border became solidified by the War of 1812 (in which many of Brant's people again fought for Britain), the United States made several attempts to deport the remaining Iroquois beyond the Mississippi. But unlike the Cherokees, the Six Nations had not reorganized themselves as modern nation-states; appearing as less of a threat to white America, they escaped the grim resolve of Andrew Jackson's "final solution." The job of removing them was never finished. By 1840, of the major Indian nations who had once peopled the eastern United States, they alone remained.

While governments and speculators had been taking the Indians' land, a third prong of civilization appeared in the form of missionaries. Attempts had been made to Christianize the Iroquois ever since the coming of Jesuits and other French priests, who had lived at Mohawk communities such as Kahnawake since the 1640s. But conversions, fewer and shallower than the fathers liked to think, were in any case confined to the Mohawk Nation. Most Iroquois still practiced the religion of their ancestors.

Protestant missionaries—mainly Lutherans, Methodists, Presbyterians, and the like—washed in with the flood of settlers to upstate New York around the turn of the century. But neither they nor their faith made a good impression on the Iroquois.

In 1805, a preacher from the Evangelical Missionary Society of Massachusetts thought he might succeed where others had failed. With backing from the federal agent, he summoned the weary Seneca chiefs to the old conference ground at Buffalo. "Brothers," he announced patronizingly, "I have not come to get your lands . . . but to enlighten your minds." The chiefs listened with mounting irritation as the young missionary droned on, telling them, "There is but one religion" and "You have never worshipped the Great Spirit in a manner acceptable to him; but have all your lives been in great error and darkness."[18]

In a scene reminiscent of the debate between Franciscans and Aztec priests nearly 300 years before, the formidable Red Jacket rose to reply. His answer is one of the best ever given to Chrisianity's claims. Which mentality, he makes one wonder, is the more primitive: that which believes itself to have a patent on truth or that which pleads for cultural diversity, for tolerance, for mutual respect?

> Brother. . . . Listen to what we say. There was a time when our forefathers owned this great island. Their seats extended from the rising to the setting sun. The Great Spirit had made it for the use of Indians. He had created the buffalo, the deer, and other animals for food. He had made the bear and the beaver. Their skins served us for clothing. He had scattered them over the country, and taught us how to take them. He had caused the earth to produce corn for bread. . . . If we had some disputes about our hunting ground, they were generally settled without the shedding of much blood. But an evil day came upon us. Your forefathers crossed the great water and landed on this island. Their numbers were small. They found friends and not enemies. They told us they had fled from their own country for fear of wicked men, and had come here to enjoy their religion. They asked for a small seat. We took pity on them, granted their request; and they sat down amongst us. We gave them corn and meat; they gave us poison in return.
>
> The white people, Brother, had now found our country. Tidings were carried back, and more came amongst us. Yet we did not fear them. We took them to be friends. They called us brothers. We believed them, and gave them a larger seat. At length their numbers had greatly increased. They wanted more land; they wanted our country. Our eyes were opened, and our minds became uneasy.

Wars took place. Indians were hired to fight against Indians, and many of our people were destroyed. They also brought liquor amongst us. It was strong and powerful, and has slain thousands.

Brother: Our seats were once large and yours were small. You have now become a great people, and we have scarcely a place left to spread our blankets. You have got our country, but are not satisfied; you want to force your religion upon us.

Brother: Continue to listen. You say that you are sent to instruct us how to worship the Great Spirit agreeably to his mind, and, if we do not take hold of the religion which you white people teach, we shall be unhappy hereafter. You say that you are right and we are lost. How do we know this to be true? We . . . only know what you tell us about it. How shall we know when to believe, being so often deceived by the white people?

Brother: You say there is but one way to worship and serve the Great Spirit. If there is but one religion, why do you white people differ so much about it? . . .

Brother: We do not understand these things. We are told that your religion was given to your forefathers, and has been handed down from father to son. We also have a religion, which was given to our forefathers, and has been handed down to us, their children. We worship in that way. It teaches us to be thankful for all the favors we receive; to love each other, and to be united. We never quarrel about religion.

Brother: The Great Spirit has made us all, but he has made a great difference between his white and red children. He has given us different complexions and different customs. . . . Since he has made so great a difference between us in other things, why may we not conclude that he has given us a different religion? . . .

Brother: We do not wish to destroy your religion, or take it from you. We only want to enjoy our own. . . .

Brother: We are told that you have been preaching to the white people in this place. These people are our neighbors. We are acquainted with them. We will wait a little while, and see what effect your preaching has upon them. If we find it does them

> good, makes them honest and less disposed to cheat Indians, we will then consider again of what you have said.[19]

Despite Red Jacket's sardonic closing, there was one group of Christians the Iroquois respected: the Quakers. They had come to America in the face of royal penalties that included the cutting off of ears and the boring of tongues with hot iron. Like the Iroquois, they had no formal temples or priests; they lived frugally and communally; they practiced what they preached. Above all, they had a policy of treating Indians honestly (though William Penn's heirs had not always lived up to it). At the Iroquois' request, Quakers acted as observers during the negotiation of Canandaigua and other treaties. They also helped the Indians adopt Western farming methods.

Like the Cherokees, the Iroquois were under intense pressure to acculturate. Some, such as Brant and Cornplanter, adopted the new ways and set an example. But the ultimate price of that was to become what Indians nowadays call an apple—red on the surface, white inside. Many sought escape from this dilemma in drink. Violence born of despair and alcohol became endemic, as it continues to be on reservations. Women aborted their babies rather than bring them into a ruined world, something that is happening among the Yanomami and other Amazon peoples at this moment. Indians, one missionary wrote of the Seneca, "bear suffering with great fortitude, but at the end of this fortitude is desperation. Suicides are frequent. . . . Their ancient manner of subsistence is broken. . . . If they build they do not know who will inhabit."[20]

The Indians' own religious values had been corroding from the day they began to hunt for foreign exchange instead of sustenance. If there was sin in native belief, this was it, as the Master of Life had warned the Delaware prophet: *Do not sell that which I have placed on the earth as food.* The Iroquois had arrived at that apocalyptic time ripe for supernatural intervention. But instead of a ghost dance, the revelation that took root among them was syncretic. It sought a middle path, a way to reconcile the gods of Europe and America. It was to be so successful that it both subsumed the ancient religion and halted the spread of Christianity to this day.

In June 1799, when the Senecas were getting ready to celebrate the Strawberry Festival, a man at the edge of death began to have visions. Until then, the man's life had mirrored the disintegration of his people. Born about 1735, he had distinguished himself in youth, when the Iroquois were still a power. His decline began when his birthplace on the Genesee River, near the modern town of Avon, New York, was taken by whites and he was forced to move to the Allegany reservation. There he contracted a wasting sickness and became alcoholic. He was "a middle-sized man, slim and unhealthy looking . . . a dissolute person and a miserable victim of the drink," wrote Arthur Parker, the Seneca ethnologist, a century later.[21] For four years the man lay bedridden in his cabin, kept alive by the care of a loving daughter. But he was not without resources: He had been born into a lordly family of the Turtle clan; he was a half-brother of Cornplanter and an uncle of Red Jacket. And the clan mothers had elected him to the sachemship that bore the title Handsome Lake, or Ganeodiyo (the Seneca equivalent of Ontario).

When spring came to Allegany in 1799, Handsome Lake was crippled by grief and paralysis. His niece, Cornplanter's daughter, had died, and he sang the holy songs of the dead not only dolefully but drunkenly. Then, filled with remorse at his sacrilege, he swore never to touch booze again. One day in June he rose from his sickbed, a pathetic specter, "yellow skin and dried bones,"[22] and collapsed in his daughter's arms. No breath passed his lips, his body was cold; it seemed that he was dead. Cornplanter came and began preparing his half-brother's corpse. But he and a nephew both noticed a warm spot near the heart. Then, slowly, breath and pulse returned, and sometime later the dead man opened his eyes. The nephew asked, "My uncle, are you feeling well?" And Handsome Lake answered, "Yes, I believe myself well. Never have I seen such wondrous visions!"[23]

He told how four heavenly messengers had come to him from the Creator with a great teaching that he called Gaiwiio, the Good Message. This he repeated fluently in council and preached throughout the Iroquois League until his death in 1815. The oral text, written down about forty years later, fills more than a hundred printed pages in the version given to Gawasowaneh (Arthur Parker) by Sosondowa (Edward Cornplanter) around 1905. These lines are from Parker's translation:

> Then said the beings, addressing me, "He who created the world at the beginning employed us to come to earth. Our visit now is not the only one we have made. . . .
>
> "Do not allow any one to say that you have had great fortune in being able to rise again. The favor of the four beings is not alone for you, and the Creator is willing to help all mankind. . . .
>
> "We will uncover the evil upon the earth and show how men spoil the laws the Great Ruler has made. . . .
>
> "Four words tell a great story of wrong, and the Creator is sad because of the trouble they bring, so go and tell your people.
>
> "The first word is *One'ga* [alcohol]. It seems that you never have known that this word stands for a great and monstrous evil and has reared a high mound of bones."[24]

The other evil words were "witchcraft," "black magic," and "abortion." Witchcraft and magic may not be pressing concerns today, but in 1800 they stimulated fear, jealousy, and discord, in white as well as Indian communities. The ban on abortion was also timely. Many pre-Columbian peoples had practiced birth control and abortion to keep their numbers in balance with the land. But in 1800, with only 4,000 Iroquois left on earth and women aborting from despair, it had to be stopped. Handsome Lake preached a moral code which, unlike ghost dances that sought to bring the dead back to life, would reverse the decline among the living.[25]

In subsequent visions, the four beings took Handsome Lake on a great shamanic journey to the sky, where they showed him many things illustrating the past and future, good and evil. He met personages—Iroquois and white, living and dead—whose deeds had a bearing on his people's predicament. Among these was George Washington, who had died in 1799. In the vision, the president of the Thirteen Fires confirmed the sovereignty of the Six Nations: "I shall let them live and go back to the places that are theirs, for they are an independent people."[26]

There was even a curious encounter with the Iroquois religion's main competitor.

> It appeared that his hands and feet were torn by iron nails. . . .
>
> Then said the man, "They slew me. . . . So I have gone home to shut the doors of heaven that they may not see me again until the earth passes away. . . .
>
> "Now it is rumored that you [Handsome Lake] are but a talker with spirits. Now it is true that I am a spirit . . . of him who was murdered. Now tell your people that they will become lost when they follow the ways of the white man."[27]

So Christ himself warns against Christianity. Yet Handsome Lake drew from Christianity—especially Quakerism—elements that could strengthen aboriginal culture and reshape it for a changed world. Most important were temperance, nonviolence, and frugality. To enforce these moral precepts, he emphasized good and evil in a more personal way than before: people could now expect to be judged in the afterlife. Red Jacket, speaking to George Washington in 1792, had said that the Great Spirit "who gives peace and prosperity . . . also sends evil," a paradox consistent with the Amerindian view (whether Iroquois or Aztec) of God as the Duality in whom all opposites are reconciled. Handsome Lake approached the problem of evil from a more Judeo-Christian perspective: God became exclusively good, and a devil, known as the Evil One, was set up against him.

Despite his warnings about white influence, Handsome Lake, through his visions, gave divine sanction to secular customs that Iroquois were obliged to adopt.

> Three things that our younger brethren [the Americans] do are right to follow.
>
> Now, the first. The white man works on a tract of cultivated ground and harvests food for his family. . . .
>
> Now, the second thing. It is the way a white man builds a house. . . .
>
> Now the third. The white man keeps horses and cattle . . . there is no evil in this for they are a help to his family.[28]

The Quakers, and President Thomas Jefferson himself, took note of the Seneca prophet's reformation and encouraged it. They saw the Good Message as a step on the road to the true faith and civilized life. What they did not see was that the Gaiwiio was also a revitalization of the old Iroquois religion. Handsome Lake endorsed the ancient ritual calendar, especially the Strawberry, Maple, and Green Corn festivals, the White Dog sacrifice, Thanksgiving, and the sacred Bowl Game. He sang and passed on the holy songs. The Great Law of the Iroquois Confederacy, taught long ago by the Peacemaker on the shore of Onondaga Lake, became in effect an "Old Testament" reinterpreted in the light of a new.

Handsome Lake's reformation offered spiritual rewards similar to those purveyed by missionaries, but did so within the flow of Iroquois culture. By meeting the white man's religion on its own ground, he neutralized it. Above all he assured the Iroquois that they would survive.

When Edward Cornplanter gave Arthur Parker the text of the Gaiwiio a century later, he also recited a fascinating legend entitled "How the White Race Came to America and Why the Gaiwiio Became a Necessity." Not part of the Gaiwiio itself, it belongs to the Iroquois Apocrypha, but like all great legends it is the essence of historical truth: "Now this happened a long time ago and across the great salt sea. . . . There is, so it seems, a world there and soil like ours. There . . . swarmed many people—so many that they crowded upon one another."

In this land, which is of course England, a young holy man, a servant of the queen, reads some ancient books about the life and death of the son of God. He then has a vision. From a window in the palace the young man sees in the river Thames a beautiful island and "he marveled that he had never seen it before." In the trees on the island stands a castle of gold, and he believes that "so beautiful a castle on so beautiful an isle must indeed be the abode of him whom I seek." He knocks at the castle's door and is greeted by "a handsome smiling man," who, he supposes, is the son of God.

> The smiling man in the castle of gold said, "I have wanted a young man such as you. . . . Listen to me and most truly you shall be rich.

> Across the ocean that lies toward the sunset is another world and a great country and a people whom you have never seen. These people are virtuous, they have no unnatural evil habits and they are honest. A great reward is yours if you will help me. Here are five things that men and women enjoy; take them to these people and make them as white men are." . . .
>
> So then the young man took the bundle containing the five things and made the bargain. He left the island and looking back saw that the bridge had disappeared, and before he turned his head the castle had gone, and then as he looked the island itself vanished.
>
> Now then the young man wondered if indeed he had seen his lord. . . . So he opened his bundle of five things and found a flask of rum, a pack of playing cards, a handful of coins, a violin and a decayed leg bone. . . . He thought the things very strange and he wondered if indeed his lord would send such gifts to the people across the water.

Still, feeling he must fulfill his promise, the young man searches for someone to take the bizarre gifts across the ocean—and finds Christopher Columbus.

The man in the golden castle begins to laugh triumphantly and say:

> These cards will make them gamble away their wealth and idle their time; this money will make them dishonest and covetous and they will forget their old laws . . . this rum will turn their minds to foolishness and they will barter their country for baubles; then will this secret poison [disease] eat the life from their blood and crumble their bones.[29]

For the man in the golden castle on the Thames is not the son of God at all, but "Hanisse'ono, the evil one."

The results are such that "even the devil himself lament[ed] that his evil had been so great." Eventually the Creator takes pity on his people, the Indians, "whom he had molded from . . . the earth of this Great

Island." He sends down his four messengers; and after many attempts, they succeed in giving their words of hope and renewal to the prophet Handsome Lake.

When Parker published this legend in his introduction to the Gaiwiio, he thought that the days of the Iroquois religion were few. The young twentieth century, he feared, would soon bury this relic of the pre-Columbian world. Parker traveled to Onondaga, the ancient capital of the Six Nations where the Peacemaker had preached long before Columbus, and where Handsome Lake, who was in a way the Peacemaker's second coming, died of old age soon after delivering his Good Message to the Confederacy Council in 1815.

"It is an odd sight, provoking strange thoughts," the Seneca ethnologist wrote, "to stand at the tomb of the prophet near the Council House and watch each day the hundreds of automobiles that fly by over the state road."[30]

But now that the twentieth century is old and dishonored, the Longhouse religion, as Iroquois often call their faith, is as strong as it has been for generations.

PART THREE

REBIRTH

ELEVEN

AZTEC

> Who has written this play that we are obliged to perform? Some crazy or euphoric executioner? Did history lie when it promised peace and progress?
>
> —Eduardo Galeano, 1982

Rebirth should really have a question mark, because although modern Maya, Iroquois, Cherokees, and Incas are pressing their claims for self-determination with renewed vigor, the forces arrayed against them are no less formidable than in the past. Some of these forces are military and political, others simply the invasive pressures of the modern world, which weigh upon all small nationalities, independent or not.

Another question mark belongs to the Aztecs. Of the five peoples in this book, they are the most difficult to define in the twentieth century. The syncretic character of their resistance—a blending with the conquerors' culture that transformed it from within—is by its very nature elusive and impossible to quantify. Are there still "Aztecs" today? If we define them narrowly as people who speak the Nahuatl language, there are perhaps only one million in a country of 80 million. But since that day in 1790 when the goddess Coatlicue returned to Mexico, modern Mexicans have had something of the ancient Mexica within them. The Aztec rebirth is also a metamorphosis.

In the late eighteenth century, a wave of revolution swept Europe and its colonies: British America in 1776; Peru in 1780; France in 1789; Haiti in 1791. But Mexico saw nothing like Tupa Amaru's bid to restore Inca rule. As Octavio Paz noted, Mexico has always been dominated by its capital; the Spanish viceroy had filled the Aztec Tlatoani's throne. The children of the Mexica rulers had long ago become part of the colonial establishment.[1] Unlike the latter-day Incas, they had no city of their own, remote from that of the invaders, in which to dream and plot, and they felt little of that repugnance which European culture had induced, like a wrongly transplanted organ, in Peru.

Worn down by the haciendas and the mines, the Indians of Mexico needed leaders, but they would not find them among descendants of their ancient kings. Instead, it was creole and mestizo idealists who tapped their deep desire for retribution. In 1810, the year modern Mexicans regard as the beginning of their independence, Miguel Hidalgo, a maverick priest, rang the liberty bells at Querétaro. "Will you free yourselves?" he called out to the crowd, waving the banner of Tonantzin-Guadalupe. "Will you recover the lands stolen three hundred years ago from your forefathers by the hated Spaniards? . . . Long live Our Lady of Guadalupe! Death to bad government! Death to the *gachupines!*"[2]

Padre Hidalgo was a creole, a Spaniard born in Mexico, but he did not shrink from using the Nahuatl pejorative *gachupín* for peninsular Spaniards.[3] His call released centuries of rage. Mobs sacked Querétaro and Guanajuato, and within weeks Hidalgo had an army of 80,000. New Spain then had about 6 million people, of whom more than half were classified as Indians; mestizos and creoles each formed about one-fifth, but peninsular Spaniards—the upper level of the colony's power structure—numbered only one third of one percent.[4] If Hidalgo had attacked Mexico City immediately, he might have taken it. But he hesitated, was captured, and died before a firing squad in 1811.

His place was taken by José María Morelos, another priest. Morelos was mestizo and even more radical. He shouted the names of Moctezuma and Cuauhtémoc and for a while controlled much of their ancient empire. But creole support waned; Mexican whites wanted independence from Spain but not genuine revolution. Victorious Indians, they feared, were unlikely to make the fine distinction between themselves and *peninsulares* when settling the score of oppression. By the end of 1815, Morelos, too, had been shot.

In 1820, Agustín de Iturbide, a colonel in the viceroy's army, stole the independence for conservative creoles simply by switching sides. A year later he took Mexico City and in July 1822 crowned himself Agustín I, Emperor of Mexico. He was an emperor in the Napoleonic mold: a caudillo with extravagant ambitions. His empire lasted seven months. There would be no Agustín II.

A liberal revolt drove Iturbide from Mexico City, Central America broke away, and the United States began its intrigue to lop off Mexico's north. Iturbide had freed New Spain from Old Spain, but freedom for the Indians and mestizos had been betrayed and would not be seriously addressed for ninety years. Iturbide's only legacy was the raw fact of independence and the choice of Mexico, the name of the Aztec city-state, for the reborn nation.

The Liberal leader, General Antonio López de Santa Anna, did not make himself emperor but surpassed in other ways the grotesque figure he overthrew. He embezzled vast sums, insisted on being addressed as Most Serene Highness, and filled the capital with ornate and costly monuments, including a marble shrine for the remains of a leg he had lost in battle.[5]

Most new nations—or old nations newly free—seem fated to civil war until they have defined the style of their polity. In Mexico, as in much of Latin America, the main protagonists were Liberals and Conservatives. Conservatives supported the Catholic church, the creole aristocracy, and the status quo; in other words, they wished to continue the business of New Spain under local management. Liberals tended to be anticlerical, positivist, and republican, with strong ties to freemasonry and a rigid faith in private property. It would be naive to think that Indian interests lay only with Liberals. The deeply religious Indians owned their land in *ejidos*—ethnic communes derived from the pre-Columbian *calpulli*. Although liberalism attracted them, it also posed serious ideological and economic threats.

This dilemma became manifest in the person of one man, the only Indian to lead an American country since precolonial times, Benito Juárez.[6] The Aztec Empire had dominated many nations and ethnic groups who were neither Aztec nor even members of the Nahua language family. Among these were the Yaqui, Tarahumara, Huichol, Maya, Mixtec, and Zapotec, all of which remain distinct cultures today.

Juárez, born in Oaxaca in 1806, was a Zapotec. Long before the Aztec Empire, his nation had built the city of Monte Albán, a magnificent complex of temples and palaces on a terraced mountain overlooking Oaxaca City. After the Spanish conquest the Oaxaca Valley had become the personal fief of Hernán Cortés and his descendants.

Juárez spoke nothing but Zapotec until the age of twelve or thirteen, when he got himself into a seminary and began to study for the priesthood. But he discovered law, and decided he could best serve his people in court. He passed his legal exams in 1831 and sat as a member of Oaxaca's congress. There he promptly introduced a bill to confiscate the Cortés property for the state.[7] He also defended poor villagers in lawsuits against powerful landowners, one of whom was the church. This experience drove Juárez to seek structural change in the Mexican republic. By 1847, the five-foot Zapotec genius with intense obsidian eyes was sitting in the national congress; later the same year he became governor of Oaxaca.

While Santa Anna's regime disintegrated and the Mexican-American War went from bad to worse, Juárez quietly gave Oaxaca frugal, honest, and inspired leadership. Among his achievements was the building of fifty schools—for girls as well as for boys. In 1855, after the flight of Santa Anna, Juárez became minister of justice in the Reform government. One of his first acts abolished military and ecclesiastical immunity from civil courts. Seen as a frontal attack on the church, the Juárez Law raised an outcry from Conservatives and split the government into moderate and radical factions. The latter, led by treasury minister Miguel Lerdo, then passed the famous Lerdo Law abolishing communal property. Though aimed at church estates, it also struck hard at Indian communes.

The Juárez and Lerdo laws were enshrined in the constitution, along with Mexico's first bill of rights. The church fought back with the sacred blackmail of excommunication. In 1858, civil war broke out, and the Liberal government was driven from Mexico City to the port of Veracruz, where Cortés had landed in 1519. Indians fought in large numbers on both sides, some outraged by the Liberal attack on ejido and church, others loyal to the Zapotec leader and his cause.

On January 10, 1861, a triumphant Juárez returned to Mexico City as president. He addressed the crowd from the balcony of the National Palace, on the same ground as the halls of Moctezuma.

> Mexicans! Upon reestablishing the legitimate Government in the ancient capital of this nation, I salute you for the return of peace and the fruits of victory won by your valiant forces. . . .
>
> Throughout the people's terrible struggle against the aristocracy transplanted from Spanish colony to independent Mexico . . . immense sacrifices have hallowed freedom in this nation. Be as great in peace as you have been in war . . . and the republic will be saved. . . .
>
> As for me, in a short time I shall hand over power to the person chosen [in new elections]. . . . Two things will fulfill my wishes: first, the sight of your happiness; and second, to earn from you, so I may hand it down to my children, the title of good citizen.[8]

There is, I think, a resonance between the Zapotec Juárez and the Cherokee Elias Boudinot. Both stood out with brilliance in the non-Indian world. Both thought they knew what was best for all. Boudinot put his faith in Christianity, Juárez in liberalism. Both rose so far and so fast that they lost sight of their own peoples' deepest needs. And both were of such integrity that they underestimated the evil in others.

For most Indians in Mexico, land was far more important than paper rights. The Zapotec president failed to save them from those who, unlike himself, were not good citizens.

> Nations are the creatures of their mythmakers; it is their image of the past that produces an image of present and future.
>
> —Charles Weeks, *The Juárez Myth in Mexico,* 1987

After Juárez won the elections of March 1861, his faith in humanity made him less ruthless with enemies than he needed to be. He pardoned rebel Conservatives and expected to be repaid by mature political debate. Instead they tried to drive him from the palace. Their chance came when Mexico suspended payment on the foreign debt accumulated by war and spendthrift tyrants.

Britain, Spain, and France, not in a mood to be patient with their creditor, formed a joint expeditionary force to occupy Veracruz and siphon off customs duties. At least that was what Britain and Spain had in mind; the French were more ambitious. Napoleon III, a man cut from the same cloth as Iturbide and Santa Anna, thought the grandeur of his name deserved an American empire. He sent troops along the route of Cortés toward the capital, but Juárez's army beat them back at Puebla on May 5, 1862. The decisive action of the day was commanded by a young brigadier who would be heard from again, Porfirio Díaz.

The French returned in strength the following year; after a long siege, Puebla fell. Juárez understood that this town (like its neighbor Cholula, where Cortés committed his first massacre) was the gateway to Mexico. Realizing that he had insufficient troops to hold the capital, he and his government withdrew northward, waging guerrilla war. The rest of the story is well known. Napoleon sat an Austrian archduke, Maximilian of Hapsburg, on the throne of Mexico. Maximilian governed conscientiously but poorly. When the French army left, he was doomed.

In 1867, the Austrian surrendered to the Zapotec. This time Juárez was not magnanimous. Remembering that Maximilian had ordered death for all *Juarista* captives, he ordered the same. On June 19, the last emperor of Mexico fell to a firing squad.

Juárez cut the size of the army, created a rural police force, spent generously on education, and, in short, laid the cornerstones of modern Mexico. But in 1872, a heart attack killed him, making Benito Juárez one of few Mexican leaders to die of natural causes in the nineteenth century. Even so, his last days were hardly peaceful. Porfirio Díaz, hero of Puebla, had run against him in 1871 and taken electoral defeat with bad grace. Supported by the Conservatives and army officers, Díaz staged an unsuccessful revolt.

In 1876, Díaz rebelled again. This time he succeeded, and the cruel third of a century known as the Porfiriate began.

The new dictator had a social Darwinist belief in progress at any cost. He concentrated power in the hands of landowners and industrialists, and let foreign capital hold Mexico in thrall as the price of development. Haciendas expanded rapidly on land seized from native communes. Dispossessed Indians were forced into serfdom on plantations; others became migrant workers in mines and Travenesque mahogany camps. Those who resisted were hunted down for use as convict labor. The proud Yaquis of Sonora were deported en masse to Yucatán and enslaved in chain gangs on henequen estates. Mexico's economy grew, but behind the railways, factories, and glittering fin de siècle buildings lay a hinterland of human misery. Díaz still gave lip service to the indigenous heritage, but his real ideology was *malinchismo,* the desire for anything foreign, a word coined from the name of the mistress of Cortés.

In 1910, aged eighty himself, the dictator celebrated the centenary of Hidalgo's revolt in characteristic style, spending more on the fiesta than the entire education budget for the year. His gala was marred by omens: one side of the Pyramid of the Sun at Teotihuacan, hastily "restored" for the event, collapsed, and a beautiful girl enthroned on a float as the symbol of the republic was found to be dead from exhaustion at the end of the day.

Later that year, Francisco Madero denounced the tyrant; rebel armies with long memories sprang up all over the nation, and in 1911 Díaz fled. But his defeat was only a beginning: the beginning of the true definition of independent Mexico, postponed for a century. The task took more than a decade and consumed 2 million lives, the life of one in every seven Mexicans.[9]

In the story of the Aztecs, the Mexican Revolution was the final battle in a war that had started four centuries ago, the final crucible in which their culture and the invading culture were fused. The Revolution was about many things, but Mexico's Indians—Nahua, Zapotec, Otomí, and the rest—fought to regain lands lost to the Spaniards and the creole landlords. For most of them, the hero was Emiliano Zapata, a Nahuatl-speaking muleteer from the wild hills of Morelos to the south of Mexico City.

A remarkable memoir of these years was dictated in the 1960s by a Nahua woman who lived through them. Doña Luz Jiménez was born at the end of the last century in Momochco Malacatepec (known in Spanish as Milpa Alta), a village on a dry plateau in the lava foothills between the volcanoes Teuhtli and Cuauhtzin, only thirty miles from central Mexico City. Today it is a suburb of the sprawling capital; then it was a rural hamlet speaking a Nahuatl "not so distant in form from that which Cuauhtémoc and Moctezuma spoke,"[10] according to the translator of her narrative. "In those days, unlike now," Luz Jiménez said, "nobody was ashamed of speaking Mexican."[11]

Her parents lived by tapping maguey cacti for *pulque*, the fermented sap, light and fizzy when young, that is the ale of the Mexican highlands. Her father also grew a little corn and beans, and climbed into the cool pine forests on the flanks of the volcanoes to make charcoal and gather wild mushrooms. A bright and ambitious girl, Luz took advantage of the schooling and Procrustean modernization imposed by Porfirio Díaz. She wanted to become a teacher. But in 1911, when she was still in her early teens, an Indian army suddenly appeared in her quiet village.

Their leader was a good-looking young man with steady eyes and a waxed mustache, Emiliano Zapata.

> The first thing we knew of the Revolution was one day when *Tlatihuani*[12] Zapata came. . . . All his men wore white clothes: white shirts, white breeches, and leather sandals. All these men spoke Mexican [Nahuatl], almost in the same way as ourselves. Tlatihuani Zapata also spoke Mexican. . . . Each man had [an icon of] the saint he loved best on his hat to watch over him. . . .
>
> Tlatihuani Zapata stood in front of his men and spoke like this to all the people of Momochco: "Join up with me! I have risen up; I have taken up arms and I bring my fellow countrymen—because we no longer want President[13] Díaz to look after us. We want a much better leader. Rise up with us, because we don't like what the rich pay us. It isn't enough for food or for clothes. I also want all the people to have their own land—so they can plant and reap maize, beans, and other crops. What do you say? Will you join us?"[14]

The people of Momochco were noncommittal. Young Luz Jiménez was pulled both ways: she admired Porfirio Díaz because of the education he had given her; she admired Zapata because he spoke the Nahuatl language and defended the Nahua peasantry, true Mexicans like herself, from the creole landlords and northern caudillos who fought over the National Palace for the next ten years. Momochco was on the battlefront between the men of the city and the men of the hills, and both brought terrible destruction.

> When the Zapatistas came, they came to kill. They killed the rich because they asked for money and they did not give it. Then they took the landlords and killed them off in the bush. . . .
>
> And in those days there began to come to Momochco certain people called Otomís and Zapotecs. The women came with their husbands; the men were with the Zapatistas. . . . When the Zapatistas passed by, different languages were heard. We heard them speaking; they spoke among themselves, but only God Our Lord knew what they were saying. . . .
>
> Then the Zapatistas went into the town of Amilco. They fired many shells from machine guns and thus they destroyed the schools. And when the buildings fell, many federal troops were buried.[15]

Later that year Zapata went to see Madero, the provisional president, in Mexico City. Madero waffled about due process and the fullness of time; Zapata picked up his carbine and pointed to the president's gold fob: if he used his gun to take that, he asked, would Madero have the right to demand it back? Madero answered yes. "Well," said Zapata, "that is exactly what has happened to us. . . . Hacendados have seized the lands of the people by force. My soldiers, the armed peasantry, and all the people expect me to tell you, very respectfully, that they wish the restitution of their lands to proceed immediately."[16] In November 1911, Zapata's *Plan de Ayala* denounced the Madero regime and called for "ejidos [land communes], townsites, and fields."[17]

It was academic: in 1913, a conservative faction backed by the United States overthrew Madero and shot him. Victoriano Huerta followed

Madero; Venustiano Carranza followed Huerta. At the convention of Aguascalientes in 1914, Zapata broke with Carranza. "Independence," shouted the Zapatista delegate, "was not independence for the Indian, but independence for the *criollo*, for the heirs of the conquerors who continue infamously to abuse and cheat the oppressed Indian."[18]

Then came the worst of times in Momochco Malacatepec. In Luz Jiménez's words, especially these passages that speak of death, one hears echoes of the Aztec account of the conquest 400 years before.

> If only you could know what happened when Zapata left us! . . . The following week these men began to arrive [from the north]; some wore earrings, others had a great gold ring in the nose. They spoke Castilian, I think, but we could hardly understand them at all. They spoke with very thick accents. They were the Carranzistas! . . .
>
> They made the Zapatistas flee towards the woods. . . . It seemed like a cloud of smoke. [But] there were no deaths on the Carranza side, nor on the Zapata side. Only the local people died—those who went early to the fields—those were the dead. A *tlachiquero* gathering his maguey sap, someone who had gone to pick herbs, and a wood cutter: those were the people whom death took on the path. . . .
>
> And one day the Carranzistas seized all the men from their houses: the boys of fifteen, those of twelve or thirteen, the old men, the young men, and the strong men; and they killed them all in the precinct of the church. . . .
>
> They killed my father and my uncles. . . . The machine gun gave just one burst. That is how they killed them.
>
> The pigs and the dogs devoured the dead.[19]

Luz Jiménez was among a handful of survivors who fled to the floating gardens of Xochimilco on the edge of Mexico City. Momochco stood empty for years, and when people began to return they found saplings growing in the fields. In March 1919, Zapata wrote an open letter to "Citizen Carranza," whose presidency he did not recognize: "It never occurred to you that the Revolution was fought for the benefit of the great masses. . . . The old landholdings . . . have been taken over by new landlords . . . and the people mocked in their hopes."[20]

One month later, Carranza had Zapata entrapped at a conference and treacherously slain by the guard of honor. "At point blank," recalled an eyewitness, "without giving him time even to draw his pistols, the soldiers who were presenting arms fired two volleys, and our unforgettable General Zapata fell never to rise again."[21]

Soon after Zapata's death, Luz Jiménez concludes her narrative, in elegant Nahuatl couplets evoking the four quarters of her world:

Nican yotlan notlatol	Here end my words
ipan Momochco Malacateticpac,	on Momochco Malacatepec,
altepetl tepetzalan,	the town between the mountains,
Teuhtli ihuan Cuauhtzin,	between Teuhtli and Cuauhtzin;
intzalan Mexico ihuan Tepoztlan.	between Mexico and Tepoztlan.[22]

The land reform for which Zapata fought and died was not seriously addressed until the 1930s, when President Lázaro Cárdenas, who named his own son Cuauhtémoc, rebuilt the ejido system.

While Indians had fought for land, the revolution's intellectuals embraced *indigenismo* (Indianism) to a degree unique in the Americas. Some, like Dr. Atl, took Aztec names; others discussed making Nahuatl the national language; and a visiting D. H. Lawrence wrote a novel in which Quetzalcoatl and Huitzilopochtli made a comeback as Mexico's gods.[23]

The greatest neo-Aztec revival was in art. Painters like Diego Rivera, José Clemente Orozco, and David Siqueiros found that the strong line, bold color, and iconic style of ancient murals and codices could become the visual language of the Revolution.[24]

As a young man, Rivera had tried and failed to kill Díaz with explosives smuggled in his paint box, but it was his great murals, done in the twenties and thirties, that slew the derivative world of the Porfiriate.[25] One walks today into the National Palace, and there is Mexico's history portrayed with astonishing vigor, wit, wonder, and anger on the walls. To see his panorama of Tenochtitlan is to travel in time. But his style is neither archaic nor pastiche. Informed by surrealism, expressionism, and socialist realism, yet never overwhelmed by them, it seems the style that modern Aztecs might be using if the conquest had never occurred.

Among Rivera's Indian faces is the face of Luz Jiménez, who sat for him in these and other works. Her story can represent that of the Aztecs in the twentieth century: a peasant caught up in the revolutionary bloodletting, immortalized in the nation's symbols, committed to the alien ideas of progress implanted by Juárez and Díaz. Her girlhood wish to be a teacher was fulfilled, late in life, in a way she could never have foreseen—teaching Nahuatl to scholars. In so doing, she created one of the last great historical narratives in the Aztec language.

Since the Revolution the indigenous side of Mexico has been diluted by the dominant world culture, especially in its gringo form. Faces on the murals may be copper, but those on television are white. And just when people of Indian descent began to take their place in seats of power and influence, there came new waves of aggressive European migrants fleeing Franco, Hitler, and Stalin. These whites, and the original creoles, still prosper out of all proportion to their numbers. People considered *indígena* have fallen since 1810 from a majority to a minority, not because of widespread intermarriage but because Mexico's modernization has brought Westernization, has made the Indian redefine himself as someone who is part European even if no white blood flows in his veins. Living Aztecs suffer discrimination while dead ones are eulogized.

But one has only to look elsewhere in the Americas to see that Mexico has confronted its history to a degree unequaled by any other nation of the misnamed New World. The national myth may be flawed, but at least it is a Mexican myth, not a European one. In Lima, Peru, a bronze Pizarro stands triumphant beside the national palace; in Mexico, there is not one statue to Hernán Cortés.

For fifty years Mexico has been ruled by the Institutional Revolutionary Party (PRI), a name that might have come from the pen of George Orwell. Though other parties exist, real power is brokered within the PRI, whose presidential candidate always wins. Much depends on the president who, for his single six-year term, wields the powers of a viceroy or a tlatoani. Since the departure of Lázaro Cárdenas in 1940, the party has become more institutional and less revolutionary. Today, as international business interests dictate the political agenda and one tenth of the population enjoys two thirds of the wealth, there are many who say that the PRI is becoming a new Porfiriate.

But the curious PRI monolith has begun to crack. In the 1988 presidential campaign, Cuauhtémoc Cárdenas broke with his father's party and took up the neglected causes of the poor. Many believed he won and was kept from office by fraud. Crowds filled Mexico City, and for the first time in centuries, *Cuauhtémoc! Cuauhtémoc!* was chanted in the central square.

This square, where the Mexica beheld their founding vision in the year Two House, or A.D. 1325, has recently seen more solid reminders of the Aztec past. In an accidental discovery equal to that of Coatlicue or the Calendar Stone, a colossal relief of Coyolxauhqui, sister of Huitzilopochtli, came to light. The find inspired the clearing of entire blocks to reveal the remains of Tenochtitlan's great pyramid and ceremonial precinct. Full study will take decades, but much has already been published by the archaeologist directing the project, Eduardo Matos Moctezuma. As his surname suggests, he is descended from the man who took Cortés by the hand and led him up the temples of Mexico in the autumn of 1519.[26]

To conclude the story of the Aztecs, here are some lines from the *Crónica Mexicáyotl*, written in epic Nahuatl by an earlier descendant of Moctezuma, his grandson Tezozomoc:

> It is told, it is recounted here how the ancients . . . the people of Aztlan, the Mexicans . . . came to [build] the great city of Mexico-Tenochtitlan. . . .
>
> Never shall it be lost, never shall it be forgotten, that which they came to do, that which they recorded in their ink and in their paintings. Their fame, their renown, their remembrance will be kept in the ages to come. . . . We shall always keep it, we who are their children, grandchildren . . . their descendants, of their colour and their blood. And they shall tell it, they shall recount it, they who are not yet living, they who are not yet born: the children of the Mexicans.[27]

TWELVE

MAYA

Thus the whirligig of time brings in his revenges.

—*Twelfth Night*, Act V, Scene 1

When Spain withdrew from Yucatán in the 1820s, its rule had lasted a full cycle of thirteen katuns—one *may*—as foretold in the Maya books of Chilam Balam.[1] But it soon became clear that independence from the Spanish Empire did not mean independence for the Maya. For them, as for all Amerindians, the so-called liberation was merely a white settler takeover, resembling that of Ian Smith's Rhodesia. At first the Indians were nonplussed. But within one katun (twenty years) of the end of Spanish rule, the Yucatec Maya would rise up in the great Caste War, "without question the most successful Indian revolt in New World history."[2]

The small settler elites of independent Yucatán and Guatemala bolstered themselves by making mestizos—those of mixed blood who aspired to Hispanic culture—into honorary whites. The two, known collectively as Ladinos, or Latins, together formed one third of the total population at most, but they had inherited Spain's imperial apparatus: her courts, militia, and jails. With that and the help of foreign interests, they created not true nations but internal colonies that exploited the indigenous majority more ruthlessly than ever. As in North America, imperial legislation that had protected Indians, however feebly, was swept away. Land recognized for centuries as communal Maya property was declared "empty" and seized by the state; it was then sold or given to white entrepreneurs who carved out haciendas and reduced the inhabitants to serfdom. For the Maya there was no redress: they could no longer appeal to Spain, and those who sought justice in Mérida or Guatemala City were judged by their oppressors. It was common practice for such courts to demand title deeds as evidence and then destroy them.

As in Peru, Indian society had been run throughout the colonial period by descendants of pre-Columbian nobility. These leaders, known in Yucatán as *batabs,* were often persons of education and substance: bilingual, literate, able to mediate between two worlds. Other prominent Mayas held local posts in the church hierarchy. Full priesthood was always denied them—a major grievance—but they were allowed to become catechists and scribes. They could read and write Maya in the Roman alphabet, were fluent in Spanish, and knew a bit of Latin. They did not confine their skills to the service of the church: such Mayas copied, enlarged, and kept alive the books of Chilam Balam.

Opportunity came when the Ladinos began fighting among themselves over whether Yucatán should be part of Mexico, as it is today, or an autonomous republic. Greatly outnumbered by Mexican forces, they had no choice but to draft Indians. To do this they relied on the batabs who, like Sir William Johnson's Mohawk chiefs, were given commissions in the army. Many Mayas were glad to enlist, believing that if they fought beside their Ladino countrymen they would earn respect for themselves and their rights. In this they were deceived, but by then they were also armed and trained.

The war between the "castes," or races, broke out at the colonial town of Valladolid, which stands in the old Itzá Maya heartland near the ruined city of Chichén Itzá. Today Valladolid is a tranquil place, its tall limestone church overlooking a plaza full of flowering trees and Maya women in pure white shifts with rich floral embroidery around the neck and hem. For 300 years this had been the center of Spanish control over the eastern half of the peninsula. Their uneasy dominion here brought out the worst in the Spaniards. After independence, Valladolid had remained a tense garrison town staffed by provincial racists who banned Mayas from the streets but made free with Maya girls in bed.

In January 1847, the Indians rioted, killing some eighty whites and sacking their houses. After a Maya noble was shot by firing squad, the riot became a general uprising. It was led by Jacinto Pat, batab of

Tihosuco, "who wrote elegant and eloquent letters, usually in Maya, in a beautiful hand,"[3] and by Cecilio Chi of nearby Ichmul. Not only were the date and place auspicious according to prophecy; international circumstances, for once, favored the Indians. Native independence movements in the New World usually fail because whites have access to weapons and external support, while Indians have not. But in 1847 Mexico and the United States were at war; Yucatán's ports were sealed by a gringo blockade, and immediately to the south lay Belize, or British Honduras, a lair of smugglers and erstwhile pirates who had no qualms about trading Maya loot for Enfield carbines.

As the war spread it became polarized along racial lines. In August the Yucatán parliament stripped Indians of citizenship and formally abolished the Maya aristocracy. Whites poured into Mérida as the Indian army took their haciendas one by one. The city became an upturned hive of refugees and rumor. Panicky whites lynched prominent Mayas, including loyal ones, who fell into their hands. They attacked outlying villages and burned the corn, which to Maya—for whom maize is the Grace of God, the material from which the human body is made—was blasphemy. The rebels considered themselves defenders of the true faith against unbelievers and barbarians, as they made clear in letters they sent to the enemy during many fruitless negotiations:

> We . . . are aware of what the whites are doing to injure us, of how many evils they commit against us, even to our children and harmless women. . . . If the Indians revolt, it is because the whites gave them reason; because the whites say they do not believe in Jesus Christ, because they have burned the cornfields.[4]

> If we are killing you now, you first showed us the way. If the homes and the haciendas of the whites are burning, it is because you first burned the town of Tepich, and all the farms where the poor Indians lived. And the whites ate all their livestock.[5]

> I inform you of the reason why we are fighting: because those Commanders and your Governor gave the order for them to kill

> us . . . old and young, and the youths they seized violently in order to shove them into their houses, which they burned. . . . The *Campechanos* [whites of Campeche, then part of Yucatán] are the ones who burned the Holy Church and the Saints which are in it; they likewise threw down the Holy Oil inside the church; there they defecated, and they stabled their horses in it, heaping the blame on us. . . . I inform you that the cause of the present war is because we have seen the slaughter of those who are of our race.[6]

When white priests tried to use the Indians' own piety to pacify them, batab Francisco Caamal gave this reply:

> I will say only one thing to you and to the venerable saintly priests. Why didn't you remember or take any notice when the Governor began to kill us? Why didn't you show yourselves or come to our aid when the whites were killing so many of us? Why didn't you do anything when a certain Father Herrera . . . put his horses's saddle on a poor Indian, and mounted on him, began to whip him, gashing his belly with his spurs? Why didn't you take pity when that happened? And now you remember, now you know that there's a true God? When they were killing us, didn't you know there was a true God? We were always commending the name of the true God to you, and you never believed . . . but rather, even in the dark of the night, you were killing us on the gallows.[7]

By the summer of 1848, the Mayas had taken most of the peninsula. The whites were bottled up in the two cities, Mérida and Campeche; many began to flee in small boats. It looked as though the prophecies of Chilam Balam were about to be fulfilled: the Spaniards were being driven back into the sea, back the way they had come three centuries before.

But on the eve of victory, the Indian advance disintegrated. Too little is known to say exactly why. Perhaps Ladino forces were able to rally (some supplies from outside managed to get through at this time); perhaps the western Mayas, ancient foes of the Itzá, refused to join the easterners; perhaps the scent of victory caused disputes among the rebel leaders. Many years later, Leandro Poot, son of a Maya commander, gave this explanation, the only one that exists from the Indian side:

> When my father's people took Acanceh they passed a time in feasting, preparing for the taking of Tiho [Mérida]. The day was warm and sultry. All at once the *sh'mataneheeles* [winged ants, harbingers of the first rain] appeared in great clouds to the north, to the south, to the east, and to the west, all over the world. When my father's people saw this they said to themselves and to their brothers, "Ehen! The time has come for us to make our planting, for if we do not we shall have no Grace of God to fill the bellies of our children." . . .
>
> And then when morning came, my father's people said, each to his Batab, "Shickanic"—I am going—and in spite of the supplications and threats of the chiefs, each man rolled up his blanket . . . tightened the thongs of his sandals, and started for his home and his cornfield. . . .
>
> Thus it can be clearly seen that Fate, and not white soldiers, kept my father's people from taking Tiho and working their will upon it.[8]

Historians far removed from the life of a farmer in the parched Yucatán bush have found this unconvincing, but it may well be exactly what happened. Huge acreages of corn had been burned in the war, so remaining stocks must have been desperately low. The rains, which usually come but once, are seldom generous. Even in a normal year, to fail to plant at the right time is to invite disaster. The ordinary soldier thought he could go home, put in his crop, and return later to finish off the whites. He had no knowledge of the international connections the Ladinos would activate as soon as they had a moment's respite, of the arms and mercenaries—including gringos—that would flood into the peninsula the moment the siege was relaxed. The batabs understood such things perfectly, but they could not overrule a man's duty to his family and his god.

The Maya regrouped after planting, but by then they had lost the initiative. The best they could do was fight a rearguard action as the Ladinos pushed them east, back to Chichén Itzá, Tihosuco, and beyond. In 1849, Jacinto Pat and Cecilio Chi were assassinated, and the new leaders saw that their only hope was to make a stand in the trackless forest of what is now Quintana Roo. This eastern third of the peninsula, bordered on the south by Belize, has more rainfall and bigger trees than the west, but its soils are poor. Few ancient Mayas had lived there, and Old World plagues had kept the colonial population sparse. Spain had lost control of the area after English pirates infested its coastal lagoons in the seventeenth century.

By 1850, war, famine, and disease had killed 250,000, half the population of Yucatán. The surviving insurgents—some 40,000 people—were disunited and desperate, more refugees than rebels, driven deeper and deeper into the forest by Ladino patrols. Then a miracle happened.

No rivers run on the limestone floor of Yucatán. Rain falls, seeps into the rock, and flows through endless subterranean caverns—the watery realm of *chac,* the tapir-snouted deity of storms and wells. Here and there, the roof of a cavern breaks through to the surface, creating a sinkhole that descends to a disk of water reflecting the marbled sky and a ring of vinedraped trees. Maya gods had always haunted these *cenotes,* these manholes to the underworld. Cenotes are the earth's eyes, where a person sees clearly, where messages are received, where supernatural journeys are begun.

The fleeing Mayas gathered at such a place in the heart of Quintana Roo. And there a small wooden cross carved on a mahogany tree spoke to them:

On the fifteenth
Of the count
Of October . . .
I began to speak . . .
I reside
In the village . . .
Of Jaguar House. . . .
There have arrived,

The day
And the hour
For me to show you
A sign . . .
Because it has come,
The time
For the uprising of Yucatán
Over the Whites
For once and for all![9]

The Cross offered divine help in the form of tactical and moral instructions. It told the Mayas that they were the chosen people, inspired them in battle, and foretold eventual victory. It rallied them like the heavenly voices heard by Joan of Arc.

In 1858 the Mayas took the fort and town of Bacalar. This did not win them back the whole peninsula, but it solidified the military front into a border between Ladino Yucatán and an independent Maya state. They then transformed their camp beside the cenote into a *noh cah,* a great town, or capital, complete with a vaulted temple, a religious school, a palace for their generals and priest-kings, and a range of barracks for the faithful who guarded the Most Holy One, God Three Persons, the strange deity known to the outside world as the Speaking Cross.

Ladinos scoffed at the new god, thinking it a childish heresy operated by ventriloquism with which the leaders exploited their followers' credulity. It was much more than that. The Maya, like the ancient Greeks, had had speaking oracles before. The cross was not so much the dead Christ's scaffold as a tree of life: the center of ceremonial space, symbol of the four directions, and the sign of water. Even the triune nature of God Three Persons had Maya as well as Christian roots: according to hieroglyphic inscriptions at Palenque, three gods were born there in 2360 B.C. And though the Cross's temple looked much like any Yucatán church, it was called Balam Na, Jaguar House, because the great jungle cat, avatar of the night sun, presided there as he had in the temples of the Classic period.

With guns and de facto recognition from the British at Belize, the state of the Speaking Cross survived for fifty years. But at the turn of the twentieth century, Porfirio Díaz decided to crush it. Many things had changed in those five decades. Above all, Western technology had run far ahead of the muskets and cannon of the Mayas. The Mexican army had machine guns, and as they advanced through the bush they laid a railway, a steel lance aimed at the jaguar's heart.

At the same time, smallpox and influenza swept through Quintana Roo. When General Ignacio Bravo took the Maya capital in 1901, only a few thousand rebels were still alive. But Mayas have a way of refusing to lie down when told they are dead. The Mexican occupation of Santa Cruz Balam Na was even less conclusive than the Spanish victory at Tayasal—the last Maya city to be conquered—in 1697. Survivors faded into the forest and waged guerrilla war on Bravo's railway. When the Revolution came and Díaz fell, the Mayas cut the steel link that chained them to the Mexican republic. Under a general of their own, Francisco May, they regained their autonomy; and the writ of Mexico did not run in central Quintana Roo until the 1930s.

In retrospect, the Caste War was not fought in vain. It was the dress rehearsal for the Mexican Revolution, when the power of the haciendas was broken at last and the Yucatec Maya won much of what their grandfathers had fought for. Today they number about a million, at least half the population of the peninsula. They seem to be achieving that most difficult feat, modernization without loss of cultural identity. Though most are corn farmers, as they have always been, there are Maya teachers, university professors, and politicians. Maya is widely spoken, women wear the embroidered cotton *huipil,* and it is a common sight to see a neat stone house with thatched roof and rounded ends—exactly like those carved more than a thousand years ago on the reliefs at Uxmal—with a truck or a motorbike parked outside.

Descendants of the Caste War Maya in Quintana Roo, who sometimes call themselves the Separate Ones, frown upon what they regard as collaboration with the enemy. Although the eagle and serpent flag of Mexico flutters above their former capital, and though the Balam Na itself has been reconsecrated to the cross of Rome, the cult of the

Speaking Cross still lives in villages throughout the forest. On special days, words from a book of Chilam Balam are still read in public at its principal shrine.

The Cross's followers believe that the Caste War never ended but is merely in a state of truce. They await a final battle when they must triumph over the Mexicans or die in the attempt. Then, according to legend, the ruined city of Chichén Itzá will come alive. Its stone warriors will march; its feathered serpents will writhe hungrily to earth. From its great cenote will emerge the Itzá king who, like Peru's Inkarí, awaits the day of retribution. The king holds a trumpet in his hands, and as each year passes he draws it a fraction closer to his lips. When he sounds the trumpet, the final battle will begin. This may end in Maya victory—or be the war of the end of the world.[10]

> The war that is coming, it will be because of hunger. . . .
> Because there isn't any justice. . . .
> The poor man, nothing is left to him. . . .
> Blood will be shed. . . .
> In all nations. The Third World War.[11]

> The U.S. armed and accompanied an invasion that liquidated by fire and sword a democratically elected government that had the subversive idea of carrying out an agrarian reform.
>
> —Eduardo Galeano, 1982

> In Argentina there are witnesses, there are books, there are films, there is proof. Here in Guatemala there is none of that. Here there are no survivors.
>
> —Edgar D'Jalma Domínguez, Guatemalan colonel, 1985

Although the followers of the Speaking Cross may dream of renewing the war against Mexico, the need for armed struggle has waned in the peninsula. The Revolution slowly transformed Yucatán into a modern and tolerably open society; the worst ghosts of the conquest have been laid. But the same cannot be said of the other half of the Maya world, Guatemala.

In February 1980, a number of Guatemalan Maya leaders gathered at Iximché, capital of the Cakchiquels who fought Pedro de Alvarado in the 1520s. The ruins are quiet and restful now—squat pyramids, flights of steps, and sunken courts set among pine trees on a hilltop. The Indians came to recall the violent days of the conquest and expose what they saw as a renewal of the five-century war between Mayas and Latins. At the end of their meeting they released a document, the Declaration of Iximché.

> We the indigenous peoples of Guatemala declare and denounce before the world more than four centuries of discrimination, denial, repression, exploitation, and massacres committed by the foreign invaders and continued by their . . . descendants to the present day. . . . The suffering of our people has come down through the centuries, since 1524, when there arrived in these lands the assassin and criminal, Pedro de Alvarado.[12]

Things were already bad by February 1980, but much worse was to come. In the next four years the Guatemalan army destroyed, by its own count, 440 villages, most of them Maya. Wholesale terror drove a million Guatemalans—one eighth of the population—from their homes. Much of this escaped the notice of the world, which focused what attention it had for Central America on more easily reported wars in El Salvador and Nicaragua.

Guatemala is five times the size of El Salvador and nearly twice as populous. Half of all Central Americans are Guatemalans, yet their forested, volcano-studded land remains obscure, known vaguely for ancient temples, Indian weaving, and tales of unrest. Although the latest phase of Guatemala's war can be seen as a struggle between right and left, such a simplistic view obscures that it is also a race war.

Guatemala is socially and politically archaic, but its archaism lies not, as Ladino Guatemalans tend to think, in the highly traditional Maya population but in the way naked power is wielded by the ruling race and class.

Guatemala has been called the South Africa of the Americas, but abuse of the Maya majority—about 60 percent of the population—by the Ladino minority has been far more ruthless, more callous, more violent, and more effective than the well-known evils of the Boer republic. Guatemala has no formal system of apartheid because it does not need one. Guatemala has no political prisoners because they are all dead.[13] The Nelson Mandelas and Desmond Tutus of Guatemala are silent in unmarked graves.

The modern assault on Maya land and labor began when Justo Rufino Barrios, a dictator of the Díaz type, came to power in the 1870s. He was a social Darwinist "liberal" committed to the most ruthless forms of modernization, which were to be financed by a miracle cash crop, coffee. The best coffee grows on mountains, and the mountains belonged to Mayas who preferred to raise corn and other things they could eat. So Barrios abolished communal land title, removed millions of acres from Indian ownership, and expanded the national army to silence any objectors. He encouraged white immigrants, notably Germans, to bolster the small elite and be the catalysts of economic growth. He built railways and a secret police force so effective that a British consul described Guatemala as "one of the most cruel despotisms the world has ever seen." Another visitor remarked, "Even drunk men are prudent here."[14] When at last Barrios died, his family absconded with the contents of the treasury and went to live in New York.[15]

His example has been followed with minor variations ever since.

Guatemala is a nation only on paper: a map line drawn around a collection of rival ethnic groups and fiercely antagonistic social classes. Though the main rift is between Indians and Ladinos, neither group is monolithic. The Mayas are subdivided into more than twenty different languages and nationalities; the term "Ladino" includes all non-Indians, from Caribbean blacks to German coffee planters, though most are physically mestizo. Political and religious differences fracture every community and organization: there are rightists and leftists, fundamentalists and Catholics on both sides of the ethnic divide. There are many poor Ladinos and a few—very few—rich Mayas. Levels of repression and unrest vary from one part of the country to another. But when one steps back from all this confusing detail, the picture resolves itself into a human pyramid with a small white elite at the top and the Maya majority at the bottom.

By Third World standards, Guatemala is rich, but its wealth is in so few hands that malnutrition, infant mortality, and life expectancy are the worst in the Western Hemisphere with the sole exception of Haiti.[16] Life expectancy for Ladinos is sixty-one, for Indians forty-five.[17] In 1980, only 27 percent of children under five showed normal physical development; malnutrition has since got worse.[18] Guatemala has never had a successful revolution or property reform. Only twice in its history has it had reasonably fair elections, and the second government to be so elected was overthrown by a CIA-sponsored coup in 1954. Ever since then, the country has been ruled by right-wing military regimes, sometimes (as now) with a facade of "low-intensity democracy."[19]

The 1954 coup crushed the democratic left. The terror that followed tore the heart out of the political center and stunted an entire generation of social, political, and intellectual growth. One hundred thousand people have been killed for political reasons and 38,000 more "disappeared," an average of ten murders a day for more than thirty years.[20] These figures do not include combatants killed in the civil war, nor peasants slain in massacres.

We hear little about this in the news. Too many journalists, priests, human rights investigators, and aid workers are among the dead. When reports do get out, the stories are so horrifying—Indian babies used as footballs, village elders herded into churches and burned alive—that decent, naive people find it difficult to believe them.

If Guatemala is the most tragic country in the Americas, it is also one of the most beautiful. Whenever its chronic war is in remission, tourists come to the misty volcanoes and whitewashed towns, the rain forest and cloud forest, the ruined cities of the ancient Maya, and above all to see the modern Mayas, who are everything a tourist desires in local color. The Mayas are warm, dignified, possessors of intriguing customs, wearers of superb handwoven clothes. They are compliant, having no power to keep intruders from their homes and shrines. "Come to Guatemala, Land of the Maya!" invites the Tourism Department, never dreaming that if Guatemala were truly democratic it would indeed be a Maya land.

Highland Guatemala is ethnically much as it was in the sixteenth century. The old Maya kingdoms are kingless, but they are still there—the Quichés in El Quiché, the Cakchiquels in Sololá, the Mams in Huehuetenango. They speak their languages, worship at the ruins of their ancient cities, and keep the old ritual calendar of Mesoamerica. This maintenance of Maya culture is itself a political act, a defiance of the Ladino state. The rhythms of the calendar anchor the Mayas to their past, to their sense of who they are, and to hope in the midst of despair. If knowledge is power, knowledge of time is perspective. The Mayas know that they have been here much longer than their conquerors; they know that all things pass.

Guatemala's Indians have tried every avenue for change: they have joined national political parties; they have formed their own; they have organized unions and cooperatives. Finally, having seen each generation of leaders tortured and gunned down, some gave up peaceful methods and joined left-wing guerrilla movements originally founded by Ladinos. Seeing Indians as the key to victory, the guerrilla armies recklessly involved rural populations they could neither arm nor protect. The Mayas fought with crude guns of pipe and wood, with deadfall traps like the ones their ancestors had used against Pedro de Alvarado; they hid in the jungles and mountains. The army had helicopters, napalm, and Uzi submachine guns. By 1985 there were 50,000 war widows and 200,000 orphans in a country of 8 million.[21]

In the mid-1980s, after one fourth of the Indians had fled their homes, the army began resettling survivors in so-called model villages. Guarded and fed by the army, allowed out only with restrictions, indoctrinated and forced to take part in "civil patrols" against their own people, the Mayas in these camps are if anything worse off than their ancestors in the Spanish *reducciones* 400 years ago.

Such comparisons with the past are germane. History is not forgotten by either side. At the height of the war, a Quiché shaman announced that Tecun Uman, the Quiché hero who fought Alvarado in 1524, had returned to earth with 2 million warriors "to bring justice to Guatemala."[22] In 1982, a wealthy landowner excused his country's conduct on these grounds: "The massacre of Indians is simply the continuation of the work of the conquest."[23]

> In their carnage the military rulers had passed beyond the ordinary classifications of political philosophy. They had become, in a word, Nazis. . . .
>
> I have never come so close to martial cruelty on such a scale.
>
> —Edward Sheehan, *Agony in the Garden,* 1989

If there is any room for hope at all, it is that Guatemala's atrocities have sown seeds that may become seeds of change. Thousands of Mayas are now in exile, where they see a different world. They have the experience of living in countries where the leaders of exploited ethnic groups are not routinely assassinated. These Mayas have begun to speak: to their kin at home and to the world.

In 1982, a young Quiché woman exiled in Paris dictated a memoir that is one of the most powerful testimonies to have come from any war. Rigoberta Menchú, then barely twenty-three, had known how to speak Spanish for only three years. Her father had given his children a Quiché upbringing at home because he feared the corrosive nature of the education offered by the Ladino state. "Don't aspire to go to school," he said, "because schools take our customs away from us."[24]

Her book, *I, Rigoberta Menchú,* has been published in eleven languages, including English. Unlike the literary creations of sympathetic outsiders, it is the rarely heard voice of the victim in all its candor and authority. She begins with childhood, with her people's customs and beliefs, with what it is to be Quiché: "We are people of maize; we are made from the white and yellow corn."[25]

She then tells of experiences that would have unhinged a lesser person. From an early age, Rigoberta traveled with her family to work on the *fincas,* the agro-export plantations. What happened there was no accident but common practice—Guatemalan mother's milk has been found to have the highest DDT levels in the Western world.[26]

> Two of my brothers died in the *finca*. The first . . . Felipe . . . died when my mother started working. They'd sprayed the coffee with pesticide by plane while we were working, as they usually did, and my brother couldn't stand the fumes and died of intoxication. The second one . . . was Nicolás. He died when I was eight. He was the youngest of all of us, the one my mother used to carry about. . . . When my little brother started crying, crying, crying, my mother didn't know what to do with him because his belly was swollen by malnutrition too. . . . The time came when my mother couldn't spend any more time with him or they'd take her job away from her. . . . He lasted fifteen days. . . .
>
> The *caporal* [overseer] told my mother she could bury my brother in the *finca* but she had to pay a tax to keep him buried there. My mother said: "I have no money at all." He told her: "Yes, and you already owe a lot of money for medicine and other things, so take his body and leave."[27]

When Rigoberta was about fourteen, her best friend María died from being sprayed in a cotton field.

During the 1970s Rigoberta's father, Vicente Menchú, became involved in a dispute with powerful Ladinos over the ownership of some fields he and other villagers had cleared. He spent the family savings on taking the matter to court, but the judges were bribed to rule against him. He was imprisoned twice. Beaten up by thugs who left him for dead, he was never able to walk properly again. During his second jail term, in 1977, he met another Indian who talked about the formation of an agrarian trade union called CUC, the Peasant Unity Committee. When he got out, Vicente Menchú became an organizer for CUC and went underground.

In September 1979, Rigoberta's youngest living brother, a boy of sixteen, was kidnaped. He reappeared a fortnight later, when the army staged a public spectacle at Chajul, in the lovely Ixil country of the northern highlands, to show how it dealt with "communist subversives." Petrocinio Menchú had had stones forced into his eye sockets, his sex organs had been mutilated, and strips of skin flayed from his face. But he was still alive.

> The lorry with the tortured came in. They started to take them out one by one. . . . My mother went closer to the lorry to see if she could recognize her son. Each of the tortured had different wounds on the face. I mean, their faces all looked different. But my mother recognized her son, my little brother, among them. . . . [He] was very badly tortured, he could hardly stand up. All the tortured had no nails and they had cut off part of the soles of their feet. They were barefoot. They forced them to walk and put them in a line. They fell down at once. They picked them up again. There was a squadron of soldiers there ready to do exactly what the officer ordered. And the officer carried on with his rigmarole, saying that we had to be satisfied with our lands, we had to be satisfied with eating bread and chile, but we mustn't let ourselves be led astray by communist ideas. . . . He started off with the Soviet Union, Cuba, Nicaragua; he said that the same communists from the Soviet Union had moved on to Cuba and then Nicaragua and that now they were in Guatemala. And that those Cubans would die a death like that of these tortured people. Every time he paused in his speech, they forced the tortured up with kicks and blows from their weapons.
>
> No-one could leave the meeting. Everyone was weeping. . . . The captain devoted himself to explaining each of the different tortures. This is perforation with needles, he'd say, this is a wire burn. . . . And the woman *campañera* [comrade, workmate], of course I recognized her; she was from a village near ours. They had shaved her private parts. The nipple of one of her breasts was missing and her other breast was cut off. . . . She had no ears. All of them were missing part of the tongue or had their tongues split apart. . . .
>
> The officer called to the worst of his criminals—the *Kaibiles* [counterinsurgency commandos], who wear different clothes from other soldiers. They're the ones with the most training, the

> most power. . . . They lined up the tortured and poured petrol on them; and then the soldiers set fire to each one. . . . They roared with laughter and cried, "Long live the Fatherland! Long live Guatemala! Long live our President! Long live the army!"[28]

It is difficult for anyone who does not know Guatemala to read such a story without wondering whether such horrors really happened. The evidence is overwhelming that they did. Reports gathered independently from refugees, priests, and diplomats have confirmed the reality of this massacre and many others like it.

Four months later Vicente Menchú, other Mayas from northern Quiché, and several Ladino supporters occupied the Spanish embassy in Guatemala City. They thought it might be possible to draw international attention to what they described as "a long history of kidnappings, torture, assassinations, theft, rapes . . . and the massacre at Chajul."[29] The occupation was peaceful; the ambassador asked the authorities not to intervene.

Hundreds of police surrounded the building and began chopping through the doors with axes. Shots were fired, a bomb was thrown, and the embassy caught fire. Of forty-one people inside, only the ambassador and a Maya (not Menchú) escaped. The next day the Maya was dragged from his hospital bed and murdered. His body turned up at the university campus, a favorite death squad dumping ground. Spain broke off diplomatic relations with Guatemala; no one was ever brought to trial.

Seven weeks later, Rigoberta Menchú's mother was kidnaped, raped, and tortured; she died where she was dumped, in the hills near their hometown. This left only three—all girls—from a family of nine.[30] One ran away to the guerrillas at the age of eight. Rigoberta became involved with a radical Catholic organization named after her father but soon realized that she had to flee the country and take her story to the world. She has been doing so ever since.

Rigoberta Menchú came to Canada in the spring of 1990. Her schedule included a two-hour talk each evening, meetings with school and church groups every day, and a visit to the Ojibway Indians of Manitoulin Island. She gave me an interview just before she was due to speak in Toronto, the first free time she had had that day. I was intimidated by the magnitude of her suffering, but her poise and warmth put me at ease immediately. Like most Mayas she is small—even in heels, she did not reach my chin. She was wearing the dress of a highland woman: a wraparound ankle-length skirt of indigo homespun, a brocade *huipil* (blouse), her hair plaited and coiled about her head. But her clothes were not the costume of any one village or group, as they would have been at home; she wore a mixture of regional styles and tallish box heels, as if to imply that she identified with all who had suffered the Guatemalan terror, be they Quiché, Ladino, or foreign. I knew her face from photographs: a calm, broad face; sadness and resolution in wide-set eyes that could no longer be surprised by anything.

I mentioned the subject of this book and asked if she had any comment on the quincentenary celebrations of Columbus's "discovery." It turned out that she had been involved in several conferences on this issue. "Back in 1982, I was at the first meeting, when the United Nations working group on the rights of indigenous peoples was formed. Now we're trying to get the UN to make 1992 the year of the declaration of indigenous peoples' rights." She smiled. "I'm practically a veteran at the UN."

Whenever she stopped speaking, tiredness seeped into those eyes, but she spoke with few pauses, in the plain, clear Spanish I knew from her book. She anticipated most of my questions.

> They [various countries] are trying to represent the quincentenary as if it were the "encounter" of two worlds, of two cultures, as if they were commemorating the beginning of what they consider progress and development, and of Latin American history.
>
> [But] the invasion was not just something that happened in the past; it is a continuing process. We would like a proper focus given to the present events. I'm referring especially to the great violations with which our peoples live—in Guatemala more than fifty thousand widows, of whom eighty percent are Indian, mothers of five or six children, battered by war, torn from their homes—these are realities that cannot remain outside any treatment of the quincentenary.

We think that for the first time, at least, we Indians will have an opportunity to express ourselves. Throughout the five hundred years there have been valuable studies, analyses, collections of data, but I'm sure that Indians have been able to speak for themselves only a few times. And each time we have tried to speak, it came as a surprise for many people of the outside world, because it was as if we Indians should not do so, or could not do so. So discrimination is very strong in our countries—and not only in Guatemala. But we Indians have resisted throughout these five centuries because we are the ancient owners of this continent.

They have robbed us of our lands, they have stripped us of a great part of our whole view of life and of the universe. Indians never regarded the natural world as if it were separate from their own lives. The mother earth is an economic resource—the basis of economic survival—but she is also the source of culture, she is our historical memory, she is our roots, she is the only reason that the Maya heritage still exists today. And in our struggle, the most important factor, the one that has generated the most conflict, is the problem of the land—the unfair distribution of land, and its abuse by scattering all kinds of toxic substances. It is the Indians' historical right to possess a part of this continent. The great majority of us live on the land, and by the land. It's the same in the case of Bolivia, in Ecuador, in Brazil, especially with the destruction of the Amazon.

I think we have begun moving towards a new conception of development, a different kind of development. [Until now] development has been part of the mentality and the interests of minority groups who have enriched themselves upon our territory—in Guatemala's case, two percent of the total population hold sixty-five percent of the most fertile lands. Through control of the agro-export business, and of the nation's wealth, they have enriched themselves and have set up, very much at the elite level, their own idea of "democracy." But what does this kind of democracy mean for us? Is it democracy to live in the worst kind of housing? To receive a wage that barely allows you to starve, that is virtual slavery on our own lands? And so many dead, so many murders, so much destruction, so much damage to our culture. So many times we have been forced to lose or put at risk many of those values we have kept for five hundred years. In short, the quincentenary has to focus on the great wounds on our continent.

By seeking true democracy, true development, and making sure that we [native and invader] at least begin to coexist, we can start to create conditions that will allow a genuine encounter of two worlds, of two civilizations, in the future.

What concerns us is the Indian of today and of tomorrow. Why should we merely survive? We need to develop our ancient culture and offer it as a contribution to the human race. I have been several times to see the Hopi, the Navajo, and the Sioux in the United States, and just now I've met Indian colleagues from here. Truly we have a lot in common in our situations, but above all in our world views, in our values, which in many of these countries have suffered so much destruction yet still endure, still persist. I think there are many things we Indians must learn from each other. For example, when the Guatemalan refugees—the great majority Indian—fled to Mexico, they received hospitality, cooperation, solidarity from their Indian brothers there. The same would happen anywhere else on the continent, and not only among Indians. There are many who understand the language of dictatorships, of repression, of disappearances, of assassinations, of evictions.

In Guatemala there also exists a veritable invasion from fundamentalist sects—evangelicals closely tied to the American right. They have begun to invade our peoples, and they are in effect trying to substitute the "low-intensity war" or "anti-communist war," as it was called, with a manipulation of religious faith. They are directly attacking the roots of the Maya.

We are tired of discrimination. In Guatemala we indigenous people are sixty-five percent of the total population; if we exist it isn't because we have been wanted, but because we have known how to hold on to things, because we have known how to form our own organizations, to build that future which we so desire.

And it has cost us dearly—so many dead—but in spite of it all we have an immense future. It is our hope that the conflict will end on the basis of justice, on the basis of equality, on the basis of significant change in the structures that have until now dominated us and imposed the conditions in which we live.

The celebration of Columbus is for us an insult. I think nobody on earth is so devoid of patriotism, of nationalism, of identity, that he would celebrate an invasion. Our peoples have struggled, through sacrifice, through misery, for all these five hundred years. Who would celebrate their own colonization?

Our struggle will not begin in 1992 and neither will it end in 1992.[31]

THIRTEEN

INCA

> It is, then, quite clear that what concerns us most about Inca civilization is not what has died but what remains.
>
> —José Carlos Mariátegui, c. 1928

> It is not the white man's civilization, nor his alphabet, that lifts the soul of the Indian. It is myth [and] revolution.
>
> —Luis E. Valcárcel, 1927

The rebellion of Tupa Amaru II in the 1780s was the first great tremor in the quake that shook the Spanish Empire apart only forty years later, but it was also the last time the Incas could mount an effective bid to recover their ancient domain. By killing Tupa Amaru, purging the latter-day Inca nobility, and suppressing Andean culture itself, the Spaniards prepared Peru for takeover by the small but powerful clique of local whites. The Incas had made their move too soon; when Spain pulled out of South America, the indigenous nation that might otherwise have regained its autonomy was headless.

Some countries win their independence; others have independence thrust upon them. Three outsiders drove Spain from Peru in the 1820s: an Argentine, José de San Martín; and two Venezuelans, Simón Bolívar and Antonio José de Sucre. Only San Martín gave any recognition to the Indian nationality, acknowledging Quechua as an official language and confirming the legal standing of the *ayllus,* the Indian communes that had been the building blocks of every Andean state since the empire of the Incas and before. These provisions were promptly overturned by Simón Bolívar, whose "liberalism," derived from Rousseau and Adam Smith, had no room for Incas. The new masters of the Peruvian republic thought that the Indians had been destroyed as a people and remade as a class of serfs.

The petty creole states that took charge of the old territory of the Tawantinsuyu—Ecuador, Peru, Bolivia, and Chile—fought with one another and their citizens throughout the nineteenth century. To pay for their ambitions, armies, and disorderly parliaments, they reimposed Indian tribute, stole Indian land, and sold their natural resources to the gringos as fast as they could.

Perhaps the saddest example is guano, a millennial crust of seabird droppings on arid islets off the Peruvian coast. The Incas had wisely mined this rich fertilizer at a rate matching its deposition. Even so, llama trains had packed thousands of tons up into the mountains each year. Spread on irrigated terraces, guano shortened the growing season of maize, giving yields that fed the empire.

Not long after Peru's independence, modern agronomy "discovered" the scientific use of fertilizer. Peru could have used this knowledge to redevelop its own agriculture and provide for its people as the Incas had. But Peru did no such thing. Instead, highland Indians, Chinese coolies, and kidnaped Polynesians were brought to the islands, chained together, and forced to dig until they dropped. Of 720 taken from Easter Island in 1863, 620 died. The guano greened distant fields in Europe and North America; it was exhausted in decades. The money it brought lasted no longer. Large sums found their way to foreign bank accounts, much went on grandiose architecture and unneeded railways, and most was squandered on an arms race that ended in the War of the Pacific (1879–1883), when Chile conquered Peru. Of the mountains of guano, there remained only a mountain of debt.

Latin America might have learned something about what was later called dependency theory. But guano was merely followed by nitrates, tin, rubber, and the rest. The "First World" of the day had sold the "Third World" insidious dreams of progress. The Incas, free of that Western myth, had planned for eternity.

After Peru lost the Pacific war, the criollo elite tried to pay off its national debt by renewing its assault on Indian property. But the Pacific war also caused the creoles to reexamine themselves and their nation. Many believed that Peru's backwardness was the fault of the Indians, whom they saw as "inherently inferior creatures doomed to be trampled under foot in the march of progress."[1] They encouraged "superior races" to emigrate from Europe and tried to destroy whatever remained of Andean culture—ideas that justified the ruthless expansion of the haciendas. But Peru's elite also had another side. Some intellectuals noted that the few successes against Chile had been won by Indian troops, and they knew that Indian Peru had been an imperial power. Those who traveled to the mountains in the spirit of Victorian inquiry saw the remains of the Tawantinsuyu and saw that it had outshone everything that followed it. *Indigenismo,* Indianism, was born.

Indigenista ideas profoundly influenced Peru's two outstanding political thinkers of the early twentieth century, the charismatic creole Haya de la Torre, founder of the populist Alianza Popular Revolucionaria Americana (APRA), and José Carlos Mariátegui, a lame mestizo with a schoolboy face who developed a distinctly Peruvian brand of Marxism. Neither of them was Indian, spoke Quechua, or had any firsthand knowledge of Andean culture, but both saw a kind of socialism in the ayllu and the Inca state and believed a new Peru could be built on such principles. The Andean utopia, popularized 300 years in the past by Inca Garcilaso, had new progeny.

Although a similar rediscovery of the pre-Columbian heritage had wrought a national transformation in Mexico, this did not happen in Peru. The landed oligarchy managed to maintain its privileges, suppress or emasculate political opposition, and reinforce its ties to foreign capital. By electoral fraud and military coupe, Haya's APRA was kept from the Pizarro Palace, whose very name was offensive to indigenous Peru.

If indigenismo remained a dream as a political movement, as a cultural force it was considerable, especially in the highlands. Andean mestizos, caught between worlds, found new meaning in the Indian heritage they had been taught to despise. In Cusco, La Paz, and other mountain towns, they began writing poetry, songs, and historical plays in Quechua. In 1889, Clorinda Matto de Turner, a Cusco woman married to an Englishman, launched the indigenista novel with her *Aves sin Nido (Birds with No Nest)*. In the 1930s, Luis E. Valcárcel, a philosopher and advocate of violent revolution, unearthed Cusco's ruins and revived *Inti Raymi*, the Inca Feast of the Sun.

The movement was sometimes romantic, naive, and inauthentic, but it prepared the ground for José María Arguedas, a writer born in 1911 whose work is widely regarded as indigenismo's highest literary expression, and not only in Peru. Unlike the others, Arguedas knew the native world from inside. The first language he learned was Quechua; the first music he heard was the stately flute and harp of the Andes. This would be unremarkable were he an Indian himself, but he was not. The son of a provincial judge in the southern Andes, Arguedas had Mediterranean features. Such children are usually given first-class treatment in middle-class Peru, but José María was abandoned at the age of three when his mother died.

For several years a foster mother raised him in Andahuaylas, a high temperate valley of cornfields and eucalyptus trees crimped by the frigid punas between Cusco and Ayacucho. A Lucana Indian who spoke only Quechua, she was José María's real parent; with her, the three-year-old white boy grew to be an Indian in a white skin. Later, when his exceptional gifts became apparent, a grandmother helped him get a formal education in return for work on her farm. From these beginnings emerged an intense young man with wiry hair, a puckered brow, and a severe toothbrush mustache that failed to hide his vulnerability. He studied in Lima and returned to the mountains as a schoolteacher; there he became a novelist, poet, musician, and ethnographer. His masterpiece is *Los Rios Profundos,* a novel of childhood published in 1958. Like much of his work, it explores the divide between the two Perus, Inca and Spanish, mountains and coast. The divide ran right through the middle of his being. It was this that gave him his insight, and it was this that drove him to suicide in 1969.

With his sensitivity, his melancholy, and his feet in two worlds, Arguedas was modern Peru's successor to Felipe Waman Puma, the writer and artist who had chronicled the wreckage of the Tawantinsuyu in his extraordinary appeal to the Spanish king. Like Waman Puma,

Arguedas wanted the outside world to know what had happened in Peru. Both men sought a way to heal the gash of conquest. Waman Puma, writing circa 1600, feared that the wound might soon prove fatal; Arguedas, writing in the 1950s, saw that Peru had not been killed but crippled. Both proposed essentially the same solution: the return of the Inca. For Waman Puma that meant self-rule under an Indian king, for Arguedas, restoration of the Inca heritage to a place of honor and influence in a new Peru, bilingual and bicultural, as he was himself.

During his years as a teacher in Sicuani and Puquio (the former near Tupa Amaru II's town of Tinta, the latter not far from Waman Puma's old home), Arguedas spent much of his time in windowless adobe huts, drinking maize beer warmed over a fire of twigs or llama dung, listening to the music and stories of the Indians. He asked them what they knew about the Incas, and their answers astonished him: Arguedas was the first ethnographer to be told the cycle of Inkarí legend, which revealed that the Inca, in a way, still lives.

When the Spaniards killed Tupa Amaru II, he enriched with a new sacrifice the mythic figure of the once and future king. Yet again, the sun darkened at noon and the Inca king retired to the underworld to restore his body and await the day of his return, for Andean time is revolutionary in the fullest sense: the past is not gone forever but merely hidden, awaiting the next *pachakuti*, the overturning of worlds, when eras will change place and the Indians will defeat the Spaniards.

In the myths Arguedas collected, the Inca messiah has two functions. He is the rectifier of the conquest, the avenger of Atawallpa and the Tupa Amarus. He is also a much older, pre-Columbian culture hero—the *first* Inca, "the original model of all things,"[2] the shaper and organizer of the world. In the following version, told by Mateo Garriaso of Puquio, Inkarí appears in both these roles.

> Inkarí rounded up the stones with a whip and commanded them. He drove them to the heights, and then he founded a city. . . .
>
> Inkarí enclosed the wind [and] tethered Father Sun. Thus Inkarí lengthened time; he made the day long, so that he could accomplish everything he had to do.

> After he had tamed the wind, he threw a golden staff from the summit of Great Osqonta mountain, saying, "May this establish Cusco." The staff . . . kept moving inland . . . until it reached the place where Cusco stands. We of today do not know how far that was. Atawallpa and the ancient ones, they knew.
>
> The king of the Spaniards seized Inkarí . . . and kept him prisoner somewhere. It is said that only Inkarí's head still exists. But from the head he is growing, growing down towards his feet. And when everything is complete, Inkarí will return.[3]

In another version from Puquio, Inkarí creates the *wamanis,* the mountain deities who watch over every Andean community and dispense the gift of fertility. They are identical with many of the great pre-Conquest *wak'as,* the tutelar gods invoked by Manku Inka and the Taki Onqoy cult of the 1560s.

> The wamanis belong to us, they are beings created by our ancient lord, Inkarí. . . .
>
> Every mountain has its wamani. The wamani gives pasture to our animals; and for us he opens his veins, the mountain streams. . . . And we receive this water from our fathers, the wamanis, because this is what our god has ordained. Our Inkarí created everything. . . .
>
> They say that nowadays he is in Cusco. . . . And they say that his hair is growing, and his body is growing downwards from his head. When he is made whole again, the final judgement will occur. . . .
>
> And so the birds down on the coast are singing, *Qosqota riy,* "Go to Cusco," *Qosqopi riy,* "In Cusco is the king."[4]

Andeans make little distinction between the Spaniards who killed Inkarí, and the "Spaniards" or "gringos" who control modern Peru. Although Peru has had some genuine reform in recent years, the small white elite—perhaps 5 percent of the population—still enjoys most of the wealth and power. Roughly half the people are mestizo, a generally urban middle class that aspires to the affluence displayed by the creoles.

The other half of the country remains predominantly Inca in language and values.

These categories are cultural as well as genetic: some "Indians" have white blood; many "mestizos" have not; many "white" families have Indian ancestors, among them Inca royalty. Nevertheless, the rich are paler than the poor, and their links are with the world beyond Peru. Racial allegiance is defined by where a person is from, what he wears, how he sees himself, and most of all by what language he speaks. The highlands are predominantly indigenous, the coast mestizo and white. By far the largest native language is Quechua, which has about 12 million speakers all told, most of them within modern Peru; Aymara, a survival of the pre-Inca Tiawanaku civilization, is common around Lake Titicaca. Dozens of smaller languages are spoken in the Amazon.

According to white Peru's national myth, these ethnic differences do not exist, or if they do they shouldn't. Ever since Areche suppressed the last Inca nobles, denial of ethnic diversity has been a tool of domination. It works like this: since Indians are by definition poor and ignorant, any who achieve wealth or education can no longer *be* Indians; instead of becoming effective leaders of their own people, they are co-opted by the values and aspirations of the white/mestizo nation. Arguedas wrote in 1965, "When people speak of 'integration' in Peru, they invariably mean acculturation . . . to Western culture; in the same way, when they speak of literacy they think of nothing but *castellanización*."[5] That last word, also much used in Guatemala, is revealing: on one level "Castilianize" means to teach Spanish; but it also means to transform someone who is not a Spaniard into a Spaniard. It is the equivalent of "Anglicize"—by no means merely a language lesson.

In 1969 the word *indio* was officially expunged and replaced by *campesino* (peasant). There were to be no Indians, mestizos, and whites anymore, only Peruvians. But when creole politicos took this message to the highlands, the Indians were not taken in. "You are not Peruvians," one replied. "You are Spaniards . . . the kindred of Pizarro. I am . . . kin of Inkarí."[6]

The following Inkarí story was told in the 1970s by Ignacio Wamani, a young Quechua speaker who migrated from Huancavelica, more than 12,000 feet up in the Andes, to a Lima slum. It shows the social order of the past as the reverse of the present. The "gringos" (which in Peru includes local whites) are subject to the Inca; they suffer privations like today's Indians. Inkarí's godly powers are focused here on control of water. In a literal sense, this recalls the Inca irrigation systems. Symbolically, the "baptism" of the water (the imposition of Christianity) makes it leave the mountains for the coast, where power now resides.

> There used to be gringos who . . . were slaves of Inkarí, and they worked without rest under his orders. But Inkarí was a good man. They say he governed the whole world: Huancayo, Cusco, the whole earth. And they say he built works so the water would stay on the heights.
>
> In those days, because he did not wish it, nothing was baptized, nobody was baptized. The people didn't live in valley towns but up high in stone houses, to which the water came by the works of Inkarí.
>
> Inkarí built Cusco . . . and there he lived, in a great and beautiful city all of stone. The whole world came to his palace, where he discussed and ordered everything.
>
> When Inkarí and his people . . . died, they went down into the underworld; and the water descended to the lowlands, and was baptized.
>
> The houses in the hills have no water anymore, only the stones remain.[7]

Ever since Pizarro founded Lima, his city has consumed the country. In 1940 Lima had half a million inhabitants;[8] in 1991, 7 million—one third of the people in Peru. For many, life in Lima is bad, but they keep coming because elsewhere life is worse.

Four centuries ago, when Waman Puma went to Lima to send his *First New Chronicle* to the Spanish king, he noted that Indians were making the same one-way journey to escape tribute, forced labor, and destruction of the Inca farming system: "The Indians leave their towns because they have nothing to eat. . . . And here [in Lima] one sees the world upside down . . . and there is no remedy."[9]

Today they flee a degraded environment and an escalating war between army and guerrillas. The price is the same: the erosion of Andean culture in a deracinated urban world. To survive in Pizarro's city, the Indians must reject their origins and language; they must try to become mestizos.

Were it not for the reference to modern powers, it would be hard to tell whether the following was written by Waman Puma or said—as in fact it was—by an Indian migrant to the Lima of today:

> In the past we ate well, men and women were sturdy, full of strength.
>
> All that is gone; and so we abandon our towns because there is no rain, there is no food, and it is impossible to work the land no matter how much one wants to. . . . People say the United States and Russia have learned how to hide the rain and water for themselves, and that's why there isn't any. . . .
>
> And so we wander here, here to the city of Lima where we eat but are destroyed. And there is no way to defend ourselves.[10]

> Underdevelopment is . . . the historical consequence of someone else's development. Some countries are poor because other countries are rich.
>
> —Eduardo Galeano, 1982

> Beginning reform is beginning revolution.
>
> —Duke of Wellington, 1830

> I abhor the atrocities of the Left even more than those of the Right, because they betray much more.
>
> —George Woodcock, 1990

One way that Andeans have tried to defend themselves is by armed insurrection. In 1885, an Indian named Pedro Atusparia seized control of the central Andes north of Lima;[11] in 1923, a rebellion in Cotabambas took the name Tawantinsuyu and announced the return of the Inca;[12] in 1927, Bolivian Aymaras sacrificed a landlord to their sacred mountain.[13]

Around 1962, Hugo Blanco, a bearded Cusco Trotskyist bilingual in Quechua and Spanish, organized peasants in the coffee-growing valleys beyond Machu Picchu, a remote region that was once part of the Neo-Inca state. Blanco hoped that by seizing estates from repressive landlords he could unleash the revolutionary potential in Andean culture and achieve the creation of "a workers' and peasants' government."[14] This is from his memoir, *Land or Death:*

> In Cusco, for centuries, the Indian had slouched along the streets with his poncho and his whispered Quechua; he had never dared, even when drunk, to mount the sidewalk or speak his Quechua out loud with his head held high. He was fearful of the *misti* [mestizo or white], who was master of the city. He fled from the authorities, or from whoever could force him to do a job for a pittance—or for nothing. . . .
>
> The mass meeting put the Indian on top of the monster. A concentration of ponchos in the main plaza, the heart of the city. At the court on the cathedral portico, which dominates the plaza like a rostrum. The odor of *coca* and Quechua, permeating the air. Quechua, out loud from the throat; Quechua shouted, threatening, tearing away the centuries of oppression.[15]

After eluding the authorities for about a year, Blanco was captured and sentenced to life in jail, where he wrote the above. But his abortive revolution had unexpected consequences. Junior Peruvian army officers, mainly coastal mestizos from the lower middle class, were appalled by what they saw when sent into the Andes. One officer reported seeing peasants shot by landowners for stealing bread.[16] They began to ask themselves why such conditions existed and what purpose was served by perpetuating them. They were also gripped by the old coastal fear of Andean retribution, of a vengeful Quechua avalanche sweeping down on the Hispanic seaboard. They saw that they had two choices: increase the level of repression—Guatemala's option—or do away with the system that made repression necessary. To their credit, they chose the latter.

In 1968, General Juan Velasco toppled an ineffectual civilian president, Fernando Belaúnde Terry, who had promised reform but failed to deliver it. Within a year of taking power, Velasco nationalized the country's oil and began serious land reform. The big sugar estates of the coast and the haciendas of the Andes were expropriated with compensation and reorganized as cooperatives. The far right called Velasco a communist, the far left (including Blanco, whom Velasco freed) called him a fascist. He was in truth a nationalist, a soldier inspired by the ideas of Garcilaso, Waman Puma, and Arguedas, looking for a way to mend Peru from its two broken halves. The United States, then preoccupied with Chile, did relatively little to unseat him.

Although he came from the coastal town of Piura (Pizarro's old base and a shrine of *hispanismo,* the opposite of Indianism), Velasco made Quechua an official language and decreed that it be taught in schools. He encouraged Andean folklore and pageantry; he made Tupa Amaru II the figurehead of his "revolution." Ruins were excavated and proudly restored; Quechua and Aymara were spoken on radio and television; Arguedas's books came out in new editions. Demetrio Tupac Yupanqui, a journalist descended from the tenth Inca emperor, wrote a Quechua political column for a leading paper.[17] Anyone traveling through the Andes by bus heard the driver's radio playing *wayno* music, lilting Quechua folk songs in the Inca tradition.

Yet on the same day that Velasco announced the land reform by quoting Tupa Amaru—*No longer shall the landlord feast on your poverty!*—he abolished the word "Indian." And the complications of the reform process—especially the clumsy attempt to drag Indian ayllus into the market economy—sometimes did more harm than good. Even if the skills, funds, and political will had been available, centuries of misuse of the land could not have been remedied quickly. In Blanco's words, the conquistadors and their republican heirs had taken "it upon themselves to destroy the terraces and murder the soil, even as they murdered the people."[18] Introductions that Europeans deemed civilizing improvements—the plow, the ox, the horse, pigs, and sheep—had brought erosion and ruin. The llama's delicate feet and mouth do not damage Andean turf; cattle and sheep do. Nutritious Andean grains such as quinoa (a Chenopodium) had been neglected or banned. The Spanish practice of *reducción*—forcing Indians to resettle in valley towns where they could be controlled—had erased scarce bottom land by building on it.

The reform got out of control. Landowners sabotaged their herds and machinery rather than see them fall into Indian hands. Peasants seized property on their own initiative from landlords, from corrupt cooperative managers (who threatened to become a new manorial class), and from each other. Food production shrank and migration to Lima accelerated.

Velasco's "revolution" had bad luck on other fronts: copper prices fell (partly because of U.S. machinations); the El Niño current crippled the fishing industry; there were earthquakes, floods, and droughts. After 1973, Chile's Augusto Pinochet provoked a military buildup that Peru couldn't afford. By 1975, Velasco had become seriously ill. A conservative subordinate removed him from office, and he died the following year.

In the beginning, the wayno singers' high-pitched voices had hailed the idealistic general as a new Tupa Amaru. But this wayno, in a mix of Quechua and Spanish, captures the disillusionment of his last days.

Kay Peru nasiunpi Hambre y miseria Manaña tukuq.	In this Peruvian nation Hunger and misery Continue without end.
Ay, haykakamaraq Wakchalla kasun . . . Kay Peru nasiunpi?	Oh, how much longer Must we be poor . . . In this nation of Peru?
Campesino runa Hatarillasunña. . . . Lima capitalpis Cojo Velasco;	People of the land Let us now awake. . . . In Lima, the capital, Velasco is crippled;

Llapam llaqtapi, Sinamos . . .	In every town, SINAMOS . . .
Wakcha runata engañan.	Deceives the poor.[19]

(SINAMOS was the agency responsible for land reform.)

In 1978, the military called a constituent assembly; in 1980, elections were held. Belaúnde Terry returned to the national palace. Unfortunately he was no more effective than before. Seduced by Reaganomics, he opened the country to foreign competition with the promise that if the rich got richer, wealth would trickle down to the poor. The poor got poorer; the economy continued to decline.

Revolutions often occur after partial reform has lifted the lid on change, and Velasco had opened a box that was not to be closed. His cultural program had resonated deeply in the Andes. Quechua an official language? Taught in schools? Broadcast nightly from the capital? Such things helped transform indigenous Peru's image of itself as friendless and defeated. But the educational reforms, sabotaged by unsympathetic teachers, became a dead letter even before Velasco's death. At the constituent assembly of 1978–1979, delegates controlled by the old oligarchy emasculated official bilingualism and tried to deprive illiterates of the vote. Without bilingual education, literacy meant literacy in Spanish, so this move was nothing less than a devious form of electoral apartheid. Universal suffrage survived, but in most other respects Hispanic culture reasserted its hegemony, offering the Indian no choices but alienation or absorption.

Like Rigoberta Menchú's father, Andeans recognize the cultural assault in schooling designed by and for a Hispanic state; and this threat has entered the cycle of legend surrounding the figure of Inkarí. In the following parable, Isidro Wamani, a monolingual Quechua speaker from the department of Ayacucho, expresses the dilemma in mythic terms, using the Andean structure of paired opposites. God has two sons: Inca and Jesus Christ. Inca develops a reciprocal relationship with Mother Earth that brings order and plenty. But Jesus defeats his Inca brother with a European weapon, writing, and allies himself with a sinister denizen of the pre-Inca world, *Ñawpa Machu,* the Ancient One.

(In the Andean scheme of alternating eras, pre-Inca and post-Inca are natural allies against Inca.) Isidro Wamani represents greater Peru as a human body, a very ancient pattern enshrined in place names. "Lima" comes from the Quechua *Rimaq*, which means "Speaker." Originally this referred to the great oracle at Pachacamac, but ever since Pizarro built his capital nearby, it has meant the power of the government, colonial or republican, to dictate.

> Peru begins in Lake Titicaca, which is the sex of Mother Earth, and ends in Quito, her forehead. It is said that Lima is her mouth and that Cusco is her beating heart. The rivers are her veins. . . .
>
> But even though Lima is earth's mouth, nobody there wants to speak our Runasimi [Quechua], not one of those "Peruvians."
>
> In the beginning, Almighty God, our Father, walked through the whole world. He had two sons: Inca and Jesus.
>
> Inca said, "Speak," and we all learned to speak, and from that day forth we have taught our children everything. Inca said to Mother Earth, "Give food," and we learned to dig and plant the earth. The llamas and cattle obeyed us. In those days we lacked for nothing. . . .
>
> Inca built Cusco, which I'm told is entirely of stone. Lima, they say, is of mud. . . . He then built a tunnel beneath Cusco, and by that tunnel he took gifts to Mother Earth; there they used to speak, and he asked her to provide everything we needed. The Inca and Mother Earth married, and they had two children. They are very beautiful children, but we do not know their names, and we do not know if they are still there, wandering underground. . . .
>
> The birth of these two children angered and hurt Holy Jesus. He had grown up into a fine strong youth, and he wanted to defeat his elder brother.

With the help of writing and supernatural forces, Jesus drives Inca into the Lima desert, where he starves to death. Jesus then begins to destroy the Andean world and the reciprocity with Mother Earth that sustained it. The story ends in hope of Inkarí.

When Inca could no longer do anything, Jesus struck Mother Earth and cut her throat. Then he made us build the churches. . . .

The Ancient One had had to stay hidden while Inca walked the earth. When he knew that Inca had died he was delighted; he enjoyed the beating of Mother Earth. The Ancient One lived inside a mountain, and the name of the mountain was School.

A little while later, Inca's children passed by, searching for their parents. The Ancient One said to them, "Come here, I will tell you where Mother Earth and Inca are." And so the children went cheerfully into School, where the Ancient One was waiting to devour them. "Mother Earth no longer loves Inca," he said. "Inca and Jesus Christ are friends now, and they live together as brothers. Look, it is written here on this paper." But the children were terrified, and they ran away.

Ever since that time, children go to school. But like the children of Mother Earth they hate school and they escape whenever they can.

Where can Inca's two sons be today? It is said that when the elder son is grown he will come back. And when he returns that will be *Punchaw Usiu,* the Last Day.[20]

In 1980, when Peru was electing Belaúnde, armed men appeared at Chuschi, a small town in Ayacucho Department, and burned the ballot boxes—on May 18, the 199th anniversary of Tupa Amaru II's execution. Peru's heady mix of racism, indigenism, Inca messianism, and desperate poverty had begun to ignite.

The new guerrillas called themselves *Sendero Luminoso,* the Shining Path, because they claimed to follow the radiant way blazed in the twenties by José Carlos Mariátegui (as did almost every faction of Peru's left). They also thought themselves the purest Maoists in the world. Apart from that, they didn't talk to the press: an air of mystery suited their taste for the portentous. When the pope came to Lima they blacked out the city so that all eyes might turn to a fiery hammer and sickle flaming on a hillside. They hung dogs from lampposts, with signs identifying the curs as Deng Xiaoping and other "traitors." On a single memorable day, they lobbed dynamite into the American, Chinese, Italian, and Chilean embassies, and the Soviet Union's cultural center. Not even the CIA thought this was the work of foreign powers.

Sendero's leader, Abimael Guzmán, had been to China in the 1960s. Later he taught philosophy at Huamanga University in Ayacucho, where he fostered a clique of ideologues committed to Mao's revolution from the countryside. He called himself the Fourth Sword of Marxism—after Marx, Lenin, and Mao—and took Comrade Gonzalo for a nom de guerre. In 1979 he went underground for the last time, and there have been no reliable sightings of him since.[21] Though in his late fifties by now, he appears on propaganda posters as a wild-eyed young man in an open-necked shirt with a moon face and big glasses, much like a manic Buddy Holly.

Ayacucho is one of the poorest, most forgotten regions of the Andes. Life expectancy is forty-five, the same as for Indians in Guatemala. Ayacucho is also strategic ground where decisive battles have been fought throughout Peruvian history. Its name, meaning "Corner of the Dead," dates from a pre-Columbian battle with the Incas; four centuries later, on the same field, Sucre beat the Spanish royalists. The heartland of the Taki Onqoy, Ayacucho supported Titu Kusi and produced Waman Puma. Guzmán, who read Andean history and recruited anthropologists, knew all this and more.

While Velasco's revolution-from-above flowered without roots, *Senderistas* were patiently forging links with Indians of the Ayacucho hinterland. They learned Quechua, became *compadres* (cogodparents), and married into far-flung villages. Sendero, they claimed, "is an ethnic, cultural movement.... It recognizes that we are a fundamentally Indian republic with a fundamentally Indian outlook.... It will win because it is fighting an unlosable war."[22] Guzmán became known in Quechua as *Puka Inti,* the Red Sun, and the word *pachakuti* emerged from mythology to be yelled on the streets.[23] It seemed as though Guzmán had tapped into the underworld of Inkarí.

He also made good use of other Andean myths, especially that of the *pishtakuq,* a ghoulish white man who kills Indians in desolate places and boils them down for their fat. The pishtakuq first appeared at the time of the Taki Onquy, when it was said that he took the fat to Spain for curing disease; nowadays he exports it for greasing machinery and making cosmetics. Like so many Amerindian legends, it is an elegant distillation of social truth: the invaders get rich on Indian sweat and vaunt those riches on their wives. It is also an echo of literal truth, of what Bernal Díaz, one of Mexico's conquerors, casually admits in his *Conquest of New Spain:* "We dressed our wounds with the fat from a stout Indian whom we had killed and cut open."[24]

After more than a decade, Sendero has acquired a sinister reputation reminiscent of Pol Pot's. To starve the cities, it has destroyed crops, livestock, and foreign-aid projects, slaughtering peasants who objected or informed. Peasants have also been killed in large numbers by the army and police. In ten years, 20,000 have died.

Expectations of Inkarí may have been aroused and fanned by Sendero, but as time passes there is less and less evidence that the movement is committed to specifically Andean concerns. It has a Spanish name and Spanish slogans; it has little support in Cusco, where Inca traditions are strongest; and its center of gravity seems to be shifting to the Lima slums and cocaine jungles. When Guzmán gave the "interview of the century" to a Lima journal in 1988, doctrinal ranting far outweighed attention to Peru's ethnic rift. By that time Osmán Morote, Sendero's leading anthropologist, was in jail. Perhaps a split in the leadership had occurred, consolidating the power of the Maoist ayatollah.[25] Like Mao, Guzmán believes in the future, not the past. But, though he may spurn the mantle of Inkarí, his authoritarianism, his obsession with order and planning, and his messianic style are all deeply Andean. They who would rule the Andes cannot escape the shadow of the Sapa Inka, any more than Mao, the anti-imperialist, could avoid becoming a new emperor.

Few think the Shining Path will ever lead to power, but what other paths are open? There is a smaller guerrilla organization named for Tupa Amaru and inspired by the Moscow of the Brezhnev years. There is the army and there is the ballot box, but the two are equally discredited. Politics is bankrupt. Everything has been tried: the old right; the new right; the new left; the old left; the army; APRA; various bits of the center. All have failed.

The 1990 elections were contested by two amateurs, Mario Vargas Llosa, the fashionable creole novelist, and Alberto Fujimori, an unknown nisei agronomist. The smooth and intellectual Vargas had immense appeal for foreign dilettantes who did not know, or chose to ignore, his long antagonism to Andean Peru. ("I've never liked the Incas," Vargas once admitted in the *New York Times;* elsewhere, he mounted sly attacks on the late José María Arguedas.)[26] Peruvian voters, many of them illiterate Indians who would have been denied the vote if Vargas's political friends had had their way, were not so easily fooled. Despite a campaign budget one hundred times greater than Fujimori's, Vargas lost.

And Cusco? What of Cusco, the Inca capital? In the twenty years I have known it, the city has grown to perhaps a quarter million. Adobe slums now climb its hills, and the rainbow flag of the Tawantinsuyu flutters in the plaza. Tourism, for all its faults, has brought a little prosperity and a sense that there is something here that the world admires. Attitudes have changed since Hugo Blanco wrote his gritty prose. Even Mario Vargas Llosa was addressed in Quechua by local dignitaries. In Cusco, if not in Lima, an Indian can get an education and a job without having to trample his identity. One has only to attend a religious fiesta or drink chicha in a rustic bar or engage a student in conversation to learn that the Inca heart still beats beneath the Inca walls. If Cusco does not follow the Shining Path, it is because it waits for something better.

One day, perhaps, Cusco will surprise Peru.

FOURTEEN

CHEROKEE

> The United States [desires] to secure to the Cherokee Nation of Indians a permanent home . . . which shall, under the most solemn guarantee of the United States, be and remain theirs forever. . . .
>
> In no future time [shall it] be included within the territorial limits or jurisdiction of any State or Territory.
>
> —Treaties of 1828 and New Echota, 1835

> Treaties were expedients by which ignorant, intractable, and savage people were induced . . . to yield up what civilized people had the right to possess.
>
> —George Gilmer, governor of Georgia, c. 1830

Years after the Cherokees were rounded up and driven along the Trail of Tears, John G. Burnett, a soldier who took part, reflected on what he and his nation had done.

> School children of today do not know that we are living on lands that were taken from a helpless race at the bayonet point to satisfy the white man's greed. . . .
>
> Murder is murder and somebody must answer, somebody must explain the streams of blood that flowed in the Indian country. . . . Somebody must explain the four thousand silent graves that mark the trail of the Cherokees to their exile.[1]

In one of those graves lay the wife of John Ross, the muttonchop-whiskered chief who had fought removal to the last, a short, thickset man with a firm Scottish jaw and the deep black eyes of a Cherokee. An American officer described Ross at this time as

> a man of strong passions and settled purposes which he pursues with untiring zeal. . . . After much attentive observation I am of [the] opinion that John Ross is an honest man and a patriot laboring for the good of his people. . . . With almost unlimited opportunities [for embezzlement] he has not enriched himself. . . .
>
> It would be strange if there was not ambition with the patriotism of John Ross, but he seeks the fame of establishing his nation and heaping benefits upon his people.[2]

The 12,000 Cherokees who survived the death march to the region that is now northeastern Oklahoma were split in two bitter factions: the National Party, headed by a grieving but unbroken Ross—by far the larger group—and the small but influential Treaty Party, headed by the newspaper editor Elias Boudinot, his brother Stand Watie, the Ridges, and others who had signed their names to the deal at New Echota in 1835. Trying to mediate between the two were the Old Settlers, about 3,000 who had migrated in earlier years, including Sequoyah, the reclusive genius who invented the syllabic Cherokee script. These now found themselves obliged to share what they had with the diseased and starving refugees.

History may judge the Treaty Party pragmatists, but to most Cherokees they were traitors. By the written and customary law of the Nation, all were marked men. Freelance execution squads, fired by an anger that had fed on every death and outrage on the march, did not wait long. In June 1839, Major Ridge was shot from his horse and his son John stabbed to death. Elias Boudinot, the white man's Indian, went to his Christian God with a tomahawk buried in his skull.

Stand Watie, who escaped somehow, held Ross responsible for the killings, though it's unlikely that the chief had ordered them. Ross's supporters had to guard him from revenge. Alarmed by the risk of civil war, Sequoyah joined with Ross and others to proclaim a new government and constitution intended to unite all Cherokees.

> Whereas our Fathers have existed, as a separate and distinct Nation, in the possession and exercise of the essential and appropriate attributes of sovereignty, from a period extending into antiquity, beyond the records and memory of man. . . . We, the people . . . do hereby solemnly and mutually agree to form ourselves into one body politic under the style and title of the Cherokee Nation.[3]

This constitution, like its 1827 predecessor, borrowed much from that of the United States, but it remained faithful to one fundamental principle of pre-Columbian America: land was still held in common by the Nation; individuals owned only their goods, houses, and improvements.

Despite Sequoyah's efforts, the uprooted Cherokees were torn by bloodshed for years. But at last the vendettas ceased and the constitution was accepted. By 1845, Stand Watie and the Treaty Party had the wisdom to direct their anger where it belonged—at the Congress of the United States:

> If there was a crime in the Treaty of 1835, it was more your crime than ours. We were all opposed to selling our country east, but . . . you abolished our government, annihilated our laws, suppressed our authorities, took away our lands, turned us out of our houses, denied us the rights of men, made us outcasts and outlaws in our own land, plunging us at the same time into an abyss of moral degradation which was hurling our people to swift destruction.[4]

In 1846, the Cherokee factions and the United States concluded a treaty by which the Nation was reunited and compensated for its losses. Once again the Cherokees demonstrated their remarkable resilience. They reopened their bilingual newspaper, now called the *Cherokee Advocate,* and built a new capital complete with Council House, Supreme Court, and other fine buildings of brick and stone. Beloved Chota had too bitter a taste to be evoked again, so they named the young city for Tahlequah (a form of Tellico), the seat of "Emperor" Moytoy a very long century before.

David Carter, editor of the *Advocate* and "a fine specimen of an enlightened Cherokee gentleman,"[5] did his best to raise morale.

> Everything about our Town is life and animation. . . . The location . . . is central and beautiful and combines advantages of good health, excellent spring water, and a plentiful supply of timber for firewood and purposes of building. The surrounding country is, in our opinion, of surpassing beauty, presenting a diversity of mountain, woodland, and prairie scenery. . . .
>
> The Supreme Court has just opened its annual session, in a new and commodious brick Court House, which in point of neatness and durability is perhaps surpassed by no building of the kind in Arkansas.[6]

The Cherokees financed their public works by shrewdly investing the $5 million they received for their old home. By the early 1850s they had built more than twenty local schools and two seminaries, one each for girls and boys. The latter were large two-story brick mansions surrounded by imposing colonnades in the antebellum style. The girls' college—a rarity in those days—reflected the high status that women enjoyed in Cherokee society, as they had since ancient times. In 1855 the Nation's press ran off more than a million pages, including various books of the Bible, the national laws, and an almanac; most of these were either bilingual or in Cherokee alone.

At the 1857 national council, a heartened Chief Ross could report: "I visited . . . the different districts to inform myself of the general condition of the country. The evidences of progress by the Cherokee people furnished by this tour was of the most cheering kind. . . . Well cultivated farms . . . well filled public schools, large and orderly assemblies, and quiet neighborhoods . . . in all the districts."[7]

Ross, known also by his Cherokee name, Kooweskoowee,[8] was elected time after time to the office of Principal Chief. Though more Scot than Cherokee in ancestry, he had won the confidence of full-bloods and traditionalists, who far outnumbered the mixed and acculturated elite. He shared their tenacious love of the hills and rivers of the old Cherokee

Nation, and while Boudinot and the Ridges had left early and in comfort to join the Old Settlers, he had stayed to the cruel end.

Ross also knew that the more the Cherokees achieved, the more the invaders, with their usual parasitism on Native Americans, would covet the improved land. In the same 1857 address to the Nation, he sounded a prophetic warning.

> If our rights of soil and self-government, of free homes and self-chosen institutions, are worth the toils and struggles of the past, they are worth present defence and continuation upon the most permanent footing. Years of trial and of anxiety, of danger and struggle, have . . . maintained the Cherokee people as a distinct community; and such must continue to be the case. . . .
>
> You cannot fail to be seriously impressed with the change of policy shown by the United States government in her dealing with the Indian tribes in the Territory of Kansas and Nebraska. And, as an evidence of the dangers with which we ourselves are threatened, I need but refer to the language [of] the present governor of Kansas . . . who, if I mistake not, was in the Senate of the United States when the removal of all the Indians from the east . . . so recently forced us from the homes of our fathers.[9]

Ross then quoted from the inaugural address of Kansas governor Robert J. Walker, exposing the menace in his oiled words. Unlike the blunt Andrew Jackson, who hated Indians and said so, this new breed of predator was skilled in the deadliest of weapons—self-interest cloaked as altruism.

> Indian territory . . . is one of the most salubrious and fertile portions of this continent . . . and it ought speedily to become a State of the American Union. The Indian treaties *will constitute no obstacle,* any more than precisely similar treaties did in Kansas; for their lands, valueless to them [but sold] for their benefit . . . would make them a most wealthy and prosperous people.[10]

The Cherokees were already wealthier and more prosperous than most frontier whites, considerably better educated, and their lands were certainly not "useless" to them. Absorption into a white state would come, but not for half a century. Yet within four years of Ross's speech a different and unforeseen calamity struck the Indian nations: the Civil War.

Less than a generation passed from the Trail of Tears to the War between the States, and only fifteen of those years were truly peaceful for the Cherokees. Even so, their population began to recover, climbing from about 15,000 (including Old Settlers) in 1839 to 21,000 by 1861.[11] These figures are important for understanding the nature of the New World holocaust. In its early stages the great death was accidental. The invaders had not planned to introduce Old World sickness, though they benefited vastly from the result. It is therefore easy for Euro-Americans to absolve themselves of this "act of God." But Cherokee demographics demonstrate clearly that Native American peoples were capable of rebuilding their numbers when they were given time and peace and a place in which to do so. Slowly, after generations of collapse, they had acquired some immunity to the foreign pathogens. By the nineteenth century, any decline was due less to smallpox per se than to endless displacement, warfare, hunger, and seizures of land. White settlers filled the country that might otherwise have fed future Indian mouths. The invaders' quest for lebensraum gave native America no chance to grow back.

Any who doubt this need look no further for a test case than Fiji and Hawaii, two Pacific island groups of comparable size with similar—and equally vulnerable—populations. In Fiji, alienation of native property and further European settlement were halted seventy-five years after first contact. Fijians kept most of their lands, continued living on them in a traditional way, and were not used as plantation labor.[12] Hawaii, on the other hand, was flooded with settlers, both white and Asian, who exploited, dislodged, *and occupied the space* of the original inhabitants. Today, half the people in Fiji are native Fijians, but a mere one percent of the people in Hawaii are indigenous Hawaiians.[13] Absolute numbers show the same contrast: 350,000 Fijians; 14,000 Hawaiians. The difference, as in America, is due to acts of man, not God.

John Ross and the traditionalists wanted to stay aloof from the white troubles. In May 1861, he wrote to the commander of the nearest Union fort: "The Cherokees have properly taken no part in the present deplorable state of affairs. . . . We do not wish our soil to become the battle ground between the states, and our homes to be rendered desolate and miserable by the horrors of a civil war."[14]

But it proved impossible to escape entanglement. Indian Territory occupied strategic ground: it lay near the Mississippi, between Texas and the rest of the states. The Indian nations were seen by both sides as an open storehouse to be plundered for supplies and cannon fodder. White armies and agitators crossed the territory at will. The Cherokee Nation's wounds, healed superficially in 1846, opened under the strain. The Americans' war became the Cherokees' war as well. White America lost 2 percent of its people in the fighting. The Cherokees, for the second time in under thirty years, lost 25 percent.[15] One woman in three became a widow; one child in four lost both parents.

Stand Watie and the Treaty Party, who had acquired a taste for the southern planter's way of life, owning taverns, mills—and slaves—supported the Confederates. Even the *Advocate*'s editor, an "enlightened Cherokee gentleman" and a Ross man, had a plantation "black with darkies."[16] Ross himself owned slaves, but as usual he put the Nation's interest ahead of his own. He knew that the only hope for Indians, however slim, lay with a strong federal government; he had not forgotten Georgia's villainy in the Cherokee removal.

But when at first it looked as though the Confederacy might win, Ross began to worry that the Cherokees would be seriously exposed. Stand Watie forced the issue by raising a Cherokee regiment for the South under his own command. A gloomy Ross told friends, "We are in the situation of a man standing alone upon a low, naked spot of ground, with the water rising rapidly all around him. He sees the danger, but does not know what to do. If he remains where he is, his only alternative is to be swept away and perish."[17]

One by one the other Civilized Tribes—the Choctaws, Chickasaws, Creeks, and Seminoles—who lived beside the Cherokee Nation in the stark rectangles they had been forced to trade for their ancient homes became allies of the South. In August 1861, Ross addressed his people, recommending "preliminary steps for an alliance with the Confederate States."[18] The alliance was signed in October. John Ross and Stand Watie publicly shook hands.

It was the biggest mistake of Ross's career. Soon the tide of war began to turn; Union forces invaded Indian Territory, seized the old Cherokee chief, and took him to Washington. Stand Watie remained in the field, declared himself principal chief, and fought on for the South. By all accounts he was a superb military leader. His men spoke of his "mysterious power" and swore they would "follow him into the very jaws of death."[19] Watie became a brigadier general in the Confederate army and went down in history as the last southern commander to capitulate. Most of his battles were against Union forces, but he also fought Cherokees loyal to the North. "I went to Tahlequah," he wrote tersely to his wife in 1863. "I had the old Council House set on fire and burned down. Also John Ross's house."[20] Soon almost everything the Cherokee Nation had built in Oklahoma lay in ruins. Thousands starved on the freezing plains, and in their weakened state fell victim to cholera and smallpox.

If truth is the first casualty of war, the second is tradition. Catastrophic war kills off the older generation and its knowledge. Traditional Cherokees—that silent majority who spoke no English, read only Sequoyan, owned no slaves, and had little use for Christianity—realized that they were in danger of losing their culture. Unlike "progressives," they did not regard white civilization as a suitable replacement. In the late 1850s, many of them formed or revived a secret organization called the Keetoowah Society, which became the core of opposition to Stand Watie, the wealthy "mixed-bloods," and the South.

Meanwhile Ross, though technically a prisoner in Washington, befriended Abraham Lincoln and did what he could to exonerate his people. "The U.S. Army in Texas and in the Indian country either joined the rebellion or fled," he told Congress. "What else could the Cherokees do than submit until the United States could assert its authority?"[21]

At last, in 1865, the war ended and Ross made his way back to the Cherokee Nation, now a land of burnt cabins with only the stone chimneys standing as forlorn monuments to its devastation. His own house was gone, and in July of that year his second wife died. He wrote to his sister-in-law from the steamboat *Iron City:* "I know that I am fast approaching my country and my people . . . but, where is that delightful home and the matron of the once happy family who so kindly and hospitably entertained our guests. Alas, I shall see them no more on earth. . . . I am here journeying . . . alone to find myself a stranger and homeless in my own country."[22]

Ross was past seventy and ailing, but his political battles were not yet over. At the first postwar council, held outside the ruins of Tahlequah, Watie's partisans tried to discredit him. And the United States tried to force massive cessions of land and sovereignty from all Indian nations on the pretext of punishing them for their southern alliance.

Ross went back to Washington in 1866 to fight the more menacing clauses of the peace treaty, especially plans to amalgamate the Indian governments and open their land to railway corporations. He fought, as he had fought before, to preserve Cherokee unity and treaty rights. On July 19, a compromise was signed by all parties. On August 1, the old chief died.

In April, Kooweskoowee had made a short speech from his sickbed; it may stand for his epitaph:

> I am an old man and have served my people and the government of the United States a long time, over fifty years. My people have kept me in the harness, not of my own seeking, but of their own choice. I have never deceived them. . . . I have done the best I could, and today upon this bed of sickness, my heart approves all I have done. And still I am John Ross, the same John Ross of former years. Unchanged! No cause to change![23]

> Observance of the strict letter of treaties with Indians is in many cases at variance with their own best interests and with sound public policy.
>
> —Commissioner of Indian Affairs, 1876

> From capitalism's point of view, communal cultures . . . are enemy cultures.
>
> —Eduardo Galeano, 1988

Once more the Cherokees patiently reconstructed their Nation. They replaced the old Council House burned by Watie with a new brick capitol—a fine example of Victorian architecture that still stands in Tahlequah. They reopened the printing press and schools; they built a large orphanage for the many children bereft by war, and, as obliged by the peace treaty, they freed their slaves and made them Cherokee citizens.

The American Civil War had been a strange half-modern conflict: trenches, exploding shells, telegraph lines; yet white men sometimes taking other white men's scalps. It had stimulated technical innovation and the beginnings of what Dwight Eisenhower later called the military-industrial complex. When it was over, the armies that had fought each other were sent West to part the last free Indians from their land. The idea was to drive the entire population of the plains to the Indian Territory where, it was supposed, they could learn the advantages of civilization from the Five Civilized Tribes.

The western tribes were as different from Cherokees as Bedouin are from Belgians. Most were nomadic buffalo hunters accustomed to roaming over large but familiar territories year after year. To think that they could all be given plows and teams and turned overnight into small farmers was absurd. But that is exactly what the United States tried to do to them, and on drylands that in the course of sixty years became a dust bowl. Nation after nation walked its own trail of tears to Oklahoma, often to find that corrupt officials had looted the supplies intended for their conversion to a settled life. War, hunger, whiskey, and sickness reduced nations that had numbered in the tens of thousands to a few hundred or a few dozen miserable survivors. Many tried to escape; others committed suicide. Those who trekked back to their old hunting grounds found few buffalo and many whites, especially soldiers. It was in these times that General Philip Sheridan, a Union war hero, made his famous remark: "The only good Indians I ever saw were dead."[24]

Thanks to new technology, the process that had taken three centuries in the East was accomplished on the plains in three decades. The repeating rifle, the machine gun, the railway, and the steamboat won the West.

William Ross, John Ross's nephew and a Princeton[25] graduate, served several terms as chief in the postwar years. Like his uncle he spent much of his time in Washington, fighting one attempt after another to violate "the most solemn guarantee of the United States" that the new Cherokee Nation should "be and remain theirs forever"—a guarantee in danger before it was forty years old.[26] Railways were the main threat. The rail companies' rights of way through the Indian Territory were corridors of white penetration. Along them came workers, migrants, speculators, and crooks of every stamp. These non-Indians lay outside the jurisdiction of the Indians' courts. Not only did they commit crimes with impunity, but their very presence as "outlaws" in the Cherokee Nation gave the United States an excuse to intervene. The old pattern that had driven the Cherokees from Georgia was reproduced in almost every detail: settler invasion, jurisdictional disputes, cessions of sovereignty and land.

In 1872, Ross protested to the United States Congress about the "soulless corporations [which] hover like greedy cormorants over this territory and incite Congress to remove all restraint and allow them to swoop down . . . destroying alike the last hope of the Indians and the honor of the government."[27]

The following year he warned the Cherokee people: "The results anticipated . . . are the gradual blending of the Indians under the same form of government . . . the allotment of their lands in severalty, the gradual extinction of all civil distinction between them and citizens of the United States, and their ultimate absorption."[28]

Meanwhile, philanthropic easterners were becoming troubled by reports of what was happening in the West. From 1869 to 1871, under President Ulysses Grant, a Seneca Iroquois held the post of Indian Affairs Commissioner, the first Indian to do so—and the last for a century. He was none other than Hasanoanda, or Ely Parker, friend and colleague of Lewis Henry Morgan. A civil engineer by training, Parker had served as a Union colonel and written with his own hand the surrender signed by Robert E. Lee at Appomattox. Although he was hounded from office by the corruption ring that made fortunes off government contracts—the very men responsible for Indians dying in filthy camps across the West—Hasanoanda was able to raise a public outcry.

> If any tribe remonstrated against the violation of their natural and treaty rights, members of the tribe were inhumanly shot down and the whole treated as mere dogs. . . . Today, by reason of the immense augmentation of the American population, and the extension of their settlements throughout the entire West . . . the Indian races are more seriously threatened with a speedy extermination than ever before.[29]

White voices joined his. In 1881, Helen Hunt Jackson published *A Century of Dishonor,* a best-selling exposé of injustice to Indians. But tragically, public agitation played into the hands of those who wanted to "help" Indians by helping themselves. Smooth-tongued "experts" proposed a solution still advocated by similar interests today: to make the Indians, whether they liked it or not, into imitation whites. The best way to do that was to give them the same property "rights"—that is, risks—as everyone else. The trouble with the Indian, assimilationists claimed, was that he had too much land and would never progress until weaned from that primitive, unchristian habit of owning it in common.

In 1887 Congress passed the Dawes Severalty Act, named after its sponsor, Senator Henry Dawes of Massachusetts, who belonged to that dangerous tribe who know a little and think it enough. Dawes had come back from a brief tour of the Indian Territory praising the Cherokee Nation in almost utopian terms, yet plotting its destruction in the same breath: "There is not a pauper in that nation, and the nation does not owe a dollar. It built its own capitol . . . its schools and hospitals. Yet the defect of the system was apparent. They have got as far as they can go, because they hold their land in common. . . . There is no selfishness, which is at the bottom of civilization."[30]

His remedy for this shocking lack of avarice was to divide Indian lands into private plots—160 acres for each family. It didn't take much arithmetic to see that this would leave a great "surplus," which would, of course, be opened to whites. So a genuine desire to help Indians was perverted into a new assault on their culture, property, and sovereignty.

In 1890 the United States annexed the western half of the Indian Territory and renamed it the Territory of Oklahoma, and in 1893 the

Cherokee Outlet—more than 10,000 square miles of prairie originally intended for Cherokee expansion—was thrown open to settlers. One hundred thousand whites swarmed over it on a single day, staking out holdings in a frenzy resembling a gold rush.[31]

When the Cherokee Nation fought the Dawes Act in the Courts, Congress answered with the Curtis Act of 1898, which dissolved the national governments of the Civilized Tribes and abolished indigenous land tenure. The bill was passed by the House after three minutes of debate.[32] Oil—a substance as deadly to Indians as gold—had been found.

As soon as word got out that the land allotment was coming, thousands of whites, with the help of crooked lawyers, got themselves enrolled as "Indians." These white "Indians" then connived with corrupt members of the mixed-blood elite in the final pillage of the Nation's patrimony. "This nefarious, tyrannical Curtis law," wrote a Cherokee named Too-Qua-Stee, "dishonors the social life of our people . . . and reduces all the noble fathers and mothers of our country to the moral condition of pimps and prostitutes."[33] Another Cherokee, Mary Cobb Agnew, reflected in 1937:

> We Indians got our homes rebuilt [after the Civil War] and were doing well when the government took another shot at us and set up the Dawes Commission. . . . We owned all the land as a whole and could farm all we wanted to as long as we didn't infringe on a neighbor's land. We had a good government of our own just like we had back in Georgia, but the white man wanted our land just as they wanted it in Georgia. . . . The white people called us barbarians, half-wits, said we couldn't run our business, etc. So they sent men out to enroll all the citizens of the Cherokee tribe. . . . I am an old woman who has lived a long time and if there ever was a race of people that was downtrodden it was the Cherokees. . . . I knew every principal chief of the Cherokees from John Ross to Tom Buffington [chief from 1899 to 1903]. Something always arose to cause the chiefs more worry than the president of the United States has today. The white man all the time wanted to get all the Indians had.[34]

In the 1880s, after touring Europe with Buffalo Bill Cody's Wild West Show, Chief Sitting Bull of the Hunkpapa Sioux observed, "The white man knows how to make everything, but he does not know how to distribute it."[35] Settlers, Sitting Bull understood, did not swarm over every inch of America because there wasn't enough land to go around—the United States had, and still has, a low population density. They hungered for land because wealth was always concentrated upward, because people were measured by what they owned, because have-nots had to plunder weaker (Indian) haves. "The love of possession is a disease with them," Sitting Bull said. "They take tithes from the poor and weak to support the rich who rule. They claim this mother of ours, the earth, for their own and fence their neighbors away."[36]

If America had been twice the size it is, there still would not have been enough; the Indians would still have been dispossessed.

In 1905, white "Indians" and Oklahoma settlers began pushing for statehood. Genuine citizens of the Five Civilized Tribes made a last bid to create a new polity of their own. If they couldn't have their nations, perhaps they would be allowed to form an Indian state. They named it Sequoyah, drafted a constitution, and applied to Washington. The idea was quashed; Congress and the president insisted that the Indian nations be swallowed by Oklahoma. In November 1907, Theodore Roosevelt, author of *The Winning of the West*, proclaimed the new state. The celebrations ended with a mock wedding between a white "Mr. Oklahoma" and a Cherokee "Miss Indian Territory."

Acculturated Cherokees who knew how to profit from severalty became prominent citizens of Oklahoma, as their descendants are to this day, but severalty offered nothing to the full-bloods. The traditionalist Keetoowahs continued to boycott registration of their lands, even refusing checks for whatever rents and royalties fell due to them. As the years passed they withdrew farther into the hills, where they restored the Cherokee religion by drawing on Creek and Iroquois traditions. Disillusioned with politics, the Keetoowahs kept the soul of the Cherokee Nation alive, as they still do, in their religious teachings handed down from the pre-Columbian world.

About a year before his death in 1918, Redbird Smith, the Keetoowahs' visionary leader, wrote in Cherokee:

This religion . . . is growth like the child—it is growth eternal. This religion does not teach me to concern myself of the life that shall be after this, but it does teach me to be concerned with what my everyday life should be.

The Fires kept burning are merely emblematic of the greater Fire, the greater light, the Great Spirit. I realize now as never before it is not only for the Cherokees but for all mankind.[37]

Only to the white man was nature a "wilderness" and only to him was the land "infested" with "wild" animals and "savage" people. To us it was tame. . . . Not until the hairy man from the east came and with brutal frenzy heaped injustices upon us and the families we loved was it "wild" for us. When the very animals of the forest began fleeing from his approach, then it was that for us the "Wild West" began.

—Luther Standing Bear, Lakota Sioux, 1933

When the original Cherokee Nation made its last preremoval land cessions in 1819, many of the "beloved towns" in the Smoky Mountains north and east of the Little Tennessee had been relinquished to white frontiersmen. Bryson City grew up near the site of Kituhwa (the ancient "mother town" from which the Keetoowah Society took its name), and the great mound of Nikwasi became encrusted with the shacks of Franklin. But apart from settlements such as these, relatively few whites occupied the mountains—the land was stony, the growing season short, and timber could be cut more easily elsewhere.

Several hundred Cherokees had managed to stay in this part of the Smokies as freeholders or squatters after the Cherokee Nation shrank to its 1819–1838 borders. They were, on the whole, the most traditional of Indians: poor, isolated, with few white genes or black slaves. But they made canny use of the law. When removal came, they argued that the Treaty of New Echota did not apply to them, as they were North Carolina citizens. Their leader, old Yonaguska, or Drowning Bear, was said to be the finest speaker of his time. Born in the mid-eighteenth century, he remembered the heyday of the hill towns and disliked the changes sweeping through New Echota. When Boudinot's Bible came out in Sequoyan script, Yonaguska listened to a chapter or two and remarked, "Well, it seems to be a good book—strange that the white people are not better, after having had it so long."[38]

Yonaguska was on his deathbed when the removal was carried out, but he strengthened his people's resolve never to abandon their ancient country. If they moved west, he foresaw, it would be only a matter of time before the white man followed them there. During 1838, about 300 other Cherokees from *within* the Nation's boundary eluded the U.S. army dragnet and hid, hungry but defiant, in the wrinkles of the Smoky Mountains. These managed to join up with Yonaguska's people, and together they became the Eastern Band of Cherokees. Their modern descendants number 9,000 and live on the Qualla Reservation, the place where four and a half centuries ago their ancestors had met that Renaissance man, Hernando de Soto.

The existence and size of this reservation—ninety square miles—are owed largely to William Thomas, a fatherless white boy whom Yonaguska raised as his own son. Thomas apprenticed himself to the local storekeeper and eventually became the area's most successful businessman, but he also taught himself law and championed the Eastern Cherokees in court throughout his life. Fully bilingual, trusted and trustworthy, he bought land for his adoptive people whenever they had money, managed their affairs, and laid the legal foundations for their survival.

In the late 1880s, James Mooney, a young anthropologist, came to Qualla and received a gift of knowledge from a medicine man named Ayuñini, or Swimmer, "a genuine aboriginal antiquarian and patriot, proud of his people and their ancient system." Swimmer opened his mind—"a storehouse of Indian tradition"[39]—and turned over his personal archive of notebooks in Sequoyan script to Mooney. The result was the superb *Myths of the Cherokee* and *Sacred Formulas of the Cherokees*, first published a century ago and reprinted in 1982 by the Eastern Cherokees' own museum. Without Swimmer's generosity, much of what is known about Cherokee history, mythology, and medicine might have been lost; indeed, it was this very fear that prompted Swimmer to reveal what he did. When he met Mooney, new mission and federal schools had been established—for the purpose of "beating the Indian" out of the young. All over North America, native children were strapped or had their mouths rinsed with soap for speaking their own languages.[40] Even Sequoyah's great invention, taught for years by Cherokee teachers, was suppressed by white pedagogues from Indian Affairs.

Although the reservation was relatively large, little of it was arable. In early years the Cherokees earned a living by growing ginseng and cutting their timber, but by the 1930s Qualla was overcrowded and desperately poor. Then came Franklin D. Roosevelt's New Deal and a new approach to Indians. Commissioner John Collier aimed to reverse the disastrous acculturation policies, announcing that his Indian Reorganization Act would begin "the process of liberating and rejuvenating a subjugated and exploited race in the midst of an aggressive civilization."[41] Use of the Cherokee language was encouraged, and a new source of income came with the opening of the Great Smoky Mountains National Park in 1934. Indians were again welcome—as woodsmen, guides, craftspeople, and "local color." Quallatown changed its name to Cherokee, North Carolina, and opened for business as a tourist attraction.

Today, if you follow Soto's route by car, you can tell you are getting near an "Indian" place because the road signs sprout large plastic arrowheads of the Flintstone type. Totem poles and teepees appear at the roadside. You encounter the Honest Injun Trading Post, the Hiawatha Trailer Park, and the Warrior Motel. You wonder how many visitors are aware that Cherokees never made totem poles (Northwest coast), never lived in teepees (Plains), and haven't used stone-tipped arrows for about 300 years. As long ago as 1752, Mankiller of Hiwassee wrote to the South Carolina governor, "In my last letter to your Excellency I desired some ammunition, but forgot flints."[42] Gunflints are much easier to make than arrowheads: evidently Cherokees had left the Stone Age by then.

To reduce their dependence on tourism, the Eastern Cherokees have recently purchased a profitable mirror factory, which they own in common—a creative blend of Indian communalism and white capitalism. They have only to lift their eyes from the gimcrack souvenirs and trailer parks to the mountain landscape, nowadays covered in a lush secondary growth of oak, hickory, and maple, to be reminded that the land, if wisely used, is everlasting.

From Qualla, the Little Tennessee, longest of "long men" in the Cherokee heartland, wriggles through the Smoky Mountains to the valley of the ancient Overhill towns. It is a two- or three-hour drive on a road pinched between the misty "proud contending tops" that inspired James Adair. When you reach the other side and travel through the parts of the Cherokee Nation that were acquired by the United States at such enormous human cost, it is a shock to see that the fertile valleys, once coveted as an "American Canaan," have been drowned. The Little Tennessee and its tributaries do not flow; they drop in lifeless, glassy steps from one concrete barrier to the next: sixteen dams in a watershed less than ninety miles long.[43] Most seem to have no purpose: they drive no turbines, they irrigate no fields. A little delving into the career of the Tennessee Valley Authority (TVA) makes one suspect that many of these reservoirs, built for "conservation" and "flood control," are nothing but pork barrels.

The latest and most controversial of these is the Tellico Dam, which killed the last wild stretch of the Little Tennessee and drowned one of the richest historical legacies in North America, including the ancient sites of Chota, Tanasi, Tellico, and Fort Loudoun. The dam had been opposed for years by Cherokees, environmentalists, historians, and any number of disinterested experts. It did not make economic sense, as its promoters well knew: "It is essential," said a TVA memo, "that we . . . apply to the Tellico project any new and different methods we can devise for justification."[44]

Among such methods was a grandiose scheme to build a model city, to be named Timberlake after the man who took Ostenaco to England in 1762. The dam was supposed to "justify" Timberlake, and vice versa, but neither project could stand alone, and it was soon clear that they couldn't stand together. But in 1979, after battles in court and shenanigans in Congress, the seventeenth and final nail was hammered into the coffin of the Little Tennessee. Peter Matthiessen, who watched the waters rise and devoted an angry chapter of his *Indian Country* to the tale, concluded: "The T.V.A. itself acknowledges that the Tellico Dam Project is a failure. Not a single industry has located there."[45]

Today, little has changed. Fort Loudoun has been reconstructed as a tourist attraction, and unless you press the staff you can be misled into thinking that this "historic site" stands on original foundations. It does not—they are under water several hundred yards away. The fort is no more genuine than its garrison of college boys in eighteenth-century fig.

Nearby, overlooking the deserted waters, is the Sequoyah Birthplace Museum, built to soothe the Cherokees for desecration of their ancient homes and graves. More than a thousand of their dead, hastily dug up in rescue archaeology, lie here beneath a monument.

It took me half an afternoon to find the site of Chota, capital of the eighteenth-century Cherokees. I knew where it was—just a few miles upstream from the fort—but getting there by small roads winding through the wooded hills was another matter. The best farmland having been flooded, it seems that only two lines of business thrive in the area today: the sale of lawn ornaments and the sale of God. Concrete "darkies" in red jackets were a hot item. If you didn't want a darkie you could take home the "Deeds and Miracles of Jesus Carved in Wood."

Several times I asked the way, but only one local citizen had ever heard of Chota, and then merely as a place to launch a boat. It was as if the Cherokee past, like the Cherokee people, had been swept away.

The road I sought was a gravel track along the shore of "Tellico Lake." The waters were still, platinum blue beneath a sharp spring sky. Wildflowers were blooming, bees at work in the sun, and the woods were bright with new leaf. People love to erect monuments to their conquests, and the TVA is no exception. At a small carpark beside the lake stood a granite plaque, informing me that Tanasi—hometown of Attakullakulla, the Little Carpenter—from which Tennessee gets its name, lay about 300 yards "west": in other words, out in the water somewhere. "Therefore," the plaque crooned, "those who reside in this beautiful state are forever linked to its Cherokee heritage." It reminded me of Adlai Stevenson's assessment of Richard Nixon as the kind of politician who could cut down a redwood tree, mount the stump, and make a speech for conservation.

Chota has a more elaborate monument. A large, low mound rising from the lake is connected to the shore by a causeway with a footpath bordered by young willows and reeds. My tread disturbed a great blue heron and some geese. At the mound, eight concrete posts have been set in a circle to represent the pillars of the townhouse that once stood here. One post has a plaque; the others bear symbols of the seven Cherokee clans. A headstone commemorates Oconostota, the Great Warrior of Chota and rival of Attakullakulla, who was buried beside this building in 1783 and dug up, along with his eyeglasses, in 1969.[46]

I sat and gazed across the lake; it was still possible to imagine the drowned river in its depths. For some moments "Chota" beguiled me, but this, too, is a fake. The great townhouse, sixty feet in diameter, did indeed stand here, but well below the waterline. The mound on which I sat was not piled up long ago by Cherokee hands, but recently by a bulldozer.

So what do we have on the land that cost so many lives? A fake fort and a fake Indian ruin presiding over each end of a fake lake. And between these two eminences lies the swollen corpse of the Long Man, in which the heritage of the Cherokees has been drowned in the name of progress. The TVA itself admits that the dam is a failure. Why not drain it? In a few years the ground would recover its fertility. Why not return the land to the Cherokees, who are becoming ever more crowded on their reservations? Some could live and farm again at their old beloved towns.

It would be but small reparation for the Trail of Tears.

At a congressional hearing on the dam in 1978, a Cherokee named Jimmie Durham gave the following speech, a speech worthy of all those who spoke so eloquently centuries ago in Chota's townhouse.

> Is there a human being who does not revere his homeland, even though he may not return? . . . In our own history, we teach that we were created there, which is truer than anthropological truth because it was there that we were given our vision as the Cherokee people. . . . In the language of my people . . . there is a word for land: Eloheh. This same word also means history, culture, and religion. We cannot separate our place on earth from our lives on the earth, nor from our vision nor our meaning as a people. We are taught from childhood that the animals and even the trees and plants . . . are our brothers and sisters. So when we speak of land, we are not speaking of property, territory, or even a piece of

> ground upon which our houses sit and our crops are grown. We are speaking of something truly sacred.[47]

Yet it would be wrong to end this story on a note of pathos, for if there is one thing that characterizes the Cherokees it is their resilience. Despite all that has happened since Hernando de Soto burst into their towns 450 years ago, the Eastern Cherokees are still living where Cherokees have lived since long before Columbus. Nor does the story of the Western Cherokees end with Oklahoma's statehood. Despite a century of effort to disperse and assimilate them, they number 80,000 today, 10,000 of whom still speak the Cherokee language.

The government of the Cherokee Nation, suppressed in the late 1890s, has been reborn at Tahlequah. In 1970, Cherokees elected their principal chief for the first time since 1898, and in 1975 they adopted a new constitution that gave traditionalists a genuine say in the Nation's affairs. The present principal chief is Wilma Mankiller, an able and dedicated descendant of her namesakes of the past.

Here is an excerpt from Chief Mankiller's State of the Nation address, given at Tahlequah on September 1, 1990:

> As we approach . . . the twenty-first century . . . I can't help but feel hopeful about our future. I think the strongest thing I see as I travel around to Cherokee communities and talk with people is their tenacity. Despite everything that's happened to our people throughout history we've managed to hang on to our culture, we've managed to hang on to our sense of being Cherokee. . . .
>
> When people ask where I want the Cherokee Nation to be in the twenty-first century I always tell them I want to enter the twenty-first century . . . not on anybody else's terms but on our own terms. . . . Two hundred years from now people will gather right here in this very place and there will still be a very strong Cherokee Nation. Someone will stand up and say that this past year's been a good year. . . .
>
> We are going to do everything in our power to make sure that the Cherokee Nation continues to exist.[48]

FIFTEEN

IROQUOIS

> [Indians] are simply living on the benevolence and charity of the Canadian Parliament, and . . . beggars should not be choosers.
>
> —John A. Macdonald, prime minister of Canada, 1885

> No nation has the right to hold a captive nation.
>
> —Mohawk Warrior Society, 1981

The rebirth of the Six Nations—the Mohawk, Oneida, Onondaga, Cayuga, Seneca, and Tuscarora—may be taken literally: there are today at least 60,000 Iroquois, more than at any time in three and a half centuries. Metaphorically, rebirth takes many forms: the spread of the Longhouse religion; the revival of languages, especially Mohawk; the growth of Iroquois nationalism.

Of the modern Iroquois, some 25,000 are Mohawks, 80 percent of whom live within the outline of Canada. In the summer of 1990, the Iroquois were suddenly reborn in white consciousness when Canadian front pages were filled for three months by what became known as the Oka Crisis or Mohawk Revolt. Canada's history—an unsightly history swept under the threadbare rug of its national myths—came back to haunt it.

When I began writing this book, I could not have imagined that the government of this country in which I live would send more than 4,000 troops—equipped with tanks, artillery, jet fighters, and helicopter gunships—against a few hundred Mohawk "warriors." Canada is a country that prides itself on its humanity and probity, on its role as peace-keeper, negotiator, and international social worker. Now one must ask, Is this sanctimonious therapist the sort who secretly commits abuse at home? To understand why Corporal Marcel Lemay of the Quebec police died in a chaotic burst of gunfire on July 11, 1990, one must know something of the hidden war that the Dominion of Canada has waged against the Iroquois Confederacy since Canada became self-governing in 1867.

By that date, the territory of the Six Nations was reduced to about fifteen scattered islands in a rising tide of whites. The largest was the Grand River tract at the west end of the Niagara peninsula, obtained by the Mohawk loyalist Joseph Brant after Britain betrayed the Indians at the 1783 Treaty of Paris. In 1784, the Crown transferred this land to "His Majesty's faithful allies . . . the said Mohawk Nation, and such other of the Six Nations as wish to settle in that quarter to take possession of and . . . enjoy forever."[1] Had it been surveyed as originally defined—a twelve-mile strip following the river from its mouth at Lake Erie to its source more than a hundred miles north—the tract would amount to 1,200 square miles. But almost from the beginning, the Iroquois and the British agreed neither on its size nor its political status. Brant had seen it as an exchange of national territory for the vast expanse of Iroquoia abandoned to the Americans. Sovereignty, he insisted, lay with the Six Nations, "a free People subject to no power upon Earth."[2] Had it been otherwise, he wrote after the British began meddling in Grand River affairs, "we would never have accepted the land." The Crown itself, he pointed out, described the Six Nations as allies, not dependents: an important distinction. "We still had opportunities left after the [Revolutionary] war of providing for ourselves in the free and independent manner natural to Indians," the august and balding chief continued. "Unhappily for us, we have been made acquainted too late with the . . . real intentions of the Ministry."[3]

Another group of Mohawk loyalists settled on the Bay of Quinte, near modern Kingston. Both Quinte and Grand River lie just outside the ancient bounds of Iroquoia, but the British offered neither territory merely from a sense of moral obligation. The Iroquois loyalists still had military clout; by helping them settle at either end of Lake Ontario, Britain was able to continue its policy of maintaining Indian buffer states along the political fault line of North America.

Brant's followers were soon joined by other Iroquois fleeing the American republic. When members of all Six Nations had arrived in force, the ancient League replicated itself like a living cell. Grand River became a new, miniature Confederacy, complete with fifty condoled chiefs (sachems chosen by clan mothers), Pine Tree Chiefs elected for merit, and its own Council Fire tended by local Onondagas. Outside Grand River, most of the Iroquois archipelago continued to regard Onondaga, New York, as its capital. Two parallel confederacies have existed ever since; the relationship between them has never been clearly defined. On rare occasions—one being the 1990 crisis—they meet in council at Onondaga. Most of the time each goes its own way.

Joseph Brant was, and still is, a controversial figure. Like many Indian leaders of his day, he advocated rapid change to a Euro-American economy. To raise money for this purpose, he leased parcels of the Grand River tract to whites. This is some of the finest farmland in Canada: corn springs almost visibly from the alluvial soil on steamy summer days, and great willows, maples, and oaks overhang the smooth water. Brant reasoned that leases to foreigners would remain under Iroquois sovereignty, but the colonial government later converted his deals into irrevocable cessions.

When the Dominion of Canada was formed in 1867, the Six Nations were left with ninety square miles on the Grand River. Canada regards this as an Indian "reserve," or reservation. The Iroquois do not. They see their remaining lands not as mere estates within Euro-American countries but as national territories. When whites assert that these could never be viable as such, Indians point out that several European nations are much smaller: the republic of San Marino, landlocked within Italy, has only twenty-four square miles, and the principality of Monaco covers a princely 370 acres. Why, they ask, should a people who have never been conquered by Canada, and have never surrendered their independence, be colonized when other small nations are free? They add that if lands unjustly taken were returned to them, their countries might not be so small.

Today the Grand River is home to about 16,000 citizens, many of whom have jobs in the white world outside. Some own ranch-style houses with double garages and late-model cars. At first glance, little distinguishes this landscape from the Canada beyond. But here and there, set back from the gravel roads among trees and well-mowed lawns, are large halls of log or whitewashed clapboard with a chimney at each gable: these are longhouses, the temples of the Iroquois faith, modern descendants of the great bark halls of pre-Columbian times. In Ohsweken, the tiny capital, stands a fine Victorian structure of ocher brick. A new sign says "Six Nations Public Library"; but over the door are the faded words COUNCIL HOUSE and the date 1863. For most of its life this building was the parliament of the Grand River Iroquois. It is older than Canada's own parliament, but Canada has driven out the assembly that sat there.

When it became clear during the late nineteenth century that the United States would not invade the British colony, Indian buffer states were no longer required. Canada, knowing that native nations held aboriginal title to large parts of North America, wanted to get rid of its indigenous rivals. The best way, short of extermination, was to absorb them. With no Indians, there could be no aboriginal claims; so the young Canadian parliament passed an Indian Act intended to promote assimilation.

This process could be hastened, Canada thought, by encouraging contact with "civilization," which often involved confining Indian children in missionary boarding schools, and shrinking the reserves, which it had come to regard as mere holding camps for a doomed race. Under the policy of "enfranchisement," Indians were expected to give up membership in their own nations forever in exchange for the privilege of voting in Canadian elections. Males received a lump sum and a piece of land—essentially a bribe—snipped from their reserve.[4] Few took the bait. Between 1876 and 1918, only 102 did so, most of them women who had married whites. Such a marriage brought automatic "enfranchisement" even though Canadian women then had no vote.[5]

The Indian Act also aimed to replace indigenous governments with a uniform system of elected band councillors who would be responsive puppets of the Indian Affairs department. "Hereditary" chiefs (an inaccurate term for Iroquois sachems) would be deposed, and matrilineality—the reckoning of descent, and hence nationality, through the female line—would end.[6] In short, the act's purpose was to destroy native nations from within by dissolving their political and family structures.

Canada began by overthrowing traditional governments on the smaller Iroquois territories of Ontario and Quebec. In the mid-1880s, Indian Affairs pressured the Bay of Quinte Mohawks, ostensibly on a trial basis, to replace their condoled chiefs with elected councilmen. The Indians put up with the new system for a couple of years, then rejected it—the adversarial style of European politics ran counter to their tradition of consensus, as did exclusion of the women's voice.

But it turned out that the "trial period" was a sham: Canada would not allow the people to restore their own system. The outraged Mohawks sent pleas to the governor general, Queen Victoria's representative in Canada.

> We . . . do not want our Council Fire extinguished, because it was the custom and manner of our forefathers. . . .
>
> We will remind you of the Covenant Chain of Peace and Friendship between the English people and the Six Nations. When our forefathers first made the Covenant Chain with the English, both parties engaged to keep the ends of it fast in their hands. . . .
>
> Brother! At the time of formation of the treaties . . . the Six Nations Indians were found and looked upon as a people, and had a systematic constitution. . . . It was understood by both parties . . . that each should maintain their own constitutions, but in the present instance, it appears that the Silver Chain is now tarnished upon these points.
>
> The Canadian Government, which does not recognize us fully, looks upon the Six Nations as minors and treats them as such.
>
> Brother! We quote the words of Lord Dufferin, one of your predecessors, saying the people of Canada and the people of Britain will not cease to recognize these obligations. . . . Never shall the word of Britain, once pledged, be broken. . . .
>
> What is your power and authority to rule our people?[7]

What indeed? But the petitions did no good. Canada recognized only the puppet council and funneled all rents, annuities, and other funds belonging to the Indians through that body.

Along the St. Lawrence, where the Iroquois first met Cartier and Champlain, are the large Mohawk communities of Kahnawake, opposite Montreal, and Akwesasne, between Montreal and Kingston. Although these had drawn close to the French for a century, they had helped the British conquer New France in 1759–1760 and welcomed large numbers of southern Mohawks during the Revolution.

In 1890 the people of Kahnawake protested, pointing out the Canadian government's lack of jurisdiction and its hypocrisy in opposing "hereditary" chiefs:

> Every nation throughout the world retains their own customs, rites, and ceremonies, and according to the British Constitution [there are] Kings, Queens, and Lords and Peers as hereditaries.
>
> Brother! We cannot account . . . why we cannot adhere . . . to our customs, rights, and ceremonies.[8]

Canada's most brutal intervention came at Akwesasne. This territory's very location should remind the United States and Canada that the Mohawk Nation is far older than they, for the map line drawn between them runs through the middle of it. Here, in 1898, the clan mothers wrote a long letter to the governor general, explaining how their system worked and insisting that they had no wish for change. Twice the women prevented elections from being held. An official of the Canadian government, sent to investigate, made a most revealing comment: the Indians, he said in his report, "might as well look for the falling of the sky as to expect recognition of their claim to hold the position of a practically independent state."[9] Very similar words would be uttered ninety-two years later by Prime Minister Brian Mulroney. The real issue, then as now, was sovereignty. And then, as now, the affair turned violent.

In March 1899, Mounted Police arrived to enforce the holding of an election. They were soon besieged by 200 Mohawks. No Mounties were hurt, but they were sent packing. Two months later they returned. Michael Mitchell, the present elected chief of Akwesasne, wrote this account of how the council he heads, and aims to reform, was installed:

> At 4:00 A.M. on May 1, 1899, Colonel Sherwood . . . came to Akwesasne, leading a contingent of police across the St. Lawrence River. They occupied the Council Hall, where they sent a message to the chiefs to attend a special meeting regarding the buying of stone [to rebuild a bridge]. . . . As the chiefs walked into the council office, they were thrown to the floor and handcuffed. One of the women notified the Head Chief, Jake Fire, and as he came through the door demanding the release of his fellow chiefs he was shot twice, the second shot being fatal. The police marched their prisoners to the tugboat and left the village. Jake Fire was shot down in cold blood while fighting for Mohawk Indian government. . . .[10]
>
> The seven chiefs . . . were imprisoned. Five of them were kept in jail for more than a year. . . .
>
> Immediately after this affair, the representatives of the government took fifteen Indians over to Cornwall and provided them with alcohol. The Indian agents told them each to nominate one of the others present. This was how the elective government under the Indian Act system was implemented at Akwesasne.
>
> This is the way Canada introduced our people to the principles of their democracy.[11]

To its credit, a white newspaper, the *Huntingdon Gleaner*, had this to say at the time:

> In reality, the whites have been the aggressors all through the wretched affair, which has had so tragic an ending. It was the whites who passed a law to interfere with the internal management of an inoffensive tribe . . . the Indians were merely resisting an attempt to change the customs that are dear to them, and which concern themselves alone. . . . They simply ask to be let alone, an independ-

ent community, ruled by themselves, and we do not see why what they ask should be withheld.[12]

> Tyranny, stupidity, and lack of vision have brought about the situation now alluded to as the "Indian Problem."
>
> —Luther Standing Bear, Sioux, 1933

> Iroquois do not wish to be subjects of any foreign nation. . . . We ask only to be left to our way and our traditions. We want the same freedom for ourselves that the whites wanted when they fled European tyranny.
>
> —Clinton Rickard, Tuscarora, 1966

When Canada entered the twentieth century, the Iroquois sachems of Quinte, Kahnawake, and Akwesasne had been overthrown, but those of Grand River still retained their ancient powers. All peoples have religious and political divisions, and the Iroquois are no exception. A small but vocal minority opposed to the traditional government had arisen at Grand River. They became known as the Dehorners because deer antlers are the insignia of a condoled chief. Some of the dissidents were non-Iroquois, such as Delawares, who had no members of their own on the council; others were young men who felt left out by their elders; most were doctrinaire Christians who thought the ancient assembly smacked of heathenism. The Canadian government conspired with this "Christian democrat" minority as a way of breaking the League in the name of electoral reform.[13]

The seriousness of this challenge prompted the Grand River sachems to renew their claim to sovereignty after the First World War, in which the Six Nations again served as Britain's allies, *not* as Canadian conscripts. The status Grand River sought was essentially that of a self-governing British protectorate. There were several such at the time, for example Tonga and Botswana, which have since become independent countries. The Six Nations did not wish to threaten Canada's legitimate interests or security; they merely wanted Canada to stop threatening theirs.

In 1919, the Grand River Council appointed a status committee led by the Cayuga sachem Deskaheh, whose English name was Levi General. In photographs and drawings, Deskaheh's calm face looks out from beneath the sacred antlers of his sachemship, his lower lip full and curled like that of a Maya lord. But there is no haughtiness, only solemn resolve. An Irish journalist who met him found "a good-looking, broad-shouldered man . . . who knows his strength and believes in it, whilst his shining eyes speak of enthusiasm and idealism."[14]

Against Deskaheh—against all Indian leaders at odds with the settler government—stood Duncan Campbell Scott, head of Indian Affairs from 1913 to 1932.[15] Scott was a time-serving mandarin but eager man of letters. He took a romantic interest in native tradition, but living natives were another matter. "I want to get rid of the Indian problem," he said in 1920. "Our object is to continue until there is not a single Indian in Canada that has not been absorbed."[16]

Scott saw himself as Canada's Kipling. Perhaps he shared Kipling's vices, but not his brilliance or his irony: for Scott, natives were indeed lesser breeds without the law. His writings, admired in their day, now seem so much Edwardian bric-a-brac: florid, ponderous, unabashedly bigoted. The Indian, Scott wrote, was "a weird and waning race . . . ready to break out at any moment in savage dances; in wild and desperate orgies."[17] Most revealing of all is one short line: "Altruism is absent from the Indian character."[18] Only someone deeply ignorant, deeply prejudiced, or both could have written that. Even Senator Henry Dawes had known enough to draw the opposite conclusion: "There is no selfishness, which is at the bottom of civilization."[19]

In the autumn of 1920, the Six Nations hired lawyers and requested a ruling on their political status from Canada's Supreme Court. The Privy Council stepped in to block the hearing. The Indians then went to the governor general.

> The Six Nations of the Grand River, with sorrow in their hearts, come to complain of wrongs done us in the name of the Dominion Government.
>
> We complain because the Ministry of the Interior has ceased to recognize our rights in the Grand River Retreat. The Ministry has

> devised and prevailed on the Dominion Government to enforce on our people, one by one, [Canadian] citizenship . . . and thus to open our domain, without our consent, to piece-meal purchase by outsiders. . . .
>
> We have no shield of our own with which to oppose the Power of Canada coming against us in our own homes. To prevent so great a wrong we offer the simple justice of our cause.[20]

When it became clear that "simple justice" would get nowhere in Ottawa, Deskaheh took the case to Britain, the nation that had granted his ancestors the Grand River "to be held . . . according to the several customs and usages of them the said Chiefs, warriors, women, and people of the Six Nations."[21] The colonial secretary, one Winston Churchill, sent the petition back to Canada. "The matters submitted," he wrote, "lie within the exclusive competency of the Canadian Government."[22] It was an interesting piece of buck-passing, in view of what would happen two years later.

During 1922, Canada's new minister of the Interior proposed a royal commission and seemed willing to negotiate with the Six Nations. But while this offer was being discussed, the Royal Canadian Mounted Police (probably at Scott's instigation) raided Grand River on the pretext of looking for moonshiners. Shots were fired; talks were broken off. Scott then stationed an RCMP detachment at Ohsweken, within yards of the brick Council House.

The Iroquois had meanwhile taken an interest in the fledgling League of Nations, which they saw as kindred to their own. In 1923, after the police invasion, Deskaheh decided to take his people's case to Geneva. Supporters organized lacrosse tournaments—an ancient Iroquoian game—to raise funds for the trip. In a brilliant move, the delegates traveled on Six Nations passports, which Switzerland accepted.[23]

Deskaheh and his American lawyer, George Decker, had prepared a sophisticated brief: *The Redman's Appeal for Justice: The Position of the Six Nations That They Constitute an Independent State*. The document included treaty texts illustrating that the Six Nations had long been regarded as a sovereign people. Deskaheh also brought antique belts, among them the famous Two Row Wampum, whose parallel lines commemorate the earliest pact between Iroquois and Europeans. The oral tradition associated with this is that the two peoples agreed to travel side by side on the same river but in their own hulls, meaning that each would retain their own law and customs; disaster would result should either try to navigate with a foot in the other's boat.

Deskaheh also produced sources likely to carry greater weight with legal minds. He quoted the landmark Cherokee decision of U.S. Chief Justice John Marshall: "Discovery could not affect the rights of those already in possession [of America] European Crowns asserted a title against other Europeans only."[24] And he clinched his argument with a more recent precedent. In 1912—only eleven years before—Britain had persuaded the United States to pay the Grand River Cayugas for pre-Revolutionary land cessions south of the border. In this case the British had themselves told the court:

> The Six Nations were recognized as independent nations and allies of the Dutch, and afterwards by the English. . . .
>
> These confederate Nations have ever since resided upon the Grand River . . . maintaining their cohesion and ancient constitution and method of government.[25]

Diplomats who had regarded the "redskin" as merely an amusing diversion from the tedium of Geneva began to suspect that he might have a case.

By the rules of the League of Nations, nonmembers needed a member to sponsor their affairs. Deskaheh first approached the Netherlands, reminding them of their old friendship with the Six Nations. Britain frightened off the Dutch by threatening to dig up *their* colonial skeletons, but not before the Iroquois petition had reached the League of Nations' secretary general, who sent a copy to Ottawa. The Canadians huffed in reply: "The claim that the Six Nations are an organized and self-governing people so as to form a political unit apart from Canada is . . . an absurd one."[26]

Deskaheh got a sympathetic hearing from the delegates of Persia, Ireland, Estonia, and Panama, whose nations knew the taste of violated sovereignty. They had also become irked by Canada's wearisome tone of moral superiority as it tried to use the League of Nations to promote its own sovereignty as distinct from that of the British Empire. Persia prepared to put the Iroquois case on the agenda for March 1924; it looked as though Canada would be seriously embarrassed.

But Britain, having dismissed all appeals from the Iroquois as beyond its jurisdiction, was willing to wield a big stick on little Canada's behalf. Suddenly these Indians' cause, described by Churchill as an exclusively Canadian concern, became "impertinent interference in internal affairs of the British Empire."[27] The Foreign Office sent threats to Teheran, Tallin, and Panama City. Deskaheh's appeal was never heard.

In October, in desperation, the Iroquois sachem wrote to King George V:

> I . . . Deskaheh of Ohsweken, have been sent forth by my people, the United Nations of the Mohawks, Cayugas, Onondagas, Oneidas, Senecas and Tuscaroras . . . to seek assistance and protection for them who are domiciled on the banks of the Grand River. . . .
>
> My People have been subjected to a tyranny, and to outrages and indignities of which nothing is known over here. . . .
>
> The Six Nations have never failed to fight in the American wars for the interests of the British Crown, the chief engagements being the Battle of the Plains of Abraham, Quebec, 1759, the Revolutionary War of 1776–7, the Battle of Queenstown Heights of 1812, and, lastly in the great European War of 1914–[18], when my People sent forth their contingent . . . and of the 300 that went forth, 260 returned.
>
> It is because of the fierce and persistent violation by Canada . . . of the rights and freedom of my People—the attempts to break down and destroy their government, the Council at Ohsweken, the attempts to deprive them of their liberty and their nationality . . . that I feel now compelled to seek Your Majesty's aid and protection.[28]

The Canadian government, meanwhile, had been working exactly as Deskaheh feared: to overthrow the assembly that dared to challenge it.

On October 7, 1924, armed police burst into the Ohsweken Council House and read a decree dissolving the Six Nations' parliament. They broke open a chest and seized documents going back to the time of Joseph Brant, many of them germane to the sovereignty case.[29] More police raided the wampum keepers' homes, taking the sacred belts, the Iroquois equivalents of flag, mace, and Magna Carta.

The invaders announced elections for a new council, to be chaired by a pistol-toting employee of Indian Affairs. Scott feared that the condoled chiefs might stand and win, but to his relief they and almost everyone else boycotted the entire process. From a population of 4,500 only twenty-seven people voted: "Christian democrats" who elected themselves.[30]

But the sachems did not give up. They have sat ever since as a government exiled in its own country, holding their meetings at the Grand River Onondaga Longhouse. In 1959 they staged a countercoup and took back their council building. Again the Mounties ousted them with clubs. For the majority at Grand River the sachems remain the true government, the only one with the authority conferred centuries ago by the divine Peacemaker. The alien democracy has never taken root: in the most recent vote for the "democratic" council, a mere 6 percent of the electorate took part.[31]

Deskaheh was still in Europe when news of the October coup reached him. He raised a new outcry in Geneva but was again turned away. The blow against his people affected him physically; he became gravely ill with lung disease. He got back to North America but had to stay south of the border on the Tuscarora reservation at Niagara, out of reach of Canadian police—an ironic reversal of Grand River history. In his memoir *Fighting Tuscarora,* Deskaheh's friend and ally Chief Clinton Rickard recalls the Iroquois patriot's last days:

> He was confined [in hospital] for eight weeks. Nine doctors who worked on him were unable to cure him. He then made a request . . . to come and stay at my home. . . . He was accordingly brought to our house from Rochester in an ambulance and we gave him a bed in our parlor.

> Our new guest now asked if I could secure a medicine man to treat him. I therefore went to his reserve. . . . Two medicine men who came to see him and who stayed in the same room with him for a week . . . brought him to the point of recovery. . . .
>
> Now I do believe that the Canadian rulers were convinced that some plot was being hatched in my house for they did a very strange thing. The government of Canada sent Royal Canadian Mounted Police over into the United States and into the Tuscarora Reservation. These mounties rode up and down in front of my house intimidating us.[32]

The United States had just passed the 1924 Immigration Act, which aimed, in part, to keep nonwhites (especially Orientals) out of the land of the free. Then as now, about half the Iroquois lived on each side of the border. Despite old treaties guaranteeing Indians free passage, the act was used against them. This Immigration Act, wrote the Tuscarora chief, "made the original inhabitants of this continent the victims of American racial prejudice. . . . Members of Deskaheh's own family, who had not seen him in two years, were prohibited from coming over."[33] The border guards also stopped Deskaheh's medicine men, a vindictive blow that sent him into an irreversible decline.

Deskaheh died on June 27, 1925. "He was only fifty-two years old," wrote Chief Rickard, "and one of the finest men I have ever met."[34] His body was taken back to Grand River and buried in the grounds of the Upper Cayuga Longhouse, a sturdy building of dovetailed logs that is still in regular use. Two thousand mourners came to his funeral. So did the police. The Mounties were planning to comb the speeches for seditious content, but they found that everything was said in Iroquois.

The following is from Deskaheh's last address, which he gave in English by radio from Rochester, New York, a few months before his death:

> My home is on the Grand River . . . where, one hundred and forty winters ago, we had a little seashore of our own and a birch-bark navy.

> You would call it Canada. We do not. . . .
>
> We didn't think we would ever live long enough to find that a British promise was not good. An enemy's foot is on our country, and George the Fifth knows it for I told him so, but he will not lift his finger to protect us nor will any of his ministers. . . .
>
> To punish us for trying to preserve our rights, the Canadian Government has now pretended to abolish our government [and] set up a Canadian-made government over us, composed of the few traitors among us who are willing to accept pay from Ottawa. . . .
>
> One word more so that you will be sure to remember our people. If it had not been for them, you would not be here. If, one hundred and sixty-six winters ago, our warriors had not helped the British at Quebec . . . it would have been a French-speaking people here today, not you. That part of your history cannot be blotted out by the stealing of our wampum belts in which that is recorded.[35]

To make life difficult for future Deskahehs, Canada passed a law to deny Indians access to the law. In 1927 it became illegal for "any person" to raise money for Indian claims.[36] This remained in effect until 1951, but there were few prosecutions. The law's drafters forgot that the Indian Act stated elsewhere: "The term 'person' means an individual other than an Indian."[37]

> The fish which . . . used to supply us with food, are now, by the dams and other obstructions of the white people, prevented from multiplying, and we are almost entirely deprived of that accustomed sustenance.
>
> —Red Jacket, Seneca, 1821

> Whenever the legislators endeavour to take away and destroy the property of the people, or to reduce them to slavery under arbitrary power, they put themselves into a state of war with the people who are thereupon absolved from any further obedience.
>
> —John Locke, 1690

By the mid-twentieth century the invaders' hunger for the land they had seized was on the wane. They had felled the timber, panned the gold, dug the coal. A hundred years of their mechanical plowing had produced far greater yields than the Indian hoe, but at enormous cost to the soils of North America. Farmsteads wrested from the Iroquois only generations before lay unkempt or abandoned, a wrack of rusty threshers, rotting barns, jalopies, and briars. The mills of which the Seneca orator Red Jacket complained had become ruins, antique shops, or quaint country inns. Industrial cities were drawing the "settler" from the land.

But although the invaders were no longer crowding in person at the Indian's threshold, their urban centers conducted a long-range assault with heavy weapons. Industry needed electrical power, and the cheapest way to get it was to build dams, and the cheapest way to build dams was to expropriate Indian land. During the high tide of American positivism—the age of tailfins, crewcuts, McCarthy, and chrome—the small archipelago remaining to the Six Nations was bulldozed, concreted, and flooded for the general good. The Iroquois lost more land in fifteen years than they had lost in the preceding century.

A slice of Onondaga, the Confederacy capital, went for a dam in the late 1940s; in the fifties, more was dug up and spread beneath the state freeway and the hole used as a dump. In the early 1960s, after court battles reminiscent of the Cherokee Removal, 10,000 acres belonging to the Allegany Senecas—a third of their total and most of the good farmland—was drowned by the Kinzua Dam. To accomplish this, Washington had to break one of the oldest treaties between Indians and the United States, the Canandaigua of 1794, which reads: "The United States will never claim . . . nor disturb the Seneca Nation." George Heron, president of the Senecas, asked, "How long is forever?"[38] In the same decade, the New York Power Authority took a bite from the Tuscaroras for its vast project at Niagara Falls. The Tuscaroras fought all the way to the Supreme Court, only to lose by one vote. "Some things are worth more than money. . . ." the dissenting judges said. "Great nations, like great men, should keep their word."[39]

But the most devastating assault came along the route that Jacques Cartier had hoped might lead to China. Here Canada initiated the

St. Lawrence Seaway, a canalization scheme that dwarfed both Panama and Suez and enabled large oceangoing ships to sail, if not to China, at least halfway across the intervening continent. Between 1954, when the work began, and 1959, when it ended, 100 square miles of property was condemned. This included the waterfront of two Mohawk territories: Akwesasne, Where the Partridge Drums, and Kahnawake, By the Rapids. "When we let the Seaway get put in," an elderly Mohawk said, "we let them take away part of our life."[40]

While they were about it, the white nations built two big power dams opposite Akwesasne. Cheap power brought aluminum smelters and foundries, transforming a quiet rural backwater into an industrial hive. Within a few years, land, water, and air were severely polluted for miles around. Cattle sickened and died; snapping turtles were found to have such high PCB levels that their flesh was technically toxic waste. First robbed, then poisoned, the Akwesasne Mohawks lost their fishing and their farms.

This judicial violence committed by the bloodless hand of compulsory purchase had violent consequences.

The Mohawks are famous for their "high steel" construction on bridges and skyscrapers, a skill they have practiced since the first iron bridges were thrown across the St. Lawrence a century ago. The fearlessness and control required for such demanding work came easily to a people who had always prized courage and stoicism. Ironworkers became the "warriors" in a changed world, traveling afar on dangerous projects, returning home with maturity and prestige. But the seaway spurred some to rediscover their warrior roots more literally. From the theft of the river and the poisoning of the land, militant Mohawk nationalism was born.

In 1972 these Mohawks reestablished the *Rotiskenhrakete,* known in English as the Warrior Society.[41] Their first move was to evict non-Indians from Kahnawake. In 1974 they occupied state land in the New York Adirondacks, proclaiming it Ganienkeh (the Mohawk name of the Mohawk Nation)—a first step toward repossession of their ancient home.[42]

Though never popular with Christian Iroquois, the Warrior Society worked closely at first with leaders of the Longhouse religion and the

Confederacy Council at Onondaga. But during the 1980s it lost the support of many mainstream traditionalists. The reasons for the split were complex, but they boiled down to questions of legitimacy and the corrupting influence of money and guns. In 1982 the Reagan administration cut funding for reservations and encouraged Indians to milk the taxpayer through bingo halls instead. Whites who had never in their lives met an Indian flocked to Indian country for a weekend flutter. At Akwesasne, where the poisoned earth offered few alternatives, bingo and other forms of gambling burgeoned under Warrior "protection." The Warriors also plied a lively cigarette trade, buying cheaply in the United States, shipping across Akwesasne into Canada without paying duty, and selling at Kahnawake to nicotine-addicted Montrealers. For centuries the white man had used alcohol to dispossess the Indian; now the Indian was using tobacco to recover some arrears.

Despite this poetic justice, many Longhouse elders became uneasy: Handsome Lake's Good Message—the Iroquois "New Testament"—emphasized temperance and pacifism; to profit from others' weaknesses, even in a good cause, was a sin. The Warriors countered that the Seneca prophet's revelations were a Quaker-influenced distortion of Iroquois belief; they harked back to the much older Great Law, which preached peace among Iroquois but considered foreigners fair game.

Mohawk longhouses divided, some staying loyal to Handsome Lake's teachings (the orthodox form at Onondaga and elsewhere throughout the Confederacy), others returning to what they saw as an older, purer way. When Red Jacket rebuffed the missionaries in 1805, he said, "We never argue about religion"; now traditionalist Iroquois became as sectarian as Belfast Christians. Old ethnic tensions also surfaced: at Onondaga the Warriors were seen as the latest in a line of "Mohawk hotheads" stretching back to Hendrick and Joseph Brant; at Kahnawake a Mohawk woman dryly told me, "The Onondagas are great philosophers. They dream. We live in reality."

Although bingo halls were legal by American law, casinos were not, and the "smuggling" angered the Canadians. The Warriors argued persuasively that the United States and Canada had only themselves to blame for the smuggling problem: when they carved up North America they should have thought twice before running their border through an unceded part of the Mohawk Nation. But the gambling issue polarized Akwesasne, inflaming old factional wounds caused by more than a century of divide and rule. Both Canada and the United States had installed puppet councils, but the condoled chiefs continued to exercise moral authority. Besides the two white nations, three lesser white regimes—Ontario, Quebec, and New York State—also claimed the right to send police and officials onto different slices of Akwesasne's thirty-six square miles. In all: eight governments (and a Warrior Society) for one community of 10,000 Indians.[43]

When the Mounties, the FBI, and local police tried to shut down the casinos, the Warriors set up patrols to stop them. "This is a sovereign nation that has existed since time immemorial and we will not tolerate any outside interference," said Ateronhiatakon, a Warrior leader using his Mohawk name. "Only the people of Akwesasne can decide their laws and their future."[44] Many antigambling Iroquois also believed in sovereignty, but they charged that the Warriors were using nationalism as a cloak for racketeering. When they appealed to outside authority, the Warriors regarded them as traitors.

The anger sown by the invader was not yet reaped by him: gun battles broke out between the Mohawk factions, and on May 1, 1990, two men died.[45] The affair had become an Iroquois civil war: Warriors and radical Mohawks against conservative Mohawks and the rest of the Confederacy.

Meanwhile, fifty miles away, a small branch of the Mohawk Nation was confronting the latest footfall of encroachment. Just west of the suburban outgrowths of northern Montreal, where the Ottawa River broadens into the picturesque Lake of Two Mountains before joining the St. Lawrence, lies the French Canadian resort town of Oka. Its small web of streets ends at a sandy escarpment rising into a still forest of evergreens with trunks as thick as wine barrels. Above the Pines, as the woods are called, are copses of sugar maple and rolling farmland, home to Kanehsatake (not to be confused with Kahnawake, the much larger Mohawk territory south of Montreal), a scattered community of about a thousand Mohawks.

The Oka land dispute is nearly three centuries old and rooted in the same cultural myopia as the pope's "donation" of America to Portugal and Spain. In 1717, the seven-year-old Louis XV of France "granted" 150 square miles of land surrounding Oka to Sulpician missionaries. From this act two fallacies arose: that the land thereafter belonged to the seigneury of Saint Sulpice and that the fathers "settled" Mohawks there. In truth, while some Mohawks were brought to the Oka mission, most had always lived there. Kanehsatake is specifically mentioned in the ancient roll call of the Iroquois Confederacy: since the days of the Peacemaker, mothers of the Turtle clan have appointed a sachem bearing the name Tekarihoken to the Onondaga Council Fire.

During the last century, the priests began selling off timber and farmland to whites, threatening to excommunicate any Indian who complained. The anger that erupted in 1990 was foreshadowed by an Oka chief in 1869:

> This land was given you in trust for the tribe to whom it belongs; and how have you betrayed that trust? By . . . filling your treasury with the proceeds of stolen property. This land is ours—ours by right of possession; ours as a heritage. . . . We will die on the soil of our fathers, and our bleaching skeletons shall be a witness to nations yet unborn.[46]

Mohawks burned down the Catholic church at this time, but the sales continued. By 1945, when the Canadian government bought what was left of the seigneury, there remained only a ragged quilt of small lots among French Canadian farms and holiday homes: less than 1 percent of King Louis's "grant." Even the creation of a federal reserve did not stop further violations. By a private member's bill in the Quebec legislature, the town council of Oka—a coterie of white businessmen eager for the tourist trade—got title to part of the Pines; in 1959 the town felled trees and built a nine-hole golf course.

The Indians protested, and in 1961 a Canadian parliamentary committee recommended urgent resolution of the Oka problem. It took Ottawa sixteen years to announce that the Mohawk claim did not meet the government's criteria: all claims dating from before the foundation of Canada in 1867 were not its problem, the Canadian government conveniently ruled.

In 1989 the burghers of Oka announced plans to expand their golf course to eighteen holes; to do that they needed more of the Pines, including disputed land beside the Indians' cemetery.

Things came to a head the following March. As the snow melted and the frost left the sandy ground beneath the trees, people from the Kanehsatake longhouse mounted a twenty-four-hour watch from a small ice-fishing shack. It began peacefully enough. Women—the owners of the land by Iroquois tradition—took their turn, and a faith-keeper came every day to offer tobacco to the sunrise before he left for his job fueling jets at Montreal airport.

But one night the fishing shack was set on fire, and rumors began circulating that the Quebec police—the *Sûreté du Québec* (SQ)—would mount an attack. More Mohawks joined the protest; roadblocks were built from logs and sand; men brought their hunting rifles. Late in April 1990, negotiators from the Quebec government, the Mohawks, and the town of Oka sat down to talks, but at that moment word came from the Pines that trucks escorted by police had been unloading long wooden boxes. It is still unclear whether the boxes contained guns, but the Mohawks believed they did. They sent out a cry for help, a cry answered by the Warrior Society. Men in camouflage fatigues came from all parts of the Mohawk Nation, identifying themselves only by Indian names and colorful noms de guerre: Lasagna, Mad Jap, Spudwrench, Wolverine, Noriega. They brought field radios and automatic weapons. They patrolled their lines on commandeered golf carts, their faces hidden by kerchiefs, war paint, and Halloween masks; one wore a Groucho Marx disguise. But behind the carnival facade lay a serious purpose—the chance for the Warriors to prove themselves, to show that they were indeed the army of the Mohawk Nation, fulfilling their ancient duty at the Confederacy's eastern door.

Joe David, a member of the Kanehsatake Bear clan who took part in the protest, showed me around Oka after the siege had ended. David is a successful painter and sculptor in his early thirties, short for a Mohawk, his eyes thoughtful, his words deliberate. He did not join the barricades until he had fasted on a hilltop and received an omen indicating that he should. A believer in nonviolence, he had never handled a gun. He had doubts about the Warriors.

> But I came to realize that their purpose for being a Warrior Society was the protection of the land and the people, regardless of what was going on at Akwesasne. I saw finally why they were invited, and why they came. There was no interest in cigarettes and gambling here. They were here for the right reasons.
>
> I spoke out against the weapons. I thought we could do a nonviolent protest like those at Temagami and other places [where Indians tried to halt logging and other intrusions unrelated to the Mohawk crisis]. But I think what turned things around for everyone here was knowing that those barricades all over Canada don't seem to be doing anything. People get clubbed and beaten and thrown in jail, and the projects end up going through. The machine is so massive that we're being rolled on, all native people. There's no way to stop it.[47]

A few days after Joe David joined up, the police attacked.[48] On the morning of July 11, a hundred armed SQ piled out of cars and vans, firing tear gas shells, smoke bombs, and concussion grenades. They charged the main barricade with a front-end loader. Gas and smoke blew everywhere. Mohawk men and women armed with anything from sticks to AK-47s were shouting, running, rubbing their eyes, throwing themselves to the ground. The police were equally confused. Then came a volley of gunfire from both sides. When the shooting ceased, the barricade still stood, the SQ had abandoned their cars, and Corporal Lemay was dead.

The police said he had been shot by the Indians; the Indians, by his own side. It would take almost a year for a Quebec coroner to release an eight-page report suggesting that a Mohawk bullet was to blame but failing to produce any solid evidence.[49] It hasn't even been established which SQ commander gave the order for the bungled raid. What *is* known is that the police were asked to act by Oka's mayor, Jean Ouellette, a prime mover in the golf course scheme.[50]

> To be unable to live as ourselves . . . in our own language and according to our own ways, would be like living without an arm or a leg—or perhaps a heart.
>
> —René Lévesque, premier of Quebec, 1968

When the police attacked at Oka, the Warriors radioed comrades twenty-five miles away in Kahnawake; within minutes, Mohawks had blocked rush-hour traffic on the Mercier Bridge and its feeder ramps. Decades ago, Kahnawake fought and lost in court to stop Montreal's freeways being driven through its territory; now those unwelcome corridors became Indian weapons. Some Mohawks hinted that if the police attacked again, the Mercier Bridge would be blown up.[51] Others talked of dropping a cantilever into the Seaway, an "ace in the hole" that would paralyze all shipping on the Great Lakes. The temptation must have been great for those who remembered Kahnawake as it had been before the huge rust-streaked vessels began sliding past their windows every few minutes, vibrating the old limestone houses and bathing the streets in sulfurous exhaust.

As time passed and a peaceful resolution seemed less and less likely, Kahnawake dug in, cutting trenches across the arterial roads. Suburbanites from neighboring Châteauguay, accustomed to traveling through Mohawk land, began to mass outside the barricades, brandishing clubs and chanting racist slogans; the burning of a Mohawk in effigy became a nightly event—at least whenever the press showed up.

"They have been inconvenienced for a few weeks," the Mohawks said. "We have been inconvenienced for centuries."

Canadian Prime Minister Brian Mulroney, a bilingual Quebecker of Irish ancestry with a long chin, twinkling eyes, and the velvet voice of a salesman, refused to get involved. Both opposition parties demanded that Parliament be recalled from summer recess; Mulroney ignored them. In the previous summer, he had recalled Parliament to deal with the weighty problem of a boatload of Sikh refugees landing in Nova Scotia, but an armed insurrection and the blockading of a city of 3 million merited neither his personal attention nor that of the country's elected representatives. Only John Ciaccia, Quebec's Native Affairs minister, would talk to the Mohawks, and whenever he seemed to be getting somewhere, hard-line members of the Quebec cabinet undermined his work.

The two white governments were carrying just as much historical baggage as the Iroquois Confederacy. If the Mohawk Nation was the Confederacy's enfant terrible, Quebec was Canada's. Mulroney had spent the previous three years trying to amend the constitution with a deal called the Meech Lake Accord, which involved transferring federal powers to the provinces in order to persuade Quebec that it would have little to gain by carrying out its frequent threats to secede. Although this giveaway of federal responsibilities was unpopular outside Quebec, provincial premiers were delighted with the chance to help themselves to a bigger slice of the national patrimony.[52] Above all, the accord alarmed the native nations, who were worried about their treaty rights and offended by the prime minister's vision of Canada as a product of "two founding peoples," both white. By a fluke, the Manitoba legislature's rules required a unanimous vote to pass the accord before the deadline. By another fluke, one member of that legislature was an Indian, the first ever to sit there.[53] Less than three weeks before the police attack at Oka, Elijah Harper, a Cree, killed the hated accord with a shake of his head and an eagle feather in his hand.

Many Quebec nationalists had never forgiven "their" Mohawks for siding with the English in 1759 and 1760; now they had a grudge against Indians in general. So did Brian Mulroney. Dispirited and perhaps vindictive, he appeared to stay aloof from the Oka crisis while directing his ministers to present it as a Quebec affair, an attitude that could only make things worse. Under Canada's constitution, Indians and Indian lands are a federal concern; Quebec did not have the jurisdiction to treat with the Mohawks.

Brian Maracle, a Mohawk writer and broadcaster from the Grand River Six Nations, sent an open letter to Mulroney that was carried by several newspapers in the third week of July.

> Dear Prime Minister Mulroney:
>
> How many more people will die before you decide to do something about the situation at Oka?

> Your people say that the Oka stand-off is a matter involving just the Mohawks and the government of Quebec. But if this is just a provincial matter, why have you sent in the RCMP and the army?
>
> The RCMP and the army are not problem-solvers. They are there to kill Indians, if they have to, and that will only trigger more problems. Solving problems is your job. . . .
>
> The dispute at Oka is no longer about a golf course. Now it's about the fight for a fundamental change in the relationship between aboriginal people and the government of Canada. . . .
>
> There is a new generation out there in Indian country . . . who feel they have nothing to lose. They may be willing to push confrontation to the limits in their territories because they may have learned the lesson of Oka—that violence works.
>
> You have the responsibility, the power and the opportunity to make peace. . . . You have the chance to build racial harmony instead of racial hatred. . . .
>
> Act now, Mr. Prime Minister . . . before more people die.[54]

It is still impossible to know precisely what happened during the eleven-week Oka siege, for Quebec has blocked all moves for an independent inquiry. The federal government, mindful of its own murky role and terrified of French separatism, dares not insist. Information from the Iroquois side is hindered by splits in the Confederacy and because many key figures are awaiting trial. What follows is an outline of the known facts.

On August 8, 1990, the prime minister announced that, at the request of Premier Robert Bourassa, he was making the army available to Quebec. Canadians learned to their dismay that their constitution allows a province to take command of the national army and turn it against its own residents. At the same time, Mulroney appointed a mediator to work out "preconditions for negotiations." On August 12, the mediator announced a draft agreement: food and medical supplies, cut off by a police cordon, would be allowed into the Mohawk camp, while a team of international human rights observers would monitor the talks. Two days later the Canadian army deployed 2,500 troops within easy striking distance of both Mohawk territories. On August 16, the promised talks began, but were broken off a week later by the Mohawks when troops moved up to the barricades. It seemed that government strategy (it was not clear which government) was to pretend to talk while tightening the military noose.

On the following weekend, both Iroquois Confederacy councils—those of Onondaga and Grand River—met in the log hall at their ancient capital near Syracuse. The meeting was chaired by Leon Shenandoah, the elderly Tadodaho, or Speaker—descendant in office of the man appointed by the Peacemaker centuries ago. Samson Gabriel, the Kanehsatake sachem bearing the name Tekarihoken, donned his antlers and addressed the Six Nations in the Mohawk language. Official interpreters rendered his words into each of the Iroquois tongues. The debate went back and forth, "across the fire" tended by the Onondagas, until all were of one mind. Neither council supported the Warriors, but both were committed to upholding Iroquois sovereignty. On August 25, they sent the following letter to Prime Minister Mulroney.

> Brother:
>
> Greetings from the combined councils of Grand River and Onondaga in Grand Council at the Onondaga Nation. Your ancestors knew our government as the Confederacy of the Five (and since 1720 Six) Nations, and France knew us as the Iroquois. . . .
>
> In the interest of peace regarding the land issue brought before us by Chief Tekarihoken (Samson Gabriel) the Six Nations Council expresses concern that the long-standing policies which have denied justice and equity in land claims in Canada is a major factor producing the current conflict at Oka, Quebec. We urge Canada's Indian claims policy be dramatically reformed to reflect an honest, just, and binding resolution of such claims. As a first step, we propose a process of negotiations between Confederacy representatives (including Kanesatake representatives) and federal and provincial representatives. . . .
>
> The Haudenosaunee (Six Nations) Council has long suffered from a Canadian policy which claims that . . . our political personality has dissolved into the past. Such injustices serve no

> purpose and create potential for chaos and disorder. . . . We urge immediate review and reconsideration of these policies.[55]

An elegant letter in the great tradition of Six Nations diplomacy, but Brian Mulroney, a small-town lawyer whose career had been built on quelling labor troubles, was hardly the man to appreciate it. Here was an offer from a body uniquely placed to seek a peaceful solution. Mulroney was being handed an opportunity to reverse Canada's disastrous policy of trampling on Iroquois sovereignty, a reversal that could make the Warrior Society redundant. The Confederacy had its own differences with the Warriors, but it retained enormous prestige among Iroquois everywhere, including many of those non-Warriors who, like Joe David, had taken up guns only because they saw no other way.

The following day, after basking in the aura of loftier matters surrounding President George Bush at Kennebunkport, Maine, Mulroney returned to Canada and made a rare statement to the press. The Mohawks' demands, he said, had become "bizarre"—they had even tried to "give themselves the status of an independent nation." Clearly Mr. Mulroney either knew nothing, or pretended to know nothing, about the shared history of Canada and the Six Nations. He and his ministers, especially Justice Minister Kim Campbell, a woman with the hectoring voice and gimlet stare of a Margaret Thatcher, tried to persuade the public that the Mohawk trouble was strictly a law-and-order matter. Why, they asked, should Mohawks fear laying down their arms in a country boasting one of the finest legal systems in the world? "The laws of a civilized nation must apply to us all," Mulroney intoned. "There can't be a double standard."[56] And Quebec's premier said that he was defending democracy against people who did not believe in it.

Perhaps Premier Bourassa had forgotten that Indians were not allowed to vote in his province until 1968; perhaps the federal minister of Justice had forgotten the infamous Canadian law, passed after the Deskaheh affair, which prevented Indians from using the law between 1927 and 1951; perhaps Mr. Mulroney did not know what his "civilized nation" had done at Akwesasne in 1899, at Grand River in 1924 and again in 1959. Perhaps he was unaware that if Indian treaties still had constitutional weight—and Canada's Supreme Court had recently ruled that they did—then the presence of Canadian police and soldiers on Mohawk territory was possibly a violation of international law.[57]

Such was the work of a prime minister who had tried to build an international reputation by grandstanding on the evils of apartheid. And the work of Quebec, a small nationality trying to preserve its distinct culture in North America, yet unwilling to concede that much older nationalities might have prior claims to the same soil.

For the Canadian public, the events were extraordinary and shocking. But for Indians the pattern was sickeningly familar. The so-called rule of law, employed relentlessly as a tool to divide and dispossess them, had finally been met by patriots in a corner with guns. This then justified the use of overwhelming force in the names of "democracy" and "civilization." Oka threatened to repeat the pattern of the Sand Creek massacre (1864), the Wounded Knee massacre (1890), the Yucatán Caste War (1847), Wounded Knee revisited (1973), and the Guatemalan army's neo-conquest of the highland Maya. Oka might have become a bloodbath such as those.

On August 26, the international human rights observers criticized Quebec and Ottawa for failing to keep the preconditions agreed to on August 12. On August 27, Bourassa cut off negotiations and ordered the army to move in. The next day, the Mohawks opened one lane of the Mercier Bridge to allow their children, the sick, and the old to leave Kahnawake before the final showdown. Police held up the convoy for two hours and appeared to stand by as a white mob, which had gathered during the delay, pelted the Indian cars with stones. Joseph Armstrong, an elderly Mohawk with a heart condition, died.

On August 29, Canadian tanks rolled up to the Kahnawake frontier; jets and helicopters roared overhead. At least 4,000 troops were now deployed in the Montreal area. But, when the only outcome seemed to be a massacre, a deal was worked out on the spot between Mohawk and army commanders. Late in the afternoon, soldiers and Warriors together began dismantling the roadblocks at the Mercier Bridge. In return, it seems, the army turned a blind eye while certain Warriors and weapons left Kahnawake by air. It was, at least, a disengagement.

The same did not happen at Oka itself. There the army advanced relentlessly on several fronts. Day after day on television, Canadians watched the tall pines crash before tanks and chain saws. Native protests broke out all over the country: in British Columbia, roads were blocked, in Ontario the railways; electricity pylons crashed to the ground. Protesters of all races marched in Toronto, Montreal, and other cities. Hundreds of Canada's most prominent citizens and organizations took out a full-page in the *Globe and Mail* condemning the government's action and demanding the recall of Parliament "to discuss the crisis and the demands of the First Nations for sovereignty."[58]

The army stopped short of overrunning the Indians' final stronghold—one building and a few acres of forest overlooking the Lake of Two Mountains. Inside were about forty Mohawks and a dozen journalists. The army surrounded the perimeter with razor wire and built searchlight towers to deprive the occupants of sleep. The Mohawks drummed and sang around a sacred fire, gaining strength and morale from the ritual power of False Faces—quizzical, grimacing masks carved from living trees—which the Iroquois have traditionally used to summon metaphysical force.

Perhaps little but the certainty of international disgrace, and the prospect of a hundred Okas across the country, prevented army tanks from rolling over the Indian camp. Journalists outside the wire were kept well away from the front and fed a bland diet of news and propaganda by affable officers. Only the handful of reporters *within* Mohawk lines had any chance of witnessing what happened; they were the main deterrent. The army tried to jam their telephones, confiscate their film when it was sent out, and block supplies, clothing, and food. Since no state of emergency had ever been declared, these actions violated the Charter of Rights, the very democracy Mulroney and Bourassa claimed to be upholding.

On September 8, Canadian soldiers crept under the wire and clubbed a Warrior named Spudwrench sleeping in his foxhole; the next day the image of his broken, bloodied head appeared on front pages and TV screens. Immediately, officialdom stepped up efforts to silence the reporters. Only hours after it showed the damaging footage of

Spudwrench, the Canadian Broadcasting Corporation mysteriously pulled out its film crew, offering the excuse that the army could no longer guarantee the safety of journalists. The excuse was absurd: the army had made exactly the same statement when the crew went *in;* and at that very moment the CBC had crews in Iraq, Lebanon, and El Salvador.

On September 18, a hundred troops supported by helicopters raided a Kahnawake longhouse, supposedly to look for weapons. The raid sparked a brawl with unarmed men, women, and children; about seven soldiers and seventy-five Mohawks were injured or badly gassed. Late that night, the Indians sent an open letter to the Canadian people:

> Since July 11, 1990, we of the Mohawk Nation and its allies have attempted to reach a peaceful conclusion to the present crisis, which has its roots long before that date.
>
> It was not our desire to avoid discussions with your civilian leadership. We had no choice! Prime Minister Mulroney and Premier Bourassa have ignored their oaths of office, by delegating their political decision-making authority to the military. . . .
>
> Your governments promised that when the Mercier Bridge was opened and all barricades were removed, discussions regarding our long-term grievances would begin. They lied. . . .
>
> Your army promised that once the roads were opened and the bridge was cleared at Kahnawake they would move no further on our territory. They lied! Since that time they have violated our sacred Longhouse, beaten our women . . . occupied our entire territory, and last night fired weapons and tear gas, and beat unarmed people.
>
> Your government told the European Parliament [which denounced Canada's handling of the crisis] that they are meeting with our representatives to end this stalemate. Once again they have lied. . . .
>
> All that we ask is for a process and not promises. All that we have ever received is promises and not action.[59]

Several more times the Oka Mohawks offered to lay down their arms if a joint commission from Quebec, Ottawa, the Iroquois Confederacy, and international human rights organizations would preside over the disengagement and judicial process. Quebec refused every time, saying, "The only negotiations the government recognizes are the army's attempt to get the surrender."[60]

On September 26, two days after Mulroney could no longer delay the sitting of Parliament, the Mohawks surprised everyone by turning an expected surrender into a breakout. Some marched hundreds of yards down the road to mingle with journalists; others, led by "Noriega," got as far as Oka town. Soldiers wrestled Mohawk men and women to the ground, fixing bayonets even though the Indians had left their weapons behind. Eventually, most of the Warriors were bundled into buses and taken to an army base for "processing."[61]

Months after it was over, Joe David, the soft-spoken artist, recalled his last hours inside the wire.

> We thought, at any minute, the shooting is going to start. I still don't know why it didn't.
>
> But we had the medicine pouches we wore around our necks; the ashes from the sacred fire. The guns were nothing. We didn't have enough ammunition to stand off the army for ten minutes. It was all symbolic.[62]

EPILOGUE

REDISCOVERY

> If [my people] are to fight they are too few; if they are to die they are too many.
>
> —Hendrick, Mohawk, 1755

> If my people are wiped out you must destroy all photographs of us, because future generations will look at our photographs and be too ashamed at such a crime against humanity.
>
> —Davi Yanomami, Yanomami, 1990

> Wherever Christians have passed, conquering and discovering, it seems as though a fire has gone, consuming everything.
>
> —Pedro de Cieza de León, c. 1550

The pine woods of Oka did indeed become a symbol—a symbol for all that the invaders have taken from the original Americans over the past 500 years. If there are grounds for optimism in 1992, it is that a country such as Canada has been shocked into reexamining its national myths. In 1990 its politicians still spoke of two founding peoples, English and French; within a year that myth was dead. In 1991 Prime Minister Mulroney announced a royal commission to examine native grievances, and the Ministry of Indian Affairs dropped its policy of ignoring claims from before 1867. The Inuit (Eskimo) and Dene of the Northwest Territories, among the few aboriginal Americans to remain a majority in their own lands, may soon create their own territorial governments.

Change can be seen in other settler countries. The United States seems at last to have recognized that Indians are there to stay. Many reservations are now internally self-governing, with powers comparable to those of states, and in 1978 the First Amendment extended protection to native religions. It has been suggested that the Navajo Nation, whose population has reached a quarter million and whose territory is more than twice the size of Israel, may become the first Indian state.[1] Even in Guatemala, there have been talks to end the war and make room for the Maya and their culture.

At the United Nations and around the world, people such as Rigoberta Menchú, the Quiché Maya activist, are talking about their ignored past and present, reminding us that their history is unfinished. And in doing this, the captive nations of America are rediscovering one another. In northern Quebec, a delegation of Kayapo came from their Amazon home to advise the James Bay Crees. In Quito, Ecuador, once the northern capital of the Inca Empire, indigenous people from throughout the hemisphere recently met to discuss their mutual problems, including how to confront the Columbus celebrations.

But there are still many causes for alarm. The Yanomami of Brazil—sometimes called the last free Indian nation—are suffering precisely the same assault that doomed the Cherokees and Sioux in the nineteenth century: invasion by a gold-hungry rabble spreading disease and laying waste the land. Throughout the Amazon basin, poor migrants are burning trees and fighting Indians for the same reasons that the Long Knives did—reasons inherent in the myths, values, and economics of Western civilization. In the United States, Supreme Court appointments during the presidencies of Ronald Reagan and George Bush have produced a bench that may hand down a new generation of anti-Indian decisions.[2] Canada's royal commission may prove to be nothing but a talking shop, while Quebec's aggressive plan to drown Cree land beneath a $12 billion hydroelectric scheme—the threat that prompted the Kayapo visit—shows that the St. Lawrence Seaway mentality is far from dead. Canadian Indians under twenty-five have the highest suicide rate in the world;[3] and Guatemala's death squads are still killing more than 2,000 people a year.

When the Anglo-Saxon and the Iberian came to the New World, each remained true to his traditions. The Spanish soldier of fortune wanted gold and serfs so that he could live the idle, domineering life. The English peasant wanted land, and to get it he did again what his forebears had done to the forebears of the Welsh. That history happened. It cannot be undone. In much of the Americas, Indians are indeed "too few to fight." The Delawares are gone from Delaware, the Massachusetts from Massachusetts. There are no Ottawas in Ottawa, nor Manhattans in Manhattan. A name on the map is often the only tombstone of a murdered people. In many places, from Newfoundland to Patagonia, even the names are dead. But as the voices that speak in this book make clear, there are also millions who survive. To ignore their existence and their wishes is to become accessories to murder. They are too many to die.

In 1933, Luther Standing Bear, a Lakota Sioux, wrote in his *Land of the Spotted Eagle:*

> The white man does not understand the Indian for the reason that he does not understand America. He is too far removed from its formative processes. The roots of the tree of his life have not yet grasped the rock and soil. The white man is still troubled with primitive fears. . . . The man from Europe is still a foreigner and an alien. And he still hates the man who questioned his path across the continent.[4]

The past cannot be changed, but what we make of it certainly can. The new nations of America will never take root in its soil until they confront what is hidden by their myths and make reparation to the survivors of the holocaust that began five centuries ago. They could start by admitting what they have done. They could start by honoring their own treaties; by ceasing to put dams, mines, and chemical dumps on the little territory the first nations have left. They could start by teaching the other side of their history—the dark side—in their schools.

The people from the "Old World" cannot go back across the sea, nor should they. And the mixed people born of both worlds can have no other home. But the intruders and their offspring can at least make room for the American peoples who remain. They can offer true equality, not annihilation disguised as "integration" or *mestizaje,* nor the fictitious liberty of citizenship in Euro-American countries where the Indian will always be outnumbered and outvoted. They can accept the right of American Indians to be free, equal, and different.

The invaders can stop "conquering and discovering." And if they begin to treat America as a home in which to live, not a treasure house to ransack—a home for the first nations as well as for themselves—they may, unlike Christopher Columbus, discover where they are.

> The history of our people needs to be told. We need to present accurately what happened in the past, so that we can deal with it in the future. . . .
>
> I don't like what has happened over the last 500 years. We can't do much about that. But what are we going to do about the next 500 years? What are we going to do about the next *ten* years?
>
> —Georges Erasmus, Dene, 1990

AFTERWORD

The British critic Cyril Connolly once remarked that the test of a book is ten years. So it is certainly gratifying for the author to see a new edition of *Stolen Continents* a decade after the first. What is less gratifying is that many of the problems that beset indigenous people ten years ago are still unresolved, in Canada and elsewhere.

Stolen Continents ended with a question asked in 1990 by Georges Erasmus, formerly president of the Dene Nation and National Chief of Canada's Assembly of First Nations. His words were prompted by the past (by the 500th anniversary of Columbus's first voyage) but directed at the future: "What are we going to do," he asked, "about the next *ten* years?" A full answer might easily fill a new book, but I will try to outline briefly some of the salient events in the Americas since *Stolen Continents* first appeared in 1992.

There has been progress. Civil wars in Guatemala and Peru have subsided. The territory of Nunavut has been created in Canada, giving real political power to Inuit in the eastern Arctic. But the past decade has also brought new troubles, such as the Zapatista revolt in Mexico and the killing of an unarmed Chippewa protester by Ontario police.

These ten years have seen great political change throughout the world. When *Stolen Continents* went to the printers, the first Gulf War and the fall of the Soviet Union were only months in the past. There was talk of a "peace dividend" and a "new world order," hope that the business of war might give way to the urgent needs of peace, especially in the so-called Third World. American triumphalists argued that democracy and free enterprise had won a Darwinian struggle between ideologies and brought us to the best of all possible worlds; there was nothing much to fight about anymore; mankind had reached the "End of History." This last view, which could only have come from a nation that seldom listens to history, now seems shockingly naive.

In reality, the collapse of the communist bloc led to a frenzy of laissez-faire capitalism on a scale unseen since the heyday of the robber barons and the World Market before 1914. In the name of free trade, nearly a hundred years of costly political and economic lessons were unlearned and replaced with a market fundamentalism as extreme as any utopian project of the left. Private interests sought to cripple the regulatory and redistributive powers of government while seizing and exploiting the last traces of the "commons"—the collective heritage of human beings—on every front: public lands and institutions, the air and water of the planet, food staples handed down from ancient civilizations, even the genes in our bodies. According to United Nations figures, by 1998 the three richest individuals had amassed a greater net worth than the poorest forty-eight countries.

The recent history of indigenous peoples has taken place within this context. It was no coincidence that the Zapatista uprising in Chiapas began on January 1, 1994, the day the North American Free Trade Agreement came into effect in Mexico. Alarmed by a return to land ownership and foreign investment policies reminiscent of Porfirio Díaz's regime, and exasperated by corruption, racism, and violent intimidation, many Chiapas Maya took up arms under the leadership of Subcomandante Marcos, who styled himself "second-in-command" to make the rhetorical point that he was acting on behalf of local community leaders. So far, world media attention and broad public support have restrained the Mexican government's response and led to round after round of inconclusive talks.

After a lifetime of power in Mexico, the Institutional Revolutionary Party (PRI) was at last defeated in the 2000 presidential elections. Victory went to the right-wing opposition led by Vicente Fox, a wealthy northern rancher. While most Mexicans welcome democratic change, the Fox government's policies have little to offer Indian communities and are likely to widen the gulf between rich and poor.

The end of the Cold War did bring one significant benefit throughout Latin America: it was no longer possible to justify violent repression on the grounds that local dissent was "communist inspired." This was especially true in Guatemala. In 1992, Maya activist and author Rigoberta Menchú won the Nobel Peace Prize and took a leading role in talks to end the Guatemalan civil war.

Menchú also sustained an attack from an American anthropologist on the reliability of her 1983 book *I, Rigoberta Menchú,* which she had dictated from memory after fleeing Guatemala in her early twenties. The attack became a news story, seized on by the right to discredit Menchú and the left in general. Menchú admitted that complex events were sometimes conflated into single scenes, and that she had added detail witnessed by others to her account. Her defenders have pointed out that such things are inevitable in a long oral narrative, and that Menchú herself stated on the book's first page that she was speaking not only for herself but also for her people. The matter is well discussed by George Lovell in the second edition of his fine Guatemalan essays, *A Beauty That Hurts* (2000). The broad truth of Menchú's testimony is no longer in doubt, having been amply borne out by official investigators of the Guatemalan tragedy.

By the mid-1990s, killings in Guatemala had declined. There was some strengthening of indigenous and democratic rights, including a major investigation by the Catholic Church into slaughters and "disappearances." Meanwhile, congressional hearings in Washington uncovered the extent of CIA involvement in the war and in specific murders of Guatemalans and Americans. Despite an army massacre of returned refugees in 1995, the former insurgents and the government signed a peace accord in December 1996. A United Nations Truth Commission was then set up. In its 1999 report, *Guatemala: Memory of Silence,* the Commission found that 93 percent of the civilian killings between 1962 and 1996—more than 200,000 all told—were the work of Guatemalan state forces. More than four-fifths of the victims were Maya.

Despite these courageous efforts to tackle terrible events, lasting change has not yet taken root in Guatemala. In 1998, Bishop Juan Gerardi, head of the Church's human rights probe, was bludgeoned to death at his house two days after releasing his report, *Guatemala: Nunca Más* [*Never Again*]. A constitutional referendum, intended to enshrine key elements of the peace accord, achieved neither a majority nor a healthy turnout at the polls. The underlying problem of land ownership has not been addressed, and the authors of the terror, mainly high-ranking army officers, have eluded prosecution. Even the ballot box seems to be failing: Alfonso Portillo, the new president who took office in January 2000, enjoys the backing of former dictator Rios Montt, whose terror campaigns during 1982–83 were found by the UN Truth Commission to have been both strategically planned and genocidal under the Geneva Convention.

In Peru, where the Sendero Luminoso insurgency raged until the early 1990s, there is now also an uneasy peace, though achieved by less admirable means. Once in power, President Alberto Fujimori implemented monetarist policies similar to those of his electoral rival, Mario Vargas Llosa. He also forged a symbiotic alliance with the head of military intelligence, Vladimiro Montesinos, a sinister figure whose ruthlessness proved a match for Sendero's. Suspected rebels were jailed without due process; many were kidnapped and "disappeared" by security forces.

In 1992, Fujimori pulled off an *autogolpe,* or self-coup, suspending Congress and ruling by decree. Many Peruvians winked at these methods when Sendero's leader, Abimael Guzmán, was captured later that year and put on show like a caged beast. The Shining Path went into decline and has never recovered. The Tupac Amaru Revolutionary Movement was dealt a similar blow in 1992, and finished off in 1997 with a bloody end to a hostage taking at the Japanese ambassador's Lima residence.

As the threat of revolution faded, Peruvians became alarmed by the brutality and corruption of their regime. In the 2000 elections, Fujimori changed the constitution to allow himself a third term and rigged his victory. The triumph was short-lived. A revived Congress overthrew Fujimori while he was on a visit to Japan. Montesinos also fled the country but was later brought to book.

The man who should have won the 2000 elections—Alejandro Toledo—was another charismatic outsider. A former shoeshine boy with a United States education, he made much of his being a *cholo,* someone of indigenous looks and modest background, like most Peruvians.

Toledo was vague on policy but drew enthusiastic crowds, especially of the poor. In 2001 he was at last elected president, with implications that are still unclear. For the first time in five centuries, an "Indian" rules Peru. This event will not end ethnic oppression overnight, but is important symbolically. Peru's racial and cultural divide is now openly recognized and talked about. Native Peru has a new sense of its identity; the words *indio* and *cholo* are not the insults they once were; public life is no longer the preserve of whites and would-be whites.

For Canada, the 1990s were a turbulent decade filled both with militancy and genuine reform. The Oka crisis brought out the worst and best in Canada: its hypocrisy and its humanity, its capacity for repression and for peace. It now looks as though 1990 may indeed have been a turning point in the shared history of First Nations and the Canadian nation. At Oka itself (Kanehsatake) and at Kahnawake, tensions between Quebec police and Mohawks continued for several years, though gradually relaxed. The Quebec police have largely been replaced by professionally trained Indian Peacekeepers on both Mohawk territories. Meanwhile, the Canadian government bought up nearly ten square kilometers (four square miles) of disputed land at Oka, and, in 2000, agreements were reached for transferring this to Mohawk jurisdiction. These measures may have defused the immediate problem, but many Mohawks resented being "given" what they regard as rightly theirs.

The much deeper issues of Iroquois sovereignty—in Ontario and the United States, as well as Quebec—remain unaddressed. In a *de facto* admission that it could not enforce its own taxation law on Iroquois, Ontario drastically reduced cigarette duties to stop the flow of tobacco through Akwesasne. There soon followed allegations of a new illegal trade: "people smuggling," or transfer of migrants across the unrecognized Mohawk frontier. The latter issue has since been inflamed by "homeland security" paranoia following the September 11 attacks (including an unwise outburst from Senator Hillary Clinton of New York). However, there seems little evidence that unlawful migration is any brisker at Akwesasne than elsewhere along the Canadian and Mexican borders. Sardonic observers have pointed out that controlling one's national frontier is a fundamental element of sovereignty; the

United States should attend to its own business in this regard and stop blaming Canadians, Mexicans, and Mohawks.

On the Iroquois cultural front, there is a continuing decline in the use of Six Nations languages, including traditional Confederacy governance and ritual, as the older generation dies off—a situation typical of most minority tongues in Canada and the world. While several thousand people still speak Mohawk at Akwesasne and Kahnawake, perhaps only a dozen first-language speakers remain at Grand River. Efforts are being made to reverse this decline. Three new Confederacy chiefs were raised last year at Grand River in the first "condolence" (installation) ceremony held in more than a decade. But the Band Council government—the only body recognized by Ottawa—gives little support to cultural projects, though it wields most of the money and power.

Since Oka there have been militant protests in British Columbia (some well-founded, others not) and at Ipperwash, Ontario, where Dudley George, an unarmed Chippewa protester, was shot dead by provincial police in 1995. The Ipperwash affair was sparked by two long-standing injustices: the "temporary" seizure during the Second World War of reserve land that was, despite promises, not returned; and an older dispute at a neighboring provincial park, which had expanded onto Indian land including a burial ground. As at Oka, both levels of white government were clearly at fault.

This was early in the regime of Premier Harris which (unlike previous Conservative governments) was on the far right and had little sympathy for underdogs of any color. It is widely alleged that Harris himself ordered the police to "get tough" with the Indians. Despite public outrage, and the fact that an officer was successfully prosecuted by the slain man's family for criminal negligence causing death, all calls for an official inquiry were blocked. However, late in 2001 Harris made a surprise announcement of his resignation "for personal reasons"—just days before a damaging book on Ipperwash, *One Dead Indian* by Peter Edwards, was due to be released.

The Ipperwash tragedy had another effect, and on the far side of the country. Alone of the Canadian provinces, British Columbia (like Australia) had long denied any recognition of aboriginal title. From the nineteenth century until the early 1990s, the province tried to maintain the convenient fiction that there could be no land claims because native people had no ancestral rights. This position was eroded by a complex series of legal decisions by the Supreme Court in Ottawa, and in 1992 the New Democratic government of British Columbia faced reality and began hearing dozens of claims. One of the most significant was a large suit by the Nisga'a people, which they had been pursuing in both Canada and Britain for at least seventy years. By 1995, the renewed Nisga'a negotiations had stalled, complicated by internal division on both sides. On the one hand, some Nisga'a (who had lost no wars and signed no treaties before) felt they were conceding too much, both in land and jurisdiction. On the other, unsympathetic whites exploited federal–provincial rivalry and called for a province-wide referendum. The Ipperwash killing showed where a failure to negotiate might lead. An agreement was reached.

The Nisga'a Treaty was ratified by the Canadian Parliament in 2000, but has since run into trouble. A new government came to power in British Columbia. Though nominally Liberal, it was, like the Harris regime in Ontario, controlled by the far right. One of its first deeds was to refuse to ratify the Nisga'a Treaty without a referendum. The vote was held, with predictable results, but was widely boycotted. Fair-minded people saw the ploy for what it was: a democratic sham, designed to undermine years of careful and difficult work by whipping up racial fears, especially in the rural hinterland where white and native interests tend to clash. Time and again in the history of race relations, self-interested majorities have used "democracy" to tyrannize minorities. The Liberal referendum on the Nisga'a Treaty was a case in point. Some likened it to inviting a barn full of cats to decide on the fate of the mice.

Despite outbreaks of white-settler intransigence, especially from provincial governments, most Canadians have become aware since the Oka crisis that if they do not achieve a just reconciliation with the original owners of this land, they face endless unrest with severe social and economic consequences for all. In 1996, the Royal Commission on Aboriginal Peoples, set up in 1991, handed down its lengthy final report. (For a summary of the report and its effects so far, see the third edition of *Canada's First Nations* by Olive Dickason, 2002, a wide-ranging work on aboriginal history and culture that is especially good on the period since the Second World War.)

While a few of the Commission's 400 recommendations have been put into practice, many problems remain. One of the most notorious is that of the Labrador Innu, which drew worldwide attention when Survival International, a London-based advocacy group, compared Canada's behavior in the region to that of China in Tibet (see *Canada's Tibet: The Killing of the Innu,* 1999). Federal and provincial governments, having assumed control of Innu territory without any basis in law, had allowed the intrusion of mining and hydro projects, while resettling the Innu in places unsuited to their way of life. Perhaps worst of all, Innu hunting lands were handed over to NATO as a testing range for low-level supersonic flights. The result was social collapse, especially at Davis Inlet. That village is now being relocated to a place of the Innu's choosing, but it will take much more than new housing to repair two generations of deliberate cultural destruction. A similar case, still unresolved, is that of the Lubicon Lake Cree in Alberta, whose unceded lands have been invaded by oil, gas, and timber companies. Efforts at reaching a solution have been sabotaged by bad faith between federal and provincial jurisdictions, a common and convenient excuse for government inaction. Canada's extreme decentralization (far greater than in comparable federations such as Australia and the United States) threatens to render the country ungovernable, not only in aboriginal affairs but in other vital areas such as enforcing environmental law and international agreements.

Under Canada's constitution, the federal government is responsible for aboriginal issues, but for the past twenty years Ottawa's powers have been leaking away to the provinces, mainly because of ill-conceived schemes to appease separatists in Quebec and parochial satraps in Alberta, British Columbia and, most recently, Ontario. Plans to reform the Indian Act, including those since the 1996 Royal Commission report, have often lost support among aboriginal people because the federal government tries to give up responsibilities without offering adequate economic bases and legal safeguards in return. There is suspicion of land settlements that come at the price of extinguishing ancient rights and institutions, a policy reminiscent of the notorious Dawes and Curtis Acts in the United States more than a century ago (see Chapter 14 of this book).

Calls for "one law for all," and "no privileges based on race" are also very much in the Dawes tradition. Sometimes they flow from a misunderstanding of the relationship between individual and collective rights (both of which have always existed under Canadian and British constitutions). Often they are a cynical strategy to dispossess Indians. Whatever the motivation, they are denials of both history and law, for one cannot commit a theft and elude responsibility on the grounds that the slate can be wiped clean unilaterally; nor can one acquire title to property through a contract and then cease fulfilling the contract's terms when they become inconvenient. The whole edifice of British and Canadian law rests on the observing of precedents that go back to Magna Carta and beyond.

Settler rights in this country depend on aboriginal rights. All public jurisdiction and private real estate in Canada are founded on this legal fact. (This is, of course, the fundamental difference between aboriginal rights and those of other ethnic minorities.) The invaders acquired this country only by making contracts with its original owners and polities. Under British and Canadian law, such contracts could (and can) only be made by the Crown. Where the Crown failed to make treaties in the past—as with the Iroquois and in British Columbia—it must do so now. As the *Gitksan-Carrier Declaration* put it succinctly in 1977: "Recognize our sovereignty . . . so that we may fully recognize yours."

Treaty terms, like those of any title deed, have to be honoured for as long as Canada exists. They can only be changed or reinterpreted with the full agreement of the legal successors of the original parties: the First Nations on one hand, the Canadian Crown on the other. Under both national and international law, the treaties *are* the Canadian state. Canadians who think Canada "gives" too much to Indians should ask themselves where this land came from, and what a reasonable payment for it might be.

Over the years since *Stolen Continents* first came out, I have been approached from time to time by people asking what they can do to help redress injustices. I usually reply that political pressure is always worthwhile: letters to one's MP or MLA, to the Prime Minister and Minister of Indian Affairs do have an effect. Politicians know that for every person who bothers to write, there are hundreds or even thousands more who have similar concerns. There are also many charities and international pressure groups who help indigenous peoples in various ways, in Canada and abroad. Here are three whose work I happen to know:

Maya Educational Foundation, based in Vermont, USA, gives scholarships to Maya students to help them complete higher education in their home countries. Address: Maya Educational Foundation, P.O. Box 38, Route 106, South Woodstock, Vermont 05071, USA. www.yaxte.org

Horizons of Friendship, based in Cobourg, Ontario, works with a range of local charities in Central America on aid and community projects. Address: Horizons of Friendship, P.O. Box 402, Cobourg, Ontario, K9A 4L1. www.horizons.ca

Survival International, based in London, England, is an advocacy group (modeled partly on Amnesty International) supporting indigenous peoples' rights worldwide. Address: Survival International, 6 Charterhouse Buildings, London EC1M 7ET, UK. www.survival-international.org

Ronald Wright, February 2003

A portion of royalties from the sale of this book helps support the Maya Educational Foundation.

NOTES

Because of the many languages in which the sources are written, it has been impossible to follow a uniform way of spelling foreign names and words. For Nahuatl, Maya, Cherokee, and Iroquois, I have used traditional spellings, keeping to one variant where alternatives occur. For Quechua, I follow the standard alphabet approved by Peru's Ministry of Education and published in a series of dictionaries and grammars in the mid-1970s. Thus Atahuallpa becomes Atawallpa; Huayna Capac becomes Wayna Qhapaq; and so forth. However, I have kept traditional spellings for well-known place names such as Cajamarca (Qasamarka), Cusco (Qosqo), and Machu Picchu (Machu Piqchu).

Translations from Spanish and Quechua are mine unless otherwise indicated in the notes and references. I have modernized archaic English spelling and punctuation when it seemed necessary.

It is notoriously difficult to show how foreign names are pronounced using English conventions, but here is a rough guide for some of the more daunting:

Cuauhtémoc	Kwow-*tay*-mok
Huitzilopochtli	Weet-see-lo-*potch*-tly
Ixtlilxochitl	Eesht-leel-*sotch*-it
Mexica	May-*she*-kah
Moctezuma	Mok-tay-*soo*-mah
Quetzalcoatl	Ket-sal-*ko*-at
Tenochtitlan	Tay-notch-*teet*-lahn
Xochimilco	Shot-chee-*meel*-ko
Gumarcaah	Goo-mar-*kah*
Iximché	Eesh-eem-*chay*
Quiché	Key-*chay*
Uxmal	Oosh-*mahl*
Xiu	She-*yu*

Pachakuti	Patch-a-*koo*-ty
Wayna Qhapaq	*Why*-na *Kah*-pak
Tanasi	Tah-nah-*see*
Tsalagi	Tsah-lah-*ghee*
Kahnawake	Gah-na-*wah*-gay
Kanehsatake	Gah-nuh-sa-*tah*-gay

AUTHOR'S NOTE

1. See McLoughlin 1984a: xvi.
2. Memorial quoted in Armstrong 1971: 145–47.

PROLOGUE

1. Good estimates of the New World's 1492 population range from 57 to 112 million. See Thornton 1987: 22–25 for a discussion.
2. J. M. Roberts, *The Pelican History of the World,* 1987: 457.
3. See *Harper's,* December 1990: 45–53. Much of this essay was given as the Neil Gunn Lecture in Edinburgh in October 1986. A version appeared in the *Times Literary Supplement,* January 30, 1987. For response, including mine, see *Harper's,* April 1991: 4–7.
4. See Martínez 1971.
5. Cook and Borah (1963) estimate the population of "Central Mexico"—roughly the Aztec Empire and a few independent states—at about 25 million.
6. Thornton 1987: 36, estimates Spain at 6.5–10 million. Hemming 1983: 24, estimates "under ten."
7. Montaigne 1988: 118–19.
8. Hemming 1983: 89.
9. Cieza de León 1986, 2: 66.
10. In Crosby 1972: 37.
11. Survival International "Urgent Action Bulletin," July 1990: 2.
12. These figures are educated guesses. Only in Mesoamerica and Peru do census records provide acceptable data. Even a conservative

interpretation of the Peruvian figures (Cook 1981: 114) shows a decline of 93 percent by 1630. In the Caribbean, collapse was close to 100 percent. In some isolated areas, such as Canada's north and parts of the Amazon, the great death did not strike until much later.

13. Roys 1967: 83.

CHAPTER ONE

1. See *National Geographic,* October 1989: 438, 440.
2. Sahagún 1956, 4: 96 (Sahagún's informants, Book 12, Chap. 9).
3. Díaz 1963: 23.
4. See León-Portilla 1969a: 257. Tezozomoc wrote *Mexicana* c. 1598 and *Mexicayotl* c. 1609, drawing on Aztec codices. Tezozomoc says (1975a: 7) "I am the great king Moteuhczomatzin's grandson."
5. Tezozomoc 1975b: 685.
6. Bierhorst 1974: 37.
7. Anthropologists and historians have tried to cast specific shades of meaning on the words "Mexica," "Aztec," and "Mexican." Strictly speaking, the Mexica were the people who lived in the place called Mexico, the capital city of the Aztec Empire and its environs. Some writers take "Aztec" to include related peoples speaking languages of the same Nahua family. For stylistic fluency, I employ these terms loosely. I use the word "Mexican" sometimes as a synonym for Mexica, sometimes to refer in a general way to inhabitants of the geographical area now covered by the Mexican republic, especially the central highlands on which the ancient Mexica left such an indelible impression.
8. Tezozomoc 1975a: 3–4.
9. Broda 1987: 151.
10. See Clendinnen 1991, Bray 1968, and Meyer and Sherman 1987, Chap. 5, for sketches of Aztec life.
11. Sahagún 1956, 4: 86 (Book 12, Chap. 3).
12. Ibid., 86–88; 1975: 11–13 (Book 12, Chaps. 3–4).
13. León-Portilla 1962: 26 (Book 12, Chap. 5).
14. Díaz 1963: 90–91.

15. In Sahagún 1989: 2.
16. Sahagún 1956, 4: 92–93; 1975: 19–20 (Book 12, Chap. 7).
17. Díaz 1963: 141, 153.
18. Ibid., 158.
19. Ibid., 143.
20. Ibid.
21. Wolf 1982: 72 (cf. Galeano 1985, 1: 55–56).
22. Díaz 1963: 152.
23. Ibid.
24. It is squatter than Egypt's Great Pyramid, but greater in volume.
25. Muñoz Camargo, quoted in León-Portilla 1969a: 59–61.
26. Díaz 1963: 199.
27. Sahagún 1956, 4: 99; 1975: 29–30 (Book 12, Chap. 11).
28. Ibid., 1956, 4: 101; 1975: 31 (Book 12, Chap. 12).
29. Díaz 1963: 214.
30. Ibid., 216.
31. Sahagún 1956, 4: 105–7; 1975: 39–40 (Book 12, Chap. 15).
32. See Matos 1988: 30, for an illustration.
33. Sources differ somewhat on this date. The Florentine Codex (Sahagún 1975: 80) and the Third *Relación* of Chimalpahin (1965: 121) give the date as 1-Wind, though elsewhere Chimalpahin has 8-Wind. The precise correlation of Mexican and Christian calendars is still open to question.
34. In Mesoamerica, as in ancient China, the throne was a mat, not a chair. (The literal meaning of the Chinese term for Chairman Mao is "Mat Master" Mao.) Moctezuma invites Cortés to "your mat, your seat."
35. The Spaniards had come down from the clouds on the volcanoes.
36. Sahagún 1956, 4: 108–9; 1975: 44 (Book 12, Chap. 16).
37. Ibid., 1956, 4: 109; 1975: 45; León-Portilla 1969b: 160.
38. Díaz 1963: 218.
39. The well-known *Codex Mendoza* includes tax lists. For another published example of an Aztec tax book, see León 1982.
40. Díaz 1963: 228.
41. In Von Hagen 1962: 132–33.

42. Díaz 1963: 229.
43. Ibid., 221.
44. *Cue* is not a Nahuatl word. The Aztec for a temple is *teocalli,* house of god.
45. Díaz 1963: 234–35.
46. Matos 1989: 206.
47. Conrad and Demarest 1984: 27.
48. Sahagún 1981: 257.
49. Díaz 1963: 222–23.
50. Ibid., 237.
51. Ibid., 242–43.
52. Ibid., 247.
53. Sahagún 1956, 4: 112; 1975: 49 (Book 12, Chap. 18).
54. Ibid. 1956, 4: 111; 1975: 48 (Book 12, Chap. 17). I have changed the order of these paragraphs.
55. Prescott n.d.: 364–65.
56. Leonardo da Vinci had died earlier that year.
57. In Von Hagen 1961: 155; 1962: 9–10.
58. Sahagún 1975: 51. Date (Old Style) after Cline, given in Brundage 1972: 330, n. 41.
59. Sahagún 1956, 4: 116–17; 1975: 55–56 (Book 12, Chap. 20). See also León-Portilla 1969b: 161–62, for another English translation of this passage.
60. Sahagún 1975: 59.
61. Brundage accepts Cline's date of June 30 for the murders, and the night of June 30/July 1 for the Noche Triste (Old Style, therefore July 9/10 Gregorian).
62. Sahagún 1981: 346–47.
63. Díaz 1963: 294.
64. Sahagún quoted in Cline 1989: 8.
65. Chimalpahin 1965: 236 (7th *Relación*).
66. Sahagún quoted in Cline 1989: 8.
67. Ixtlilxochitl 1956: 194.
68. The Aztecs had two kinds of projectile: arrows, and darts or short spears launched by *atlatl.*

69. Sahagún 1956, 4: 125–26; 1975: 67–68 (Book 12, Chap. 24).
70. Ibid., 1975: 71–72 (Book 12, Chap. 25).
71. Motolinía quoted in Crosby 1972: 52.
72. Crosby 1972: 44.
73. Dobyns 1983: 13.
74. Sahagún 1956, 4: 136–37; 1975: 83–84 (Book 12, Chap. 29).
75. Brundage 1972: 278.
76. I have made this line agree with Berlin's translation in Brundage 1972: 286.
77. Garibay 1964a: 50. There is also a longer excerpt in León-Portilla 1980: 53–54.
78. See Brundage 1972: 289. Accounts vary as to where and how Cuauhtémoc surrendered. Brundage accepts Cline's view that he surrendered from a boat on Aug. 14, a day after the city fell.
79. León-Portilla 1969a: 210; 1980: 62.

CHAPTER TWO

1. See Lovell and Lutz 1992. While the Indian population of Central America is about the same then as now (most being Mayas), the non-Indian population of the whole region is some 20 million. However, in Guatemala and Yucatán, Indians account for half or more of the total.
2. The Gregorian calendar, introduced by Pope Gregory XIII, was not adopted by Britain until 1751, when its suppression of eleven days incited mobs to riot, demanding their eleven days of life.
3. Hammond 1982: 292–93.
4. The last dated monument at Tikal (Stela 11) was erected on the day 10. 2. 0. 0. 0. in the Maya Long Count, equivalent to Aug. 15, 869. No Classic Petén city has a date later than 10. 4. 0. 0. 0. or Jan. 18, 909. See Morley and Brainerd 1983: 548–603 for a useful summary and tables.
5. A fourth codex, known as the Grolier, surfaced in 1971. In Toltec-Maya style, it appears to date from the thirteenth century. The poorly preserved text is concerned with the Venus cycle.

6. See Brinton 1969b, Recinos, Goetz, and Chonay (and Morley) 1953; Tedlock 1985.
7. Xahil 1980: 39.
8. Ibid., 164. I have corrected Recinos's early dates by two days because he equates 1-Hunahpu with Apr. 12, 1524, when it seems much more likely that it was Apr. 14. See Xahil page 27. All these dates are Old Style, or Julian (to convert to Gregorian, add ten days so that Apr. 14 becomes Apr. 24). After Sept. 10, 1541 (10-Tihax), Recinos's dates and mine are in step.
9. The Xahils use a "revolution" that took place in 1493 as a datum point, like revolutionary France's Year Zero. The "year" they are counting is a special unit of 400 days.
10. Xahil 1980: 95–96.
11. Ibid., 97.
12. León-Portilla 1980: 96–100.
13. In Xahil 1980: 100 n. 228.
14. Xahil, 100–101.
15. The name of this day, *Hunahpu* in Maya, should really be translated as Sun or Lord. I have chosen its Aztec equivalent, Flower, for the sake of consistency.
16. Xahil 1980: 101.
17. Ibid.
18. Ibid., 102–3.
19. Ibid., 103.
20. Ibid., 103–4.
21. Obviously he was baptized later. His Maya name was his birthday, Six Dog, or Vakaki Tzii.
22. Xahil 1980: 105–6.
23. Ibid., 107.
24. Ibid., 107–8.
25. Handy 1984: 21.
26. Xahil 1980: 108–10.
27. The Maya name for this volcano, Hunahpu, is the same as the day Sun or Flower in the calendar.
28. Xahil 1980: 110–11.

CHAPTER THREE

1. In Heyerdahl 1974: 99. See Porras. 1986: 54–55.
2. Porras 1986: 54–55. Also quoted in Hemming 1983: 25.
3. Hemming 1983: 262.
4. Chamberlain 1982: 25–27.
5. In Todorov 1984: 149 (from Las Casas's *Historia* 3, 58).
6. Galeano 1985: 60.
7. Speakers of Quechua more often call it Runasimi, Mouth of the People.
8. The brothers were Gonzalo, Hernando, and Juan. Pedro Pizarro, a young cousin whose account of the conquest is most valuable, was also present.
9. See Ascher 1981 and Julien 1988.
10. Morris and Thompson 1985: 82.
11. Cieza de León 1986, 2: 54–55, 66.
12. Morris and Thompson 1985: 96, 100.
13. Wari and Tiawanaku, ruined cities near Ayacucho and the south shore of Lake Titicaca, respectively, could have been the capitals of two smaller empires rather than one.
14. The Indian chronicler Waman Puma calls the time before the Incas *Awqa Pacha,* the Age of War.
15. The origin of the name is uncertain. It may be a corruption of Virú, a coastal valley.
16. Arguedas, quoted in Pease 1976: 31.
17. Wayna Qhapaq can be translated as Young Lord. In modern Quechua *qhapaq* means "rich"; in Inca times the word implied munificence, not unlike the original meaning of "lord" in Old English: keeper of loaves.
18. Cieza de León 1986, 2: 179.
19. Pizarro 1986: 49.
20. Besides Pizarro, there is the strange case of Alejo García, who penetrated the Inca Empire from the Amazon in the mid-1520s. He led Paraguayans in raids on Inca towns in eastern Bolivia, but was driven back.

21. Informed estimates range from 6 to 32 million. I have chosen 20 million as a compromise and because it is the population of modern Peru. Though there was no Inca city comparable in size to modern Lima, it is clear that the highlands supported far more people in Inca times than they do today.
22. See Crosby 1972: 56.
23. His manuscript is dated 1613 but must have taken many years to prepare. He seems to have been a minor nobleman from the Tinta region southeast of Cusco, probably a local lord with marriage ties to the Incas. He claims that some of his forebears were baptized at Cajamarca.
24. Pachakuti Yamki, whose spelling is erratic, also gives this name as Mihicuacamayta; it's not clear to me how it should be written.
25. Pachakuti Yamki Sallqamaywa 1968: 311.
26. Pizarro 1986: 49–50.
27. Numbers vary. Prescott (n.d.: 891, 897) gives 180 men and 27 horses, reinforced with 100 men and more horses before reaching Tumbes. He adds (914) that 177 set out for Cajamarca, 67 of those being cavalry. Hemming (1983: 27) says that about 60 men were left behind in Piura.
28. Waman Puma 1980a: 353–54.
29. Estete quoted in Hemming 1983: 30.
30. Pizarro 1986: 31, 28.
31. Todorov 1984: 80–81.
32. Hemming 1983: 31.
33. Ibid., 45
34. Titu Kusi Yupanki 1973: 131.
35. Ibid., 15–16.
36. Xerez quoted in Hemming 1983: 49.
37. Hernando Pizarro quoted in ibid., 35.
38. Estete quoted in ibid., 36.
39. Some sources say it was triangular, which would have been unusual. More likely it was a trapezoid, a shape the Incas favored for plans as well as elevations.
40. Pizarro 1986: 36.

41. Prescott n.d.: 940.
42. Perhaps from Huancavelica, which became a notorious mining center in colonial times.
43. Waman Puma 1980a: 353, 357.
44. Ibid., 357.
45. Hemming 1983: 42.
46. This text, which was translated into Spanish for Titu Kusi, uses the word *oveja,* "sheep." Just as the Aztecs called horses "deer," the Spaniards called llamas and alpacas "sheep," and the usage stuck for years.
47. Titu Kusi Yupanki 1973: 18 (order of paragraphs changed).
48. Waman Puma 1980a: 343.
49. See Prescott n.d.: 365, n. 16.
50. Lara 1947: 193–94.

CHAPTER FOUR

1. See Lockhart 1972: 80–81; my calculations are at a gold price of $400 per ounce.
2. Dobyns 1983: 12.
3. See Garcilaso 1951, xxi ff.
4. I know of three analyses: that of Mooney (1900), the De Soto Commission (Swanson 1939), and Hudson et al. (1984). The latter differs markedly from the first two, but I find it unconvincing; the authors' unwillingness to equate Chalaque with Tsalagi (Cherokee) seems perverse. I have chosen to follow Mooney, more or less; he knew the country, its place names, and ruins better than any subsequent observers.
5. Bourne (Ranjel) 1904, 2: 99.
6. Bourne (Elvas) 1904, 1: 66–67.
7. Bourne (Ranjel) 1904, 2: 98–99, 101.
8. Garcilaso 1956: 220–27.
9. Bourne 1904, 1: 66.
10. Garcilaso 1956: 220, 229.
11. There is an l/r substitution between some dialects of Cherokee.

12. Bourne (Ranjel) 1904, 2: 103–4.
13. Mooney (1982: 194) says that Juan Pardo visited Cofitachiqui in 1567, and Torres in 1628. But there is no further record of the lady.
14. Also written Guaxule in some chronicles.
15. Bourne (Elvas) 1904, 1: 72.
16. Garcilaso 1951: 236.
17. Mooney 1982: 196–97.
18. Bourne (Elvas) 1904, 1: 73–74.
19. Plates and other artifacts from Etowah, Georgia, are shown in Willey 1966: 300–308.
20. Bourne (Elvas) 1904, 1: 77.
21. Willey 1966: 298; Scarre 1988: 230–31.
22. Waldman (1985: 22) and Scarre (1988: 230) estimate 75,000 and 38,000, respectively, for Cahokia and its suburbs.
23. Dobyns quoted in Crosby 1972: 39.
24. See Jennings 1976: 30.
25. Jones 1982: 22.
26. McLoughlin 1986: 5.
27. Bartram (1955: 271) saw "several Indian mounts or tumuli, and terraces, monuments of the ancients, at the old site of Keowee." Much of the area is now drowned by dams.
28. Based on Cuming's journal in Williams 1928; details of the townhouse are mainly from Bartram 1955: 296–99.
29. Cuming in Williams 1928: 125–26.
30. Raymond Demere to Gov. Lyttleton, July 30, 1757. McDowell 1970: 391–96.
31. Adair 1968: 379.
32. Kelly 1978: 10, 3. See also S. Williams 1928: 127–28 n. 19, for a shortened and slightly different version. Attakullakulla's claim to be the only survivor was supported independently by Gov. Glen in 1752—see McDowell 1958: 228.
33. Felix Walker quoted in Brown 1938: 8.
34. The exact date is unknown. Some favor 1781 or '82; certainly he was dead by 1785.
35. Brown 1938: 43, 45.

36. In Foreman 1943: 79.
37. Felix Walker's narrative quoted in Brown 1938: 8.
38. According to Woodward (1963: 65). Brown (1938: 44) says this was at the signing in September.
39. Cuming's Journal, Williams 1928: 129.
40. According to Woodward (1963: 66). Brown says it was Oukou-Ulah. Attakullakulla had several names during his life. He was then known as Oukounaco, White Owl.
41. Williams 1928: 142.
42. Ibid., 143.
43. Ibid., 141 (articles dated Sept. 7 and 9, 1730). Brown 1938: 44.
44. De Brahm quoted in Williams 1928: 193.
45. Ibid., 27, n. 13.
46. Letter of Abraham Wood in ibid., 28.
47. De Brahm quoted in Chapman 1985: 115.
48. Estimates differ wildly because scholars agree neither on the density nor the territorial extent of the ancient Cherokees; I see little reason for thinking that their territory was any smaller in the fifteenth century than it was in the eighteenth. Before ceding any land to the British, they controlled about 100,000 square miles while most of their towns lay within a 15,000-square-mile heartland. Dobyns's (1983: 42) average of 2.53 persons per square kilometer for the Mississippi drainage yields a figure of 98,250 people in the Cherokee heartland alone and 655,000 all told. There may have been about five smallpox plagues before the documented one of 1738.
49. See Timberlake 1971: 92–93; Brown 1938: 32.
50. Bartram 1955: 381.
51. In Brown 1938: 79.
52. See Woodward 1963: 43.
53. Brown 1938: 31.
54. Skiagunsta speaking to Gov. Glen, Nov. 15, 1751. McDowell 1958: 180.
55. It has recently been shown that some inauthentic versions of Chief Seattle's famous speech are in circulation. However, these are

modern distortions, and the circumstances of the original have been clarified. See Kaiser 1987.

56. See Boyd 1938: 46, where Canasatego repeats everything to an interpreter.
57. See Dobyns 1983: 15; Adair 1968: 227–33; Woodward 1963: 68.
58. Skiagunsta to Gov. Glen, July 7, 1753. McDowell 1958: 453.
59. Bartram 1955: 270–71.
60. Adair 1968: 233.
61. Ibid.
62. Mooney 1982: 353, 507.
63. William Martin quoted in King and Olinger 1972: 226.
64. In Corkran 1962: 15. Said in 1751.
65. McDowell 1958: 183.
66. Around 1712, the Cherokees sent 100 men to help the British drive the Tuscaroras north, where they became the sixth nation in the Iroquois Confederacy—see Chap. 6.
67. Caneecatee [*sic*] to Glen, Apr. 29, 1752. McDowell 1958: 258–59. (Converted from reported to direct speech.)
68. In Corkran 1962: 60. It is not certain who the boy was, but he may well have been the future guerrilla chief Dragging Canoe.
69. Brown 1938: 55.
70. In ibid., 81.
71. Ibid., 58.
72. Ibid., 79–80.
73. Ibid., 82.
74. Waldman 1985: 104.
75. In Brown 1938: 91.
76. See Corkran 1962: 189. Mooney (1982: 42) says the Cherokee delegation numbered 32.
77. Corkran 1969: 219.
78. Ibid., 245.
79. In Brown 1938: 109.
80. Ibid., 111.
81. In Corkran 1962: 268–69.
82. In Brown 1938: 119–20.

83. See note on Ross in ibid., 473 n.
84. Woodward 1963: 85.
85. Described by Brice and William Martin. Quoted in King and Olinger 1972: 226.
86. Brown 1938: 203.
87. In ibid., 127–28.
88. Ibid., 130.
89. See map in McLaughlin 1986: 28.
90. Brown 1938: 14.
91. The Cherokees and other eastern nations regarded the Delawares as the oldest people in the land and therefore addressed them as "grandfathers."
92. In Brown 1938: 10. The speech is sometimes attributed to Oconostota, but this seems unlikely in the circumstances.

CHAPTER FIVE

1. In Boyd 1938: xxxvii, from Witham Marshe's *Journal* . . . (published 1884).
2. Boyd 1938: 78.
3. In Campbell and Campbell 1981: 92; Armstrong 1971: 12; Tooker 1988: 308–9; see also *National Geographic* 172, no. 3 (Sept. 1987): 399. Wording varies slightly in these sources. Franklin made much of the Iroquois model in the Albany Plan of 1754, a congress attended by Iroquois and other Indian delegates. See Johansen 1990: 283.
4. See Campbell and Campbell 1981: 93; Parker 1968, 1: 11.
5. See Grinde 1977, Johansen 1982, and Weatherford 1988: 137. For an acrimonious debate on the extent and nature of Iroquois influence, see Tooker (1988) and Johansen's reply (1990).
6. Franklin observed: "Many of their names are English. [They] give themselves, and their children, the names of such English persons as they particularly esteem." Smyth 1905, 4: 291.
7. Morgan 1972: 77.
8. See ibid., x.

9. Engels 1972: 96.
10. See Tuck 1967: 78.
11. "Iroquois" is not an Iroquois word; neither is "Mohawk." Mohawks call themselves Kanienkehaka (or Ganienkehaga), People of the Land of Flint. See Akwesasne Notes 1986: 1–12.
12. In Reaman 1967: 18.
13. Graymont 1972: 9. This was a town of the Hurons, who lived in much the same way.
14. Parker 1968, 3: 41.
15. Ibid., 11.
16. Parker spells it Adodarho. Names and titles vary in the six languages of the Iroquois.
17. Parker 1968, 3: 30–32, 45.
18. It has not been proved that these Iroquoians were Mohawks, but Mohawks were living there when Montreal was founded in the 1640s, and they are living there today.
19. McMillan 1988: 61; McNaught 1976: 21.
20. See Trigger 1987: 177–208.
21. See Jennings 1976: 15–31.
22. See Dobyns 1983: 42 for the higher figure, Thornton 1987: 32 for the lower.
23. See Jennings 1984: 35–36, 125 n. Starna's figures cited by Jennings (8,258–17,116 for pre-1630 Mohawk alone) imply a total Iroquois population of about 36,000 to 75,000.
24. W. Campbell 1849: 260.
25. Adriaen Van der Donck quoted in Jennings 1976: 24. However, recent excavations by Gary Warrick and Dean Snow have not shown evidence of pandemics in sixteenth-century Iroquoia.
26. Gilbert 1989: 27; Bailyn 1986: 24–25; *Encyclopaedia Britannica*, 1911, vol. 27: 635. Most were British.
27. Jennings 1984: 93.
28. Trigger 1987: 764.
29. Jennings 1984: 95.
30. 1753. In Axtell 1981: 172.
31. O'Callaghan 1856, 3: 428–29.

32. Jennings 1984: 131.
33. Reaman 1967: 37. Denonville reported 400,000 *minots* of corn. (A minot is three bushels.) Domestic hogs were adopted by the Indians from early colonists, as were peach and apple orchards.
34. O'Callaghan 1856, 3: 534. Sachems of the Six Nations (*sic*) to Dongan, Feb. 13, 1688.
35. Bailyn 1986: 24 gives a figure of 27,000 French migrants for the whole of Canada in 1608–1760. See "The Making of Canada," *National Geographic* 179, no. 3 (March 1991) for an estimate of only 10,000 migrants to the St. Lawrence during the same period.
36. No written text of the treaty exists; either it has been lost or the Dutch omitted to put it on paper.
37. McDowell 1958: 92–93; £85 is equivalent to about £5,100, or $8,600, at 1991 values.
38. Boyd 1938: 78.
39. Ibid., 26–27.
40. Ibid., 28.
41. Ibid., 51–52.
42. Jennings 1984: 360.
43. O'Callaghan 1856, 6: 781–83.
44. Ibid., 788.
45. Ibid., 854–55.
46. In Wallace 1945: 390.
47. O'Callaghan 1856, 6: 871.
48. See Blanchard 1980: 245–46.
49. See Jennings 1988: 419, 440.
50. Wallace 1970: 117–18.
51. Ibid., 120.
52. In MacGregor 1990: 56–57. Germ warfare had earlier practitioners, but disease vectors were poorly understood before this time.
53. See Jennings 1988: 446–48.
54. See Bailyn 1986: 44–49, 576–82.
55. Ibid., 579.
56. Kelsay 1984: 171.
57. In ibid., 166.

58. Ibid., 172.
59. In Graymont 1972: 99.
60. Stone 1969, 1: 176.
61. Ibid., 187.
62. See Wallace 1970: 130–34.
63. Apr. 10, 1780, in Graymont 1972: 231.
64. Washington quoted in Waldman 1985: 111. Figures from Wallace 1970: 194.
65. Gen. James Clinton quoted in Bonvillain n.d.: 53.
66. Feb. 5, 1781, quoted in Graymont 1972: 240. This George Clinton is not to be confused with an earlier governor, Admiral George Clinton.
67. Brant to Johnson, Dec. 25, 1782. Quoted at length in Kelsay 1984: 336.

CHAPTER SIX

1. This account is by the Texcoco historian Ixtlilxochitl 1956: 226.
2. Cuauhtémoc's end is told in a fascinating Maya document. See Scholes and Roys 1948: 367–72, 383–92. See also León-Portilla 1969b: 167–69.
3. Díaz 1963: 239.
4. A reference to the "year-bearers"—the days that started and named the Mesoamerican years.
5. The texts were translated into Spanish by the Mexican scholar Miguel León-Portilla. My translation is from León-Portilla 1980: 23–24.
6. From the introduction in ibid., 24.
7. León-Portilla 1980: 25–28.
8. See Brading 1984: 14–15.
9. Gruzinski 1989: 33.
10. Lafaye 1976: 140.
11. For example, Carlos Ometochtzin, burned for idolatry in 1539. Gruzinski 1989: 34.
12. Ibid., 54.

13. Ibid., 61–62.
14. Lafaye 1976: 211.
15. Sahagún 1981: 329.
16. Cline 1989: 1.
17. León-Portilla 1969b: 15.
18. Cline 1989: 11 n., 14.
19. Bierhorst 1985: 341. (Contractions removed and quotes added for the second speech.)
20. Ibid., 219–21.
21. Borah and Cook cited in Meyer and Sherman 1987: 212.
22. Bierhorst 1985: 299.
23. Ibid., 361.
24. Anderson et al. 1976: 177–89.
25. Paraguay, which arose from the confinement of the Guarani in Jesuit missions, is a special case. The country is predominantly mestizo in character, but the first language of conversation is often Guarani.
26. Chimalpahin 1965: 274, 20.
27. Ibid., 274–75.
28. Antonio de León y Gama quoted in Matos 1988: 24.
29. Lafaye 1976: 195, 197.

CHAPTER SEVEN

1. In Clendinnen 1987: 29.
2. See Clendinnen 1987: 36 and n. 23, 212.
3. Ichcaanziho is a longer form of Tiho's name, meaning "Tiho-Born-of-Heaven."
4. León-Portilla 1980: 90–92.
5. See Clendinnen 1987: 66–71.
6. The "years" of a katun were rounded off at 360 days, so the full cycle is actually about 256.27 of our years.
7. Brinton (1882) quoted in Roys 1967: 186 n.
8. Edmonson 1982: xiv.
9. Roys 1967: 77–79 (some changes in format).

10. Craine and Reindorp 1979: 65–68, 78, 81, 86–87.
11. See Wright 1989: 338–39.
12. Landa 1982: 104.
13. Clendinnen 1987: 72.
14. In ibid., 1987: 74.
15. Landa 1982: 107.
16. Ibid., 104–5.
17. Official testimony quoted in Clendinnen 1987: 76.
18. Figures in ibid.
19. In Landa 1978: 115–17 (minor changes).
20. Katuns are named for the day on which they end, which is always Ahau, the Sun Lord, equivalent to the day Flower of the Aztecs. The associated number varies.
21. Roys 1967: 82–83.
22. See ibid., 83 n. The Thompson correlation has since been accepted by most scholars.
23. When Ralph Roys worked on the Chumayel in 1928, he tracked down Hoil's descendants; one was a caretaker at Uxmal, another a brakeman for Yucatán Railways. See Roys 1967: 6–8.
24. Ibid., 143.
25. More precisely, 256.27 of our years—see note 6 above.
26. Roys 1967: 136–38.
27. Ibid., 112, 148, 169.
28. See Perera and Bruce 1982 and Bruce 1974.
29. Bricker 1981: 75.

CHAPTER EIGHT

1. It was also known in Inca times as Inti Wasi, Sun House (not to be confused with the sun temple in the city itself, which was called Qorikancha, Golden Court). Like the Mesoamerican feathered serpent, the dualism of ancient Peru was expressed by a composite beast, the bird-feline. Cusco's plan represented both a stylized puma and a hawk. The sawtooth terraces of Saqsawaman were at once the puma's jaw and the hawk's chevron tail.

2. Cieza de León 1986, 2: 148 (order of sentences changed).
3. Francisco de Toledo, March 25, 1571, quoted in Pardo 1970: 144.
4. Hemming 1983: 18.
5. See ibid., 570 for details.
6. Pizarro 1986: 99–101.
7. Hemming 1983: 184–85.
8. Titu Kusi 1973: 37.
9. Ibid., 38–39.
10. Ibid., 74–75
11. Nowadays this river is also called Vilcanota and Urubamba.
12. Titu Kusi 1973: 81.
13. A brother of Francisco.
14. Collapiña et al. 1974: 9.
15. Titu Kusi 1973: 90.
16. Ibid., 90–91.
17. Collapiña et al. 1974: 75.
18. Titu Kusi 1973: 112.
19. See ibid., 6 (intro.). The first Inca, child of the sun, was Manku Qhapaq.
20. Waman Puma 1936: 443. Waman Puma clearly means that Chillche, a Cañari, did the poisoning for Carlos Inca, Alonso Atauchi, and others who feared Sayri Tupa's rehabilitation.
21. Rodríguez de Figueroa quoted in Hemming 1983: 334.
22. Cook 1981: 94, 114. His figure for precontact is 9 million; the Tawantinsuyu's population may have been at least twice that.
23. Millones 1973a: 87. See Molina quoted in Wachtel 1977: 180. He says there would be a "vuelta," i.e., a pachakuti.
24. In modern Peru, and in much of the literature, this name is written Tupac Amaru, likewise Sayri Tupac, Tupac Yupanqui, etc. The colonial Incas themselves usually wrote it Tupa Amaru or Topa Amaro, never Tupac, a variant apparently invented by Garcilaso. In recent works the form Thupa is also used.
25. See Burga 1988: 117.
26. See Hemming 1983: 638.
27. In ibid., 449.

28. Titu Kusi 1973: 94–98.
29. Sir Paul Rycaut published the first complete English translation in 1688. Like Livermore's modern translation (1966), it includes Garcilaso's much longer Part 2, dealing mainly with postconquest matters, which originally appeared shortly after his death in 1616. Inca Garcilaso died on or about April 23, the same day as Shakespeare or Cervantes, or both—there is some confusion between Gregorian and Julian calendars.
30. See Zamora 1988.
31. Garcilaso 1688: 150. Garcilaso seems to be citing the authority of a lost manuscript by Padre Blas Valera in this chapter.
32. Waman Puma 1980b, 2: 446; 1980a: 1025. (I prefer Pease's punctuation.)
33. Ibid., 1980a: 1025; 1980b, 2: 446–47.
34. Ibid., 1980a: 857–58, 876–78, 885.
35. Ibid., 889.
36. Ibid., 888–89. For discussions of Waman Puma's ideas, see Wachtel 1973: 163–228, and Ossio 1973: 153–213.
37. O'Phelan 1985: 285–98.
38. The chronicler Pachakuti Yamki Sallqamaywa gives Diego Felipe Kunturkanki as the name of his own father. Pachakuti Yamki lived at the right time and place for these two Kunturkankis to have been the same man; however, the chronicler makes no mention of Tupa Amaru's daughter and gives a different woman as his mother. Has anyone solved this puzzle?
39. See table in O'Phelan 1985: 47. A 1795 census of the Peruvian viceroyalty (excluding what is now Bolivia) gave the population as 1.15 million, of which about 60 percent were Indians, 22 percent mestizos, and 12 percent Spaniards; 7 percent were black—half slaves, half free.
40. See, for example, Stern 1982 on Huamanga. This book also has a good chapter on the Taki Onqoy.
41. See Garcilaso 1985, 1: xl–xli (intro.). Bishop Moscoso of Cusco, formerly a friend of Tupa Amaru, thought that the Inca had read too much Garcilaso.

42. Szeminski 1987: 177.
43. Lewin 1957: 394.
44. Guardia Mayorga 1973: 255.
45. L. Campbell 1987: 125. Unfortunately, the painting hasn't survived.
46. See Szeminski 1987: 185–86.
47. Lewin 1957: 464–65.
48. See ibid., 396 and notes, and 745. There are four versions of this remark. This one, recalled by José Gabriel's brother, Juan Bautista Tupa Amaru, is also in Valcárcel 1977: 128.
49. This account is given in full by Lewin 1957: 497–98.
50. In Rowe 1976: 35–36.

CHAPTER NINE

1. In Evans 1977: 179.
2. Henry Stuart's account, Saunders 1968, 10: 773. Unfortunately, the Indian talks in this document are given as reported speech. Brown (1938: 139, 142, etc.) freely converted them to "direct" speech. I have done the same, but have stuck more closely to Stuart's wording.
3. Saunders 1968, 10: 774, 776.
4. Ibid., 777.
5. Ibid., 778.
6. Ibid., 779.
7. William Tatham quoted in Williams 1921: 176.
8. In ibid., 176–78. Also in *Journal of Cherokee Studies* 1, no. 2 (Fall 1976): 128–29.
9. Waldman 1985: 112.
10. Carter 1976: 10.
11. Ibid., 11.
12. See Mooney (1982: 490) for this speech and interesting notes re "War Women."
13. Sevier later became the first governor of Tennessee and a congressman.
14. Chapman 1985: 107.

15. See Wallace 1970: 160; Brown 1938: 322–27.
16. In McLoughlin 1986: 49.
17. Ibid., 33.
18. Jefferson quoted in McLoughlin 1984a: 15.
19. Ibid., 49.
20. In ibid., 150 (Thurman Wilkins trans.).
21. Ibid., 142 (McLoughlin trans.).
22. See ibid., 1986: 181.
23. From Mooney 1973: 676–77, quoted in McLoughlin 1984a: 138. For a fine study of the Plains ghost dances, see *We Shall Live Again* (1986) by Russell Thornton.
24. McLoughlin 1986: 187.
25. See Wilkins 1986: 69.
26. See Ehle 1988: 120.
27. See McLoughlin 1986: 193–95.
28. Wilkins 1986: 15.
29. In ibid., 45–46.
30. See Perdue 1983: 80 n.
31. In Wilkins 1986: 6.
32. In McLoughlin 1986: 449.
33. In Carter 1976: 83.
34. William Chamberlain quoted in McLoughlin 1986: 353.
35. Ehle 1988: 69.
36. See A. Wallace 1970: 148. Brodhead, in his 1781 "squaw campaign," murdered captive Delaware women and children. In 1782 American militia murdered 90 pro-American Christian Delawares.
37. The full address, with notes, is in Boudinot 1983: 65–83.
38. Woodward 1963: 158–59.
39. McLoughlin 1984a: 26.
40. Ross to Senecas, Apr.14, 1834, in Ross 1985, 1: 284–87.
41. Quotations in Woodward 1963: 171. See also Castile 1979: 194. O'Brien (1989) briefly discusses the legal implications.
42. Ridge to Ross, Feb. 2, 1833, in Ross 1985, 1: 260.
43. Boudinot 1983: 88.
44. Ibid., 27.

45. Mooney 1982: 127–28.
46. Ibid., 127.
47. Ibid.
48. King and Evans 1978: 183.
49. Mooney 1982: 97; King and Evans 1978: 183. The wording differs somewhat in the two accounts.
50. In Brown 1938: 495.

CHAPTER TEN

1. In Gilbert 1989: 58.
2. In Wallace 1970: 197.
3. See Fenton (1989) for the division of the League, its political problems, and the return of eleven wampum belts to Grand River in 1988. For more on wampum, see Williams 1990.
4. Wallace 1970: 198.
5. Waldman 1985: 114.
6. Stone 1866: 132–33.
7. See Wallace 1970: 160; Brown 1938: 322–27.
8. Stone 1866: 169–70.
9. Ibid., 105.
10. Ibid., 170–76. I have changed the position of the first paragraph. The emphasis is in the original.
11. Ibid., 468.
12. Ibid., 469.
13. Ibid., 471–72.
14. The Canandaigua treaty is also known as the Pickering Treaty. See Parker 1967: 135.
15. Pickering Treaty in Deskaheh 1924: 39–42.
16. In Stone 1866: 475.
17. Ibid., 477–78.
18. Stone 1866: 273.
19. Ibid., 273–76. The speech was printed in 1811 by James D. Bemis, editor of Canandaigua's first newspaper, which published several of Red Jacket's speeches during his lifetime. Many bilingual

Senecas lived in the area, so the translations may be considered especially reliable.

20. In Wallace 1970: 201.
21. Parker 1968, 2: 9.
22. Ibid., 22.
23. Ibid., 24.
24. Ibid., 24–27.
25. Thornton (1986) argues convincingly that some ghost dances also achieved practical recovery.
26. Parker 1968, 2: 66.
27. Ibid., 67–68.
28. Ibid., 38.
29. Ibid., 16–19.
30. Ibid., 7.

CHAPTER ELEVEN

1. See Octavio Paz, *Posdata* (1970); Brading 1984: 82.
2. In Meyer and Sherman 1987: 287–88. (There are different versons of Hidalgo's words.)
3. In his *Diccionario de Aztequismos*, Cabrera (1975: 80) suggests that *gachupín* comes from *cactli,* footwear, and *chapín,* a Spanish word for high heels typical of the conquerors.
4. See Meyer and Sherman 1987: 218.
5. Ibid., 332.
6. Other leaders have had Indian ancestry, but Juárez was the only ethnic Indian, born and raised in an indigenous culture.
7. Roeder 1968, 1: 55.
8. In Galich 1974: 81–82.
9. See Meyer and Sherman 1987: 552. They consider 1.5 to 2 million a moderate estimate. Others go as high as 3 million. The population was about 15 million in 1910 and 14 million in 1920.
10. Jiménez 1968: 12. This is from the introduction by the memoir's translator, Fernando Horcasitas. See also Bierhorst 1990: 24–25, for mention of Jiménez and the modern Nahua.

11. Jiménez 1968: 20–21.
12. *Tlatihuani,* sir or señor, is the modern Nahuatl version of the Aztec emperor's title *Tlatoani,* Speaker.
13. The Nahuatl term for president is *totatzin,* our father. The other word used here for leader, ruler, or community—*altepetl*—is the Aztec word for town or city-state. See Broda et al. 1987: 93.
14. Jiménez 1968: 104–5.
15. Ibid., 110–15. For comments on the Nahuatl style, see the Foreword by Miguel León-Portilla, 7–9.
16. In Mayo 1978: 310.
17. In Meyer and Sherman 1987: 514–15.
18. Antonio Díaz Soto y Gama quoted in ibid., 536.
19. Jiménez 1968: 119–21, 132–33.
20. In Meyer and Sherman 1987: 548.
21. Ibid., 549.
22. Jiménez 1968: 150–51.
23. *The Plumed Serpent* (1926), however flawed it may be as a novel, caught the spirit of the times.
24. Rivera's wife, Frida Kahlo, a major painter in her own right, explored a more personal use of pre-Columbian and colonial symbols.
25. Mayo 1978: 388.
26. In Spanish-speaking countries, both parents' surnames are used. He is descended through his mother, whose maiden name is Moctezuma.
27. Tezozomoc 1975a: 3–5.

CHAPTER TWELVE

1. By modified Itzá chronology, which lengthened the katun. A true katun is 7,200 days, about 256.27 solar years.
2. Bricker 1981: 87.
3. Ibid., 98.
4. Quoted in Reed 1964: 48.
5. Francisco Caamal et al. to Domingo Bacelis and José Dolores, Feb. 19, 1848. In Careaga n.d.: 33–34; also quoted in Bricker 1981: 97–98.

6. Unsigned to Victor García, Mar. 18, 1848; quoted in Bricker 1981: 98.
7. Francisco Caamal et al. to Domingo Bacelis and José Dolores, Feb. 19, 1848. In Careaga n.d.: 33–34; also quoted in Bricker 1981: 94. (My translation differs slightly from Bricker's.)
8. In Reed 1964: 99.
9. Bricker 1981: 104, 156.
10. See Sullivan 1989: 84–87.
11. Ibid., 178–79 (Sullivan trans.).
12. Much of the text is in Mondragón 1983: 12–22.
13. See Wright 1987: 44; Sheehan 1989: 272.
14. In Handy 1984: 63.
15. Ibid.
16. And for some statistics, Bolivia, a much poorer country than Guatemala.
17. Painter 1987: xvii.
18. Ibid., 3.
19. Ibid., 88.
20. Simon 1987: 14.
21. See Sheehan 1989: 275; Rigoberta Menchú quoted below in this chapter.
22. Carmack 1988: 67–69.
23. In McClintock 1985: 258–59.
24. Menchú 1984: 169–70.
25. Ibid., 1985: 41, 92.
26. See Barry et al. 1983: 29.
27. Menchú 1984: 38–40.
28. Ibid., 176–79.
29. In Handy 1984: 247.
30. Figures from Menchú speech, Toronto, June 1, 1990.
31. Translated and edited from taped interview, June 1, 1990.

CHAPTER THIRTEEN

1. Werlich 1978: 142.
2. Arguedas quoted in Pease 1976: 31.

3. Arguedas and Ortiz 1973: 220–21. Collected by Arguedas in Puquio in the 1950s.
4. Ibid., 222–23. The ending is a pun; the Quechua word *riy* can be the verb "to go" or a word for "king" (from Spanish *rey*).
5. Arguedas 1987b: 24–25.
6. In Pease 1973: 451.
7. León 1973: 348.
8. Werlich 1978: 21.
9. Waman Puma 1980a: 1027, 1025–26; 1980b, 2: 446–47.
10. León 1973: 346–47.
11. See Alba 1985.
12. Stern 1987: 179.
13. See Langer 1990.
14. Blanco 1972: 28. Note his comments on *ayllu*.
15. Ibid., 47.
16. I am grateful to Mark Day for this instance from an interview of his with a Peruvian officer.
17. *El Comercio*. The column was called Kaypin Rimayku, which means "Here *We* Speak."
18. Blanco 1972: 28.
19. Montoya 1987: 665–67. Song composed during land takeovers in Uranmarca, Andahuaylas.
20. Ortiz 1973: 238–43, collected in 1971 and first published in *Educación*, no. 7, Lima.
21. See Gonzalez 1986; Gorriti 1990a, 1990b.
22. Shakespeare 1988: 165.
23. See DeQuine 1984: 613.
24. Díaz 1963: 143. See also Wright 1983: 20; Stern 1987: 170–71 n.
25. I am grateful to Mark Day for this speculation.
26. See, for example, *Entre Zapos y Halcones,* Vargas's speech of acceptance into the Academia Peruana de la Lengua Española in 1977. This attempts to explain away the social injustices portrayed in Arguedas's work as stemming more from the author's childhood than the reality of Peruvian sierra life. One could say the same of Dickens.

CHAPTER FOURTEEN

1. Full text in King and Evans 1978: 180–85.
2. Major Ethan Allen Hitchcock quoted in Foreman 1989: 322.
3. Act of Union, July 12, 1839; this and the constitution are in Starr 1969: 121–30.
4. In Reed 1979: 158; Wilkins 1986: 3–4.
5. *Fort Smith Herald,* July 18, 1849. In Foreman 1989: 403.
6. Ibid., 369–70.
7. Ross 1985, 2: 404.
8. The name, which is that of a large bird, is also spelled Guwisguwi (Brown 1938: 473).
9. Ross 1985, 2: 405–8. I have changed the position of the last sentence.
10. Gov. Robert J. Walker, as quoted by Ross 1985, 2: 408 (my emphasis).
11. G. Foreman (1989: 418–19) reports 21,000 Indians, 1,000 whites, and 4,000 blacks in the Nation in 1859.
12. I outlined the reasons in *On Fiji Islands* (1986).
13. Excluding part Hawaiians, who account for about 15 percent.
14. Ross 1985, 2: 468–69.
15. Woodward (1963: 312) cites census figures showing a drop from 18,000 to 13,566.
16. In Foreman 1989: 403.
17. In Moulton 1978: 172.
18. Ross 1985, 2: 479–81. Address of Aug. 21, 1861.
19. In Woodward 1963: 277.
20. Ibid., 287.
21. Ross 1985, 2: 591 (speech given June 14, 1864).
22. Ibid., 646.
23. In Woodward 1963: 302.
24. In Dee Brown's excellent *Bury My Heart at Wounded Knee* (1981: 166).
25. Princeton was called the College of New Jersey until 1896.
26. In Jackson 1881: 294.
27. In Woodward 1963: 317.

28. Ibid., 318.
29. In Brown 1981: 172.
30. Hendrix 1983a: 32. See also Campbell and Campbell 1981: 99–100. Dawes wrote this in 1883.
31. See Woodward 1963: 320.
32. Moses and Wilson 1985: 128–29.
33. In ibid., 129.
34. In Woodward 1963: 320–21.
35. In Vestal 1957: 251–55.
36. In Turner 1974: 255.
37. In Hendrix 1983b: 84–85.
38. Mooney 1982: 163.
39. Ibid., 236.
40. See Neely 1979: 167, and Wright 1988 for Canadian examples.
41. In Perdue 1989: 98.
42. McDowell 1958: 254–55.
43. See Wheeler and McDonald 1986: 25.
44. In ibid., 24.
45. Matthiessen 1985: 133.
46. See King and Olinger 1972.
47. In Matthiessen 1985: 126–27.
48. Mankiller 1990: 11.

CHAPTER FIFTEEN

1. Haldimand Grant in Deskaheh 1924: 44–45. See also Titley 1986: 112. The grant was confirmed by the Simcoe Deed of 1793; see Deskaheh 1924: 51–53, and Titley 1986: 133.
2. In Bourgeois 1986: 3.
3. Brant to Captain Green, Dec. 10, 1797. Quoted in Cork 1962: 94–95.
4. See ibid., 121–22.
5. Frideres 1988: 12. The full federal franchise was not extended to Canadian women until 1918.
6. An 1890 amendment gave Indian Affairs power to impose changes without band consent. See Titley 1986: 113.

7. In Blanchard 1980: 363–65.
8. Ibid., 366.
9. McCrea quoted in ibid., 369.
10. There is confusion in the records as to whether the victim's surname was Fire or Ice. Sally Benedict, an Akwesasne historian, explained it to me as follows. There were two brothers, known in English as Jacob and John Fire. The confusion began because John was generally called Jake. Since his Mohawk name referred to ice, people called him Jake Ice to distinguish him from his brother Jacob Fire. The man shot was therefore John "Jake Ice" Fire.
11. Mitchell 1989: 118–19.
12. In Blanchard 1980: 372.
13. "Christian Democrats," in this sense, was coined by Mohawk writer Brian Maracle.
14. In Rostkowski 1987: 445.
15. His title was Deputy Superintendent General, but the deputy was in fact the head.
16. In Asch 1984: 62–63. Scott's draconian schemes included Bill 14, which sought to eliminate Indian "agitators" by making them into de jure whites through compulsory enfranchisement. This legislation was repealed a year later when Mackenzie King came to power, but not before it drew many to Deskaheh's cause.
17. In Titley 1986: 31–32.
18. Ibid., 34.
19. In *Journal of Cherokee Studies* 6, no. 2 (1981): 100.
20. Deskaheh et al. to the Duke of Devonshire, May 10, 1921. Canada, Indian Affairs, RG10, vol. 2285, file 57, 169.
21. Simcoe Deed, in Deskaheh 1924: 51–53.
22. Ibid., 22.
23. Noon 1949: 59.
24. Deskaheh 1924: 16.
25. Ibid., 9.
26. In Veatch 1975: 93.
27. Ibid., 98.

28. Deskaheh to George V, Oct. 22, 1924. Canada, Indian Affairs, RG10, vol. 2286, file 57, 169.
29. It is believed that some were never seen again.
30. Paul Williams and Robert Jamieson agree on 27 (personal communications, 1990). See also Noon 1949: 64–65.
31. Paul Williams, personal communication.
32. Rickard 1973: 63–64.
33. Ibid.
34. Ibid., 65.
35. In Akwesasne Notes n.d.: 13–20.
36. Section 141 of the Indian Act (1927).
37. In MacGregor 1990: 57.
38. See Hauptman 1986: 105–22.
39. Justice Hugo Black quoted in ibid., 174.
40. In Blanchard 1980: 459.
41. Pindera 1991: 34.
42. They first seized an abandoned camp at Moss Lake, which Gov. Mario Cuomo of New York persuaded them to exchange for state land nearer to Akwesasne in 1977.
43. Hauptman 1986: 145.
44. In *Globe and Mail,* May 5, 1990.
45. Matthew Pyke and Harold Edwards.
46. Chief Joseph Onasakenrat in Parent n.d.: 107–8.
47. Edited from taped interview, Nov. 21, 1990.
48. See Pindera 1991 for a good summary of the Oka dispute and profile of Joe David.
49. *Globe and Mail,* May 28, 1991.
50. See "Chronology of Main Events in Oka Dispute," *Globe and Mail,* Sept. 3, 1990.
51. Ibid., July 14, 1990.
52. The notable exception was Newfoundland's Clyde Wells, who blocked a federal move to get around the Manitoba impasse.
53. *Toronto Star,* Sept. 8, 1990.
54. Maracle 1990.
55. Iroquois Confederacy to Brian Mulroney, Aug. 25, 1990.

56. CBC TV *Newsworld,* Aug. 27, 1990; *Globe and Mail,* Sept. 3, 1990.
57. See Clark 1990a, 1990b.
58. *Globe and Mail,* Sept. 6, 1991.
59. Faxed press release dated Sept. 19, 1990.
60. *Toronto Star,* Sept. 22, 1990.
61. See "Mohawk Warriors . . ." by André Picard and Geoffrey York, *Globe and Mail,* Sept. 27, 1990.
62. In Pindera 1991: 39.

EPILOGUE

1. See Thornton 1987: 185.
2. Eddie Lazarus, personal communication, 1991.
3. Reported by CBC TV *Journal,* June 18, 1991.
4. Standing Bear 1978: 248.

BIBLIOGRAPHY

Adair, James. 1968 [1775]. *The History of the American Indians*. New York: Johnson.

Adorno, Rolena. 1982. (ed.) *From Oral to Written Expression: Native Andean Chronicles of the Early Colonial Period*. Syracuse: Syracuse University Press.

—. 1986. *Guaman Poma: Writing and Resistance in Colonial Peru*. Austin: University of Texas Press.

Akwesasne Notes. 1986. *Basic Call to Consciousness*. Rooseveltown, N.Y.: Mohawk Nation.

—. n.d. [c. 1975]. *Deskaheh: Iroquois Statesman and Patriot*. Rooseveltown, N.Y.: Mohawk Nation.

Alba Herrera, C. Augusto. 1985. *Atusparia y la Revolución Campesina de 1885 en Ancash*. Lima: Ediciones Atusparia.

Anderson, Arthur, Frances Berdan, and James Lockhart. 1976. *Beyond the Codices: The Nahua View of Colonial Mexico*. Berkeley: University of California Press.

Arciniegas, Germán. 1963. *Biografía del Caribe*. Buenos Aires: Editorial Sudamericana.

Arguedas, José María. 1958. *Los Rios Profundos*. Lima: Editorial Losada.

—. 1984. *Katatay*. Lima: Editorial Horizonte.

—. 1987a. *Indios, Mestizos y Señores*, 2d ed. Edited by Sybila Arredondo de Arguedas. Lima: Editorial Horizonte.

—. 1987b [1965]. "El Indigenismo en el Perú." In Arguedas 1987a: 11–27.

Arguedas, José María, and Alejandro Ortiz Rescaniere. 1973. "Tres Versiones del Mito de Inkarri." In Ossio 1973: 217–36.

Armstrong, Virginia I., ed. 1971. *I Have Spoken: American History Through the Voices of the Indians*. Chicago: Swallow Press.

Asch, Michael. 1984. *Home and Native Land*. Toronto: Methuen Press.

Ascher, Marcia and Robert. 1981. *Code of the Quipu*. Ann Arbor: University of Michigan Press.

Axtell, James. 1981. *The European and the Indian*. Oxford: Oxford University Press.

—. 1988. *After Columbus*. Oxford: Oxford University Press.

Bailyn, Bernard. 1986. *Voyages to the West*. New York: Knopf.

Bannon, John Francis, S. J., ed. 1966. *Indian Labor in the Spanish Indies*. Boston: D. C. Heath.

Barrera Vásquez, Alfredo. 1984. *Códice de Calkiní, Cantares de Dzitbalché*. Campeche: CORACEC.

Barry, Tom, Beth Wood, and Deb Preusch. 1983. *Dollars and Dictators*. London: Zed Press.

Bartram, William. 1955 [1791]. *The Travels of William Bartram*. New York: Dover.

Bennett, Philip. 1984. "Corner of the Dead." *The Atlantic*, May 1984, 28–33.

Berkhofer, Robert F. 1978. *The White Man's Indian*. New York: Knopf.

Bierhorst, John, ed. and trans. 1974. *Four Masterworks of American Indian Literature*. New York: Farrar, Straus and Giroux.

—. 1985. *Cantares Mexicanos: Songs of the Aztecs*. Stanford: Stanford University Press.

—. 1990. *The Mythology of Mexico and Central America*. New York: Morrow.

Blanchard, David. 1980. *Seven Generations: A History of the Kanienkehaka*. Kahnawake: Kahnawake Survival School.

Blanco, Hugo. 1972. *Land or Death: The Peasant Struggle in Peru*. New York: Pathfinder.

Boldt, Menno, and J. Anthony Long, eds. 1985. *The Quest for Justice: Aboriginal Peoples and Aboriginal Rights*. Toronto: University of Toronto Press.

Bonner, Raymond. 1988. "Peru's War." *The New Yorker*, January 4, 31–58.

Bonvillain, Nancy, ed. n.d. *Studies on Iroquoian Culture*. Albany: State University of New York, Occasional Publications in Northeastern Anthropology, no. 6.

Boudinot, Elias. 1983. *Cherokee Editor: The Writings of Elias Boudinot.* Edited by Theda Perdue. Knoxville: University of Tennessee Press.

Bourgeois, Donald J. 1986. *The Six Nations Indian Land Claim to the Bed of the Grand River.* Toronto: Queen's Printer for Ontario.

Bourne, Edward Gaylord, ed. and trans. 1904. *Narratives of De Soto,* 2 vols. New York: A. S. Barnes.

Boyd, Julian P., ed. 1938. *Indian Treaties Printed by Benjamin Franklin 1736–1762.* Philadelphia: Historical Society of Pennsylvania.

Brading, D. A. 1984. *Prophecy and Myth in Mexican History.* Cambridge, Eng.: Centre of Latin American Studies.

Bray, Warwick. 1968. *Everyday Life of the Aztecs.* New York: G. P. Putnam's Sons.

Bricker, Victoria R. 1981. *The Indian Christ, the Indian King.* Austin: University of Texas Press.

Brinton, Daniel G. 1969a [1884]. *The Lenape and Their Legends.* New York: AMS.

—. 1969b [1885]. *The Annals of the Cakchiquels.* New York: AMS.

Broda, Johanna, David Carrasco, and Eduardo Matos Moctezuma. 1987. *The Great Temple of Tenochtitlan.* Berkeley: University of California Press.

Brody, Hugh. 1981. *Maps and Dreams.* Vancouver, B.C.: Douglas and McIntyre.

Brotherston, Gordon. 1979. *Image of the New World.* London: Thames and Hudson.

Brown, Dee. 1981. *Bury My Heart at Wounded Knee.* New York: Simon and Schuster.

Brown, John P. 1938. *Old Frontiers.* Kinsport, Tenn.: Southern Publishers.

Bruce, Robert D., ed. 1974. *El Libro de Chan K'in.* México D.F.: INAH.

Brundage, Burr Cartwright. 1972. *A Rain of Darts: The Mexica Aztecs.* Austin: University of Texas Press.

Burga, Manuel. 1988. *Nacimiento de una utopía: Muerte y resurrección de los incas.* Lima: Instituto de Apoyo Agrario.

Burns, Allan F. 1977. "The Caste War in the 1970's: Present-Day Accounts from Village Quintana Roo." In Jones 1977: 259–73.

Cabrera, Luis. 1975. *Diccionario de Aztequismos.* México D.F.: Ediciones Oasis.

Calvert, Peter. 1985. *Guatemala: A Nation in Turmoil.* Boulder, Colo.: Westview Press.

Campbell, Janet, and David G. Campbell. 1981. "Cherokee Participation in the Political Impact of the North American Indian." *Journal of Cherokee Studies* 6, no. 2 (Fall): 92–105.

Campbell, Leon G. 1987. "Ideology and Factionalism during the Great Rebellion, 1780–1782." In Stern 1987: 110–39.

Campbell, William W., ed. 1849. *The Life and Writings of DeWitt Clinton.* New York: Baker and Scribner.

Careaga Viliesid, Lorena. n.d. [c. 1980]. *Lecturas Básicas para la Historia de Quintana Roo.* Chetumal, Q. R.: Fondo de Fomento Editorial del Gobierno.

Carmack, Robert M. 1988. *Harvest of Violence: The Maya Indians and the Guatemalan Crisis.* Norman: University of Oklahoma Press.

Carrasco, David. 1982. *Quetzalcoatl and the Irony of Empire.* Chicago: University of Chicago Press.

Carter, Samuel. 1976. *Cherokee Sunset.* New York: Doubleday.

Castanien, Donald G. 1969. *El Inca Garcilaso de la Vega.* New York: Twayne.

Castile, George Pierre. 1979. *North American Indians: An Introduction to the Chichimeca.* New York: McGraw-Hill.

Chamberlain, Robert S. 1982. *Conquista y Colonización de Yucatán.* México D.F.: Porrúa.

Chapman, Jefferson. 1985. *Tellico Archaeology.* Knoxville: Tennessee Valley Authority.

Chimalpahin Cuauhtlehuanitzin, [Don Domingo] Francisco de San Antón Muñón. 1965. *Relaciones Originales de Chalco Amaquemecan.* Translated by Silvia Rendón. México D.F.: Fondo de Cultura Económica.

Cieza de León, Pedro de. 1986, 1. *Crónica del Perú, Primera Parte.* Edited by Franklin Pease. Lima: Universidad Católica del Perú.

—. 1986, 2. *Crónica del Perú, Segunda Parte.* Edited by Francesca Cantú. Lima: Universidad Católica del Perú.

Clark, Bruce 1990a. *Native Liberty, Crown Sovereignty.* Montreal: McGill-Queen's University Press.

—. 1990b. "Indian Heroes, Government Outlaws." *Globe and Mail,* September 26.

Clendinnen, Inga. 1987. *Ambivalent Conquests*. Cambridge: Cambridge University Press.

—. 1991. *Aztecs: An Interpretation*. Cambridge: Cambridge University Press.

Cline, Howard F., ed. 1989. *Conquest of New Spain: 1585 Revision*. Salt Lake City: University of Utah Press.

Coe, Michael D. 1987. *The Maya*. London: Thames and Hudson.

Collapiña, Supno, y Otros Quipucamayos. 1974. *Relación de la Descendencia, Gobierno y Conquista de los Incas*. Introduction by Juan José Vega. Lima: Ediciones de la Biblioteca Universitaria.

Collier, George A., Renato I. Rosaldo, and John D. Wirth, eds. 1982. *The Inca and Aztec States, 1400–1800*. New York: Academic Press.

Conrad, Geoffrey W., and Arthur A. Demarest. 1984. *Religion and Empire*. Cambridge: Cambridge University Press.

Cook, Noble David. 1981. *Demographic Collapse: Indian Peru, 1520–1620*. Cambridge: Cambridge University Press.

Cook, Noble David, and W. George Lovell, eds. 1991. *"Secret Judgments of God": Old World Disease in Colonial Spanish America*. Norman: University of Oklahoma Press.

Cook, Sherburne F., and Woodrow Borah. 1963. *The Aboriginal Population of Central Mexico on the Eve of the Spanish Conquest*. Berkeley: University of California Press.

Cork, Ella. 1962. *The Worst of the Bargain*. San Jacinto, Calif.: Foundation for Social Research.

Corkran, David H. 1962. *The Cherokee Frontier*. Norman: University of Oklahoma Press.

Craine, Eugene R., and Reginald C. Reindorp, trans. 1979. *The Codex Pérez and the Book of Chilam Balam of Maní*. Norman: University of Oklahoma Press.

Crosby, Alfred W. 1972. *The Columbian Exchange*. Westport, Conn.: Greenwood Press.

—. 1986. *Ecological Imperialism*. New York: Cambridge University Press.

Degregori, Carlos Iván. 1988. *Sendero Luminoso*. Lima: Instituto de Estudios Peruanos.

Deloria, Vine. 1970. *We Talk, You Listen*. New York: Macmillan.

DeQuine, Jeanne. 1984. "The Challenge of the Shining Path." *The Nation*, December 8, 610–13.

Deskaheh (Levi General) and Six Nations Council. 1924. *The Redman's Appeal for Justice*. Brantford, Ont.: Wilson Moore.

Díaz, Bernal. 1963 [c. 1575]. *The Conquest of New Spain*. Translated by J. M. Cohen. Harmondsworth, Eng.: Penguin.

Dickason, Olive. 1984. *The Myth of the Savage*. Edmonton: University of Alberta Press.

Dobyns, Henry F. 1983. *Their Number Become Thinned*. Knoxville: University of Tennessee Press.

Edmonson, Munro S., trans. 1982. *The Ancient Future of the Itzá : The Book of Chilam Balam of Tizimín*. Austin: University of Texas Press.

—. 1986. *Heaven Born Mérida and Its Destiny: The Book of Chilam Balam of Chumayel*. Austin: University of Texas Press.

Ehle, John. 1988. *Trail of Tears*. New York: Doubleday.

Engels, Friedrich. 1972 [1884]. *The Origin of the Family*. Moscow: Progress Publishers.

Erasmus, Georges. 1990. "Speech on Planned Celebration of 1992." *Canadian Forum* 68, no. 784 (January): 16–17.

Evans, E. Raymond. 1977. "Notable Persons in Cherokee History: Dragging Canoe." *Journal of Cherokee Studies*, no. 1 (Winter): 176–89.

Farriss, Nancy M. 1984. *Maya Society Under Colonial Rule*. Princeton: Princeton University Press.

Feest, Christian F., ed. 1987. *Indians and Europe*. Aachen, Ger.: Edition Herodot.

Fenton, William N. 1987. *The False Faces of the Iroquois*. Norman: University of Oklahoma Press.

—. 1989. "Return of Eleven Wampum Belts to the Six Nations Confederacy on Grand River, Canada." *Ethnohistory* 36, no. 4 (Fall): 393–410.

Finger, John R. 1984. *The Eastern Band of Cherokees*. Knoxville: University of Tennessee Press.

Flores Galindo, Alberto, ed. 1976. *Túpac Amaru II*. Lima: Retablo de Papel Ediciones.

Foreman, Carolyn Thomas. 1943. *Indians Abroad, 1493–1938*. Norman: University of Oklahoma Press.

Foreman, Grant. 1987 [1938]. *Sequoyah*. Norman: University of Oklahoma Press.

—. 1989 [1934]. *The Five Civilized Tribes*. Norman: University of Oklahoma Press.

Foster, Tom. 1990. "Warrior Society's Militant Message." (Syracuse, N.Y.) *Post-Standard*, July 9.

Frideres, James S. 1988. *Native Peoples in Canada*. Toronto: Prentice-Hall.

Fried, Jonathan L., Marvin E. Gettleman, et al., eds. 1983. *Guatemala in Rebellion*. New York: Grove Press.

Fuentes, Carlos. 1985. *Latin America at War with the Past*. Toronto: CBC Enterprises.

Galeano, Eduardo. 1983. "Did History Lie When It Promised Peace and Progress?" Translated by Marianne Dugan and Ernesto Castillo. In Fried et al. 1983: 318–323.

—. 1985, 1987, 1989. *Memory of Fire*, 3 vols. Translated by Cedric Belfrage. London: Quartet.

—. 1988. "The Blue Tiger and the Promised Land." Translated by Liz Herron. *New Statesman* 115, no. 2976: 16–18.

Galich, Manuel, ed. 1974. *Benito Juárez, Pensamiento y Acción*. Havana: Casa de las Américas.

Garcilaso de la Vega, El Inca. 1688 [1609]. *The Royal Commentaries of Peru*. Translated by Sir Paul Rycaut. London: Christopher Wilkinson.

—. 1951 [1605]. *The Florida of the Inca*. Austin: University of Texas Press.

—. 1956. *La Florida del Inca*. México D.F.: Fondo de Cultura Económica.

—. 1966. *Royal Commentaries of the Incas*. Translated by Harold V. Livermore. Austin: University of Texas Press.

—. 1985. *Comentarios Reales de los Incas*, 2 vols. Edited by Aurelio Miró Quesada. Caracas: Biblioteca Ayacucho.

Garibay Kintana, Angel María, trans. 1964a. *La Literatura de los Aztecas*. México D.F.: Joaquín Mortiz.

—. 1964b. *Poesía Náhuatl. 1: Romances de los Señores de la Nueva España*. México D.F.: UNAM.

—. 1965. *Poesía Náhuatl. 2: Cantares Mexicanos*. México D.F.: UNAM.

—. 1968. *Poesía Náhuatl. 3: Cantares Mexicanos*. México D.F.: UNAM. See also Sahagún 1956.

Gibson, Charles. 1964. *The Aztecs Under Spanish Rule*. Stanford: Stanford University Press.

Gilbert, Bil. 1989. *God Gave Us This Country*. New York: Atheneum.

González, Raúl. 1986. "Gonzalo's Thought, Belaúnde's Answer." *NACLA Report on the Americas* 20, no. 3 (June): 34–36.

Gorriti, Gustavo. 1990a. "The War of the Philosopher-King." *The New Republic*, June 18, 15–22.

—. 1990b. *Sendero: Historia de la Guerra Milenaria en el Perú*. Lima: Apoyo.

Graymont, Barbara. 1972. *The Iroquois in the American Revolution*. Syracuse: Syracuse University Press.

Green, L. C., and Olive P. Dickason. 1989. *The Law of Nations and the New World*. Edmonton: University of Alberta Press.

Grinde, Donald A. 1977. *The Iroquois and the Founding of the American Nation*. San Francisco: Indian Historian Press.

Gruzinski, Serge.1989. *Man-Gods in the Mexican Highlands*. Translated by Eileen Corrigan. Stanford: Stanford University Press.

Guardia Mayorga, César A. 1973. *Gramática Kechwa*. Lima: Los Andes.

Gulick, John. 1960. *Cherokees at the Crossroads*. Chapel Hill: University of North Carolina Press.

Hale, Horatio, ed. 1963 [1883]. *The Iroquois Book of Rites*. Toronto: University of Toronto Press.

Hamilton, Charles, ed. 1972 [1950]. *Cry of the Thunderbird: The American Indian's Own Story*. Norman: University of Oklahoma Press.

Hammond, Norman. 1982. *Ancient Maya Civilization*. Cambridge: Cambridge University Press.

Handy, Jim. 1984. *Gift of the Devil: A History of Guatemala*. Toronto: Between the Lines.

Hauptman, Laurence M. 1981. *The Iroquois and the New Deal*. Syracuse: Syracuse University Press.

—. 1986. *The Iroquois Struggle for Survival*. Syracuse: Syracuse University Press.

Hemming, John. 1983. *The Conquest of the Incas*. Harmondsworth, Eng.: Penguin.

Hendrix, Janey B. 1983a. "Redbird Smith and the Nighthawk Keetoowahs." *Journal of Cherokee Studies* 8, no. 1 (Spring): 22–39.

—. 1983b. "Redbird Smith and the Nighthawk Keetoowahs." *Journal of Cherokee Studies* 8, no. 2 (Fall): 73–86.

Heyerdahl, Thor. 1956. "Archaeological Evidence of Pre-Spanish Visits to the Galápagos Islands." *American Antiquity* 22, no. 1, pt. 3 (supplement).

—. 1974. *Sea Routes to Polynesia*. London: Futura.

Hudson, Charles, Marvin T. Smith, and Chester B. DePratter. 1984. "The Hernando de Soto Expedition: From Apalachee to Chiaha." *Southeastern Archaeology* 3, no. 1 (Summer): 65–77.

Innes, Hammond. 1969. *The Conquistadors*. London: Collins.

Ixtlilxochitl, Fernando de Alva. 1956. *Relación de la Venida de los Españoles y Principio de la Ley Evangélica*. In Sahagún 1956, 4: 187–276.

Jackson, Helen Hunt. 1881. *A Century of Dishonor*. New York: Harper & Bros.

Jennings, Francis. 1976. *The Invasion of America*. New York: Norton.

—. 1984. *The Ambiguous Iroquois Empire*. New York: Norton.

—. 1988. *Empire of Fortune*. New York: Norton.

Jiménez, Luz. 1968. *De Porfirio Díaz a Zapata: Memoria Náhuatl de Milpa Alta*. Edited and translated by Fernando Horcasitas. México D.F.: UNAM.

Johansen, Bruce. 1982. *Forgotten Founders*. Ipswich, Mass.: Gambit.

—. 1990. "Native American Societies and the Evolution of Democracy in America, 1600–1800." *Ethnohistory* 37, no. 3 (Summer): 279–90.

Johansen, Bruce, and Roberto Maestas. 1979. *Wasi'chu: The Continuing Indian Wars*. New York: Monthly Review.

Jones, Dorothy V. 1982. *License for Empire: Colonialism by Treaty in Early America*. Chicago: University of Chicago Press.

Jones, Grant D. 1977. (ed.) *Anthropology and History in Yucatán*. Austin: University of Texas Press.

—. 1989. *Maya Resistance to Spanish Rule*. Albuquerque: University of New Mexico Press.

Josephy, Alvin M. 1971. *Red Power*. New York: American Heritage Press.

Julien, Catherine J. 1988. "How Inca Decimal Administration Worked." *Ethnohistory* 35, no. 3 (Summer): 257–79.

Kaiser, Rudolf. 1987. "Chief Seattle's Speech(es): American Origins and European Reception." In Swann and Krupat 1987b: 497–536.

Kelley, David H. 1976. *Deciphering the Maya Script*. Austin: University of Texas Press.

Kelly, James C. 1978. "Notable Persons in Cherokee History: Attakullakulla." *Journal of Cherokee Studies* 3, no. 1 (Winter): 2–34.

Kelsay, Isabel Thompson. 1984. *Joseph Brant*. Syracuse: Syracuse University Press.

Kendall, Ann. 1973. *Everyday Life of the lncas*. New York: G. P. Putnam's Sons.

King, Duane H., ed. 1979. *The Cherokee Indian Nation*. Knoxville: University of Tennessee Press.

King, Duane H., and Jefferson Chapman. 1988. *The Sequoyah Legacy*. Vonore, Tenn.: Sequoyah Birthplace Museum.

King, Duane H., and E. Raymond Evans, eds. 1978. "The Trail of Tears: Primary Documents of the Cherokee Removal." *Journal of Cherokee Studies* 3, no. 3 (Summer): 129–90.

King, Duane H., and Danny E. Olinger. 1972. "Oconastota." *American Antiquity* 37, no. 2 (April): 222–28.

Krotz, Larry. 1990. *Indian Country*. Toronto: McClelland & Stewart.

Lafaye, Jacques. 1976. *Quetzalcóatl and Guadalupe*. Chicago: University of Chicago Press.

Landa, Diego de. 1978 [1937]. *Yucatan Before and After the Conquest*. Translated by William Gates. New York: Dover.

—. 1982 [1566]. *Relación de las Cosas de Yucatán*. México D.F.: Porrúa.

Langer, Erick D. 1990. "Andean Rituals of Revolt: The Chayanta Rebellion of 1927." *Ethnohistory* 37, no. 3 (Summer): 227–53.

Lara, Jesús. 1947. *La Poesía Quechua*. Cochabamba, Bolivia: Imprenta Universitaria.

Las Casas, Bartolomé de. 1984 [1552]. *Brevísima Relación de la Destrucción de las Indias*. México D.F.: Fontamara.

León, Nicolas. 1982. *Códice Sierra*. México D.F.: Editorial Innovación.

León Caparó, Raúl. 1973. "La Mitología Andina en una Barriada de Lima." In Ossio 1973: 339–53.

León-Portilla, Miguel. 1962. *The Broken Spears*. Translated by Lysander Kemp. London: Constable.

—. 1969a. *Visión de los Vencidos*. Havana: Casa de las Américas.

—. 1969b. *Pre-Columbian Literatures of Mexico*. Translated by León-Portilla and Grace Lobanov. Norman: University of Oklahoma Press.

—. 1973. *Time and Reality in the Thought of the Maya*. Boston: Beacon Press.

—. 1978. *Literatura del México Antiguo*. Caracas: Biblioteca Ayacucho.

—. 1980. *El Reverso de la Conquista*. México D.F.: Editorial Joaquín Mortiz.

Lewin, Boleslao. 1957. *La Rebelión de Túpac Amaru*. Buenos Aires: Librería Hachette.

Lipschütz, Alejandro. 1963. *El Problema Racial en la Conquista de América y el Mestizaje*. Santiago de Chile: Editora Austral.

Llorente, J. A. 1984. "Vida de Fray Bartolomé de Las Casas, Obispo de Chiapa, en América." In Las Casas 1984: 123–200.

Lockhart, James. 1972. *The Men of Cajamarca*. Austin: University of Texas Press.

Lovell, W. George. 1985. *Conquest and Survival in Colonial Guatemala*. Montreal: McGill–Queen's University Press.

—. 1988. "Surviving Conquest: The Maya of Guatemala in Historical Perspective." *Latin American Research Review* 23, no. 2: 25–57.

Lovell, W. George, and Christopher H. Lutz. 1992. "The Population History of Spanish Central America." In *The Peopling of Latin America*. Edited by Robert McCaa. Oxford: Oxford University Press.

Lyons, Oren. 1985. "Traditional Native Philosophies Relating to Aboriginal Rights." In Boldt and Long 1985: 19–23.

MacGregor, Roy. 1990. *Chief*. Markham, Ont.: Penguin.

Mankiller, Wilma. 1990. "State of the Nation Address." *Cherokee Advocate* 14, no. 11 (November): 1, 10–11.

Maracle, Brian. 1990. "Standoff Is a National Crisis." *Toronto Star*, July 21.

Mariátegui, José Carlos. 1967. *Siete Ensayos de Interpretación de la Realidad Peruana*. Lima: Biblioteca Amauta.

Martínez Peláez, Severo. 1971. *La Patria del Criollo*. San José, Costa Rica: Editorial Universitaria Centroamericana.

Matos Moctezuma, Eduardo. 1988. *The Great Temple of the Aztecs*. Translated by Doris Heyden. London: Thames and Hudson.

—. 1989. *The Aztecs*. Translated by Andrew Ellis. New York: Rizzoli International.

Matthiessen, Peter. 1985. *Indian Country*. London: Collins Harvill.

Mayo, Samuel H. 1978. *A History of Mexico*. Englewood Cliffs, N.J.: Prentice-Hall.

McClintock, Michael. 1985. *The American Connection*. London: Zed Books.

McDowell, William L., Jr., ed. 1955. *Colonial Records of South Carolina: Journals of the Commissioners of the Indian Trade, 1710–1718*. Columbia: South Carolina Archives.

—. 1958. *Colonial Records of South Carolina: Documents Relating to Indian Affairs, 1750–54*. Columbia: South Carolina Archives.

—. 1970. *Colonial Records of South Carolina: Documents Relating to Indian Affairs, 1754–65*. Columbia: University of South Carolina Press.

McLoughlin, William G. 1984a. *The Cherokee Ghost Dance*. Macon, Ga.: Mercer University Press.

—. 1984b. *Cherokees and Missionaries, 1789–1839*. New Haven: Yale University Press.

—. 1986. *Cherokee Renascence in the New Republic*. Princeton: Princeton University Press.

McLuhan, T. C. 1971. *Touch the Earth: A Self-Portrait of Indian Existence*. New York: Touchstone, Simon and Schuster.

McMillan, Alan D. 1988. *Native Peoples and Cultures of Canada*. Vancouver, B.C.: Douglas and McIntyre.

McNaught, Kenneth. 1976. *The Pelican History of Canada*. Harmondsworth, Eng.: Penguin.

Memmi, Albert. 1965. *The Colonizer and the Colonized*. Translated by Howard Greenfield. New York: Orion Press.

Menchú, Rigoberta. 1984. *I, Rigoberta Menchú*. Translated by Ann Wright. London: Verso.

—. 1985. *Me Llamo Rigoberta Menchú*. Edited by Elizabeth Burgos. México D.F.: Siglo Veintiuno.

Meyer, Michael G., and William L. Sherman. 1987. *The Course of Mexican History*. Oxford: Oxford University Press.

Miller, James R. 1989. *Skyscrapers Hide the Heavens*. Toronto: University of Toronto Press.

Millones, Luis. 1973a. "Un Movimiento Nativista del Siglo XVI: El Taki Ongoy." In Ossio 1973: 83–94.

—. 1973b. "Nuevos Aspectos del Taki Ongoy." In Ossio 1973: 95–102.

Mitchell, Chief Michael. 1989. "Akwesasne: An Unbroken Assertion of Sovereignty." In Richardson 1989, 107–36.

Mondragón, Rafael. 1983. *De Indios y Cristianos en Guatemala*. México D.F.: Copec.

Montaigne, Michel de. 1988 [1588]. *Essays*. Translated by J. M. Cohen. Harmondsworth, Eng.: Penguin.

Montoya, Rodrigo, Luis Montoya, and Edwin Montoya. 1987. *La Sangre de los Cerros: Urqukunapa Yawarnin*. Lima: Mosca Azul.

Moody, Roger, ed. 1988. *Indigenous Voice: Visions and Realities*. London: Zed Books.

Mooney, James. 1973 [1896]. *The Ghost Dance Religion*. Washington, D.C.: Smithsonian.

—. 1982 [1900]. *Myths of the Cherokee and Sacred Formulas of the Cherokees*. Cherokee, N.C.: Cherokee Heritage Books.

Morgan, Lewis Henry. 1972 [1851]. *League of the Iroquois*. Secaucus, N.J.: Citadel Press.

Morley, Sylvanus G., and George W. Brainerd. 1983. *The Ancient Maya*, 4th ed. Revised by Robert J. Sharer. Stanford: Stanford University Press.

Morris, Craig, and D. E. Thompson. 1985. *Huánuco Pampa*. London: Thames and Hudson.

Morris, Walter F. 1987. *Living Maya*. New York: Harry N. Abrams.

Morse, Bradford, ed. 1989. *Aboriginal Peoples and the Law*. Ottawa: Carleton University Press.

Moses, Lester George, and Raymond Wilson, eds. 1985. *Indian Lives*. Albuquerque: University of New Mexico Press.

Moulton, Gary E. 1978. *John Ross, Cherokee Chief*. Athens: University of Georgia Press.

Nabokov, Peter, ed. 1978. *Native American Testimony*. New York: Harper & Row.

Nairn, Allan, and Jean-Marie Simon. 1986. "Bureaucracy of Death." *The New Republic* 194, no. 26: 13–17.

Neely, Sharlotte. 1979. "Acculturation and Persistence among North Carolina's Eastern Band of Cherokee Indians." In Williams 1979: 154–73.

Noon, John A. 1949. *Law and Government of the Grand River Iroquois.* New York: Viking Fund Publications in Anthropology No. 12.

O'Brien, Sharon. 1989. *American Indian Tribal Governments.* Norman: University of Oklahoma Press.

O'Callaghan, E. B., et al., eds. 1856–1861. *Documents Relative to the Colonial History of the State of New York,* 11 vols. Albany: Weed, Parsons.

O'Phelan Godoy, Scarlett. 1985. *Rebellions and Revolts in Eighteenth Century Peru and Upper Peru.* Köln, Ger.: Böhlau Verlag.

Ortiz Rescaniere, Alejandro. 1973. "El Mito de la Escuela." In Ossio 1973: 237–50.

Ossio, Juan M. 1970. "The Idea of History in Felipe Guaman Poma de Ayala." B. Litt. thesis, Oxford University, Department of Anthropology.

—. 1973. (ed.) *Ideología Mesiánica del Mundo Andino.* Lima: Ignacio Prado Pastor.

Pachakuti Yamki Sallqamaywa, Juan de Santacruz (Pachacuti Yamqui Salcamaygua). 1968 [1613]. *Relación de Antigüedades deste Reyno del Perú.* Madrid: Atlas (*Biblioteca de Autores Españoles* 209: 279–319).

Pagden, Anthony. 1982. *The Fall of Natural Man.* Cambridge: Cambridge University Press.

Painter, James. 1987. *Guatemala: False Hope, False Freedom.* London: Catholic Institute for International Relations.

Pardo, Luis A. 1970. "La Fortaleza de Saccsayhuaman." *Saqsaywaman,* no. 1 (July): 89–157. Cusco: Ministerio de Educación Pública.

Parent, Amand. n.d. [c. 1885]. *The Life of Reverend Amand Parent.* Toronto: William Briggs.

Parker, Arthur C. 1967 [1926]. *The History of the Seneca Indians.* Port Washington, N.Y.: Ira J. Friedman.

—. 1968. *Parker on the Iroquois.* Edited by William Fenton. Syracuse: Syracuse University Press.

Paz, Octavio. 1990. "The Power of Ancient Mexican Art." *The New York Review of Books,* December 6, 18–20.

Pearce, Roy Harvey. 1965. *The Savages of America: A Study of the Indian and the Idea of Civilization.* Baltimore: Johns Hopkins University Press.

Pease, Franklin. 1973. "El Mito de Inkarrí y la Visión de los Vencidos." In Ossio 1973: 439–58.

—. 1976. *Los Ultimos Incas del Cuzco*. Lima: Ediciones P.L.V.

Perdue, Theda. 1980. (ed.) *Nations Remembered: An Oral History of the Five Civilized Tribes, 1865–1907*. Westport, Conn.: Greenwood Press.

—. 1989. *The Cherokee*. New York: Chelsea House. See also Boudinot 1983.

Perera, Victor, and Robert D. Bruce. 1982. *The Last Lords of Palenque*. Boston: Little, Brown.

Pindera, Loreen. 1991. "The Making of a Warrior." *Saturday Night* 106, no. 3 (April): 30–39.

Pizarro, Pedro. 1986 [1571]. *Relación del Descubrimiento y Conquista de los Reinos del Perú*. Edited by Guillermo Lohmann Villena. Lima: Universidad Católica.

Ponting, J. Rick, ed. 1986. *Arduous Journey: Canadian Indians and Decolonization*. Toronto: McClelland and Stewart.

Porras Barrenechea, Raúl. 1986. *Los Cronistas del Perú*. Lima: Banco de Crédito del Perú.

Powless, Irving. 1988. "The Sovereignty and Land Rights of the Houdenosaunee." In Vecsey 1988: 155–61.

Prescott, William H. n.d. [1843; 1847]. *History of the Conquest of Mexico and History of the Conquest of Peru*. New York: Random House, Modern Library.

Randall, Robert. 1982. "Qoyllur Rit'i, an Inca Fiesta of the Pleiades: Reflections on Time and Space in the Andean World." *Bulletin de l'Institut Français des Etudes Andines* 11, no. 1: 37–81.

—. 1987. "Del Tiempo y del Río: El Ciclo de la Historia y la Energía en la Cosmología Incaica." *Boletín de Lima* 9, no. 54: 69–95.

Reaman, G. Elmore. 1967. *The Trail of the Iroquois Indians*. Toronto: Peter Martin.

Recinos, Adrián, ed. & trans. 1950. *Memorial de Sololá, Anales de los Cakchiqueles*. México D.F.: Fondo de Cultura Económica. See also Xahil 1980.

Recinos, Adrián, Delia Goetz, and Dionisio José Chonay, trans. 1953. *The Annals of the Cakchiquels*. Norman: University of Oklahoma Press.

Recinos, Adrián, Delia Goetz, and Sylvanus G. Morley, trans. 1953. *Popol Vuh*. Norman: University of Oklahoma Press.

Reed, Gerard. 1979. "Postremoval Factionalism in the Cherokee Nation." In King 1979: 148–63.

Reed, Nelson. 1964. *The Caste War of Yucatán*. Stanford: Stanford University Press.

Richardson, Boyce, ed. 1989. *Drum Beat*. Toronto: Assembly of First Nations.

Rickard, Chief Clinton. 1973. *Fighting Tuscarora*. Edited by Barbara Graymont. Syracuse: Syracuse University Press.

Roeder, Ralph. 1968. *Juárez and His Mexico*. New York: Greenwood Press.

Ross, Chief John. 1985. *The Papers of Chief John Ross*, 2 vols. Edited by Gary Moulton. Norman: University of Oklahoma Press.

Rostkowski, Joëlle. 1987. "The Redman's Appeal for Justice: Deskaheh and the League of Nations." In Feest 1987: 435–54.

Rowe, John. 1976. "El Movimiento Nacional Inca del Siglo XVIII." In Flores Galindo 1976: 11–66.

Roys, Ralph L. 1967. *The Book of Chilam Balam of Chumayel*. Norman: University of Oklahoma Press.

Sahagún, Bernardino de. 1956 [c. 1555]. *Historia General de las Cosas de Nueva España*, 4 vols. Edited and translated by Angel María Garibay. México D.F.: Porrúa.

—. 1975 [c. 1555]. *Florentine Codex: General History of the Things of New Spain Book 12*. Translated by Arthur J. O. Anderson and Charles E. Dibble. Santa Fe, N.M.: The School of American Research and University of Utah.

—. 1981. *El México Antiguo*. Edited by José Luis Martínez. Caracas: Biblioteca Ayacucho. See also Cline 1989.

Saunders, William L., ed. 1968 [1886–1907]. *The Colonial Records of North Carolina*, 10 vols. New York: AMS.

Scarre, Chris. 1988. *Past Worlds*. London: Times Books.

Schele, Linda, and Mary Ellen Miller. 1986. *The Blood of Kings*. New York: George Braziller.

Schele, Linda, and David Freidel. 1990. *A Forest of Kings*. New York: William Morrow.

Schlesinger, Stephen, and Stephen Kinzer. 1983. *Bitter Fruit: The Untold Story of the American Coup in Guatemala.* New York: Doubleday.

Scholes, France V., and Ralph L. Roys. 1948. *The Maya-Chontal Indians of Acalán-Tixchel.* Washington, D.C.: Carnegie Institution.

Shakespeare, Nicholas. 1988. "In Pursuit of Guzmán." *Granta,* no. 23 (Spring): 149–95.

Sheehan, Edward. 1989. *Agony in the Garden.* Boston: Houghton Mifflin.

Simon, Jean-Marie. 1987. *Guatemala: Eternal Spring, Eternal Tyranny.* New York: Norton.

Slattery, Brian. 1984. "The Hidden Constitution: Aboriginal Rights in Canada." *American Journal of Comparative Law,* no. 3: 361.

Smyth, Albert Henry, ed. 1905–1907. *The Writings of Benjamin Franklin,* 10 vols. New York: Macmillan.

Standing Bear, Luther. 1978 [1933]. *Land of the Spotted Eagle.* Lincoln: University of Nebraska Press.

Starr, Emmet. 1969 [1921]. *History of the Cherokee Indians.* New York: Kraus.

Stern, Steve J. 1982. *Peru's Indian Peoples and the Challenge of the Spanish Conquest.* Madison: University of Wisconsin Press.

—. 1987 (ed.) *Resistance, Rebellion, and Consciousness in the Andean Peasant World.* Madison: University of Wisconsin Press.

Stone, William L. 1866. *The Life and Times of Sa-go-ye-wat-ha, or Red Jacket.* Albany, N.Y.: Munsell.

—. 1969 [1838]. *Life of Joseph Brant.* New York: Kraus.

Sullivan, Paul. 1989. *Unfinished Conversations.* New York: Knopf.

Swann, Brian, and Arnold Krupat, eds. 1987a. *I Tell You Now: Autobiographical Essays by Native American Writers.* Lincoln: University of Nebraska Press.

—. 1987b. *Recovering the Word: Essays on Native American Literature.* Berkeley: University of California Press.

Swanton, John R., ed. 1939. "Final Report of the United States De Soto Expedition Commission." *House Document 71,* 76th Cong., 1st Sess., Washington, D.C.

Szeminski, Jan. 1987. "Why Kill the Spaniard? New Perspectives on Andean Insurrectionary Ideology in the 18th Century." In Stern 1987: 166–92.

Taylor, Gerald, ed. 1987. *Ritos y Tradiciones de Huarochirí*. Lima: IEP.

Tedlock, Barbara. 1982. *Time and the Highland Maya*. Albuquerque: University of New Mexico Press.

Tedlock, Dennis, trans. 1985. *Popol Vuh*. New York: Simon and Schuster.

Tezozomoc, Fernando Alvarado. 1975a. *Crónica Mexicáyotl*. Translated by Adrián León. México D.F.: UNAM.

—. 1975b. *Crónica Mexicana*. México D.F.: Porrúa.

Thompson, J. Eric. 1950. *Maya Hieroglyphic Writing*. Washington, D.C.: Carnegie Institution.

—. 1966. *The Rise and Fall of Maya Civilization*. Norman: University of Oklahoma Press.

Thornton, Russell. 1986. *We Shall Live Again*. Cambridge: Cambridge University Press.

—. 1987. *American Indian Holocaust and Survival*. Norman: University of Oklahoma Press.

Timberlake, Lieutenant Henry. 1971 [1765]. T*he Memoirs of Lieut. Henry Timberlake*. New York: Arno.

Titley, E. Brian. 1986. *A Narrow Vision*. Vancouver: University of British Columbia Press.

Titu Kusi Yupanki, Diego de Castro (Titu Cussi Yupangui). 1973 [1570]. *Relación de la Conquista del Perú*. Lima: Biblioteca Universitaria.

Todorov, Tzvetan. 1984. *The Conquest of America*. New York: Harper & Row.

Tooker, Elisabeth. 1988. "The United States Constitution and the Iroquois League." *Ethnohistory* 35, no. 4 (Fall): 305–36.

—. 1990. "Rejoinder to Johansen." *Ethnohistory* 37, no. 3 (Summer): 291–97.

Trigger, Bruce G. 1969. *The Huron: Farmers of the North*. New York: Holt, Rinehart and Winston.

—. 1987. T*he Children of Aataentsic*. Montreal: McGill–Queen's University Press.

Tuck, James A. 1967. "The Howlett Hill Site: An Early Iroquois Village in Central New York." In *Iroquois Culture, History, and Prehistory*. Albany: New York State Museum 1967, 75–79.

Turner, Frederick W. 1974. *North American Indian Reader*. New York: Viking.

Valcárcel, Carlos Daniel. 1977. *Túpac Amaru*. Lima: Universidad Nacional Mayor de San Marcos.

Veatch, Richard. 1975. *Canada and the League of Nations*. Toronto: University of Toronto Press.

Vecsey, Christopher, and William A. Starna, eds. 1988. *Iroquois Land Claims*. Syracuse: Syracuse University Press.

Vestal, Stanley. 1957. *Sitting Bull, Champion of the Sioux*. Norman: University of Oklahoma Press.

Villa Rojas, Alfonso. 1945. *The Maya of East Central Quintana Roo*. Washington, D.C.: Carnegie Institution (publication 559).

Viola, Herman J. 1981. *Diplomats in Buckskin*. Washington, D.C.: Smithsonian.

Von Hagen, Victor Wolfgang. 1961. *The Aztec: Man and Tribe*. New York: Mentor.

—. 1962. *The Ancient Sun Kingdoms of the Americas*. London: Thames and Hudson.

Wachtel, Nathan. 1973. *Sociedad e Ideología*. Lima: IEP.

—. 1977. *The Vision of the Vanquished*. New York: Barnes and Noble.

Waldman, Carl. 1985. *Atlas of the North American Indian*. New York: Facts on File.

Wallace, Anthony F. C. 1970. *The Death and Rebirth of the Seneca*. New York: Knopf.

Wallace, Paul A. W. 1945. *Conrad Weiser: Friend of Colonist and Mohawk*. Philadelphia: University of Pennsylvania Press.

Waman Puma, Felipe (Phelipe Guaman Poma de Ayala). 1936 [1615]. *Nueva Corónica y Buen Gobierno*, facsimile ed. Introduction by Richard Pietschmann. Paris: Institut d'Ethnologie.

—. 1980a. *El Primer Nueva Corónica y Buen Gobierno*. Edited by John Murra, Rolena Adorno, and Jorge Urioste. México D.F.: Siglo Veintiuno.

—. 1980b. *Nueva Corónica y Buen Gobierno*. Edited by Franklin Pease. Caracas: Biblioteca Ayacucho.

Weatherford, Jack. 1988. *Indian Givers*. New York: Crown.

Weaver, Sally. 1981. *Making Canadian Indian Policy*. Toronto: University of Toronto Press.

Weeks, Charles A. 1987. *The Juárez Myth in Mexico*. Tuscaloosa: University of Alabama Press.

Werlich, David P. 1978. *Peru, A Short History*. Carbondale: Southern Illinois University Press.

Wheeler, William Bruce, and Michael J. McDonald. 1986. *TVA and the Tellico Dam*. Knoxville: University of Tennessee Press.

White, Lynn. 1967. "The Historical Roots of Our Ecological Crisis." *Science* 155, no. 3767: 1203–7.

Wilkins, Thurman. 1986. *Cherokee Tragedy*. Norman: University of Oklahoma Press.

Willey, Gordon R. 1966. *An Introduction to American Archaeology*. Englewood Cliffs, N.J.: Prentice-Hall.

Williams, Paul. 1980. "The Chain." LL.M. thesis, York (Ontario) University, Osgoode Hall Law School.

—. 1990. "Reading Wampum Belts as Living Symbols." *Northeast Indian Quarterly* 7, no. 1 (Spring): 31–35.

Williams, Samuel Cole. 1921. "William Tatham, Wataugan." *Tennessee Historical Magazine* 7, no. 3 (October): 154–79.

—. 1928. (ed.) *Early Travels in the Tennessee Country 1540–1800*. Johnson City, Tenn.: Watauga Press.

Williams, Walter L., ed. 1979. *Southeastern Indians Since the Removal Era*. Athens: University of Georgia Press.

Wilson, Edmund. 1960. *Apologies to the Iroquois*. New York: Farrar, Straus and Cudahy.

Witt, Shirley Hill, and Stan Steiner. 1972. *The Way: An Anthology of American Indian Literature*. New York: Knopf.

Wolf, Eric R. 1982. *Europe and the People Without History*. Berkeley: University of California Press.

Woodward, Grace Steele. 1963. *The Cherokees*. Norman: University of Oklahoma Press.

Wright, Ronald. 1983. *Worlds in Reverse: Indian Response to the Spanish Conquest* (transcript of radio series). Toronto: CBC Enterprises.

—. 1984. *Cut Stones and Crossroads*. New York: Viking Penguin.

—. 1987. "The Death List People." *Saturday Night* 102, no. 5 (May): 44–52.

—. 1988. "Beyond Words." *Saturday Night* 103, no. 4 (April): 38–46.

—. 1989. *Time Among the Maya*. New York: Weidenfeld and Nicolson.

—. 1990. "Does Canada Want a Wounded Knee?" *Globe and Mail*, August 30.

Xahil, Hernández, et al. 1980. [c. 1550–1604]. *Memorial de Sololá, Anales de los Cakchiqueles*. Guatemala: Piedra Santa. Reprint of Recinos 1950. See also Brinton 1969b.

York, Geoffrey. 1989. *The Dispossessed*. Toronto: Lester and Orpen Dennys.

Zamora, Margarita. 1988. *Language, Authority, and Indigenous History in the Comentarios Reales de los Incas*. Cambridge: Cambridge University Press.

Zuidema, R. Tom. 1983. "Hierarchy and Space in Incaic Social Organization." *Ethnohistory* 30, no. 2: 49–75.

—. 1990. *Inca Civilization in Cuzco*. Austin: University of Texas Press.

ACKNOWLEDGMENTS

This book stands on many shoulders. I owe the first and greatest debt to the indigenous Americans whose words appear on these pages; they, not I, have told their story. Pioneering scholars rescued chapters of that story from oblivion. Daniel Brinton made early translations from languages as diverse as Cakchiquel and Delaware. Richard Pietschmann published Felipe Waman Puma's chronicle after its three centuries in manuscript; Rolena Adorno and Juan Ossio have interpreted its message. José María Arguedas gave voice to the Inca world, both ancient and modern. Ralph Roys and Adrián Recinos introduced the twentieth century to the great books of the Maya. Angel María Garibay did the same for Aztec literature, and Miguel León-Portilla amplified Garibay's work and first drew public attention to the eloquence and importance of what he named "the vision of the vanquished." Among other works that were source and inspiration for my own, those of John Bierhorst, Gordon Brotherston, Dee Brown, Inga Clendinnen, Vine Deloria, Munro Edmonson, John Hemming, David Kelley, George Lovell, Peter Mathews, Luis Millones, Robert Randall, Linda Schele, Barbara and Dennis Tedlock, Nathan Wachtel, and Tom Zuidema immediately come to mind. And in a class of its own stands Eduardo Galeano's splendid *Memory of Fire*.

Peter Davison, the book's principal editor, helped define *Stolen Continents* by asking the right questions. Grant McIntyre, Iris Skeoch, and Gerry Morse also gave valuable editorial advice. Michael Poole, David Suzuki, John Kennedy, Hugh Gauntlett, and James Murray were generous with support and ideas in the early days; Milena Tulk contributed research. Farley Mowat, Brian Maracle, Bella Pomer, George Lovell, Joe Fisher, and Kirsten Hanson read the manuscript, in whole or in part, at various stages. My wife, Janice Boddy, neglected her own work to read all of it once and some parts more times than she might care to remember; as always, her critique was indispensable. I owe another large debt to Janice, to my parents, Shirley and Edward Wright, and to Claire and Farley Mowat for everything from blind faith to hot meals and stiff drinks during low ebbs in my morale.

I also wish to thank the following for their kindness and cooperation: Robert Antone; Sally Benedict; Thomas R. Berger; Patricia Boddy; Doug Caldwell (and CBC Radio's "The House"); Nilda Callañaupa; Linda Cree; Edward Dahl; Joe David; Walter David, Sr.; Mark Day; Louise Dennys; Dale Dione; Georges Erasmus; Tom Foster (and the [Syracuse, N.Y.] *Post-Standard*); Paul Geraghty; Elizabeth Graham; Ian Graham; Rayna Green; John Hemming; Robert Jamieson; Susan Jefferies; Lenore Keeshig-Tobias; Duane H. King; Thomas King; Erica Landry; Robert Loescher; Floyd Lounsbury; Oren Lyons; Alberto Manguel; Wilma Mankiller; Peter Mathews; Rigoberta Menchú; John Mohawk; Barbara Moon; Gertrude Nicks; Joe Norton; Theda Perdue; Loreen Pindera; Irving Powless; Lorna Ross; Barbara Stith; Maria Tippett; Bruce Trigger; Billy Two Rivers; Eva Varangu (and CBC Radio's "Sunday Morning"); Herman Viola; Evelyn Loft Watts; Sally Weaver; Paul Williams; Penny Williams; Geoffrey York.

My thanks to the Ontario Arts Council for its support.

Excerpts from *The Book of Chilam Balam of Chumayel*, translated into English by Ralph L. Roys. Copyright © 1967 by the University of Oklahoma Press. Used by permission.

Excerpts from *The Conquest of New Spain* by Bernal Díaz, translated into English by J. M. Cohen, Copyright © 1963 by J. M. Cohen. Used by permission of Penguin Books, Ltd.

Excerpt from "Burnt Norton" *(Four Quartets)* by T. S. Eliot. Copyright © 1943 by T. S. Eliot, renewed 1971 by Esme Valerie Eliot. Courtesy of Faber and Faber Ltd., and used by permission of Harcourt Brace Jovanovich, Inc.

Excerpts from *I, Rigoberta Menchú: An Indian Woman in Guatemala*, edited by Elisabeth Burgos-Debray, translated into English by Ann Wright. Copyright © 1984 by Verso Editions. Courtesy of Verso Editons.

Excerpts from *Ideología Mesiánica del Mundo Andino*, edited by Juan Ossio. Copyright © 1973 by Juan Ossio. Courtesy of Juan Ossio.

Excerpts from *De Porfirio Díaz a Zapata*, edited and translated by Fernando Horcasitas. Copyright © 1968 by UNAM. Courtesy of Universidad Nacional Autónoma de México.

Excerpts from *El Reverso de la Conquista*, edited and translated by Miguel León-Portilla. Copyright © 1964 by Editorial Joaquín Mortiz. Courtesy of Editorial Joaquín Mortiz.

Excerpt from "Akwesasne: An Unbroken Assertion of Sovereignty," by Grand Chief Michael Mitchell. Copyright © 1989 by the Assembly of First Nations. Courtesy of Grand Chief Michael Mitchell.

Excerpt from "State of the Nation Address" by Principal Chief Wilma Mankiller. Copyright © 1990 by Wilma Mankiller. Courtesy of Principal Chief Wilma Mankiller.

Excerpt from "Standoff Is a National Crisis," by Brian Maracle. Copyright © 1990 by Brian Maracle. Courtesy of Brian Maracle.

Excerpts from taped interviews. Courtesy of Rigoberta Menchú, Joe David, and Irving Powless.

INDEX